WITHDRAWN

TECHGNOSIS

myth, magic + mysticism

TECHGNOSIS

in the age of information

ERIK DAVIS

Harmony Books / NEW YORK

Published by Harmony Books, a division of Crown Publishers, Inc., 201 East 50th Street, New York, New York 10022. Member of the Crown Publishing Group.

Random House, Inc. New York, Toronto, London, Sydney, Auckland
www.randomhouse.com

HARMONY and colophon are trademarks of Crown Publishers, Inc.

Printed in the United States of America

Library of Congress Cataloging-in-Publication Data
Davis, Erik.
    TechGnosis : myth, magic, and mysticism in the age of information /
  by Erik Davis.—1st ed.
       p.   cm.
    Includes bibliographical references and index.
    1. Information technology—Religious aspects. I. Title.
  BL265.I54D38 1998
   303.48′33–dc21   98-19389   CIP

ISBN 0-517-70415-3

10 9 8 7 6 5 4 3 2 1

First Edition

FOR MY FOLKS

contents

acknowledgments

It would be impossible to fully trace the network of minds and hearts that helped bring this book into being, but some specific shout-outs are definitely in order. A number of the ideas animating *TechGnosis* have been pulsing in my brain for nearly a decade, and I am indebted to a handful of teachers and editors who have helped me shape them into worthy prose at various stages of my writing career: my undergraduate thesis advisers at Yale, Richard Halpern and David Rodowick; former *Village Voice* editors Jeff Salamon, Scott Malcolmson, Lisa Kennedy, and Joe Levy; *Gnosis* editors Jay Kinney and Richard Smoley; and ace cyber-critic Mark Dery, who asked me to write the essay that formed the seed crystal for the present work. Even more invaluable have been the countless kaleidoscopic conversations about philosophy, science, and spirit I have had over the years with my great friends Julian Dibbell, JP Harpignies, and Marcus Boon, all of whom challenged me to find my own weird path into technoculture and to face the difficulties of writing it down head-on.

My buddy Dan Levy harangued me into shaping my stray thoughts into a book project, and then convinced someone to actually buy it. Relationships with huge and distant corporations can be rocky: thanks to Harmony editors Andrew Stuart, who swooped in midway to save the day with his generous attention and sharp suggestions, and Peter Guzzardi, who kindly shepherded *TechGnosis* through the end game. The book you hold would be a flabbier and more error-ridden thing were it not for the perceptions, pens, and pencils of my manuscript readers, who, if they have not already been mentioned, include Margaret Wertheim, papa Russ Davis, Rachel Koenig, David Ulansey, Jeff Gorvetzian, and my mother Sandra Zarcades, who lent her razor-sharp copy-editing skills to many of its drafts.

Wef Linson helped me keep perspective throughout the daily grind with his spiritual ruminations and carefree cracks, while the Midtown Niki Starving Writers Fund allowed me to focus on the task at hand. Thanks as well to the large circle of comrades and netminds who took the time to swap ideas, give me encouragement, or feed me nifty memes: Peter Lamborn Wilson, Mark Pesce, Scott Durham, Spiros Antonopoulos, Molly McGarry, Manuel DeLanda, Hermano Vianna Jr., Jordan Gruber, Terence McKenna, Charles Cameron, Tom Lane, James O'Meara, Paul Miller, Kate Ramsey, Konrad Becker, Craig Baldwin, Sam Webster, Mark Stahlman, and Grampa Jake, who sent me a steady stream of juicy newspaper clippings from the desert heartland. In particular, Pit Schultz, Diana McCarty, and the nettime crew plugged me into a community of technology critics whose trenchant debates helped me keep my cosmological feet on the ground.

Everyone knows that no single individual can write a book, even though one person, i.e., me, must take responsibility for its perhaps inevitable flaws and errors. This does not mean that writing *TechGnosis* did not sometimes make me feel as though I were alone in the Siberian wastes, trying to claw my way out of an ice cave with a toothbrush and a Bic lighter. I thank all gods for my love, Jennifer Dumpert, who not only scraped me up from the bottom of the barrel on a regular basis, but whose wisdom, patience, and incisive feedback helped me weave this labor into a life of riches.

All that remains is the possibility of communication.
—Captain Jean Luc-Picard

TECHGNOSIS

INTRODUCTION
crossed wires

This book is written in the shadow of the millennium, that arbitrary but incontestable line that the Western imagination has drawn in the sands of time. It is also written in the conviction that one hardly needs to be decked out in a biblical sandwich board or wired to the gills with the latest cyborg gear to feel the glittering void of possibility and threat growing at the heart of our profoundly technologized society. Even as many of us spend our days, in that now universal Californiaism, surfing the datastream, we can hardly ignore the deeper, more powerful and more ominous undertows that tug beneath the froth of our lives and labors.

You know the scene. Social structures the world over are melting down and mutating, making way for a global McVillage, a Gaian brain, and a whole heap of chaos. The emperor of technoscience has achieved dominion, though his clothes are growing more threadbare by the moment, the once noble costume of Progress barely concealing far more wayward ambitions. Across the globe, ferocious postperestroika capitalism yanks the rug out from under the nation-state, while the planet spits up signs and symptoms of terminal distress. Boundaries dissolve, and we drift into the no-man's zones between synthetic and organic life, between actual and virtual environments, between local communities and global flows of goods, information, labor, and capital. With pills modifying personality, machines modifying bodies, and synthetic pleasures and networked minds engineering a more fluid and invented sense of self, the boundaries of our identities are mutating as well. The horizon melts into a limitless question mark, and like the cartographers of old, we glimpse yawning monstrosities and mind-forged utopias beyond the edges of our paltry and provisional maps.

Regardless of how secular this ultramodern condition appears, the velocity and mutability of the times invokes a certain supernatural quality that must be seen, at least in part, through the lenses of religious thought and the fantastic storehouse of the archetypal imagination. Inside the United States, within whose high-tech bosom I quite self-consciously write, the spirit has definitely made a comeback—if it could be said to have ever left this giddy, gold rush land, where most people believe in the Lord and his coming kingdom, and more than you'd guess believe in UFOs. Today God has become one of *Time*'s favorite cover boys, and a Black Muslim numerologist can lead the most imaginative march on the nation's capital since the Yippies tried to levitate the Pentagon. Self-help maestros and corporate consultants promulgate New Age therapies, as strains of Buddhism both scientific and technicolor seep through the intelligentsia, and half the guests on *Oprah* pop up wearing angel pins. The surge of interest in alternative medicine injects non-Western and ad hoc spiritual practices into the mainstream, while deep ecologists turn up the boil on the nature mysticism long simmering in the American soul. This rich confusion is even more evident in our brash popular culture, where science-fiction films, digital environments, and urban tribes are reconfiguring old archetypes and imaginings within a vivid comic-book frame. From *The X-Files* to occult computer games, from *Xena: Warrior Princess* to *Magic: The Gathering* playing cards, the pagan and the paranormal have colonized the twilight zones of pop media.

These signs are not just evidence of a media culture exploiting the crude power of the irrational. They reflect the fact that people inhabiting all frequencies of the socioeconomic spectrum are intentionally reaching for some of the oldest navigational tools known to humankind: sacred ritual and metaphysical speculation, spiritual regimen and natural spell. For some superficial spiritual consumers, this means prepackaged answers to the thorny questions of life; but for many others, the quest for meaning and connection has led individuals and communities to construct meaningful frameworks for their lives, worldviews that actually deepen their willingness and ability to face the strangeness of our days.

So here we are: a hypertechnological and cynically postmodern culture seemingly drawn like a passel of moths toward the guttering flames of the premodern mind. And it is with this apparent paradox in mind that I have written *TechGnosis*: a secret history of the mystical impulses that continue to spark and sustain the Western world's obsession with technology, and especially with its technologies of communication.

My topic may seem rather obscure at first, for common sense tells us that mysticism has no more in common with technology than the twilight cry of wild swans has with the clatter of Rock'em Sock'em Robots. Historians and sociologists inform us that the West's mystical heritage of occult dreamings, spiritual transformations, and apocalyptic visions crashed on the scientific shores of the modern age. According to this narrative, technology has helped disenchant the world, forcing the ancestral symbolic networks of old to give way to the crisp, secular game plans of economic development, skeptical inquiry, and material progress. But the old phantasms and metaphysical longings did not exactly disappear. In many cases, they disguised themselves and went underground, worming their way into the cultural, psychological, and mythological motivations that form the foundations of the modern world. As we will see throughout this book, mystical impulses sometimes body-snatched the very technologies that supposedly helped yank them from the stage in the first place. And it is these technomystical impulses—sometimes sublimated, sometimes acknowledged, sometimes masked in the pop detritus of science fiction or video games—that *TechGnosis* seeks to reveal.

For well over a century, the dominant images of technology have been industrial: the extraction and exploitation of natural resources, the mechanization of work through the assembly line, and the bureaucratic command-and-control systems that large and impersonal institutions favor. Lewis Mumford called this industrial image of technology the "myth of the machine," a myth that insists on the authority of technical and scientific elites, and in the intrinsic value of efficiency, control, unrestrained technological development, and economic expansion. As many historians and sociologists have recognized, this secular image was framed all along by Christian myths: the biblical call to conquer nature, the Protestant work ethic, and, in particular, the millennialist vision of a New Jerusalem, the earthly paradise that the Book of Revelation claims will crown the course of history. Despite a century of Hiroshimas, Bhopals, and Chernobyls, this myth of an engineered utopia still propels the ideology of technological progress, with its perennial promises of freedom, prosperity, and release from disease and want.

Today a new, less mechanized myth has sprung from the brow of the industrial megamachine: the myth of information, of electric minds and boundless databases, computer forecasts and hypertext libraries, immersive media dreams and a planetary blip-culture woven together with global telecommunication nets. Certainly this myth still rides atop the same mechanical behemoth that lurched out of Europe's chilly bogs and conquered the globe, but for the most part, *TechGnosis* will focus on information technologies alone, placing them in their own, more spectral light. For of all technologies, it is the technologies of information and communication that most mold and shape the source of all mystical glimmerings: the human self.

From the moment that humans began etching grooves into ancient wizard bones to mark the cycles of the moon, the process of encoding thought and experience into a vehicle of expression has influenced the changing nature of the self. Information technology tweaks our perceptions, communicates our picture of the world to one another, and constructs remarkable and sometimes insidious forms of control over the cultural stories that shape our sense of the world. The moment we invent a significant new device for communication—talking drums, papyrus scrolls, printed books, crystal sets, computers, pagers—we partially reconstruct the self and its world, creating new opportunities (and new traps) for thought, perception, and social experience.

By their very nature, the technologies of information and communication—"media" in the broad sense of the term—are technocultural hybrids. On the one hand, they are crafted things, material mechanisms that are conceived, constructed, and exploited for gain. But media technologies are also animated by something that has nothing to do with matter or technique. More than any other invention, information technology transcends its status as a thing, simply because it allows for the incorporeal encoding and transmission of mind and meaning. In a sense, this hybridity reflects the age-old sibling rivalry between form and content: the material and technical structure of media impose formal constraints on communication, even as the immediacy of communication continues to challenge formal limitations as it crackles from mind to mind, pushing the envelope of intelligence, art, and information flow. By creating a new interface between the self, the other, and the world beyond, media technologies become *part* of the self, the other, and the world beyond. They form the building blocks, and even in some sense the foundation, for what we now increasingly think of as "the social construction of reality."

Historically, the great social constructions belong to the religious imagination: the animistic world of nature magic, the ritualized social narratives of mythology, the ethical inwardness of the "religions of the book," and the increasingly rationalized modern institutions of faith that followed them. These various paradigms marked their notions and symbols in the world around them, using architecture, language, icons, costumes, and social ritual—and often whatever media they could get their hands on. For reasons that cannot simply be chalked up to the desire for power and conformity, the religious imagination has an irrepressible and almost desperate urge to remake the mental world humans share by communicating itself to others. From hieroglyphs to the printed book, from radio to computer networks, the spirit has found itself inside a variety of new bottles, and each new medium has become, in a variety of contradictory ways, part of the message. When the Norse god Odin swaps an eye for the gift of the runes, or when Paul of Tarsus writes in a letter that the Word of God is written in our hearts, or when New Age mediums "channel spiritual information," the ever-shifting boundaries between media and the self are redrawn in technomystical terms.

This process continues apace, although today you often need to dig beneath the garish, commercialized, and oversaturated surface of the information age to find its archetypes and metaphysical concerns. The virtual topographies of our millennial world are rife with angels and aliens, with digital avatars and mystic Gaian minds, with utopian longings and gnostic science fictions, and with dark forebodings of apocalypse and demonic enchantment. These figures ride the expanding and contracting waves of media fads, hype, and economic activity, and some of them are already disappearing into an increasingly market-dominated information culture. But though technomystical concerns are deeply intertwined with the changing sociopolitical conditions of our rapidly globalizing civilization, their spiritual forebears are rooted in the long-ago. By invoking such old ones here, and bringing them into the discourse and contexts of contemporary technoculture, I hope to shine a light on some of the more dangerous and unwieldy visions that charge technologies. Even more fundamentally, however, I hope my secret history can provide some imaginal maps and mystical scorecards for the metaverse that is now swallowing up so many of us, all across network earth.

○

You may think you are holding a conventional book, a solid and familiar chunk of infotech with chapters and endnotes and a linear argument about the mystical roots of technoculture. But that is really just a clever disguise. Once dissolved in your mindstream, *TechGnosis* will become a resonating hypertext, one whose links leap between machines and dreams, information and spirit, the dustbin of history and the alembics of the soul. Instead of "taking a stand," *TechGnosis* ranges rather promiscuously across the disciplinary boundaries that usually chop up the world of thought, drawing the reader into a fluctuating play network of polarities and hidden networks. The connections it draws are many: between myth and science, transcendent intuition and technological control, the virtual worlds we imagine and the real world we cannot escape. It is a dreambook of the technological unconscious. Perhaps the most important polarity that underlies the psychological dynamics of techno-mysticism is a yin and yang I will name *spirit* and *soul*. By soul, I basically mean the creative imagination, that aspect of our psyches that perceives the world as an animated field of powers and images. Soul finds and loses itself in enchantment; it speaks the tongue of dream and phantasm, which should never be confused with mere fantasy. Spirit is an altogether different bird: an impersonal, incorporeal spark that seeks clarity, essence, and a blast of the absolute. Archetypal psychologist James Hillman uses the image of peaks and valleys to characterize these two very different modes of the self. He notes that the mountaintop is a veritable logo of the "spiritual" quest, a place where the religious seeker overcomes gravity in order to win a peak experience or an adamantine code worthy of ruling a life. But the soul forswears such towering and otherworldly views; it remains in the mesmerizing vale of tears and desires, a fecund and polytheistic world of things and creatures, and the images and stories that things and creatures breed.

Spirit and soul twine their way throughout this book like the two strands of DNA, both enchanting and spiritualizing media technologies. On the one hand, we'll see that technologies can serve as the vehicles for spells, ghosts, and animist intuitions. On the other, they can provide launching pads for transcendence, for the disembodied flights of gnosis. The different "styles" of spirit and soul can even be seen in the two basic encoding methods that define media: analog and digital. Analog gadgets reproduce signals in continuous, variable waves of real energy, while digital devices recode information into discrete symbolic chunks. Think of the difference between vinyl LPs and music compact discs. LPs are inscribed with unbroken physical grooves that mimic and re-present the sound waves that ripple through the air. In contrast, CDs chop up (or "sample") such waves into individual bits, encoding those digital units into tiny pits that are read and reconstructed by your stereo gear at playback. The analog world sticks to the grooves of soul—warm, undulating, worn with the pops and scratches of material history. The digital world boots up the cool matrix of the spirit: luminous, abstract, more code than corporeality. The analog soul runs on the analogies between things; the digital spirit divides the world between clay and information.

In the first chapter, I will trace the origins of these two strands of technomysticism to the ancient mythological figure of Hermes Trismegistus, a technological wizard who will inaugurate the dance between magic and invention, media and mind. Tracing this hermetic tradition into the modern world, I will discuss how the discovery of electricity sparked animist ideas and occult experiences even as it laid the groundwork for the information age. Next, I will recast the epochal birth of cybernetics and the electronic computer in a transcendental light provided by the ancient lore of Gnosticism. Then I'll show how the spiritual counterculture of the 1960s created a liberatory and even magical relationship to media and technology, a psychedelic mode of mind-tweaking that feeds directly into today's cyberculture. Finally, I'll turn to our "datapocalyptic" moment and show how the UFOs, Gaian minds, New World Orders, and techno-utopias that hover above the horizon of the third millennium subliminally feed off images and compulsions deeply rooted in the spiritual imagination.

Given the delusions and disasters that religious and mystic thought courts, some may legitimately wonder whether we might not be better off just completing the critical and empirical task undertaken by Freud, Nietzsche, and your favorite scientific reductionist. The simple answer is that we cannot. Collectively, human societies can no more dodge sublime imaginings or spiritual yearnings than they can transcend the tidal pulls of eros. We are beset with a thirst for meaning and connection that centuries of skeptical philosophy, hardheaded materialism, and an increasingly nihilist culture have yet to douse, and this thirst conjures up the whole tattered carnival of contemporary religion: oily New Age gurus and Pentecostal crusaders, existential Buddhists and liberation theologians, psychedelic pagan ravers and grizzled deep ecologists. Even the cosmic awe conjured by science fiction or the outer-space snapshots of the Hubbell telescope calls forth our ever-deeper, ever-brighter possible selves.

While I certainly hope that *TechGnosis* can help strengthen the wisdom of these often inchoate yearnings, I am more interested in understanding how technomystical ideas and practices *work* than I am in shaking them down for their various and not inconsiderable "errors." Sober voices will appear throughout my book like a chorus of skeptics, but my primary concern remains the spiritual imagination and how it mutates in the face of changing technologies. William Gibson's famous quip about new technologies—that the street finds its own uses for things—applies to what many seekers call "the path" as well. As we will see throughout this book, the spiritual imagination seizes information technology for its own purposes. In this sense, technologies of communication are always, at least potentially, technologies of the sacred, simply because the ideas and experiences of the sacred have always informed human communication.

By appropriating and re-visioning communication technologies, the spiritual imagination often fashions symbols and rituals from the technical mode of communication it employs: hieroglyphs, printing press, the online database. By reimagining technologies in this way, new meanings are invested into the universe of machines, and new virtual possibilities emerge. The very ambiguity of the term *information,* which has made it such an infectious and irritating buzzword, has also allowed old intuitions to pop up in secular guise. Today, there is so much pressure on information—the word, the concept, the stuff itself—that it crackles with energy, drawing to itself mythologies, metaphysics, hints of arcane magic. As information expands beyond its reductive sense as a quantitative measure of meaning, groups and individuals also find room to resist and recast the dominant technological narratives of war and commerce, and to inject their fractured postmodern lives with digitally remastered forms of community, imagination, and cosmic connection.

Of course, as any number of "new paradigm" visionaries or *Wired* magazine cover stories prove, it's easy to lose one's way in the maze of hope, hype, and novelty that defines the information age. As any extraterrestrial anthropologist beaming down for a look-see would note, the computer has definitely become an idol—and a rather demanding one at that, almost as thirsty for sacrifice as the holy spirit of money itself. Since the empire of global capitalism is wagering the future of the planet on technology, we are right to distrust any myths that obscure the enormous costs of the path we've taken. In the views of many prophets today, crying in and for the wilderness, the spiritual losses we have accrued in our haste to measure, exploit, and commodify the world are already beyond reckoning. By submitting ourselves to the ravenous and nihilistic robot of science, technology, and media culture, we have cut ourselves off from the richness of the soul and from the deeply nourishing networks of family, community, and the local land.

I deeply sympathize with these attempts to disenchant technology and to deflate the banal fantasies and pernicious hype that fuel today's digital economy. In fact, *TechGnosis* will hopefully provide some ammo for the debate. But as both the doomsdays of the neo-Luddites and the gleaming Tomorrowlands of the techno-utopians prove, technology embodies an image of the soul, or rather a host of images: redemptive, demonic, magical, transcendent, hypnotic, alive. We must come to grips with these images before we can creatively and consciously answer the question of technology, for that question has always been fringed with phantasms.

One thing seems clear: We cannot afford to think in the Manichean terms that often characterize the debate on new technologies. Technology is neither a devil nor an angel. But neither is it simply a "tool," a neutral extension of some rock solid human nature. Technology is a trickster, and it has been so since the first culture hero taught the human tribe how to spin wool before he pulled it over our eyes. The trickster shows how intelligence fares in an unpredictable and chaotic world; he beckons us through the open doors of innovation and traps us in the prison of unintended consequences. And it is with a bit of the trickster's spirit— mischievous, riddling, and thoroughly cross-wired—that I shoot these media tales and technological reflections into the towering din.

I

imagining technologies

Human beings have been cyborgs from year zero. It is our lot to live in societies that invent tools that shape society and the individuals in it. For millennia, people not so dissimilar to ourselves have constructed and manipulated powerful and impressive technologies, including information technologies, and these tools and techniques have woven themselves into the social fabric of the world. Though technology has only come to dominate and define society within the lifetimes of a handful of human generations, the basic equation remains true for the whole nomadic trek of *homo faber*: Culture *is* technoculture.

Technologies concretely embody our ability to discover and exploit natural laws through the exercise of reason. But *why* do we choose to exploit certain natural laws? In what manner and toward what ends? Though we may think of technology as a tool defined by pragmatic and utilitarian concerns alone, human motivations in the matter of technology are rarely so straightforward. Like the rationality we carry within our minds, whose logical convictions must make their way through the brawling, boozing cabaret of the psyche, technologies are shaped and constrained by the warp and woof of culture, with its own peculiar myths, dreams, cruelties, and hungers. The immense machineries of war or entertainment can hardly be said to proceed from rational necessity, however precise their implementation; instead, we find their blueprints inked upon the fiery human heart.

The interdependence of culture and technology means that the technologies of the premodern world, despite being the most logical of crafted objects, nonetheless had to share the cosmic stage with any number of gods, sorceries, and animist powers. As the French anthropologist of science Bruno Latour explains, premodern and indigenous people wove everything—animals, tools, medicine, sex, kin, plants, songs, weather—into an immense collective webwork of mind and matter. Nothing in this webwork, which Latour calls the anthropological matrix, can be neatly divided between *nature* and *culture*. Instead, this matrix is composed of "hybrids"—"speaking things" that are *both* natural and cultural, real and imagined, subject and object. As an example, think of a traditional Inuit who hunts and kills a caribou. On one level, the animal is a fat, tasty object that he and his tribe exploit in perfectly reasonable ways that satisfy human needs and desires. But along with providing sustenance and nifty threads, the caribou is simultaneously a sacred spirit, a numinous actor in a cosmological drama ritually maintained by the prayers, perceptions, and rituals of Inuit life. The caribou and the weapon, as well as the dream that sent the hunter on his way that morning, are all hybrids; all are part of a collective song that can never be fully resolved as mythology or concrete reality.

We don't generally think this way today because we are basically moderns, and modernity is partly defined by the enormous conceptual barrier erected between nature and culture. In his book *We Have Never Been Modern,* Latour dubs this wall the "Great Divide" and places its foundations in the Enlightenment, when Descartes's mechanistic thought invaded natural philosophy and the cornerstones of modern social institutions were laid. On the one side of the Great Divide lies nature, a voiceless and purely objective world "out there," whose hidden mechanisms are unlocked by detached scientific gentlemen using technical instruments to amplify their perceptions. Human culture lies on the other side of the fence, "in here," a self-reflexive world of stories, subjects, and power struggles that develop free of nature's mythic limitations. The Great Divide thus disenchants the world, enthroning man as the sole active agent of the cosmos. From within the paradigm of the Great Divide, technology is simply a tool, a passive extension of man. It does not have its own autonomy; it simply acts upon, but does not change, the world of nature.

So far this is relatively routine stuff. Where Latour parts ways from most thinkers is his provocative insistence that the modern West never really left the anthropological matrix. Instead, it used the conceptual sleight of hand of the Great Divide to deny the ever-present reality of hybrids, those "subject/objects" that straddle the boundaries between nature and culture, agency and raw material. This denial freed the West from the inherently conservative nature of traditional societies, where the creation of new hybrids—new medicines or weapons—was always constrained by the fact that their effects were felt throughout the entire matrix of reality. By denying hybrids, modern Europe paradoxically wound up cranking them out at an astounding rate: new technologies, new scientific and cultural perspectives, new sociopolitical and economic arrangements. The West drastically reconstructed "the world" without acknowledging the systemic effects that its creative activities had on the interdependent fabric of society—let alone the more-than-human world of rock and beast that provides the material for that fabric.

Today, when human societies are more densely interconnected than ever before, Latour argues that we can no longer sustain the illusion of the Great Divide. Each new hybrid that arrives on the scene—test tube babies, Prozac, the sequencing of the human genome, space stations, global warming—pushes us further into that no-man's-land between nature and culture, an ambiguous zone where science, language, and the social imagination overlap and interpenetrate. We begin to see that everything is connected, and this recognition invokes premodern ways of thinking. Latour uses the example of ecological fear, comparing it to the stories of Chicken Little. Now "we too are afraid that the sky is falling. We too associate the tiny gesture of releasing an aerosol spray with taboos pertaining to the heavens."[1] We return—with some profound and irreducible differences—to the old anthropological matrix. "It is not only the Bedouins and the !Kung who mix up transistors and traditional behaviors, plastic buckets and animal-skin vessels. What country could not be called 'a land of contrasts'? We have all reached the point of mixing up times. We have all become premodern again."[2]

If Latour is right, and I believe he is, then we have some important stories to tell about the ways that modern technologies have become mixed up with other times, other places, other paradigms. Though the bulk of this book focuses on the mystical currents coursing through the information technologies of the scientific era, this first chapter turns to more ancient wellsprings. By delving into some of the ways that the Greco-Roman world imagined mechanical invention and information technology, we will discover some of the icons, myths, and mystic themes that populate the archetypal strata of the modern technological psyche.

Ancient Greece glowed with the first blush of the West's tragicomic romance with science, for it was the Greeks who first embraced the amazing belief that we could really *know* things, in the full philosophical sense of the term. But even before the Apollonian rise of Greek rationalism, which led to the construction of everything from astronomical computers to pneumatic automata, the ancient poems of Homer dripped with a pagan materialism that exulted in technology. Though Homeric verse was the product of an archaic and oral society, it did not reflect the deep immersion in the more-than-human world of weather and tree and beast that marks most indigenous lore. In those more "ecological" worldviews, the mythic perceptions of human beings were immersed in nature; the world was seen through the lens of animism, a magical mode of thought that reads and experiences the surrounding world as a living field of psychic presences.

Though the animist traces of the gods are everywhere in Homer, the spirits of the bush have retreated, and what comes to the fore—besides powerfully human personalities and concerns—are the enchantments of human craft. As Samuel C. Florman writes in *The Existential Pleasures of Engineering,* "We emerge from the world of Homer drunk with the feel of metals, woods and fabrics, euphoric with the sense of objects designed, manufactured, used, given, admired, and savored."[3] The ancient bards who collectively composed the Homeric epics even went so far as to imagine man-made objects that could reproduce the demiurgic spellcraft of their own chants. In a famous passage in the *Iliad,* the crippled blacksmith god Hephaestus hammers out a great shield for Achilles (an early instance of the military-industrial complex driving technological development). With the aid of comely androids, "handmaids of hammered gold who looked like living girls," the god fashions a bronze plate that he magically decorates with all the heavens and the earth. The shield's intricate scenes of battle, harvest, and celebration come to life like a metallurgic cartoon, forming the first virtual media in Western literature, a most ancient artifact of what Disney now calls "imagineering." But Hephaestus also limps along on withered limbs, anticipating the great insight that both Plato and Marshall McLuhan would later insist upon: that technologies extend our creative powers by amputating our natural ones.

Another Greek tale implies that this fundamental disequilibrium in the order of things is the essence of both man and technology. After the gods give Epithemeus the task of creating living creatures, the Titan—whose name means "afterthought"—botches the job. He grafts all the useful DNA into animals, so that when man finally crawls out of the Titan's lab he is nothing more than a soft and mewling babe, without courage, cunning, or fur. In desperation, Epithemeus turns to his brother Prometheus, who is graced with the more auspicious name of "forethought." Thinking ahead, Prometheus gives humans their upright gait and makes them tall and far-seeing like the gods. Then the Titan flies to heaven and steals the fire from the sun, which he bestows upon our still rather clueless ancestors. "Though feeble and short-lived," reads one ancient verse, "Mankind has flaming fire and therefrom learns many crafts."[4] Zeus is not impressed with this unauthorized transfer of power and chains Prometheus to a rock for his crimes, where he remains until Heracles releases him. But the Titan's rational fire sparks the technocultural imagination of the West to this day. Free-thinkers from the Enlightenment on have embraced the Promethean flame as an antiauthoritarian symbol of human self-determination, while neo-Luddites demonize it as a corrosive and destructive force that may well reduce the earth to a crisp.

Though the tongues of the Promethean flame will wag throughout this book, our main focus remains, not the technologies of power, but the technologies of communication, and the myths and mysteries that enchant those media. And the obvious Attic psychopomp for such mysteries is Hermes, the messenger and mediator of gods and men, souls and meanings, trivia and trade. Of all the godforms that haunt the Greek mind, Hermes is the one who would feel most at home in our wired world. Indeed, with his mischievous combination of speed, trickery, and profitable mediation, he can almost be seen as the archaic mascot of the information age. Unlike most archetypal figures, who lurk in the violent and erotic dreamstuff beneath the surface of our everyday awareness, Hermes also embodies the social psychology of language and communication. He flies "as fleet as thought," an image of the daylight mind, with its plans and synaptic leaps, its chatter and overload. Hermes shows that these minds are not islands, but nodes in an immense electric tangle of words, images, songs, and signals. Hermes rules the transtemporal world of information exchange that you and I are participating in right now, myself as I tap out these pixelated fonts and you as you absorb their printed twins through your eyeballs and into your brain.

More than a mere delivery boy, Hermes wears a host of guises: con artist, herald, inventor, merchant, magus, thief. The Romans called him Mercury, the name that came to grace the solar system's smallest and fastest orb, as well as the moist element beloved by later alchemists. Those of us familiar with the logo of the floral delivery service FTD will recognize Hermes at once: a young, androgynous man, with a bumpkin's cap that betrays his humble origins and a pair of winged sandals that show his addiction to speed. To round out the image, all we need to do is restore Hermes' caduceus, the magic rod topped with two serpents twining like the double helix of DNA—a fit device for a god who brings the twists and turns of information to life.

Already in Homer, Hermes is a multitasking character. The figure who flits through the *Iliad* as a messenger and thief becomes in the *Odyssey* a guide of souls and a shamanic healer, curing Odysseus from Circe's witchy poison. But the god really doesn't find himself at center stage until the pseudo-Homeric *Hymn to Hermes,* written around the sixth century B.C.E. The poem begins with the nymph Maya, lately loved by Zeus, giving birth to a boisterous child. Leaping instantly out of his crib, the babe Hermes dashes into the outside world, where he happens upon a turtle. He kills the creature, takes up its shell, and invents the lyre, becoming "the first to manufacture songs." Lord of the lucky find, Hermes crafts opportunity like those brash start-up companies that fill a market niche by creating it in the first place. Even as he's improvising a crass ditty, he ponders his next scheme: to steal cattle from his rival, the golden god Apollo.

The Greeks make no bones about it: Hermes is a thief. (During one festival on the island of Samos, people honored the god by gleefully committing highway robbery.) But Hermes' banditry should not be confused with appropriations based on raw power. The information trickster works through cleverness and stealth; he is not the mugger or the thug, but the hacker, the spy, the mastermind. When Hermes makes off with Apollo's cattle, he sports specially designed footwear that leaves no tracks, and he forces the animals to walk backward in order to trick his pursuers. When Apollo finally catches up with the kid, Hermes fools him by proclaiming oaths that, like the slickest legal contracts, do not mean what they seem to say. He tells the god of truth that "I don't have any information to give, and the reward for information wouldn't go to me if I did."[5] Finally, the duo journey to Olympus to resolve the conflict. Hermes gives Apollo the lyre, which so pleases the archer that he lets Hermes keep the cattle and grants the young demigod a measure of divine power and prestige.

The conflict between the aristocratic lord Apollo and the young upstart god is instructive. Apollo can be considered the god of science in its ideal form: pure, ordering, embodying the solar world of clarity and light. Hermes insists that there are always cracks and gaps in such perfect architectures; intelligence moves forward by keeping on its crafty toes, ever opening into a world that is messy, unpredictable, and far from equilibrium. The supreme symbol for the fecund space of possibility and innovation that Hermes exploits is the crossroads—a fit image as well for our contemporary world, with its data nets and seemingly infinite choices. In ancient days, the Greeks marked crossroads, village borders, and household doorways with the *herm,* a rectangular pillar surmounted by the head of Hermes (and graced as well with a healthy phallus). At the base of these pillars, hungry travelers would sometimes chance upon offerings to the god—offerings they would duly steal, not to thwart Hermes but to honor the lucky finds he bestows. Some herms were later replaced with wooden posts used as primitive bulletin boards; it may be that the word *trivia* (literally, three roads) derives from the frequently inconsequential nature of these postings.

Crossroads are extremely charged spaces. Here choices are made, fears and facts overlap, and the alien first shows its face: strange people, foreign tongues, exotic and delightful goods and information. Crossroads create what the anthropologist Victor Turner calls "liminal zones": ambiguous but potent spaces of transformation and threat that lie at the edge of cultural maps. Here the self finds itself beyond the limits of its own horizon. "Through Hermes," the mythographer Karl Kerényi writes, "every house became an opening and a point of departure to the paths that come from far off and lead away into the distance."[6] As Norman O. Brown points out in his study *Hermes the Thief,* the liminal quality of the crossroads also derives from the more mundane traffic of trade. In archaic times, the exchange of goods often took place at crossroads and village borders; these swaps were fraught with ambiguity, for they blurred the distinction between gift, barter, magic, and theft. As the commercial networks of the Greek city-states developed, this economic border zone eventually shifted from the wild edges of the village into the more organized markets at the heart of the new urban centers. The outside was swallowed within. Hermes became *agoraios,* "he of the agora," the patron saint of merchants, middlemen, and the service industry, while the god's epithet "tricky" came to mean "good for securing profit."[7]

Certainly Hermes would approve of the Internet, a mercurial network of far-flung messages that functions as a marketplace of ideas and commodities. Accessed through the domestic threshold of home computers, the Net opens up a technological liminal zone that swamps the self with new paths of possibility. Indeed, the mythic attraction of the Net turns on some of the very same qualities associated with the youthful trickster: speed, profit, innovative interconnection, the overturning of established orders. Of course, the information superhighway is also "mythic" in the more modern and critical sense of the term: a strategic distortion, a mirage, a social lie. The utopian rhetoric of the Internet paves over a host of troubling issues: the hidden machinations of the new corporate media powers, the potentially atomizing effects of the terminal screen on social and psychological life, and the bedeviling issue of access, as communication technologies hardwire the widening global gap between rich and poor. But Hermes prepares us for such dangers, because the merchant of messages traffics with deception: He lies and steals, and his magic wand closes human eyes forever, drawing us into the deep sleep of forgetting.

Hermes embodies the mythos of the information age not just because he is the lord of communication, but because he is also a mastermind of *techne,* the Greek word that means the art of craft. Brown points out that in Homer's tongue, the word for "trickiness" is identical to the one for "technical skill"—such as the skill that Hephaestus displays when he forges Achilles' magic shield. Hermes thus unveils an image of technology, not only as useful handmaiden, but as trickster. For all its everyday efficacy, technology stands on shifting ground, giving us at once more and less than its spectacular powers first suggest. Brown insists that Hermes' trickery is not merely a rational device, but an expression of magical power. The god's magic is ambiguous, because we cannot clearly distinguish the clever ruse from the savvy manipulation of some unseen natural fact. With such Hermetic ambiguity in mind, we might say that technology too is a spell and a trick, a device that crafts the real by exploiting the hidden laws of nature and human perception alike.

The Divine Engineer

Hermes the messenger helps us glimpse the powerful archetypal connections between magic, tricks, and technology. But the god does not bloom into a genuine Promethean technomage until he heads south, across the wine-dark sea, to Egypt. Here, in the centuries before the birth of Jesus, the religious imagination of the Hellenistic world crossbred Hermes with the Egyptian scribal god Thoth to create one of the great matinee idols of esoteric lore: Hermes Trismegistus. A thoroughly fabricated figure, the "Thrice-Great" Hermes was nonetheless considered to be a historical person well into the Age of Reason, an error which had considerable consequences, as we shall see. For Hermes Trismegistus does not just capture the ancient world's technological enthusiasm; he also comes down to us as one of the leading lights of the Western mystical tradition, a tradition whose psychospiritual impulses and alchemical images will haunt this book as they have haunted Western dreams.

To appreciate Trismegistus, this golden, hybrid god-man, we need to take a snapshot of Egypt in the age of antiquity. In particular, we need to turn our historical imaginations to the great cosmopolis of Alexandria, founded by Alexander the Great at the mouth of the Nile. With its sophisticated arts and sciences, enormous ethnic and religious diversity, and deeply polyglot culture, Alexandria resonates with our contemporary urban culture like no other city of the ancient world. It is a sister city across time. Under the relatively enlightened despotism of the Ptolemys, a Macedonian dynasty that began ruling Egypt in the fourth century B.C.E., the city of Alexandria became the scientific and technological capital of the Hellenistic world. Ptolemy II oversaw the construction of the massive Pharos lighthouse, the redigging of the ancient Suez Canal, and the establishment of a university whose famous library attempted to collect and systematize the whole of human knowledge for the first time in history. With the king's agents scattered across the known world digging up scrolls on every possible subject, the library eventually contained half a million volumes. According to Galen, one of the Ptolemys was such an information maniac that he would simply confiscate any books found on docked ships in the harbor, keep the ones the library needed, and compensate their hapless owners with copies on cheap papyrus. He even took out an interlibrary loan from Athens, borrowing the works of Sophocles, Euripides, and Aeschylus and then forfeiting his deposit rather than return the originals.

Athens may have been the home of the poets and philosophers, but during its heyday, Alexandria was home to the tinkerers. Ctesibius built singing statues, pumps, and the world's first keyboard instrument, while Philo of Byzantium constructed war machines and automated "magic theaters." And in the first century following the birth of Jesus, when the library had long declined and Roman rule could barely constrain the city's religious and political upheavals, Heron hit the scene. Known as *mechanikos*, the Machine Man, Heron invented the world's first steam engine, developed some sophisticated surveying tools, and crafted handy gizmos like a self-trimming oil lamp. Technically speaking, Heron's clever inventions were particularly notable for their incorporation of the sorts of self-regulating feedback control systems that form the bedrock of cybernetics; like today's toilets, his "Inexhaustible Goblet" regulated its own level with a floating mechanism. But what really stirred Heron's soul were novelties: pneumatic gadgets, automata, and magic theaters, one of which rolled itself before the audience on its own power, cranked through a miniature three-dimensional performance, and then made its own exit. Another staged a Dionysian mystery rite with Apollonian precision: Flames leapt, thunder crashed, and miniature female Bacchantes whirled madly around the wine god on a pulley-driven turntable.

There was nothing particularly sacrilegious about Heron automating the sorts of cult rituals so popular in his day. For centuries, the statues in Egyptian temples had been outfitted with nodding heads and long tubes that could produce the illusion of talking gods. Heron simply took religious technology a step further, engineering "divine signs" for temples: singing birds, invisible trumpet blasts, and mirrors that conjured spooks. He invented an automatic door opener triggered whenever the temple priest lit a fire. Some gadgets just saved the priests time, such as a slot machine that dispensed ritual cleansing water, described in Heron's *Automata* under the irresistible title of "Sacrificial Vessel That Flows Only When Money Is Introduced." But most of his gadgets were wondrous rather than useful—magical machines that paradoxically eroded the cultural authority of the very rational know-how that stimulated their design in the first place. In his book *The Ancient Engineers*, L. Sprague de Camp goes so far as to lay some blame on Heron for "the great wave of supernaturalism that finally killed Roman science."[8]

Still, Roman science must itself take some of the blame for the supernatural riot of astrology, Oriental cults, and strange machines that attended the slow decline of the Empire. As the historian of technology Robert Brumbaugh put it, since the Romans "had already created an objective, impersonal mechanized environment . . . we would expect mechanical ingenuity to move toward amusement, surprise, and escape."[9] And, by extension, toward the kind of popular religious experiences that the Machine Man helped engineer. Heron was not just some cynical Oz propping up decadent priests; he was designing popular spectacles designed to catalyze ecstasy and wonder, classical analogs of the raves or theme parks of our time. Taking Brumbaugh's comment to heart, it might be said that we too live in a time when an impersonal mechanized environment and a rising tide of ecstatic technologies are helping to erode the authority of reason and spark a resurgence of supernatural desires and apocalyptic fears. With such contemporary parallels definitely in mind, the great classical scholar E. R. Dodds dubbed the final centuries of the Roman Empire "an Age of Anxiety," arguing that the regimented and mechanical efficiency of the empire could no longer bottle up the chaos growing inside the souls of its subjects and outside its civic walls.

As the authority of Greek rationalism waned, people began fretting over the perennial existential questions: what was the purpose of life, the value of the body, the fate of the earth, the future of civilization? Traditional answers tasted stale, and the power of the old prophets and Rome's state religion sputtered in the face of new (or renewed) religious forces trickling in from the margins of the empire—astrology, Oriental cults, Christianity, apocalyptic prophecies. Alexandria was ground zero for this almost desperately exuberant period of religious reinvention; during Heron's time, the city's religious climate rivaled the ecumenical fusions, eclectic hybrids, and chiliastic pop cults of our own day. Hellenic Neoplatonism intermingled with Egyptian sorcery, Christianity won its first converts, and pagan philosophers swapped apocalypses with Jewish mystics. Gnostic rumors were whispered in the wings, and even a handful of Buddhist monks dropped some dharma into the stew.

But it was the mystery cults centered around gods like Isis and Mithras that broke all attendance records with their promise of esoteric information and ecstatic revelation. These cults possessed many of the same selling points that have lured modern Western seekers to the East: exoticism, a promise of spiritual experience rather than dogma, and an opportunity for religious reinvention in a time of cultural dissolution. This longing for spiritual experience was coupled with an equally familiar eclecticism: the Gnostic heretic Carpocrates was reported to worship images of Homer, Pythagoras, Plato, Aristotle, Christ, and Saint Paul, while the emperor Alexander Severus kept statues of Abraham, Orpheus, Christ, and Apollonius of Tyana in his personal shrine. Dodds cuts to the anxious heart of this spiritual smorgasbord in terms that many globe-trotting seekers today can second: "There were too many cults, too many mysteries, too many philosophies of life to choose from: you could pile one religious insurance on another, yet not feel safe."[10]

Within Alexandria's hothouse religious atmosphere, the gods were constantly being remixed and retooled. Terra-cotta figures from the time show Egyptian deities cavorting in Greek togas, while Alexandria's powerful patron god Sarapis was a hybrid from the very foundations of the city, a combination of the Egyptian bull-god Apis, Osiris, Zeus, Pluto, and the physician god Asclepius. This is the eclectic spirit of recombinant religion that led to the fusion of the Greek Hermes with the Egyptian god Thoth, the ibis-headed "hypomnematographer," or secretary to the gods, who ruled over two of the most powerful and mysterious technologies in Egypt: magic and hieroglyphs. Out of this crossbreed emerged Hermes Trismegistus.

Unlike both Thoth and Hermes, Trismegistus was not considered a god but a human being, a great wisdom figure who lived at the golden dawn of history. Along with his command of sacred knowledge, Trismegistus also served as a culture hero, a kind of Egyptian Prometheus. Hecateus of Abdera identified him as the inventor of writing, music, and games, while Artapan insisted that Trismegistus taught the Egyptians about water pumps and war machines as well as showing them how to lift stones with cranes. In the *Picatrix*, a medieval Arabic tome that contains a welter of occult materials, we find a powerful image of Trismegistus that strikes such a strangely familiar chord, it is worth quoting at length:

> Hermes was the first who constructed images by means of which he knew how to regulate the Nile against the motion of the moon. This man also built a temple to the Sun, and he knew how to hide himself from all so that no one could see him, although he was within it. It was he, too, who in the east of Egypt constructed a City twelve miles long within which he constructed a castle which had four gates in each of its four parts. On the eastern gate he placed the form of an Eagle; on the western gate, the form of a Bull; on the southern gate, the form of a Lion, and on the northern gate he constructed the form of a Dog. Into these images he introduced spirits which spoke with voices, nor could anyone enter the gates of the City except by their permission. . . . Around the circumference of the City he placed engraved images and ordered them in such a manner that by their virtue the inhabitants were made virtuous and withdrawn from all wickedness and harm.[11]

So much of the twentieth century is anticipated in this description. For the modern technocratic state, there is no symbol more empowering than the regulation and exploitation of rivers. Here Trismegistus achieves this goal, not with brute machines, but with a *symbolic technology:* magical images that tap the hidden currents of the cosmos. But Trismegistus's technologies aren't just magical; they are also utopian. The very intelligence of their design and placement instills goodness within his city's inhabitants, while also protecting them from the dark side of human passions.

The vision of an engineered utopia will return in a variety of guises throughout this book, because technological development in the West has often been driven, and embraced, by the utopian imagination. Pagan utopias like the one in the *Picatrix* would inspire the rational utopias concocted by European thinkers from the Renaissance onward, utopias that would in turn influence the construction of the modern world. But the most important mythic blueprint for future techno-utopians would remain the New Jerusalem, the adamantine hypercity that descends from the apocalyptic skies at the end of the New Testament's Book of Revelation. As a futuristic image of heaven on earth, the New Jerusalem would directly inspire the secular offspring of Christianity's millennialist drive: the myth of progress, which holds that through the ministrations of reason, science, and technology, we can perfect ourselves and our societies.

The *Picatrix* reminds us that utopian thought is technological from the beginning. Trismegistus's magic kingdom is a perfectly designed cybernetic environment, whose feedback mechanisms automatically amplify human virtue even as they dampen human wickedness. As such, the city also anticipates the modern calculus of control that the social critics of the Frankfurt School dubbed "instrumental reason," a calculus of domination that organizes society according to technical manipulation. At its worst, this logic of social engineering leads to the totalitarian state, with its cold logic of indoctrination, security, and control. The Trismegistus we meet in the *Picatrix* is a vision of the magus as Big Brother: Hiding in his panoptic surveillance tower, Hermes controls the gates to his city while extending his power through commanding images that dominate the urban landscape like the hulking statues of Soviet realism or the talking automata of Disneyland. Of course, Trismegistus's aims are no more nefarious than were Heron's when he helped Egyptian priests technologize the supernatural. Most of us would like to live in a more peaceful, virtuous, and wondrous world. But as we will see throughout this book, the magical idea that engineering will create such a world is an ominous and tricky dream, though it seems a mighty difficult dream to shake.

Inscribing the Mind

Though Hermes Trismegistus was renowned for his engineering prowess, the sage's technowizardry also extended into the more incorporeal realms of the human mind. In Plato's *Phaedrus,* for instance, Socrates tells a fascinating little tale about Thoth, the Egyptian god of magic and invention who would mutate in the Alexandrine mind into Trismegistus. According to Socrates, one day Thoth approached King Thamus with an offer of a brand-new *techne:* writing. By giving the gift of writing to the king, Thoth hoped to pass on its wonders to all of the Egyptian people, and he promised Thamus that the new invention would not only augment memory, but amplify wisdom as well. Thamus carefully considered the matter, weighing the pros and cons of this major communications upgrade. Finally, the king rejected the gift, saying that his people would be better off without the new device. And reading between the lines of the story, it's clear that Socrates and Plato agree.

Before we consider the king's gripes, let it be said as frankly as possible: Writing is a machine. Over eons, human beings have invented widely different systems of visually encoding language and thought, and these various pictograms, ideograms, and alphabets have been inscribed and reproduced using a wide variety of secondary inventions—ink, papyrus, parchment, bound codexes, woodblocks, mechanical printing presses, billboards, photocopying machines, and electronic computer screens. The material history of writing is an utterly technological tale.

Though writing has become the most commonplace of information technologies, it remains in many ways the most magical. Brought into focus by properly educated eyes, artificial glyphs scrawled onto the surface of objects leap unbidden into the mind, bringing with them sounds, meanings, and data. In fact, it is very difficult to gaze intentionally upon a page of script written in a known language and *not* automatically begin reading it. The ecophilosopher David Abram notes that, just as a Zuni elder might focus her eyes upon a cactus and hear the succulent begin to speak, so do we hear voices pouring out of our printed alphabets. "This is a form of animism that we take for granted, but it is animism nonetheless—as mysterious as a talking stone."[12] We forget this mystery for the same reason we forget that writing is a technology: We have so thoroughly absorbed this machine into the gray sponge of our brains that it is extremely tough to figure out where writing stops and the mind itself starts. As Walter Ong notes in *Orality and Literacy,* "More than any other single invention, writing has transformed human consciousness."[13]

King Thamus decided that his subjects were better off without this particular transformation. Anticipating Marshall McLuhan's notion that new technologies amputate as much as they amplify, Thamus realized that writing would actually destroy memory by making it dependent on external marks; comparing the memories of people today with the great bards of yore, one is hard-pressed to disagree. More important, Thamus feared that writing would erode the oral context of education and learning, allowing knowledge to escape from the teacher-student relationship and pass into the hands of the unprepared. Consumers of books would then ape the wise, presenting a superficial counterfeit of knowledge rather than the real deal.

There is no little irony in Plato's tacit support of Thamus, and not just because you can find a copy of the *Phaedrus* in the philosophy section of your local bookstore. As a number of scholars have shown, Plato's very philosophy—that architecture which in some distant sense still frames the Western mind, and which inspires much of the mystical lore we will encounter in this book—was the product of a mind that had been thoroughly restructured by the technology of writing. And not just any technology of writing. Plato's mind was marked by the alphabet, the most powerful of all scribal hacks.

The alphabet did not arise in a void. At the time it was invented, around 1500 B.C.E., humans had been living with different forms of writing for millennia. Indeed, if we expand the semiotic notion that human thought is born amidst signs inscribed in space, then it might be said that writing arose at the very moment we might reasonably call the minds of our small hairy ancestors "human." In such a scenario, however, early humans weren't the first ones chiseling inscriptions. Nature unfolded the first text, a flowing scroll of birdflight and bone and pawprint, animated and mapped with sense. As the human imagination flowered, we began to make what we saw, drawing pictures of discrete objects and patterns on caves and rockwalls. These images were virtual traces of the world that everywhere swallowed us up, and eventually these traces grew into picture writing, the cartoon ancestors of hieroglyphs.

Not all of humanity's earliest working symbols were sensual reflections of the surrounding visual world. The naturalistic images created by paleolithic people were often paired with highly abstract designs and glyphs. Around 20,000 years ago, when humans first started crafting bulbous goddess figurines, curious wands also began popping up in southern Europe. Made of bone or antler horn, these batons were etched with sets of simple lines or dotlike pits. Though the etchings on these artifacts were never considered writing, they seemed to represent a discrete digital system of encoding data. Eventually someone dug up a baton that confirmed such suspicions: The bone's sixty-mark notation functioned as a lunar calendar, covering a period of seven and a half months. Though the batons were crafted at a time when our minds were presumably immersed in the animist matrix of enchanted nature, they also represent the growing ability to abstract, symbolize, and dissect the flux of the world. These moonbones may be our first information technology.

The first true writing was itself packed with data. Around six thousand years ago, simple pictograms appeared on temple records in Mesopotamia. These pictorial glyphs mimicked the things that priests wanted to keep track of—basically commodities like cows and sacks of grain. In the third millennium B.C.E., Sumerians took to using clay tablets and reed styluses for such scribblings, with the result that their writing dispensed with curved lines and became far more abstract in appearance. At the same time, parallel writing systems like Egyptian hieroglyphs remained visually tied to the sensual world and were filled with images of beasts and plants and riverflow. Partly for these reasons, Egyptian writing retained a large measure of the animist magic of archaic perception. Like many ancient peoples, the Egyptians believed that a name captured the essence of a thing, but they also held that such supernatural power lived in the inscriptions themselves—that spelling was, in fact, a spell. One ancient text tells us that the high priest of Setne-Khamwas once dissolved one of Thoth's occult texts in a bit of beer and then drank the brew to receive the god's wisdom.

Though early writing was powerful enough to encode elaborate myths, its representational capacity did not extend to human vocal sounds—these marks were mute, like highway signs or religious icons today. But in Mesopotamia and Egypt, picture writing gradually became mixed up with phonetic signs: signs that denote the *sounds* of spoken language, rather than simply words, ideas, or things. The writing machine began to simulate human talk. Finally, in the fifteenth century B.C.E., a few centuries before Moses hightailed it out of Egypt, a Semitic people living in the South Sinai made one of the most genuinely revolutionary breakthroughs in the history of media, one that pushed the writing machine's envelope of phonetic capture and visual abstraction to a new plateau of power and control. They invented the alphabet.

With a small handful of letters, the alphabet arrested the evanescent flux of spoken language, although initially it could only represent the sounds of consonants. The alphabet was an eminently practical code. Besides being easy to learn, it enabled the same set of letters to capture different spoken languages. The Phoenician traders who plied the eastern Mediterranean knew a handy device when they saw one, and they spread these garrulous marks across the ancient world like a virus. In the eighth century B.C.E., Phoenician ships brought the alphabet to Greece.

The infection progressed slowly, and it wasn't until Plato's time that the alphabet began to saturate elite society. Born in 428, the philosopher was among the first generations of young boys who were systematically taught to read. He was also destined to conjure up one of the top-selling metaphysical notions of all time, a notion that irrevocably marked the rationalism, religion, and mysticism of the Western world: the theory of the forms. Plato held that another world exists beyond the realm of temporal flux and gross matter that we perceive with our senses. This other-world is a pure and timeless realm of perfect ideas; the sensual things we perceive around us are only faded Xeroxes of these ideal forms. In his famous allegory, Plato wrote that we are like people chained in a cave with our backs to the fire. We cannot see the true objects whose shadows are cast on the wall before us; instead we become entranced with their flickering, insubstantial reflections. The philosopher's goal is to turn away from these fetching simulacra and to live and think in accordance with the intelligible realm of the forms, a realm of genuine knowledge that reveals itself through reason.

In *Preface to Plato,* the scholar Eric A. Havelock argues that the realm of the forms may also have revealed itself to Plato through the alphabet. Havelock points out that the etymological root of the term *idea,* which also gives us the word *video,* has a visual connotation. Havelock argues that Platonic forms were conceived as analogies to visible forms, not just the perfect shapes of geometry, but the visible forms of the alphabet. Like letters, Platonic ideas were immobile, isolated, and devoid of warmth and secondary qualities; they seem to transcend the world at hand. As David Abram observes, "The letters, and the written words that they present, are not subject to the flux of growth and decay, to the perturbations and cyclical changes common to other visible things; they seem to hover, as it were, in another, strangely timeless dimension."[14] Abram also points out that the Greek alphabet was the first writing machine to capture vowels as well as consonants, thus completing the technological colonization of the spoken world. Abstract form came to rule embodied sense. The oracular animism that once echoed through hieroglyphs died away, and the Greeks began to associate truth with what was eternal, incorporeal, and inscribed.

Information technology may thus form the matrix of Greece's revolutionary philosophical turn. With their minds partly reformatted by alphabetic literacy, the rationalist Greek philosophers who followed Plato were able to detach their thoughts from the flowing surfaces of the material world. Nature became an impersonal and objective domain that could be dissected and analyzed in order to yield rational and general laws based on cause-and-effect explanations. Democritus, a contemporary of Plato, was the first to argue that the holistic tapestry of the cosmos was actually made up of discrete atoms. Not coincidentally, Democritus compared this atomic structure to the way that written words were formed from the bits of the alphabet.

The power and knowledge unleashed by literate rationalism was extraordinary; it paved the way, however indirectly, for modern Europe's technoscientific triumph. But like all powerful technologies, Thoth's useful tool transformed the user as well. For once the writing machine is interiorized to some degree, it can serve as both the most abstract and most intimate of mirrors; with it (literally) in mind, the self can reflect upon itself, sharpening the scalpel of its own introspection and setting itself against the external world. As Marshall McLuhan argued, "The alphabet shattered the charmed circle and resonating magic of the tribal world, exploding man into an agglomeration of specialized and psychically impoverished individuals or units, functioning in a world of linear time and Euclidian space."[15]

It wasn't until the modern era that this sense of rational detachment and alienated reflection came to dominate and define the experience of being an individual human being—an experience that, as McLuhan and others have argued, was aided and abetted by the printing press. For Plato, literate introspection may have catalyzed something far more mystical: his revolutionary belief that an incorporeal spirit lurks within the self, and that this immortal spark of intelligence is independent of the speaking, breathing body. The psychology is understandable. Just as letters and written words hold their truths above the fleeting world of flesh, and even keep a dead man's words alive, so may readers suspect that their own literate minds belong to a similarly timeless realm of transcendental essences.

Plato was not the first Greek to believe that a deathless wraith sluiced through our mortal meat. Before him, both the Orphics and Pythagoreans insisted that human beings contained an incorporeal, perpetually reincarnating soul—a notion they probably picked up from archaic shamanic lore that trickled down from Scythia and Thrace. Plato was influenced by both of these mystic sects, but while the Orphics and the Pythagoreans described the soul in the slippery lingo of myth and symbol, Plato gave the idea a metaphysical and cosmological foundation, thus wedding it to his broader rationalist project. Indeed, Plato's simultaneous embrace of rational thought and mysticism underscores one of the suspicions that guide this book: that the works of reason cannot be so easily riven from more otherworldly pursuits.

Plato calls his intelligible soul the *psyche,* and it takes shape against the powerful backdrop of his metaphysical map of cosmic reality. For Plato, the planet earth is the dusty basement of a multilayered cosmological high-rise. In the penthouse suite reside the pure and perfect forms, and it is there that our rational souls are born. Once we descend the elevator into incarnation, however, this immortal essence is submerged in the slothful bags of fluid and bone we lug about planetside. For Plato, as for the Neoplatonist mystics that followed him, the goal of the philosopher was to transcend the gravitational tug of the body in order to launch what the scholar Ioan Couliano calls the "Platonic space shuttle." In this visionary flight, the rational spark ascends to the heavens where it glimpses its own essential divinity amidst the world of the forms—a transcendental twist on the old shamanic plunge into the belly of the earth.

Plato's metaphysical cosmology would come to exert an enormous influence on the Western psyche, encouraging the transmutation of the earthy soul into the invisible inwardness of the spirit. By the time of Jesus, a few hundred years after the philosopher's death, the transcendental drive that Plato articulated in philosophical terms had already manifested itself as a peculiarly dour and increasingly offworld spiritual temperament. Gazing with homesick longing at the heavens, many seekers sought gnostic escape, the ascetic mastery of the body, or an otherworldly journey into the realms of apocalyptic vision. For the most extreme, the natural world itself came to be seen as a prison, even though Plato and most Neoplatonists embraced the earth as a "visible God" that reflected the harmony of the higher spheres. Instead, the religious self of late antiquity—at least in some of its many manifestations—found itself facing a chasm between the timeless heavens of the transcendent godhead and the demon-haunted mud puddle where our bodies copulate, sicken, and die.

Obviously the alphabet alone cannot be blamed for this binary sense of transcendental estrangement between earth and the divine. But as the literary scholar David Porush points out, "Every time culture succeeds in revolutionizing its cybernetic technologies, in massively widening the bandwidth of its thought-tech, it invites the creation of new gods." The written word, more an artifact of a human and mental world than an ecological or embodied one, speaks at one remove from the natural world, and thus stands against the pagan ways of those who live amidst the animist powers and images of that world (the Oriental mystery cults paid notoriously scant attention to texts). Porush argues that the invention of the phonological alphabet "almost certainly made the idea of an abstract monotheistic God thinkable for the first time."[16]

Porush is not thinking about Plato here, but about the Jews, whose reliance on the abstract space of the Hebrew alphabet seems consonant with the Hebraic religious innovation of a single overseeing god whose rule of law, enshrined in the narrative and legal writings of the Torah, enforces a tribe's sense of spiritual separation from their neighbors. That's why God sends down inscribed tablets of instruction from the spiritual mountaintop, and why he simultaneously condemns the golden idols that stir the imaginations of the people below. Though Jewish religious life remained focused on temple sacrifices and a priestly caste for more than a millennium, sacred writings still formed a matrix of divine authority. Moreover, the Torah was, and is, treated as a fetishistic object of cultic reverence; to this day, Orthodox Jewish men strap *tefillin*—boxes containing small pieces of parchment inscribed with scripture—on their forehead and arm during morning prayers.

Following the destruction of the Second Temple in 70 C.E., when priestly sacrifices ceased and the Jews were scattered from Palestine, Hebrew texts became the central locus of religious activity. In a sense, the Torah replaced the Temple, becoming the textual architecture of the Jewish people, their virtual homeland. What Christians call the "Old Testament" was finally canonized, and the rabbis began writing down the oral Torah, which had been passed down by word of mouth for centuries as a supplement to the written Torah. The study of Torah itself became a sacred act, while the exegetical literature of the Talmud developed an immense hypertextual literature that allowed people to both regulate and debate every facet of their lives. (Modern printed editions of the Talmud anticipate hypertext technologies, embedding the text within a complex nest of cross-references, notes, commentaries, commentaries on commentaries, and links.) On the one hand, the Jews emphasized the absolute authority of a sacred piece of writing; in the second century, for example, Rabbi Ishmael commanded the scribes to be "vigilant in your occupation, for your labor is the labor of heaven. Were you to diminish or add even one letter, you would destroy the entire universe."[17] At the same time, the endless feedback loops of Talmudic commentary, with its dialectical dance between metaphor and literal command, demonstrate that the technology of the word is embedded in a changing social world and can never capture the ever-transcending spirit of the divine. Though God's name can be written, it remains literally unpronounceable, and thus ultimately unknowable.

The interpretive elaboration of Torah was a godsend for the Jews, for the activity was concrete enough to knit them into a community of interpretation and rootless enough to follow them everywhere they wandered. Besides naming the body of Jewish lore, the notion of Torah also served as a sacred symbol, one that exerted a profound influence on Western mysticism. According to the *Sefer Yetsirah*, an important mystical text written between the third and sixth centuries, the twenty-two letters of the Hebrew alphabet—along with the ten *Sefiroth*, or number-spheres—constitute a kind of cosmic DNA code. As the text proclaims, "[God] drew them, hewed them, combined them, weighed them, interchanged them, and through them produced the whole creation and everything that is destined to be created."[18] This alphabetic line of mystical thought, amplified with Neoplatonic metaphysics, would later blossom into Kabbalah. In the thirteenth century, Kabbalists like Abraham Abulafia used Hebrew letters as objects of ecstatic meditation, recombining them in their imaginations to engender alphabetic rapture, while others employed a variety of decoding techniques based on the substitution and transposition of letters to squeeze esoteric meanings from the written Torah.

By acknowledging the mystic multiplicity of the text while emphasizing the profoundly human activity of commentary and interpretation, the Jews helped avoid the world-loathing and apocalyptic transcendentalism that often marked the other great religion of the book to emerge from the ancient world: Christianity. Arising from the religious carnival of the late Roman empire, Christianity stood out in stark contrast to the pagan mystery cults by giving pride of place to text. Though the early Christians emphasized the verbal broadcast of the *kerygma,* the "good news" of redemption through Christ, they also came from Jewish roots, and embraced the writing machine with an unprecedented passion. Even before the gospel stories of Jesus gained prominence, letters from the apostles and early Church leaders circulated widely through the budding Christian world, helping to spread the gospel while stitching together far-flung and often persecuted communities. Paul's mission was in many ways defined by his powerful and widely disseminated correspondence, which drew part of its considerable authority from his brilliant sampling of Jewish texts. As Christianity grew, believers cranked out an astronomical number of tracts, epistles, commentaries, homilies, martyr acts, and synodical communications, and these writings were consumed with a passion and seriousness unparalleled in the pagan world. As Harry Gamble writes in *Books and Readers in the Early Church,* "For Christians, texts were not entertainments or dispensable luxuries, but the essential instruments of Christian life."[19]

These instruments also took an unusual technological form. During the rise of the Christian church, the vast majority of Jewish and pagan texts continued to be written on papyrus scrolls. But for reasons that are still being chewed over, Christians embraced the codex—basically the same bound and covered leaf book you're now holding in your hands. At the time, most pagans regarded the codex as nothing more than an ephemeral notebook, private and utilitarian rather than literary. Most scholars believe that Christians welcomed the new storage device for similarly practical reasons. The codex book was economical, easy to lug around from town to town, and it allowed for random access—a handy feature when you are citing scripture to prove a point in the timeworn manner of biblical exegetes.

Unlike the Torah scroll, the codex book was never explicitly worshiped as a cultic object, nor was the language of its composition—the street Greek that served as the ancient world's *lingua franca*—considered the unique tongue of God. Christians were more interested in the text as a vehicle for the transmission of the *logos,* God's spoken word and transcendental plan. At the same time, the codex format helped generate a distinctly Christian sense of religious authority. Gamble argues that by binding Paul's correspondence in one volume, which Christians began doing at an early date, letters that had been aimed at individual churches took on the universal "broadcast" quality of scripture. As the volume of sacred writings grew, the codex format stuck because it served as an excellent structure of religious authority. When the final cut of the Bible was made in the fourth century, the bound book allowed orthodox compilers to create an "official edition" that could dispense with any spurious, strange, or heretical texts—especially those that might call into question the supreme validity of the now institutionalized Roman Church.

Though more than willing to bring the illiterate into the fold, Christianity can almost be defined by the archetype of the Book: singular, universal, possessing a crisp beginning and a dynamite end. From the multimedia illuminations of medieval manuscripts to the mass market success of the Book of Common Prayer to the "literal word" preached by today's Bible thumpers, the medium of the book has structured the Christian religious temperament, encouraging both its fetish for rule and its thirst for transcendent inwardness. Unlike the book of the Jews, with its endless nest of commentary and debate, the technology of the Christian word has more often been associated with the immediacy and presence of direct transmission, of communication in the most idealized and absolute sense of the word.

Faiths based on revealed scripture, which Muslims call the religions of the book, insist on the profound distinction between letter and spirit. But the real action may lie in the feedback loops that cross this rather mysterious divide. Reading *inspires,* opening up vistas of meaning and interpretation that further unfold the self, even as this freedom is ultimately limited by the horizon of the text, the reader, and history itself. Fundamentalist certitude to the contrary, working with scriptures is a tricky and open-ended process, because the machinery of text can never contain and control all its own meanings. It is no accident that the name of Hermes appears in *hermeneutics,* the science and methodology of scriptural interpretation—a "science" that is really more of an art. When the historian of religion Mircea Eliade complained that "we are condemned to learn about the life of the spirit and be awakened to it through books,"[20] he didn't acknowledge that this living spirit is in many ways the spirit *of* books. Reading cannot contain religious experience, but it can certainly catalyze it, as no less august a figure than Saint Augustine discovered on the day he finally found the Lord.

Augustine's famous conversion experience appears in his *Confessions,* which is often considered to be the first true autobiography. Reading the book, one senses a quality of internal struggle and anxious self-reflection not found in other ancient writings, as if the slow alchemy of the literate self is finally coming to boil. Before his conversion, Augustine tells us, he was a passionate follower of Manichaeism, a strongly dualistic gnostic religion that pitted the world of light against the world of matter. Dissatisfied with the mediocre Manichean intellectuals of the day, Augustine then discovered Neoplatonism, whose contemplative religion of inwardness gave him a mystical glimpse of the "changeless light" of God. Yearning for the Platonic rocket-ride, Augustine nonetheless came to believe that the flesh could not be broken without the grace of the Christian God. Unfortunately, his proud and apparently rather randy will refused to submit to the ascetic yoke of Jesus, and this conflict launched the man into profound existential torment.

One day, with his "inner self" feeling like "a house divided against itself," Augustine plopped down in the garden outside his home and had what we would now call a nervous breakdown. Weeping, he heard a child in the distance, chanting a nonsense rhyme: *Tolle, lege, tolle, lege.* "Take it and read, take it and read." Taking the rhyme as a message from God, Augustine went inside and, employing a bit of textual divination popular in the ancient world, randomly opened up a copy of Paul's Epistles, and let his eyes fall where they would: ". . . put on the Lord Jesus Christ, and make no provision for the flesh, to gratify its desires" (Rom. 13:14). Augustine snapped. He was born again, a soul freed from the urgings of nature by the fleshless message of a book. The chicken scratch of Sumerian bureaucrats had blossomed into an oracular delivery mechanism for the Word of God, one powerful enough to trigger the speck of essence within—and to prove that humble infotech may, in time, boot up the sacred self.

Humanist Hermetica

Although a detailed history of the relationship between the writing machine and the Western spirit lies outside the framework of this book, we cannot leave the ancient world without cracking open one more text: the *Corpus Hermeticum.* An esoteric patchwork of alchemical, astrological, and mystical writings compiled from the second to the fourth centuries C.E., the *Hermetica* was mythically considered to be a single work composed by our old friend Hermes Trismegistus. While a distinctly Christian aroma wafts through its pages, the *Hermetica* remains a pagan text, one steeped in popular Platonism and marked by the offworld religious temperament of late antiquity. The book presents an image of human beings as star-beings in corporeal disguise. Its various writings imply that, through a kind of alchemy of the soul, at once philosophical and mystical, the budding Hermeticist can transmute the clay of his lower nature into the golden light of *gnosis,* a mystic flash of luminescent knowledge that awakens the divine intelligence at the heart of the self. Alongside this transcendental mysticism, the *Hermetica* also embodies the mechanistic imagination of Egyptian sorcery. As Garth Fowden explains in *The Egyptian Hermes,* the archetypal Egyptian wizard was a kind of divine technologist; his power "was considered to be unlimited, certainly equivalent to that of the gods, once he had learned the formulae by which the divine powers that pervaded the universe could be bound and loosed."[21] The *Hermetica* thus presents itself as a spiritual operating manual for worlds both near and far.

The modern world owes more to the *Hermetica*'s mystical mixture of gnostic psychology and occult mechanics than one might suppose. The book reentered the Western imagination during the Italian bloom of Renaissance humanism, the first really modern moment in history. Working on Arabic translations of old Greek and Latin texts, scholars in the bustling, entrepreneurial city-state of Florence—the launching pad for the new intellectual era—reacquainted Europe with Greco-Roman civilization. Hermes Trismegistus still possessed a mighty reputation, one that put him on a par with the prophet Moses. So when the Florentine industrialist and multinational financier Cosimo de Medici finally got his hands on an Arabic copy of the *Hermetica,* he ordered Marsilio Ficino to stop translating Plato and get to work on the old wizard instead.

Renaissance intellectuals imbibed the *Hermetica* like a metaphysical ambrosia distilled from the dawn of time. When Pico della Mirandola famously proclaimed "what a miracle is man" in his groundbreaking humanist screed *Oration on the Dignity of Man,* he was announcing the revolutionary conviction that human beings were the arbiters of their own fate. But Pico was also quoting the *Hermetica* word for word, reframing its alchemical dream of self-divinization for the more dynamic world then emerging from the static cosmos of the Middle Ages. Man was to be a magus, blessed with the access codes of cosmos and mind, making himself up as he went along. In the *Oration,* Pico quotes the Supreme Maker: "We have made you a creature neither of heaven nor of earth, neither mortal nor immortal, in order that you may, as the free and proud shaper of your own being, fashion yourself in the form you may prefer."[22] In this statement are the seeds of the modern world: Humanity slips into the cockpit, fuels up on reason, will, and imagination, and sets off on a forward-looking flight unrestrained by religious authority or natural curbs. We are self-made mutants, the "free and proud" shaper, of our own beings—and, perhaps inevitably, of the world at large.

The cosmology of the *Hermetica* proved irresistibly interactive to men like Pico and Ficino, encouraging an instrumentalist attitude toward a universe suffused with energy and force. The *Hermetica* pictured the cosmos as a living soul, a magnetic network of correspondences that linked the earth, the body, the stars, and the remote spiritual realms of the godhead. This *anima mundi* could be accessed and tweaked by the symbolic rituals of ceremonial magic, even by a deeply pious Christian Neoplatonist like Ficino. Employing a multimedia array of tools that included talismans, stones, gestures, and scents, mages like Ficino would invoke and redirect this resonating array of phantasms and forces. To tap the love vibe, for example, the magician would wait until the planet Venus floated into a beneficent stellar way station, at which point he would ritually deploy those objects and elements associated with his Venusian goal: copper and rose, the lamp and the loins, and talismans inscribed with the iconography of the goddess.

Contemporary psychologists like James Hillman and Thomas Moore have taken up Ficinian magic as a model for the archetypal psychology they call "soul-work." These thinkers believe that much of the withering anomie of modern life might be overcome by a return to the enchanted but dynamic cosmos of the Renaissance Hermeticists. But the blend of humanist confidence and cosmic manipulation found in Renaissance occultism also foreshadowed the knowledge-hungry and instrumental attitude toward the world that, after a number of twists and turns, came to dominate the technoscience of modern civilization. According to Frances Yates, one of the great historians of the hermetic tradition, "the Renaissance conception of an animistic universe, operated by magic, prepared the way for the conception of a mechanical universe, operated by mathematics."[23] As Yates points out, the figure of the Renaissance magus reinvented the modus operandi of human will. "It was now dignified and important for man to operate; it was also religious and not contrary to the will of God that man, the great miracle, should exert his powers."[24] Ultimately, these powers were not directed toward the mystical goal of self-divinization, but toward the creation, through technology, of the millennial kingdom that crowns the Christian myth.

Of all hermetic arts, it is alchemy that most directly anticipates modern science and its passion for material transformation. This should not be too surprising, for the fiery hieroglyphic dramas of alchemy originally drew their lore from metallurgy, one of the most powerful and mysterious technologies of the ancient world. As Eliade argues in his great study *The Forge and the Crucible,* metallurgists were the hacker wizards of their day, animist engineers who snatched the materials gestating in the cavernous womb of Mother Nature and sped up their organic evolution in the artificial vessel of the forge. Draped with taboos, their labor was an *opus contra naturum*—a work against nature, as the alchemists would later say. From this metallurgic opus derived the most stereotypical goal of the alchemist: the transmutation of coarse metals like lead into gold, a quest to create free value from worthless ore that apparently led the most profane alchemists to counterfeit coin.

The history and symbolism of alchemy is full of paradoxes and bedeviling obscurities, and we should not be surprised to find that the lord of the work was Mercurius, the god whose metallic namesake captures the quicksilver intelligence and deep ambiguity of the art itself. Like the slippery figure of Hermes, alchemy places a tremendous emphasis on polarity, on the dynamic, erotic, and highly combustible interaction—or *conjunctio*—of contrary elements and states of being. This propulsive ambiguity is also reflected in the question all alchemical scholars must confront as they investigate the history of the art: What were these fellows actually *doing*? Was the Great Work physical or spiritual, sexual or imaginal, grubby or contemplative? The language and imagery of alchemy conjure up grimy laboratories of bubbling alembics, broiling furnaces and putrefying muck, and it seems quite evident that many alchemists were occupied with practical chemical researches into the formation of gold and other metals. At the same time, the work of Carl Jung and others has clearly established that alchemy was also a language of archetypal symbolism that did its dirty work in the virtual labs of the soul.

For the mystics of alchemy, the psyche is not fixed in stone. Instead, its coarse or base qualities could be refined through psychological and perhaps physiological techniques that drew their inspiration from metallurgic lore. In China, where metal was considered a fifth element alongside earth, water, fire, and wood, this tradition of "internal alchemy" focused rather obsessively on creating the elixir of immortality. In the Islamic world and Europe, alchemists sought the famous philosopher's stone—an ambiguous and mercurial icon that simultaneously signified a real rock, an extraordinary tincture, and the ultimate goal of transmuting stuff (including the body) into immortal spirit. Among Christian alchemists, the *lapis philosophorum* became associated, not only with Christ the redeemer, but with the salvation of the world itself—a cornerstone, as it were, of the future New Jerusalem.

Far from leading to brain-rotting superstition, the magical animism of alchemy and other hermetic arts helped spur those practices and paradigms now known as science. The hermetic worldview created men like Paracelsus, a wandering healer and alchemist of the early sixteenth century who rejected the Aristotelian medical lore the Church still embraced in favor of investigating the body itself. Now considered the origin of modern medical pharmacology, Paracelsus's researches were embedded within a deeply magical worldview awash with spiritual agencies and millennialist dreams of human perfection. The next century brought tremendous leaps in what was then called "natural philosophy," but from optics to astronomy to chemistry, many of these findings first crystallized in an occult crucible. Isaac Newton played a pivotal role in establishing the mechanistic view of the cosmos that overthrew Neoplatonism, dominated physics until the twentieth century, and continues to influence science's basic orientation toward the natural world. But even as Newton publicly participated in Britain's newly established Royal Society, which had elected reason as the sole arbiter of natural philosophy, he remained privately committed to the magical wonders of hermetic science and burnt plenty of midnight oil pouring over alchemical tomes.

By the close of the seventeenth century, the historical dynamic unleashed by science could only proceed by banishing the soul from the landscape of things. The art of alchemy, the supreme Western hybrid of material investigation and psychic introspection, was sliced into exoteric and esoteric wings, chemistry and the occult. Latour's Great Divide was constructed: a sky-high conceptual wall separating the now blind and mute world of nature from the endlessly mutable world of culture and its merely human meanings. But though the technological projects of empirical science and the alchemical projects of mystical gnosis would come to seem as different as apples and orangutans, in a sense they both derive from the archetype of the hermetic magus. Ioan Couliano explains:

> Historians have been wrong in concluding that magic disappeared with the advent of "quantitative science." The latter has simply substituted itself for a part of magic while extending its dreams and its goals by means of technology. Electricity, rapid transport, radio and television, the airplane, and the computer have merely carried into effect the promises first formulated by magic, resulting from the supernatural processes of the magician: to produce light, to move instantaneously from one point in space to another, to communicate with faraway regions of space, to fly through the air, and to have an infallible memory at one's disposal.[25]

Couliano reminds us that while technology has certainly hastened the horsemen of secular humanism and the rise of mechanistic ideology, it has also subliminally reawakened and fleshed out images and desires first cooked up in the alchemical beakers of hermetic mysticism. The powerful aura that today's advanced technologies cast does not derive solely from their novelty or their mystifying complexity; it also derives from their literal realization of the virtual projects willed by the wizards and alchemists of an earlier age. Magic is technology's unconscious, its own arational spell. Our modern technological world is not nature, but augmented nature, super-nature, and the more intensely we probe its mutant edge of mind and matter, the more our disenchanted productions will find themselves wrestling with the rhetoric of the supernatural.

the alchemical fire

Of all the forces crackling through the cosmos, electricity most embodies the spirit of modernity. Investigators first began experimenting with electricity during the Enlightenment, and within two centuries the West had tamed and ruled its powerful mysteries. Technologies of communication and control now utterly depend on the electrical grid, and our minds have grown quite comfortable—perhaps too much so—with the electron's conquest of shadows, stars, and silence. Electricity feeds modernity; it is our profane illumination.

But for all its practicality, the behavior of electricity itself is rather bizarre. Most of the dynamic nonbiological phenomena we encounter on a regular basis—paper airplanes, rush-hour fender benders, speeding tennis balls—can be dissected with the tools of classical physics, and classical physics does not make too many outrageous claims on the contemporary imagination. But electricity is an altogether different kettle of fish—to say nothing of the counterintuitive shenanigans that go down in the invisible world of electromagnetic fields and frequencies, which even now are saturating your body with traffic reports, pop songs, and other incorporeal communiqués.

Let's just take your nearest working household appliance, which presumably is plugged into an enormous decentralized electric grid. The current for this Internet of power alternates its positive and negative poles sixty times a second (fifty if you're reading in Europe). That's pretty quick, but more remarkable still is the superman pace that the current itself keeps as it hurtles along the line, which happens to be nothing less than the speed of light. Now, you may wonder what exactly this "current" is that could enable it to hustle along at such a healthy clip. Your high school science teacher would tell you that this flow consists of little specks of energetic charge called electrons, which are actually moving relatively slowly as they alternate back and forth across the copper atoms that make up your wire. But just as water molecules can move relatively slowly beneath fast-moving ocean waves, these electrons are also *communicating their energy,* and it is this "energy"—a pattern of current and voltage—that trucks along at the universal speed limit.

As if that isn't odd enough, any gadget actually sucking energy from the electric grid—say, a toaster—also generates an electromagnetic field (actually a combination of electric and magnetic fields). This field will induce a mild current flow in any nearby conductor, including your body, even if no physical contact is involved. The field itself, they tell us, is composed of "lines of force," which have nothing to do with acupuncture meridians or the layout of Stonehenge but are nonetheless more than passing strange. Technically speaking, the lines of force emanating from your toaster actually tweak stellar nebulae at the farthest ends of God's great universe. And lest you believe that such remote control represents the kind of spooky action-at-a-distance that science abhors, a quantum physicist would calmly explain that electromagnetic fields are no less real than light, and that they simply transmit their force through particles, like bosons and such, that pop in and out of "virtual existence."

You may take all this as a matter of course, but such curiosities cannot help but stimulate some people's cosmological imaginations. Perhaps it is our fate as moderns to exploit the sublime for the banal, but the fact that we use the electromagnetic dimensions for heating up Pop-Tarts and transmitting golf tournaments should not blind us to the sorts of profundities they can sound. Like the moon's tidal tug, or the luminous aurora of northern climes, or a sunbeam fractured into rainbow, these arresting forces cannot help but generate cosmic meditations along with intellectual curiosity and utilitarian plots. Vibrating in the gap between life and physics, between matter and the unseen ether, electricity inhabits a liminal zone that calls down spirits and sublimities out of thin air.

"Do we really know what electricity is?" asks Lama Anagarika Govinda, a German scholar who became one of the earliest Western converts to Tibetan Buddhism. "By knowing the laws according to which it acts and by making use of them we still do not know the origin or the real nature of this force, which ultimately may be the very source of life, light, and consciousness, the divine power and mover of all that exists."[26] Maybe yes, maybe no; what's important is that electricity's uncanny play leads us to ask, not how it works or how it can be captured in jargon, but what it *is*. This is the kind of natural philosophy that can set one wondering about the whole enchilada of space and time, mind and bodies. For electricity does not just catapult your imagination into the metaphysical empyrean; it also grounds you on the earth. Govinda compares its curious properties to the animistic myths of traditional societies, myths "which only express what the poets of all times have felt: that nature is not a dead mechanism, but vibrant with life, with the same life that becomes vocal in our thoughts and emotions."[27]

As we'll see, the romance of electricity and animism is an old one in the Western imagination. Govinda's vitalist interpretation of electric current, which loosely links it to the "life force" of the body and nature, is only one of a number of archetypes and intuitions that make up what I'll call, ignoring the technical differences between the forces involved, the "electromagnetic imaginary." Since the seventeenth century, the electromagnetic imaginary has seeped into religion, medicine, and technology, and over that time has probably led to more metaphysical speculations, heretical claims, and wacky gizmos than any other natural force. Much of this chapter traces the electromagnetic imaginary through the eighteenth and nineteenth centuries, when electricity catalyzed the kind of heady enthusiasms that data devices do today. In fact, the transformation of electrical current into a communicating medium, which took place in the mid-nineteenth century, represents perhaps its most remarkable mutation: from energy into information.

From the outset, I urge you to resist the temptation to write off the electromagnetic imaginary as pseudoscientific dreck or the manipulative lies of quacks. For one thing, even the nuttiest notions about material reality emerge from our need to stitch together, however provisionally, the world we feel with the world we know. Moreover, we make the historical determination between "real" science and wild-eyed speculations in the rearview mirror, and even then, only selectively. For all its skeptical rigor, science and its truth-claims can never be completely distilled from the cultural and mythic murk that characterizes all human societies. Latour's Great Divide is full of secret passageways and cosmological cracks; scientists too are shadowed by looming dreams, and stake their claims alongside pregnant intuitions and metaphysical imaginings. As the French historian of science Michel Serres put it: "The only pure myth is the idea of a science devoid of all myth."[28]

The word *electricity* entered the English tongue in a 1650 translation of a treatise on the healing properties of magnets by Jan Baptist van Helmont, a Flemish physician and Rosicrucian who worked on the borderline between natural magic and modern chemistry. Though Helmont abandoned the hoary doctrines of the four elements, he remained spiritually committed to the alchemy of "pyrotechnia," the Paracelsan labor of the forge. As an incorporeal force coaxed out of matter, the quicksilver spunk of electricity signified for many of Helmont's ilk the spiritual energies pregnant in the physical universe, the elixir of the World Soul, the spark of Creation. Many of the earliest books on electricity described the force in distinctly alchemical terms, dubbing it the "ethereal fire," the "quintessential fire," or the "desideratum," the long-sought universal panacea. Now that electronics, electric power, radio waves, and microwaves form the energetic matrix of the information age, the patterns of the electromagnetic imaginary have in many cases just slipped right into the technological unconscious. As the historian Dennis Stillings argues, "Material science could not pull itself clear from the psychological residuum that adhered to electrical theorizing, thus permitting the symbols carried by electricity to drive modern science toward accomplishments that strongly echo the goals of alchemy."[29] Electricity, in particular, would carry three different aspects of the alchemical imagination into the modern world: the fascination with the vitality of bodies, the desire to spiritualize material form, and the millennarian drive to transmute the energies of earth into the divine realization of human dreams.

The Body Electric

For the natural philosophers and tinkerers of the eighteenth century, electrical experimentation was a calling worthy of the most hackerish obsessions. One such electrogeek was the young Benjamin Franklin, who built a name for himself by knocking together electrostatic machines and writing intelligent articles on the mysterious force. Franklin was the first to recognize that the "electrical fluid" was polarized into what he described as "positively" and "negatively" charged states. Franklin also reasoned that when differently charged bodies came into contact with one another, the fluid equalized itself—which is exactly what happened when the young fellow launched his famous kite from a Maryland tobacco field in 1752. Grasping the soaking kite string, Franklin felt a "very evident electric spark" blast through his hearty frame to loose itself in the earth. Not only did Franklin prove that lightning was a form of electricity, but he also came up with the practical idea for the lightning rod—having, for an instant, actually become one.

Besides inspiring a lifesaving invention, Franklin's kite trick resonated on the archetypal plane. The thunderbolt had been an active symbol of the wrath of the gods since time immemorial, and Franklin forced that crackling shaft of judgment to run aground. The fact that it was a future framer of the American Constitution who both tamed and demystified heaven's numinous bolts only underscored the Prometheanism of the act. Franklin's lightning rod was another declaration of independence—from needless death, from a wrathful sky-god, from an enchanted earth. As the epigram on a French bust of Franklin put it, "He wrested the flash of lightning from heaven, and the scepter from the tyrants."[30]

But Franklin was not the first electrofreak to catch thunderbolts. A Moravian monk named Prokop Divisch actually invented the lightning rod a few years before Franklin, though Divisch's instrument met with considerably less success on the tradition-bound Continent. The monk's absence from the annals of popular science is also emblematic of the different faces of electricity. Where Franklin stands as a visible monument to the secular conquest of electricity in the pursuit of natural dominion, Divisch and his theosophical speculations open up the esoteric dimension of the electrical imaginary, one that finds in the "balsam of nature" an incandescent symbol of spiritual power.

In his book *The Theology of Electricity,* the German scholar Ernst Benz explains how Divisch's work was taken up by Friedrich Christoph Oetinger, the Protestant dean of Württemberg and the founder of a deeply theosophical strain of German Pietism. Oetinger and the other "electrical theologians" in his circle were the Fritjof Capras of their day—spiritual thinkers who attempted to integrate their understanding of science into a mystical view of the universe. While English Deists like John Toland and Thomas Woolston pounced on magnetic or electrical forces as demystifying explanations for Christ's miracles (loaves and fishes—zzzaapp!), Oetinger's crew of natural philosophers went the other direction. They electrified theology, revising the image of man and earth in the process.

They began, as you might guess, at the beginning of things. The Book of Genesis claims that on the first day of creation, God turns on the cosmic light switch and calls it good. But Oetinger noticed that, according to the text, the Lord doesn't get around to creating the sun, the moon, and the stars for another couple of days. So what exactly was this first "light," and where did it go once Sol rose over Eden? Oetinger believed that the first light was actually the "electrical fire," which penetrated and stimulated the primeval chaos, giving it form and energy. After the sun and moon hit the scene, this essential light disappeared into the fabric of things, popping up only during special occasions, like thunderstorms or the manipulation of electrostatic machines by curious monks.

Far from simply absorbing electricity into existing Christian cosmology, Oetinger's electrical imagination opened up a rather radical and animistic vision of nature. In his view, the world was not a lump of blind clay whose life force directly depended on a transcendent God, nor were its physical forms solely derived from the divine cookie cutters that the Lord used during the first week of creation. Instead, the weird sparks collected by Divisch's lightning-catchers furnished Oetinger with proof of the *anima mundi,* the living World Soul. Matter was endowed *from the beginning* with spirit, life, and intelligence, and it constantly strives to manifest new forms and new comminglings. This deeply evolutionary notion anticipates the "Creation Spirituality" discussed by the contemporary Green Christian Matthew Fox, another theosophical Christian who displaces the top-down control of the transcendent Creator by embracing the immanent bloom of nature.

At a time when philosophers and scientists were dividing human beings into mind and body, reason and mechanical matter, Oetinger and friends insisted on the Neoplatonic view of humanity as a threefold creature of body, soul, and spirit. Oetinger agreed with his fellow theologians that when God scraped up the clay to create Adam, he exhaled a rational spirit into his body. But for Oetinger, that dust was already animated by the electrical fire, the "balsam of nature" that allowed the body to heal and constantly renew itself. Along with our rational souls, we also lug around a natural or animal soul, an electric body responsible for sensory and physical functions, for order and motion, growth and healing. We share this soul with animals, as the mad-hatter poet Christopher Smart claims in "Jubilate Agno," his 1760 ode to his cat Jeoffrey:

> For by stroking of him I have found out electricity.
> For I perceived God's light about him both wax and fire.
> For the electrical fire is the spiritual substance which God sends from
>   heaven to sustain the bodies both of man and beast.[31]

Oetinger thus used the new scientific object of electricity to "emphasize the rootedness of man's spiritual life in the organic structures and physico-chemical processes of his bodily existence."[32] Like other natural philosophers and mystics of his era, Oetinger recharged the ancient image of the animal soul in a bath of electrical fluid.

In scientific terms, the notion that bodies possess an independent life force is known as vitalism, a doctrine that stands in heretical opposition to the dominant mechanistic picture of organic bodies as juicy biological automata devoid of any magic spark. When Luigi Galvani hooked up frog legs to various metals and electrostatic machines in the 1790s, he believed that the flow of current he discovered was evidence for such an élan vital. Count Alessandro Volta soon proved that, while animal tissues did carry an electrical charge, Galvani had actually stumbled onto the principle of the battery—only one in a long series of victories by the mechanists over the vitalist camp. But that triumph didn't keep a nephew of Galvani's from hooking up Volta's batteries to the decapitated bodies of criminals—a gory attempt to engender life that echoes down to us in Mary Shelley's Gothic science-fiction story *Frankenstein*. This archetypal tale of electro-Prometheanism, which casts electricity as the bridge between science and creation, may be fiction, but it lurks in the shadows of laboratories even today—the embryo of Dolly, the adult sheep cloned in 1997 by Scottish researchers, was kicked into action with a few drops of the electrical fluid.

Frankenstein was a cautionary tale, part of the Romantic reaction to Enlightenment hubris. But the electromagnetic imaginary would also become a positive pole of the Romantic imagination. The idealist philosopher Schelling, the deep ecologist of his day, embraced the juice as a sign of the World Soul, while the literary master and freelance scientist Goethe would speak of an electric life that dynamically bound things together through sympathetic powers of attraction and repulsion. Electricity also became an image of the Romantic spirit itself. "I am electrical by nature," wrote Ludwig von Beethoven. "Music is the electric soil in which the spirit lives, thinks, and invents."[33]

As electricity seized the Romantic imagination, alchemically minded natural philosophers like J. W. Ritter also insisted upon the magnetic pole of the World Soul. Though the exact relationship between electricity and magnetism would not be fleshed out for many decades, Ritter's polarized view made symbolic sense. Magnetism is the hypnotic yin to electricity's yang, a dark moon-tug rather than a jolt of solar fire, and its attractive magic has been associated with animist powers for millennia. To ward off demonic diseases, the Sumerians inscribed healing sigils on magnetic amulets dedicated to Marduk—He Who Causes Action at a Distance. Paracelsus used magnets to balance the vital energies of the body, while Oetinger held that charged chunks of iron would amplify the electrical fire in the body.

Without a doubt, though, the supreme wizard of magnetic healing was Franz Anton Mesmer, known today either as the king of charlatans or the man who inadvertently spawned psychoanalysis. Born in 1732, Mesmer earned his doctor's degree from the University of Vienna, where he wrote his dissertation about the influence of the planets on the mundane world. To explain how astrological forces could produce action at a distance, Mesmer posited a subtle fluid that he called the *fluidium,* a diaphanous medium that communicated moon vibes to the ocean tides as surely as it allowed Venus and Jupiter to tweak human fate. The fluidium took shape against the Newtonian concept of the ether, an invisible fluid that permeated space and that served as the static medium for gravitation and magnetism, as well as sensations and nervous stimuli. For Newton, the ether served to explain how the solar system's distant bodies communicated with one another, while also topping off a universe that abhorred a vacuum. But as Mesmer's own work shows, the ether also served as a halfway house for all sorts of animist intuitions and spooky forces that refused to accept the gears and levers of mechanistic cosmology. Given Newton's own alchemical side, this should not be surprising; Newton himself imagined that the ether was flush with a vital spirit, and even his language of gravitational "attraction" carried a trace of Eros, the spiritual glue that Neoplatonists believed held the cosmos together.

When Mesmer came to name the property of the human body that was plugged into the fluidium, he wavered between magnetism and electricity, but settled on "animal magnetism," a term he took from the esoteric Jesuit Athanasius Kircher. Mesmer wrote that "all bodies [are], like the magnet, capable of communicating this magnetic principle; that this fluid penetrates everything and can be stored up and concentrated, like the electric fluid; [and] that it [acts] at a distance."[34] Mesmer never strictly identified animal magnetism with mineral magnetism, but the "occult" behavior of the latter enabled him to carve out room for notions and practices that tapped the old dreams of sympathetic magic. Though Mesmer's wild science allowed these dreams to surf into the modern world on magnetic waves, the man's ultimate goal was to restore balance and "perfect harmony" to the body's polarized energies. His vision of healing was basically indistinguishable from Chinese medicine, which also holds that a vital spirit infuses the body, and that disease results from blockages in this dynamically balanced network of polarized energetic flows.

Not that Mesmer was above goofing around with actual magnets. In his early therapies, Mesmer would "charge" chunks of iron by passing his hands over them, and then move these metals in the general vicinity of his patients' bodies. Over time, Mesmer abandoned the notion that magnets alone could hold healing charge, and he started magnetizing everything but the kitchen sink—bread, china cups, wood, dogs. Some patients wore magnetized clothes and read magnetized books, while others took their cures from the *baquet*: a bucket filled with water, iron shavings, and glass shards, whose iron handles allowed a number of patients to become magnetized simultaneously. Eventually, Mesmer realized that *he himself* was the magnet, and that he could put patients into trance just by staring into their eyes or having them gaze at his fingers. Though we now associate the verb *mesmerize* with the induction of a stoned-out trance, Mesmer's magic fingers apparently catalyzed riproaring hysterical fits that had a lot more to do with primal scream therapy than with the placid nod of hypnotic regression.

Mesmer did not attempt to explain fully the energies he trafficked in or to justify them in the scientific terminology of the day. He regarded animal magnetism as a sixth sense that, like all senses, cannot be described but only experienced. But though he was fond of wizard capes and magic wands, Mesmer remained in his own mind a figure of the Enlightenment; he insisted that his powers were in no way mystical and that animal magnetism was a real force in the world. Nonetheless the Viennese medical establishment was not impressed with Mesmer's magnetic razzle-dazzle, and the adoration the public lavished on the charismatic fellow only made the situation worse. The good doctor was hounded out of Vienna and fled to pre-revolutionary Paris, where he promptly became the toast of a town flush with new ideas and revolutionary energies. Hundreds of patients whose maladies could not be leeched from their veins found substantial cures with Mesmer's techniques. But despite his impressive record, a commission of doctors and scientists appointed by the French government, including Benjamin Franklin, proclaimed Mesmer a fraud. To explain away his successes, the

Paris commission invoked a force that the skeptical crusaders of scientific reductionism continue to roll out to this day: the "imagination." Mesmer himself acknowledged that a "rapport" had to exist between himself and the patient, and that strictly organic complaints were not always treatable. But though Mesmer had clearly tapped into the tremendous healing energies of the human bodymind, such ambiguous power—erotic, mercurial, almost revolutionary—was too convulsive to admit within the increasingly rationalistic framework of medical thought as it attempted to remake itself into a modern science.

Luckily, Mesmer's students had no such qualms, and in pursuing magnetic experiments, they laid the groundwork for psychotherapy. The Marquis de Puységur, in particular, placed increasing emphasis on the role of the magnetizer's "will" in the whole operation, and he began to uncover the enormous power of what psychologists call suggestion and transference. Working with peasants far from the bustle of Paris, Puységur guided his patients toward the somnambulant haze we now associate with being "mesmerized." Once satisfactorily zapped, these unlettered manual laborers would take on entirely new and seemingly autonomous personalities, diagnose their own cures, and spontaneously perform apparent feats of clairvoyance and telepathy. As the historian Robert Fuller points out, "Puységur found himself the Columbus of a strange, new world—the human unconscious."[35]

A few decades later, the British doctor James Braid came up with the term *hypnotism* to describe such magnetic procedures, and researches into the hypnotic state would eventually lead a young Sigmund Freud to develop his early theories of the unconscious. Though little was left of Mesmer's original tactics at that point, Freud did resemble the old magnetizer in attempting to heal the nervous conditions of his patients by exploring altered states of consciousness in a "scientific" manner, all the while exploiting the almost magical rapport between patient and doctor. Freud also used electrical metaphors in his description of the psyche. But though psychoanalysis considerably refined Mesmer's models of the mind, it paid a steep price for abandoning the image of a real medium that plugged the mind into the vital matrix of the cosmos. Cut off from the transpersonal interactions of Mesmer's fluidium, psychic life became imprisoned inside the skull, a solitary fluctuation stuck inside an electro-thermodynamic machine.

As mesmerism lost its popularity in nineteenth-century Europe, it became a veritable fad in the United States. Thousands submitted to the magnetizing hands of wandering mesmerists for their rheumatism, menstrual aches, migraines, and melancholia. In a very American turn, mesmerism also became something of a sideshow, and many magnetizers built careers out of the same sorts of titillating stunts that hypnotists perform in nightclubs today. At the same time, more serious mesmerists were penetrating the myriad dimensions of human consciousness, and they exploited quasi-electromagnetic language every step of the way. Ascending through a Neoplatonic high-rise of altered states, mesmerized subjects reported feeling "tingling sensations" or "vibrations" flowing through them. Some experienced "waves of energy" and saw auras of light. In the deepest trances, something like cosmic consciousness kicked in, as the subject's mind, it was said, achieved identity with the force of animal magnetism itself. Clairvoyance, telepathy, and other parapsychological oddities emerged—phenomena that the mesmerist Stanley Grimes chalked up to the *ethereum,* a "material substance occupying space, which connects the planets and the earth, and which communicates light, heat, electricity, gravitation, and mental emanations from one body to another and from one mind to another."[36] Notice that, along with physical forces, Grimes's ethereum also communicates "mental emanations"—i.e., information.

While the mesmerists were uncovering the ethereum through their patients' netherminds, measurable electromagnetism was also beginning to radically reconfigure the official scientific picture of the cosmos. In the 1830s, the great British experimental scientist Michael Faraday made a phenomenal discovery: Changing the electrical current in a wire coil somehow induced an energetic fluctuation in a nearby coil. This decidedly bizarre action-at-a-distance, which came to be called electromagnetic induction, is the driving force behind electrical power plants to this day—and the inspiration as well for any number of pseudoscientific explanations for occult phenomena. For his part, Faraday explained the rather mysterious force connecting the two coils as a "wave of electricity." Pointing to the strange patterns that iron filings create around the end of a magnet, Faraday also suggested that electromagnetic "fields" consisted of "lines of force," vibrating patterns that spread throughout space.

Faraday initially considered these images of fields and lines of force as nothing more than useful fictions, but he gradually accepted them as basic descriptions of reality. This was no small step for the self-proclaimed "natural philosopher," who, as a profoundly religious man, believed deeply in the underlying unity of nature and God. Electromagnetic induction gave him a demonstration of such invisible unity, and these undulating waves and fields eventually led Faraday to reject the reigning materialist dogma that held that the atoms of the cosmos were little blobs of stuff. Humbly, Faraday suggested a new vision of the cosmos: Corporeal reality was in essence an immense sea of vibrations and insubstantial forces.

In the 1860s, James Clerk Maxwell translated Faraday's experimental findings into the language of mathematics, synthesizing optical, magnetic, and electrical phenomena into four magnificent equations that governed the whole of electromagnetic reality. In doing so, Maxwell predicted the existence of the electromagnetic spectrum whose waves we now exploit for everything from broadcasting Spice Girls singles to reheating meat loaf to analyzing the chemical composition of Alpha Centauri. Maxwell showed that light—the ultimate symbolic manifestation of divinity—was itself only a certain range of frequencies that happened to stimulate the two photosensitive orbs lodged in the human skull. Certain advanced solutions of his equations also suggested the existence of a parallel cosmos, a mirrored universe where electromagnetic waves move backward in time.

Faraday's and Maxwell's discoveries were major paradigm busters, Einstein calling their work the "greatest alteration in the axiomatic basis of physics—in our conception of the structure of reality."[37] The electromagnetic universe set the stage for the final deconstruction of atomic materialism: the dissolution of the ether, the emergence of Einsteinian space-time, and ultimately the arrival of quantum mechanics and its colossal oddities. In terms of the scientific imagination, Faraday's discovery of electromagnetic induction was the tincture that catalyzed the final transmutation of matter into spirit, a tough-minded alchemy that revealed the physical universe to be an enormous vibrating mantra of potent nothings.

Such a powerful cosmological shift could not help but impact the esoteric imagination as well. By the late nineteenth century, when electromagnetic science began seeping into the popular mind, mesmerism had pretty much packed it in. But a far more influential occult science arose, one that fleshed out the electromagnetic universe with a rich brew of esoteric lore. The Theosophical Society was founded in 1875 by Col. Henry Steel Olcott and Madame Helena Petrovna Blavatsky, a pudgy, crafty, cigar-smoking trickster from Russia. The movement combined the pulp appeal of popular magic with headier mystic thought; Blavatsky's endless books are cut-and-paste collages of Freemasonry, Hermeticism, potted "Eastern" metaphysics, and her own science-fiction tales of telepathic Tibetan masters and Atlantean cataclysms. But as the historian Joscelyn Godwin argues, Blavatsky's group also represented Enlightenment values that had nothing to do with Buddha's claim to fame and everything to do with the freethinking spirit of progress. The Theosophists loathed conventional Christianity, embraced emancipatory social movements, and called for a new global politics of "universal brotherhood." They were the gnostics of modernism.

As such, the Theosophists mixed and matched their mysticism with the new evolutionary and electromagnetic worldviews of science. As monists, the Theosophists set themselves a double task: to fit the so-called "gross" world of matter into an incorporeal universe of spirit, and to weave the higher realms into an evolutionary and lawful description of the cosmos. Mind and matter thus became the same cosmic substance at different stages of evolution, "stepped down," as *Hinduism Today* recently noted in an article about Theosophical Hindus, "somewhat as a transformer steps down the mighty power of electricity."[38] Given their debt to Indian Vedanta and hermetic Neoplatonism, Theosophists rejected materialism out of hand; they put mind well before matter and embraced the notion that our "thought-currents" had the power to create reality itself. But they reframed this ancient view by latching onto the language of etheric waves, vibrations, cosmic frequencies, and fields of force. The Theosophical cosmos was a giant hum, whose lowest and most coarse "vibrations" made up the material world and whose "higher planes" were carried on "higher" frequencies, all of which interpenetrated simultaneously and invisibly in the here and now, just like Maxwell's spectral waves.

The Theosophical attempt to inject spiritual qualities into a universe colonized by physics was also accompanied by the West's first great spiritual turn to the East. While a vibrating cosmos of incorporeal forces and radiating waves left little room for a God skilled at molding clay or constructing clocks, it was rather more accommodating to *impersonal* conceptions of the absolute—conceptions that the Theosophists snatched from Buddhism and the loftier strains of Hinduism. Theosophy's use of electromagnetic Vedanta to build a bridge between mind and matter continues to percolate through New Age physics and pop Hinduism to this day. The language that William Irwin Thompson once used to describe the worldview of yoga has a deeper source than he probably suspected: "Consciousness is like an FM radio band: as long as one is locked into one station, all he receives is the information of one reality; but if . . . he is able to move his consciousness to a different station on the FM band, then he discovers universes beyond matter in the cosmic reaches of spirit."[39]

Thompson's analogy is apt, for along with electrifying the occult universe, Theosophy also unveiled an image of an interactive body that could actively explore these vibrating planes. Reconfiguring the mystical "sheaths" of Hindu anatomy, the Theosophists argued that the body contains a Petrushka doll of spirit vehicles. Immediately up the stepladder from the flesh is the etheric body, which is basically analogous to the vital soul we have been tracking through this section. Vibrating at a slightly higher frequency than the etheric body is the famous astral body, which, in the proper circumstances, can temporarily abandon the mortal coil to surf through the astral plane, a dreamlike collective realm of fleshless and hyperreal "thought-forms"—the Theosophical version of a virtual world.

Theosophy thus represents a gnostic drift away from the body, a dematerializing tendency that in the next section we will link with the rise of new technologies that "outer" the self. In his poem "I Sing the Body Electric," Walt Whitman gave voice to the opposite tendency in the electromagnetic imagination. For Whitman, electric life meant the erotic life, and his love of bodies, his desire to "charge them full with the charge of the soul," only led him to embrace the most exuberant of heresies: that the body *was* the soul. Unlike the mesmerists, who pointed to the new technology of photography as proof that the physical world was really made up of the mental vibrations of light, Whitman recognized that the vital spirit of electromagnetism—with its lightning strikes of charge, its dynamic polarities and visceral attractions—was more a language of Eros than a mantra of transcendence. After all, Mesmer's original magnetic techniques had nothing to do with the inner planes and everything to do with stoking the convulsive life of desire in order to heal real bodies.

For many magnetic researchers and "alternative" healers in the nineteenth century, the force of electricity offered a literal key to the vital energy of the body. By the close of the century, electricity had become thoroughly identified in the popular mind with healing—especially in America's popular mind, which is more popular than most. Electricity was accepted as the active therapeutic agent in pills, soaps, teas, and lotions, and a host of electrical and magnetic devices were used to treat every remedy under the sun. U.S. congressmen even "took" electricity in a specially outfitted basement room in the Capitol. But in 1909, wary of all the free-form healing this electromania encouraged, the government issued the Flexner Report, which sought to upgrade and standardize medical education and health care throughout the country. Besides condemning the popular and efficacious practice of homeopathy and institutionalizing the AMA's arrogant reign of allopathic medicine, the report declared that electrical potentials and magnetic energies played no vital role in physiology or biomedicine. The animal soul, which had long surfed the waves of the electromagnetic imaginary, was repressed by mainstream American medicine.

The Flexner Report was also an attempt to control the meaning of new technologies of the body. By the early twentieth century, diagnostic machines were replacing the sensitive "instrument" of a doctor's own sensations and perceptions, while the previously invisible domains of disease were being probed with microscopes and X-ray radiation technology. But while the use of medical technology to gather information was considered acceptable, the notion that technologies could detect, channel, or amplify the energies of life itself became anathema. The report not only outlawed the whole bizarre array of electrical and electromagnetic contrivances, but ensured that even tough-minded doctors researching bioenergy and the possibility of "energetic" healing technologies would find themselves clutching a one-way ticket to the gulags of quackdom. The only exception to this rule was, strangely enough, research into the healing powers of radiation, one of the twentieth century's most lethal invisible obsessions.

Bioenergy proved a powerful siren, however, and its song has enchanted much of the gadgetry of alternative medicine in the twentieth century. Just as Kirlian photographers unveiled a "secret life of plants," so too did heretical healers jury-rig a secret life of machines. In the 1940s, Dr. Albert Abrams, a professor of pathology at Stanford University, came up with the theory of radionics, which held that each organ, tissue, or agent of disease has a unique vibrational rate, or resonance—an idea Abrams partially developed from watching the great tenor Enrico Caruso shatter a glass with his voice. Abrams applied his theory to the construction of a healing technology: black boxes that basically consisted of a series of dials that could rotate a tiny bar magnet. This magnet in turn was suspended near a small well that held the "witness," or tissue from the patient. The practitioner would tweak the dials until she got a positive "reading" from the witness. Spiffed up to Tom Mix standards by Abrams's rather enthusiastic followers, this simple gadget allegedly not only diagnosed disease but could also "broadcast" healing vibrations from the healer to the patient. As you might expect, Abrams's black boxes were officially condemned as magical fetishes, and the FDA imprisoned the L.A. chiropractor Ruth Drown, a radionics zealot who claimed she could derive photographs of diseased organs and tissues from nothing more than a patient's drop of blood. For his part, Abrams maintained that the radionic talent lay more in the practitioner than in the instrument; the black box thus functioned rather like a twentieth-century version of the rods and pendulums that dowsers still use to intu-itively find water, cure disease, and geomantically read the invisible information of the landscape.

Chinese acupuncturists also treat the body as a landscape of energetic flows, or *chi*. While the meridian lines that channel chi somewhat over-lap the electrochemical grid of the nervous system, the stuff also seems to leak out of whatever conceptual maps Western medicine tries to impose on it in order to explain its efficacy. Like the electromagnetic image of the energy body, chi seems to vibrate in the tingling gap between meat and soul. But in the 1950s, the physician Dr. Reinhardt Voll found that healers could map and realign acupuncture points with electrical devices; today computerized versions of his bioenergetic machines abound in Europe, and many acupuncturists also charge up their needles with low levels of electric current.

Probably the most famous example of a modern vitalist technology is Dr. Wilhelm Reich's orgone accumulator. Reich believed in better living through orgasms, and his groundbreaking research into the muscular basis of anxiety and neuroses set the stage for many of today's schools of therapeutic bodywork. Reich also believed that the pulsing, bluish vesicles he glimpsed in high-quality optical microscopes in the 1940s were *bions,* the basic unit of a new kind of energy, a vital force that Reich named the "orgone." Reich held that pulsating waves of orgone energy permeated the universe, and that they could be captured in a box he created from alternating layers of organic and inorganic material. Once so confined, the orgone could heal cancer and produce low-level electric current. But though some people swear by Reich's contraption to this day, the FDA was no more impressed with these orgone accumulators than they were with their inventor's orgasmic theories. In the 1950s, the feds impounded and destroyed Reich's equipment, literally burned his books, and threw the doctor in prison for contempt of court. He died there a few years later, a broken man convinced that Christ was a messenger from the cosmic orgone and that UFOs were ripping off Earth's vital energy.

Though most Western doctors continue to reject the idea of bioenergy, many are coming to recognize the power of alternative healing therapies such as acupuncture, breathwork, visualization, and post-Reichean bodywork. In a large part, these practices depend upon the archetype of the living and communicating bodymind, a field of vital psychic energy that can be tapped and redirected by patient and physician alike. The technocultural paradox is that, in the West anyway, this premodern image of the vital soul was kept alive during the reign of reductionist medicine partly through the language, example, and even technologies of electricity, which thus took on a certain heretical charge it retains to this day. Though few practitioners of alternative medicine actually exploit electric current today, electric flows and magnetic fields have provided fruitfully fuzzy analogies for those energetic, psychological, spiritual, or erotic dimensions of life that healers are increasingly folding back into their treatments.

But it now appears that the balsam of nature may be biting back. Today your average human body bathes in a discordant symphony of weak magnetic fields, produced by battery-powered gadgets, microwave transmitters, airport security systems, and the almost universal background buzz that leaks out of the electric power grid that feeds radios, televisions, stereos, and computers. A number of people, both within and outside of the alternative medical community, have come to suspect that some of this electromagnetic radiation—especially Extra-Low Frequencies (ELF) waves—is producing subtle but nasty effects on biology and behavior. A number of controversial studies suggest that living near beefy power lines or staring at VDTs all day long may produce a variety of disorders, ranging from severe depression to ragged immune systems to having kids with leukemia. Though most scientists write off such fears as "power line paranoia," these scientists are part of a system that places physics above mind and life force, and that has spent nearly a century deliberately marginalizing research into bioenergy. The result of this is that even the most hardheaded and legitimately concerned investigators of "electropollution" find themselves forced into the shadowlands that border the electromagnetic imaginary, where paranoia and conspiracy lurk.

Some mystics are worried as well. One particularly dark reading of electropollution is provided by William Irwin Thompson, whose powerful writings navigate the treacherous waters between science, myth, and cultural history. One of Thompson's crankier notions concerns the contemporary status of our "etheric body," which Thompson argues acts as a kind of subtle energetic armor that protects physical reality from the terror, chaos, and devouring phantasms of the astral plane. Because we are now bombarding our vibrating etheric wet suits with the "electronic noise" of ELFs and microwaves, and rending them even more with consciousness drugs, synthetic mediascapes, and, yes, loud music, "the astral plane is leaking into the threadbare and worn-out physical plane."[40] With our etheric body in tatters and the techniques necessary to navigate the astral realms long forgotten, postmodern culture is joysticking its way into the ferocious maw of collective hallucination.

For Thompson, the vampirization of our etheric juices reaches its apogee with the gloves, body suits, and head-mounted displays of virtual reality technologies—gear that allows for the total electromagnetic colonization of the energy body and the astral body alike. But while some see the inbreeding of virtual and energetic bodies as perverse, even demonic, others find it can be almost angelic. One of the most riveting and visceral virtual reality technologies to date is Osmose, a high-end electronic art installation created by the Canadian Char Davies in the mid-1990s. Exploiting the same graphics programs that conjured *Jurassic Park*'s dinosaurs to life, and running on SGI hardware normally reserved for big-budget science and military simulations, Osmose swallows the participant—suitably swathed in electronic gear—into a sensuous, luminous, and deeply enveloping dreamworld of cloud forests, dark pools, and verdant canopies. Using spatial ambiguity and tricks of light, Osmose conjures up the perceptual high of a walk in the woods; many "immersants" feel at once immaterial and embodied, like angels moving with animal grace. Some immersants emerge from Davies's dappled and vibrating pixelscape weeping or lingering in trance; others have compared their trips to lucid dreams or out-of-body experiences.

With its simultaneously intuitive and sophisticated virtual aesthetic, Osmose is a powerful example of how technological environments can simulate something like the old animist immersion in the World Soul, organic dreamings that depend, in power and effect, upon the ethereal fire. Besides pointing to a healing use of virtual technologies, Osmose also reminds us how *intimate* we are with electronics, in sight and sound, in body and psyche. Our language drips with electromagnetic metaphors, of magnetic personalities and live wires, of bad vibes and tuning out, of getting grounded and recharging batteries. Whether or not the body radiates a polarized energy soul, the self is now swaddled in electromagnetic skin.

Specters of the Spectrum

In the middle of the nineteenth century, electricity underwent a rather alchemical transformation that was destined to transmute modern society as well. The medium of this revolutionary change was the brain of one Samuel Morse, a man who, historians of technology note, had a rather crude grasp of the electromagnetic mysteries. But though Morse lacked the seat-of-the-pants hacker spirit so prevalent in the early days of electrical invention, he was without a doubt blessed with a formidable insight: If electric current could be squeezed through a wire, then "intelligence might . . . be instantaneously transmitted by electricity to any distance."[41] The ethereal fire was about to be stepped up, as it were, into an even more incorporeal realm. Energy would vaporize into information, and this in turn would change the way that humans found themselves reflected in technology.

After convincing Congress to plow $30,000 into his project, Morse strung up a wire between Baltimore and Washington, D.C. The first official message careened along that Baltimore–D.C. line in 1844, and it was a strangely oracular pronouncement: "What hath God wrought!" This bit of scripture was suggested by the daughter of the U.S. commissioner of patents, though Morse himself surely concurred with the sentiment; besides being the son of a staunch evangelist, he would later transfer a good portion of his considerable fortune to churches, seminaries, and missionary societies. Still, the first telegraphed message reads as much like an anxious question as a cry of glee, and today we know the answer: What God wrought, or rather, what men wrought in their God-aping mode, was the information age.

Morse's system was not just electrical (and hence, effectively instantaneous); it was *digital*. The electric current that ran along telegraph wires was itself an analog medium, flowing in the undulating waves that everywhere weave the world. But by regularly breaking and reestablishing this flow with a simple switch, and by establishing a code to interpret the resulting patterns of pulses, Morse chopped the analog dance into discrete digital units, dots and dashes that signified. But what really defines the telegraph as the first neural net of the information age was how rapidly it infiltrated and changed the world, especially the exuberantly industrializing United States. With Morse code in hand, railroads improved their ability to move goods over America's vast distances, newspapermen sped up the perceived pace of historical events, businessmen upped their managerial control (and their stress), and stock markets started pulsing in synch. A decade after Morse's first line, 30,000 miles of wire webbed the United States; by 1858, the first trans-Atlantic cable snaked through the inky depths; and well before the end of the century, the British had stitched together their global empire, laying cable from London to Yemen to Darwin, Australia.

As with most new media of the nineteenth century, the telegraph charged the popular imagination. Even before Morse laid his first cable, F. O. J. Smith, one of his most vocal supporters in Congress, was weighing in with the kind of information puffery that continues to spill from the lips of media moguls today:

> The influence of this invention over the political, commercial, and social relations of the people of this widely-extended country . . . will . . . of itself amount to a revolution unsurpassed in moral grandeur by any discovery that has been made in the arts and sciences. . . . Space will be, to all practical purposes of information, completely annihilated between the States of the Union, as also between the individual citizens thereof.[42]

It's tempting to chalk up this garrulous hype to the fact that Smith was a secret partner in Morse's project, but that would misrepresent the intensity of the telegraphic enthusiasm among both the masses and the elite. After the trans-Atlantic cable was laid, fifteen thousand New Yorkers—few of whom would benefit directly from the wire—celebrated with the largest parade the city had ever seen. One newspaper complained that the cable was "pronounced next only in importance for mankind to the 'Crucifixion.' "[43]

The analogy was apt, for in nineteenth-century America, the enthusiasm for religion and for technology fed off and amplified each other. It was an era of tremendous technological utopianism, when books appeared with titles like *The Paradise Within the Reach of All Men,*

Without Labor, by Powers of Nature and Machinery. And accomplishments like the Erie Canal seemed to justify such hopes. But this techno-utopianism also drew its spunk from the same religious enthusiasm that made the young nation a fiery carnival of revivalism, spiritual experimentation, and progressive communes. The gray-faced Calvinism that dominated workaholic American Christianity became flush with perfectionism—the belief that both self and world possessed a boundless potential for improvement. The revivalist spirit, with its dreams of the coming millennium, was in turn confirmed by the explosion of new machines and engineering feats. These accomplishments gave rise to what the historian Leo Marx called the "technological sublime," as the awesome and frightening grandeur that the Romantic poets associated with nature became attached to new technologies. The telegraph, with its instantaneous transcendence of space, was embraced as a particularly glowing sign of the young land's self-imagined destiny: to build heaven on earth.

Later in this book, we will show how such sublime technological utopias came to roost inside those contemporary data networks whose roots lie in Morse's wires. But what interests us here is how the telegraph's "annihilation" of space and time also started chipping away at the boundaries of the American self. For as is always the case with a powerful new medium, the mere existence of the telegraph shook up the established containers of identity. Writing about the telegraph in *Understanding Media,* Marshall McLuhan argued that "whereas all previous technology (save speech, itself) had, in effect, extended some part of our bodies, electricity may be said to have outered the central nervous system itself."[44] For McLuhan, Morse's electric ganglion was only the first in a series of media—radio, radar, telephone, phonograph, TV—that served to dissolve the logical and individualistic mindframe hammered out by the technologies of writing and especially the modern printing press. Instead, the telegraph sparked the "electric retribalization of the West," a long slide into an electronic sea of mythic participation and collective resonance, where the old animist dreams of oral cultures would be reborn among electromagnetic waves. But McLuhan also saw the collective "outering" caused by the telegraph as the technological root of the age of anxiety. "To put one's nerves outside," he wrote, "is to initiate a situation—if not a concept—of dread."[45]

Both religion and the occult derive much of their power from simultaneously stimulating and managing dread: the anxieties that dog the perpetually shifting boundaries of the self, and especially the ultimate borderland of death. As new technologies begin to remold these very same boundaries, the shadows, doubles, and dark reflections that haunt human identity begin to leak outside the self as well, many of them taking up residence in the virtual spaces opened up by the new technologies.

So while daylight America confidently telegraphed its exploding commercial designs, the nightside of the American mind found itself wrestling with ghosts. In 1848, the Fox family started hearing creepy knocks and mysterious thumpings in their humble Hydesdale cottage in upstate New York. Such eerie rappings pop up regularly in folklore, and they are usually attributed to the poltergeists still tracked by contemporary ghost busters. But the three Fox sisters did something unprecedented in the annals of strange phenomena: They started rapping back. To improve communication, the sisters convinced the spirit—supposedly a murdered peddler whose bones lay beneath their home—to respond to their queries with a simple code. One knock for yes, two for no—a spectral echo of the dots and dashes then hurtling through wires across the land.

The cottage in Hydesdale was the launching pad for Spiritualism, a modern quasi-religion of necromantic information exchange that would grow so popular as to pose a genuine threat to mainstream Christianity. By the 1870s, there were approximately eleven million Spiritualists in the United States and countless more across the world, a large number of them among the upper classes. Following the Fox sisters' simple astral telegraphy, Spiritualist media improved considerably: more complex alphabetic codes, chalk slates, "spirit-scopes," automatic writing, Ouija-like planchettes, and, of course, the human vocal cords of the usually female medium. Spiritualist séances were all about vibes; solemnly plunging rooms into darkness, and frequently asking sitters to join hands to get the currents flowing, mediums would conjure up an emotion of dread fascination. Though many of the spirits spouted the sort of vapid utopian prophecies found in many channeled teachings today, most Spiritualist chat served a far less metaphysical goal: to establish an intimate link between living souls and their departed friends and family.

Spiritualism did not arise from thin air. Humans have probably been ringing up their ancestors since the days of flint and moonbones; by the time of the Fox raps, America already had Shakers channeling Native American hierophants and Stateside mesmerists interrogating spirits through their zonked-out patients. But Spiritualism's own John the Bap-

tist was one Andrew Jackson Davis, an American visionary who channeled Swedenborgian travelogues of the incorporeal worlds in the early
decades of the nineteenth century. In 1845, Davis, who attributed supernatural powers to electromagnetism, claimed that a "living demonstration" of spiritual communication was at hand, and that "the world will
hail with delight the ushering in of that era when the interiors of men
will be opened, and the spiritual communion will be established such as
is now being enjoyed by the inhabitants of Mars, Jupiter and Saturn."[46]
We'll pick up this note of science fiction later in this book; what's worth
noting here is that, just as McLuhan held that electric technologies "outered" the central nervous system, so did Davis associate extraterrestrial
spiritual communication with the unfolding of the interior self.

Whatever the status of Davis's prophecy, and whether or not the Fox
sisters were faking it, as they themselves sometimes later claimed, Spiritualism was the first popular religion of the information age. As such, it
was bound up from the beginning with the electromagnetic imaginary
and the telegraph's groundbreaking transformation of electricity into
information. During the 1850s, the movement's most popular newspaper was called the *Spiritual Telegraph,* and Isaac Post, one of the earliest
investigators of the Fox phenomenon, concluded that "the spirits chiefly
concerned in the inauguration of this telegraphy were philosophic and
scientific minds, many of whom had made the study of electricity and
other imponderables a specialty in the earth-life."[47] (Benjamin Franklin
was a frequent caller.) Spiritualists like Allan Kardec and scientists like
Michael Faraday both looked to electricity to explain the raps, creaks,
and table-hops that occurred during séances. In a history of the movement penned in 1869, the Spiritualist Emma Hardinge wrote:

> From the first working of the spiritual telegraph by which invisible
> beings were enabled to spell out consecutive messages, they [the spir-
> its] claimed that this method of communion was organized by scien-
> tific minds in the spirit spheres; that it depended mainly on the
> conditions of human and atmospheric magnetisms.[48]

Reflecting the confident enthusiasm that technology sparked in so many
nineteenth-century Americans, Hardinge implied that the inhabitants
of the spirit world actually *invented* the spiritual telegraph, and
that its status as a technology imbued it with "concrete and scientific

characteristics" lacking in the oracular mumblings of earlier occultists. Hardinge even claimed that the spirits chose the Fox cottage because its "aura" made the abode a good battery.

The electromagnetic imaginary thus continued to shape the image of the human soul, although now the seat of vitality had passed, perhaps significantly, from the living to the dead. The conflation of mediumship and the electric telegraph also served as palpable proof that science and engineering would penetrate the invisible realms and make the marvelous real and pragmatic. Spiritualists were united in their rejection of supernaturalism, their belief in natural law, and their conviction that the afterlife was just another frontier to be conquered by the march of progress. This can-do pragmatism was reflected not only in the "inventions" reportedly handed down by some spirits, but also in the movement's anxious attempts to present itself as an empirical science. Mercilessly aping scientific rhetoric, Spiritualists took records of séances using the same objective, value-free language of names, dates, and factoids that still marks the annals of parapsychology. As the scholar R. Laurence Moore points out, Spiritualists "slavishly imitated scientific method to the point of shunning subjectivity and inwardness as things which really didn't count."[49]

All this helps explain one of the many parallels between Spiritualism and today's New Age channeling: the banality of most of the chat emerging from beyond the veil. During séances, the dullest of information played an important role, since mediums needed to produce concrete chunks of data unknowable through other means—events, names, dates—in order to prove to séance-goers that their dead relations were truly in the house, and that neither the spirits, nor the mediums themselves, were frauds. Séance-goers were also treated to vague techno-utopian prophecies which claimed that social progress and spiritual uplift would ride in on the back of technological advances. Like most New Agers today, Spiritualists held quite progressive views, embracing abolitionism and other reforms as well as loosening the straitjacket of gender roles and Christian sexual mores. The movement played a particularly pivotal role in kickstarting the emancipation of women, who for the first time were able to gain a public voice, albeit a borrowed one. But while séance-goers shared the progressive temperament of the New England Transcendentalists, they had none of that more elite group's aesthetic inwardness, and Emerson damned the movement as "the rat hole of revelation."

Reading through Spiritualist material, one can come to the conclusion that death does little more than dull one's wits. Neither the mediums nor the spirits on the other side undergo any significant transformation or evince much insight. But the tedium of this otherworldly datastream is itself deeply indicative of American culture's tendency to view technical systems of communication under the sign of the sublime. Because of this, the system itself (be it a spiritual telegraph or a computer network) carries a "revolutionary" charge more potent and substantial than any of the actual messages that pass along the line. Just as the early radio enthusiasts were usually more excited about establishing a link with some far-flung fellow geek than in having an interesting conversation, the mere delivery of information from the spiritual world was sufficient to establish the divine reality of the spiritual telegraph itself. As the New England Spiritualist Association declared in 1854, "Spirits do communicate with man—that is the creed."[50] The medium really was the message.

By the 1860s and 1870s, mediums had become the professional pop stars of the Victorian era. Though contacts with relatives who had "passed on" remained a crucial draw, attendees were increasingly treated to occult sideshows, as tables rapped and danced across the room, mediums levitated, hands and gooey ectoplasm materialized out of thin air, and musical instruments played creepy jigs in the dark while the medium remained bound and gagged. The loquacious spirits of the earlier years gave way to more rambunctious ghosts, suggesting a tendency all too familiar today: the transformation of a communications medium into consumer spectacle.

As charismatic mediums brought their increasingly elaborate stunts into the homes of the gentry here and abroad, scientists and debunkers inevitably came a-calling. Though countless mediums were revealed as frauds (without necessarily diminishing their subsequent business), a surprising number of serious scientists and engineers wound up as enthusiastic Spiritualists, even in the face of condemnation and official ridicule. Returning from the tropics, where he concocted a theory of evolution roughly parallel to Darwin's, the naturalist Alfred Russel Wallace plunged into controlled empirical studies of Spiritualism. After seeing mediums like Mrs. Guppy pop six-foot sunflowers out of nowhere, Wallace came to the conclusion that some of its phenomena were "proved, . . . quite as well as any facts are proved in other sciences."[51] Cromwell Varley, an electrical engineer who worked on the Atlantic telegraph cable, was an ardent believer, and attempted to demonstrate the existence of materialized spirits by hooking them up to galvanometers. In his later years, Thomas Edison tried to hack a radio device that would establish a telepathic channel between the worlds. Even expert magazines like the *Electrical Review,* which mocked amateur electricians and their cranky ideas, occasionally included stories of ghostly entities who intervened to operate electrical equipment.

Perhaps the most prominent scientist to fall for the spirits was Sir William Crookes, one of the most visionary physicists of Victorian England. When Crookes announced his intention to expose "the worthless residuum of Spiritualism," the more sober wings of society applauded; little did they know that the man had already satisfactorily used mediums to contact his drowned brother. Crookes employed various electrical instruments in his investigations and took scores of spirit photographs—one of the more popular uses of the new technology. Crookes's Spiritualist imagination even seeped into his science. Experimenting with the effects of electricity on gases enclosed in otherwise evacuated tubes, he discovered ghostly effects similar to the flashing, smoky lights he had witnessed at many séances. Crookes thought he had found another way to communicate with the dead; what he had actually discovered was the phosphorescent effect that cathode rays have on certain materials in a vacuum tube—a discovery that would eventually conjure up those rather vacuous ghosts that flit across television sets today.

This strange feedback between magic and machines was hardly unprecedented. As a few historians have observed, the popular scientific demonstrations that packed public lecture halls during the late nineteenth century were sometimes difficult to distinguish from the spectacles of occultism. According to one contemporary account, the "Finale" of a Boston lecture given by representatives of the Edison Company in 1887 was nothing less than a séance: "Bells rung, drums beat, noises natural and unnatural were heard, a cabinet revolved and flashed fire, and a row of departed skulls came into view."[52] Of course, such performances were framed in the context of science's technological conquest of mystery. But as far as popular perception was concerned, it was just the new shamans chasing the old ones out of town. As the cultural theorist Avital Ronell points out, "Science acquires its staying power from a sustained struggle to keep down the demons of the supernatural with whose visions, however, it competes."[53]

In this sense, the fact that Spiritualism's occult funhouse sucked in so many prominent scientists simply reflects the larger cultural confusion caused by the explosive growth of science and technology during the industrial revolution. Consciously or not, many Victorians were coming to realize that the empiricism and materialism that was handing over so many goodies was also eroding the metaphysical ground of their immortal souls. Mere Christianity, bereft of magic and sputtering before the selection pressures of Darwinism, would hardly suffice to stem the tide of a meaningless cosmos. What better salve than Spiritualism, the most materialistic and empirical religion imaginable?

Such considerations help us understand the otherwise rather paradoxical fact that the final decades of the nineteenth century, when the machine age was plunging full steam ahead, were actually boom years for pop mysticism, occult science, and decadent romanticism. On the one hand, Mesmerism, Spiritualism, Theosophy, and Mary Baker Eddy's "Christian Science" all expressed the desire to ensoul science, to overcome the growing divide between rationalism and religion. But the occult cosmologies and consciousness-tweaking practices of these groups also helped create new and sometimes eerie ways of imagining and experiencing the self at a time when the ghostly demarcations of identity were shifting in the face of new technologies of information and reproduction. Daguerreotypes, phonographs, telegraphs, telephones— all these nineteenth-century media siphon a bit of soul into an artifact or an electric herald. The story of the self in the information age is thus the story of the afterimages of the psyche, of those reflections and virtual doubles that are exteriorized, or outered, into technologies. The astral body of the Theosophists was simply the imaginal form of the "you" that appears on a photographic plate.

Such technological doublings also triggered the ancient dread of the *doppelgänger,* that psychic simulacrum of the self that moves through the world on its own eerie accord. Freud dubbed the dread produced by the doppelgänger "the uncanny," though the original German word *unheimlich* carries the additional meaning of feeling not-at-home. Freud himself connected the unheimlich to the queer feelings one gets from dolls and automata, but in *The Telephone Book,* Avital Ronell also links Freud's technological uncanny with Alexander Graham Bell's revolutionary device. Ronell's text is a fascinating and typographically brazen book that grounds an extended meditation on electric speech, schizophrenia, and Heidegger within the history of Bell's technology, but the occult portion of her tale centers on Bell's own shadowy double: Thomas

Watson, the electricity geek immortalized in Bell's famous (though probably mythical) cry: "Watson, come here! I want you!"

Though Bell came up with the notion of translating the vibrating pressures of the human voice into an electrical signal that could pass along a wire, Watson actually built most of the man's early devices. Like a lot of the electrical hackers at the time, Watson combined loads of practical know-how with weak and frequently wacky theories about the mysterious fluid itself—theories that, in Watson's case, were mixed up with his occult notions. Watson's diary shows him glimpsing auras and having chats with morning glories; as Ronell writes, he was "capable of rendering public such statements as 'believing as I do in reincarnation.' "[54] As a member of the Society for Psychical Research, Watson treated Spiritualism as a nonmystical science, and he initially concluded that, just as "a telegraph instrument transforms pulsations of electricity into the taps of the Morse code," so too did mediums transform energetic radiations into raps and knockings.[55] Later Watson accepted the "disembodied spirit" theory, a theory that, as his diary notes, leaked into his researches with Bell. "I was now working with that occult force, electricity, and here was a possible chance to make some discoveries. I felt sure spirits could not scare an electrician and they might be of use to him in his work."[56] Attempting to create a phone line that could both send and receive signals, Bell and Watson "talked successfully" by sending a weak current through a séancelike circuit made up of a dozen people holding hands, and in their later demonstration lectures, the dynamic duo conjured up various telephonic tricks that delivered all the thrills and chills of a magic show.

In a sense, the telephone is the ultimate animist technology. We associate sentient life with what communicates, and here was an inert thing full of voices. As the emperor of Brazil exclaimed when he first heard the gadget, "My God, it talks!" These days, of course, we are used to talking machines, and the ubiquity and pragmatism of the telephone has chased such animist perceptions back into the bush. And yet a spectral ambiguity continues to linger about the device. Does it talk, do we talk through it, or are those vibrations only the ghosts of ourselves? When we pick up a receiver and hear no dial tone, why do we say that the line is "dead"? A phone ringing in the middle of the night can be a terrifying thing, and not only for the ill tidings it may bring. Crank callers have long exploited the dread produced when we pick up the receiver and find "no one" there. Or think of the outgoing messages we leave on our answering machines. "I am not here right now," we say, which of course begs the inevitable question: If we are not there, then who is speaking? Such an apparently trivial question becomes palpably eerie to anyone who has reached the answering machine of the recently deceased and heard the chipper messages of the dead.

The telephonic uncanny has a political dimension as well. Throughout the twentieth century, modern state institutions have often deployed their power through intelligence organizations devoted to surveillance, and the telephone served as a prime site for such activities. Today's agents of surveillance, corporate as well as state, have also colonized much of the electromagnetic spectrum, from infrared cameras to spy satellite frequencies to devices capable of reading the electromagnetic impulses vibrating off of distant VDTs. But the telephone remains paradigmatic, since the mere *possibility* that unknown and unseen agents are bugging your line is enough to puncture the psychological intimacy afforded by a phone call, transforming your humble handset into an insidious tentacle of unwanted and invisible powers.

However legitimate, fears of electromagnetic surveillance also inform one of the great schizophrenic motifs of the twentieth century: the conviction that nefarious quasi-telepathic forces are using transistor radios, TVs, dental fillings, or microwave signals to colonize brains and manipulate behavior. Such paranoid superstitions are usually couched in stories of KGB agents or extraterrestrial probes or CIA mind-control experiments—secular mythologies appropriate for the now outered electronic self, open and exposed to the attentions of those unseen agents who lurk everywhere in information space. But the motif can be traced back to the very onset of the telephonic era, to the 1870s, when Thomas Watson met a man who swore that two prominent New Yorkers had connected his brain to their telephone circuit in order to harangue him incessantly with all sorts of "fiendish suggestions—even murder." The man even offered to let Watson lop off the top of his head so that the electrical engineer could see how the contraption worked.

As daemonic allegories of media manipulation and modern propaganda, these scenarios of electromagnetic mind control are hardly inaccurate. But their essence remains thoroughly occult, bound up with the hypnotic specters and mesmerizing powers that have always inhabited the electromagnetic imaginary. The characters in Bram Stoker's *Dracula,* published in 1897, are constantly mediating themselves through telephones, phonographs, telegraphs, and typewriters; as Sadie Plant explains, "The vampires return to a ticker-tape world of imperceptible communications and televisual speeds."[57] Half a century later, the Swedish researcher Konstantin Raudive claimed that magnetic tape recordings of silence often turn out, on repeat listenings, to contain distinct voices; devotees of "Electronic Voice Phenomenon" have tuned in to similar murmurs on nonbroadcast radio frequencies, sounds that some interpret as the voices of the dead. During the Vietnam War, the U.S. military would even fly helicopters over Vietcong villages, blasting eerie tapes of the "ancestors" in an attempt to rattle the enemy's nerves.

The fact that such phantasms, concocted and not, continue to haunt the fringes of the electronic world underscores an argument running throughout this book. Modern media fire up magical or animist perceptions by technologically stretching and folding the boundaries of the self; these perceptions are then routinized, commercialized, exploited, and swallowed up into business as usual. To tune in to such fears and glimmerings, you need to crack open the mundane casing of ordinary technologies and trace their archetypal wiring. Then you might find yourself, if only for a moment, tapping into the electromagnetic unheimlich. The spirits speak: In the information age, you are never at home.

Like a Flash of Lightning

Throughout the nineteenth century, the symbols and practices surrounding electricity kept something of the old alchemical fire alive. Electric vitalism and magnetic trances nursed the spirit of animism in an age of rising mechanism. Electrical communication, the photographic capture of light waves, and the discovery of the electromagnetic spectrum all helped dissolve the world of atomic materialism into a spectral cosmos of disembodied vibration. But electricity and the electromagnetic spectrum also came to embody the more Promethean and techno-utopian dimension of the alchemical mind.

Like the ancient metallurgists before them, the Renaissance alchemists worked *contra naturum,* against nature, artificially accelerating the evolutionary potential of the world. Christian alchemists identified this labor, not only with the immortal redemption of the individual, but with the creation of the celestial kingdom glimpsed at the close of Revelation. It's a good bet that for many alchemists this millennialist *lapis* corresponded to a mighty potent state of mystic consciousness, but the symbol of the celestial city hovering at the close of space-time was also interpreted as a blueprint for material history. And it was in this meatier sense that the millennialist urge slipped into the modern ideology of technological progress, especially in the United States. By the end of the nineteenth century, when electricity began to generate power and "faery castles" of lightbulbs fought back the ancient enemy of night, electricity itself took on this millennialist charge.

Of all the Private who laid the wiring for this electric New Jerusalem, none dreamed harder than Nikola Tesla, who never met a natural force he didn't want to harness for humanity. An ethnic Serbian born in Croatia, Tesla came to America as a penniless young man, with dreams of wooing the great Thomas Edison with his impressive designs. When Tesla died in 1943, he had more than 700 patents under his belt, and could lay claim to having invented or discovered the induction motor, the polyphase alternating-current (AC) system, the Tesla coil transformer, fluorescent lights, and the principle of the rotating magnetic field. He dabbled with X rays and wireless communication before, respectively, Roentgen and Marconi. He tamed Niagara Falls to illuminate a city, and his AC induction generators and electrical motors continue to generate light and power across the globe. Even as modern civilization levitates above the belching turbines of the industrial age into the virtual empyrean, it continues to owe much of its lifeblood to Tesla.

Tesla was also the ultimate visionary crank, and to this day, both the man and his notions radiate a powerfully uncanny and mercurial aura. Tesla's habits were severely odd, his speculations both wild and prophetic, and his most spectacular (and unproved) claims vaulted over the primitive science fiction of his day. Tesla was no Spiritualist—his belief that human beings were meat machines pretty much staved off any lapses into occult theorizing. On the other hand, the inventor was not above chatting with the Theosophical cover boy Swami Vivekananda when the guru hobnobbed his way through Western cities in the 1890s; subsequently Tesla began to occasionally slip Vedic notions about prana and akasha into his writings on the "luminiferous ether."

But the reason that Tesla cuts such an enigmatic figure is that he seemed to possess an intuitive, visceral, almost supernatural knowledge of the electromagnetic mysteries, and investigators are still picking up the strings he left dangling. According to Tesla's own memoirs, his inventions sometimes popped into his head fully formed, as if he had simply downloaded the prototypes from the astral plane. The notion of a motor capable of generating alternating current—perhaps his most important invention—came to the young engineering student one day when he was strolling with a friend in a park in Budapest. Moved by the stunning sunset, Tesla recited a verse from, of all things, Goethe's *Faust;* in a moment "the idea came like a flash of lightning."[58]

Years later, Tesla's alternating current system was sold to the American tycoon George Westinghouse. This pitched the young inventor into a fierce public battle with Thomas Edison, who wanted his own direct current system to power the land. The "War of the Currents" unveiled the dark side of the electromagnetic imaginary, injecting morbid spectacle into late-nineteenth-century electrical culture. The two warring camps publicly electrocuted animals using their rival's systems— grotesque performances that inevitably gave rise to the first electrocution of a condemned prisoner. Edison arranged to use Tesla's system to execute one William Kemmler, but Edison's engineers botched the job and Kemmler had to be zapped twice. This gory sacrifice on the altar of electric utopia was widely reported by the popular press; *Scientific American* had already praised the method of dispatch, arguing that such "death by lightning" would "imbue the uneducated masses with a deeper terror."[59]

For his own public performances, Tesla preferred spectacles with a more crowd-pleasing if Faustian bent. Partly to prove the safety of his system, which eventually won the field, Tesla would saturate himself with electricity, passing hundreds of thousands of volts through his glowing body. In the words of the *Electrician:* "Who could . . . remain unimpressed in the face of the weird waving of glowing tubes in the suitably darkened room, and the mysterious voice issuing from the midst on an electrostatic field?"[60] The machine that generated some of Tesla's spectacular onstage fireworks was the famous induction coil that still bears his name. Small Tesla coils are widely used in TV sets and electronic gear, but their larger kin are most famous for helping generate the tremendous artificial lightning storms that dance about Doctor Frankenstein's laboratory in James Whale's classic film version of the tale.

Like many of Tesla's inventions, the Tesla coil exploits the principle of resonance, which has become such a common trope in contemporary thought as to warrant a brief description here. Not so much a law of nature as a deep habit, resonance pops up across the board, emerging in electrical systems, steam engines, and molecular dynamics, as well as

Tuvan overtone chanting and the tuning of TV sets. Everything vibrates, and when the oscillating vibrations of different systems coincide, or resonate, large quantities of energy can be exchanged from one system to the other. That's why powerful singers can shatter wineglasses; by energetically belting out a tone that matches the resonant frequency of the container, they are able to amplify the vibrations until the vessel explodes.

During the summers of 1899 and 1900, when he built a lab in Colorado Springs, Tesla performed experiments that pushed his own resonant intuitions into heights worthy of the great and terrible Oz. In a remarkable symbolic act, Tesla became the first Promethean to actually *generate* lightning, producing flashes over a hundred feet long. Investigating the natural lightning storms endemic to the region, Tesla also made the astonishing discovery that the planet itself generated stationary waves. As he put it, "The earth was . . . literally alive with electrical vibrations."[61] With these planetary waves in mind, Tesla conjured his most enigmatic notion: that the earth itself could be used as a resonant conductor, a kind of vibrating tuning fork that could broadcast power freely across the globe. After performing one experiment in Colorado, Tesla claimed that he had sent electrical energy back and forth across the entire planet without losing any energy along the way. Inspired by the natural laws he claimed to have discovered, Tesla imagined a wireless power network that could produce an earthly paradise. Broadcast power would transform ice caps into arable land, clean up cities, and abolish war, poverty, and hunger. Though some free energy freaks are still convinced that Tesla discovered some still-untapped electromagnetic phenomenon, most scientists today put this particular dream of his into the crank box.

Tesla electrified techno-utopianism, but he also tapped into the dark side of the force. Beneath his arcadian visions lies a violent world of electrocution, death rays, autonomous weapons, and wireless mind control. In the 1890s, popular periodicals reported that Tesla had secretly invented electromagnetically guided torpedoes—rumors that proved to be true. As he grew older and more destitute, the inventor became increasingly obsessed with wireless mayhem on a mass scale. Tesla painted scenarios of horrifying "death rays" and robot warriors that would supplant human soldiers—smart weapons similar to those now making their way through the ranks of the U.S. military machine. But

Tesla's most apocalyptic claim was his assertion that by keying into the resonant frequency of the earth, he could split the planet like an "apple"—a fit image of knowledge gone awry.

Even during his mind-blowing Colorado experiments, Tesla was savvy enough about human nature to recognize that a global fountain of power alone would not ensure utopia. So Tesla coupled his plans for broadcast power with the wireless delivery of information—what we now call radio. As he wrote in the *Electrical Experimenter:*

> The greatest good will come from the technical improvements tending to unification and harmony, and my wireless transmitter is preeminently such. By its means the human voice and likeness will be reproduced everywhere and factories driven thousands of miles from waterfalls furnishing the power; aerial machines will be propelled around the earth without a stop and the sun's energy controlled to create lakes and rivers for motive purposes and transformation of arid deserts into fertile land.[62]

Though Tesla ended up never building his great wireless transmitter, his vision of a global high-voltage Emerald City still glitters over the technological horizon. Like many techno-utopians today, Tesla held the curious belief that *technical* solutions to the problem of global communication would magically dissolve the social and political antagonisms that beset humankind. When Tesla wrote that "Peace can only come as a natural consequence of universal enlightenment," he was not just calling for the global imposition of modern cultural values about reason and progress. He was also suggesting that this "universal enlightenment" could be incarnated in the all-pervading waves of the wireless, just as today's Internet boosters believe that the decentralized structure of the Net will automatically instill the information age with a democratic and participatory politics.

The similarity between these two technical dreams should not be surprising. For just as online enthusiasts project their utopias into the unformed "space" of cyberspace, so did Tesla and other radioheads project their hopes into the wide open spaces of the electromagnetic spectrum. Though Maxwell had predicted the existence of radio waves in the 1860s, it took later technologists like Tesla and Marconi to prove that the invisible waves could be used as a medium of communication. Once tapped by technology, radio reproduced the now familiar pattern of intense technical development and the usual fatuous prophecies about world peace, democratic communication, and cultural transformation. Radio also attracted legions of hackers—hobbyists, teenage and otherwise, who endowed their home-brewed crystal sets with an undeniable charge of wonder, invention, and anarchic play. Weenies across the globe chatted up a storm while making important discoveries about the spectrum, especially on the shortwave side of things.

By the 1920s, however, federal and commercial interests began stringing regulatory barbed wire across the once many-to-many spectrum, professionalizing and segmenting a free-range medium into the commercial broadcast market we know today. But even as the airwaves began filling up with baseball play-by-plays and ads for laundry soap, radio freaks still heard some strange and otherworldly sounds in their crude headphones—cosmic echoes of the spooks that once haunted the old magnetic ethereum. Thomas Watson got an early taste of such unearthly transmissions late at night in Bell's lab, when he would listen to the snaps, bird chirps, and ghostly grinding noises that hopped along the telephone circuit. "My theory at this time was that the currents causing these sounds came from explosions on the sun or that they were signals from another planet. They were mystic enough to suggest the latter explanation but I never detected any regularity in them that might indicate they were intelligent signals."[63] Though the noises he heard may well have had terrestrial origins, Watson made the mind-blowing discovery that electromagnetic waves enabled human ears to directly perceive emanations from the cosmos. And like countless others after him, Watson could hardly suppress the intuition that such whispers from space might hold meanings both mystic and informational.

Watson was not the only electrofreak to believe that he was picking up play-by-plays from other planets. During the eventful Colorado summer of 1899, Tesla also picked up transmissions on his 200-foot radio tower, strangely rhythmic tones that led him to tentatively conclude that he was "the first to hear the greeting of one planet to another." Though astronomers would later tune in to such stellar pulses on a regular basis, Tesla's public announcement of this first hidey-ho from Venus or Mars (the most likely choices) was met with derision. But Tesla held firm. "Man is not the only being in the Infinite gifted with mind."[64] Never one to turn down the opportunity for feverish ponderings, Tesla even speculated that aliens might already move among us—*invisibly.*

For decades after Tesla received his transmissions, many wireless operators picked up powerful, persistent, and seemingly unexplainable signals, some of which were reported to be Pynchonesque repetitions of the letter *V* in Morse code. Marconi himself claimed to have received such signals on the low end of the longwave spectrum, and in 1921 flatly declared that he believed they originated from other civilizations in space. On August 24, 1924, when Mars passed unusually close to the earth, civilian and military transmitters voluntarily shut down in order to leave the airwaves open for the Martians; radio hackers were treated to a symphony of freak signals. Scientists today would describe the bulk of these sounds as sferics—a wide range of amazing radio noises stirred up by the millions of lightning bolts that crackle through the atmosphere every day. Skeptics would chalk up the rest to the human imagination and its boundless ability to project meaningful patterns into the random static of the universe. But this argument, however true in its own terms, distorts the larger technocultural loop: New technologies of perception and communication open up new spaces, and these spaces are always mapped, on one level or another, through the imagination.

For millennia, the hardwired side of human perception has been limited to the peculiar sensory apparatus constructed by our DNA, an apparatus that partly determines the apparent nature of "the world." In this sense, dogs and bees and jellyfish—with their own unique ratios of sense and perception—live in a different world than we do. New technologies of perception thus unfold a new world, or at least new dimensions of universal nature. When ocular instruments extended human sight toward Galileo's moons or Hooke's microscopic cells, these tools created new regions of causal explanation and knowledge. But they also evoked a sense of wonder and mystery, forcing us to reconfigure the limits of ourselves and to shape the human meaning, if any, of the new cosmological spaces we found ourselves reflected in.

In the book *Stockhausen: Towards a Cosmic Music,* the German avant-garde composer Karlheinz Stockhausen describes the human body as an incredibly complicated vibrating instrument of perception. The composer, who travels the vast spaceways that link electronic music and mysticism, argues that the "esoteric" is simply that which cannot yet be explained by science. "Every genuine composition makes conscious something of this esoteric realm. This process is endless, and there will be more and more esotericism as knowledge and science become increasingly capable of revealing human beings as perceivers."[65] And transmitters as well. Spiritual or not, we are beings of vibrating sensation, floating in an infinite sea of pulsing waves that roll and resonate between the synapse and the farthest star.

the gnostic infonaut

In 1945, near the village of Nag Hammadi, an Egyptian peasant with the heavyweight name of Muhammad 'Ali stumbled across an old jar. Standing with his fellows beside the crumbled talus of the Jabal al-Tarif, 'Ali hesitated a moment before opening the container, knowing that such an ancient vessel might well contain a nefarious *jinn*. But 'Ali was not really a superstitious man, or at least not a squeamish one (a month later, he would hack his father's murderer to bits). And so he smashed open the jar, wherein he discovered a number of leather-bound scriptures written in Coptic, a form of Hellenized Egyptian prevalent during the late Roman Empire. The texts were not scrolls but codices, ancestors of the bound book, and they contained the largest cache of original Gnostic writings ever discovered.

'Ali could not read Coptic, and after wrapping the volumes up in his cloak, he deposited the booty with his mother. Apparently more interested in their value as fuel than as data, she tossed some of the documents on the fire. When the police came to question 'Ali about the blood feud his family was embroiled in, he hid some of the books with a local priest. Others were sold to neighbors for peanuts, and eventually Bahij 'Ali, the one-eyed outlaw of al-Qasr, got his hands on most of the texts, which he promptly palmed off to a number of antiquities dealers in Cairo. A portion of one codex was smuggled out of the country, and eventually purchased by Carl Jung.

Everyone who knows something of Gnosticism knows this tale, told and retold until it seems a myth worthy of Indiana Jones. And no wonder. The discovery of ancient things, of tombs and mummies and musty scrolls, is about as close as moderns usually get to the ancient sense of revelation. Impoverished peasants are transformed into so many Aladdins; archaeologists and bespectacled Near Eastern scholars become the hierophants of secrets from a mysterious past. In the popular mind, the simple *fact* of the discovery is often more exotic than its purported contents; the collective imagination rushes into the gap between the first tentative newspaper reports and the careful pronouncements made by scholars years later. It's as if the serendipitous delivery of ancient data threatens to change everything, to reveal that our history, our faiths, and even ourselves are not what we were taught to believe. Such popular desires cropped up around the Dead Sea Scrolls, discovered two years after the Nag Hammadi texts by shepherd boys in the Qumran caves above Palestine's great saline lake. When a ferocious scholarly war over information control kept the translations of the texts out of the public eye, popular rumors claimed that an academic cabal was suppressing secrets that could knock the cornerstone out of the vast edifice of historical Christianity. But while the Qumran materials proved that Jesus was hardly the only messianic Jewish radical in town, the Church easily withstood the eventual publication of the Scrolls, proving once again that the shifting veils that cloak secrets are often far more fascinating than the naked truths themselves.

Many such veils cloak Gnosticism, a mystical mode of Christianity that arose in late antiquity, held a rather sour view of material life, and embraced the direct individual experience of *gnosis*—a mystical influx of self-knowledge with strong Platonic overtones. Unfortunately, even this relatively basic definition of Gnosticism would be meat for the hawks of Near Eastern academe, since the origins, rituals, philosophy, and influence of the Gnostics are notoriously difficult to reconstruct. This ambiguity, combined with the bad press piled on by a Roman Church desperate to maintain ideological control, has made Gnosticism a kind of Silly Putty religious stance, capable of representing any number of different philosophies and practices. Before 1945, almost everything known about early Gnostic thought came through the writings of its orthodox enemies, who were not exactly inclined to cut the "heretics" much slack. But Ali's jar contained something different. Unlike nearly all the texts from the ancient world that we can read today, the Nag Hammadi codexes weren't copies of copies of copies, endlessly xeroxed by erring scribes and meddling redactors over the centuries. Though the texts themselves may have been compiled and buried by orthodox Pachomian monks, the Gnostic signals themselves come to us unsullied, straight from the ancient horse's mouth.

Given the aura that surrounds such discoveries, the timing of Nag Hammadi's unexpected blast from the past has led some myth-minded moderns to suspect that something more than happenstance was afoot. After all, history too has its poetic logic; apparently random accidents can strike deep chords of synchronicity, especially once those events are

played through the organ of the mind, with its constant search for harmony and melody. In the words of June Singer, a contemporary Jungian
gnostic of sorts, "What a coincidence, what a meaningful coincidence,
that those Egyptian peasants stumbled upon that jar just at the end of
the Second World War, after the Holocaust and after the dropping of the
atomic bombs on Hiroshima and Nagasaki."[66] Singer points out that the
Nag Hammadi codexes themselves tell us to pay attention to the timing
of their return to the world. The tractate known as the *Gospel of the
Egyptians* claims:

> The great Seth wrote this book with letters in one hundred and thirty
> years. He placed it in the mountain that is called Charaxio, in order
> that, at the end of the times and eras, . . . it may come forth and reveal
> this incorruptible, holy race of the great savior.[67]

Now, 1945 was not exactly the end of times and eras, though one can
forgive the citizens of Hiroshima, Nagasaki, and Dresden for thinking
otherwise. But the atomic bomb was destined to inflict a world-rending
dread on postwar life, and its solar powers were shrouded from the
beginning with apocalyptic imagery. Immediately following that summer's first Trinity test blast, in the New Mexican wasteland known as
the Jornado del Muerto, Robert Oppenheimer recalled a quotation from
the *Bhagavad-Gita:* "Now I am become Death, the destroyer of worlds."
In the next decades, many feared that a cataclysmic incandescence was
only a red phone call away, though few expected a savior any more holy
than the tense stalemate of detente.

Despite the danger that wayward nuclear weapons still pose today,
the mushroom cloud has mostly evaporated in our imaginations, dissi-
pating into a more amorphous apocalyptic atmosphere laced with air-
borne viruses, biological weapons, toxic fumes, and greenhouse gases.
With this in mind, we might even say that the most world-shaking
explosion in the 1940s was not atomic but *informational*. When Marshall McLuhan perversely described the atomic bomb as "information,"
he probably was testing out one of his patented rhetorical shocks. But
he may have glimpsed a deeper revelation as well. For if the information age was born in the electric nineteenth century, and nurtured in the
first decades of the radio-crazed twentieth, World War II marked its
glorious coming-of-age.

This rite of passage was certainly not without its nightmares, especially when it came to the electronic media's increasing ability to mesmerize hearts and minds. Technology critics who fear the power of mass media thought control still point to the German fascists, whose culture industry engineered a dark consensus reality with fiendish acumen. In the words of Albert Speer, the showman behind the Third Reich's Nuremberg pep rallies,

> Hitler's dictatorship was the first dictatorship of an industrial state in this age of modern technology, a dictatorship which employed to perfection the instruments of technology to dominate its own people . . . 80 million persons could be made subject to the will of one individual.[68]

Besides staging megawatt mass spectacles, the Nazi propagandists exploited the sonorous immediacy of the radio with sorcerous brilliance, allowing Hitler to, as he himself put it, make his way with the ease of a somnambulist. To fight the Axis powers, the Allies also exploited new information technologies to the max. In both theaters of war, radar played a pivotal, if often overlooked, role, with microwaves giving the Allies a distinct tactical edge toward the end of the war, especially in coordinating D day and the bombing raids on Germany. The war also saw the creation of the Z-3, the world's first programmable digital computer, invented in 1941 by an ardent Nazi and used to design some of Germany's flying bombs. Secret codes were cranked out on both sides of the barbed wire fence, and in Britain, Alan Turing used some of the earliest digital computers to unscramble German Enigma messages. Such efforts also fired up the burners for the kind of code paranoia that would come to typify postwar espionage, as civilian censors among the Allies, fearing the propagation of encrypted information, went so far as to rearrange stamps on outgoing letters, ban crossword puzzles and toddler drawings from the mail, and in one case spin the dials on an entire shipment of watches to scramble any possible hidden messages.

Following 1945, the war's intense electronic development found its way into civilian life, especially in the United States. ENIAC, the first electronic programmable computer, made its U.S. debut in 1946, stirring the public imagination with the "electronic genius" of its "superbrain." A few years later, Bell Labs' revolutionary transistor started replacing the vacuum tubes previously used in computers and other electronic devices, initiating the spiral of miniaturization and circuit-board complexity that has led us today to the brink of nanotechnology and quantum computing. In the late 1940s, theoretical developments like information theory and cybernetics laid the groundwork for new forms of information-driven social organization, while consumer culture kicked into electric overdrive. The first generation of media mutants was born, baby boomers destined to grow up in the first modern suburbs, soak up the first commercial television broadcasts, and blow their minds and turn global culture inside out when they eventually got their gadget-happy hands on electric guitars, Marx, and LSD (whose psycho-shamanistic powers were first uncorked at a Swiss pharmaceutical corporation in 1943).

But what does this explosion of information culture and electronic media have to do with a stack of Coptic religious texts crumbling in a jar in upper Egypt? Obviously, an incalculable historical, cultural, and spiritual divide exists between the mystical aspirations of ancient dualists and the cultures and concepts that would come to surround information and its technologies in the twentieth century. But from a hermetic perspective, which reads images and synchronicities at least as deeply as facts, the mythic structures and psychology of Gnosticism seem strangely resonant with the digital zeitgeist and its paradigm of information. As we'll see, Gnostic myth anticipates the more extreme dreams of today's mechanistic mutants and cyberspace cowboys, especially their libertarian drive toward freedom and self-divinization, and their dualistic rejection of matter for the incorporeal possibilities of mind. Gnostic lore also provides a mythic key for the kind of infomania and conspiratorial thinking that comes to haunt the postwar world, with its terror of nefarious cabals, narcotic technologies, and invisible messengers of deception.

Gnosis forms one of the principal threads in the strange and magnificent tapestry of Western esotericism, and I must emphasize that my use of its lore is not intended to belittle its possibly illuminating powers. Hermetic scholars or occult Traditionalists would write off any similarities between Gnostic religion and contemporary technoculture as, at best, the latter's demonic and infantile parody of the former. But the authenticity of spiritual ideas and religious experiences does not really concern me here; rather I am attempting to understand the often unconscious metaphysics of information culture by looking at it through the archetypal lens of religious and mystic myth. Inauthentic or not, these patterns of thought and experience have played and continue to play a role in how humans relate to technology, and especially the technologies of information. But before we crack open the techgnostic jar and let its speculative genies loose, it seems important to wrestle a bit with the concept of information itself, that strange new angel that lends its name to our age.

The Mythinformation Age

Information gathering defines civilization as much as food gathering defines the nomadic cultures that preceded the rise of urban communities, agricultural surplus, and stratified social hierarchies. From the moment the first scribe took up a reed and scratched a database into the cool clay of Sumer, information flow has been an instrument of human power and control—religious as well as economic and political. It is hardly accidental that the first real writing machine emerges hand in hand with urban civilization, nor that the technology was initially devoted to recording the transfer of goods into the hands of priests.

But it wasn't until the twentieth century that information became a thing in itself. People began to devote themselves more and more to collecting, analyzing, transmitting, selling, and using the stuff. Even more significantly, they built machines to automate and perform these tasks with a level of power and efficiency far beyond the builders themselves, and this information combustion fueled the expanding apparatus of science, commerce, and communications. In many people's minds, what was once merely a category of knowledge began to mutate into a new unit of reality itself, one that took its place alongside matter and energy as one of the fundamental building blocks of the cosmos. If electricity is the soul of the modern age, information is its spirit.

In the simplest everyday terms, "information" suggests a practical chunk of reified experience, a unit of sense lodged on the hierarchy of knowledge somewhere between *data* and *report*. Though an essentially incorporeal and "mental" element, information nonetheless seems to derive from the external physical world, tightly bound to mundane materials like newsprint or a thermometer or sound waves emerging from a herald's mouth. Information emerges in the spark gap between mind and matter. In the middle of the twentieth century, scientifically rigorous definitions of the stuff began to appear, definitions that were destined to invade biology, social science, and popular culture, thereby transforming our understanding of ourselves and our social institutions.

Computers brought the logical machinery of data processing into every-day life, while new communication technologies wove human beings into a global web of messages and signals.

Inevitably, information became one of those concepts whose meaning expands even as it begins to evaporate. You could fill a million Dust-busters with the fuzzy thinking that "information" has produced, especially as the technical term collided with social and cultural forms of knowledge. At the same time, the constantly shifting borderlines around the term have lent the concept an incorporeal mystique; despite its erst-while objectivity, information has become an almost luminescent icon, at once fetish and logos. Straddling mind and matter, science and psyche, hard drives and DNA, information has come to spawn philosophies both half-baked and profound, while also reconstructing, perhaps danger-ously, our images of the self and its cosmic home. Gnosticism is hardly the only passageway into the storehouse of archetypes lurking beneath the secular mask of information, but it underscores the metaphysical patterns and Promethean fire that the new category of reality unleashed into the postwar mind.

In the late 1940s, a Bell Labs researcher named Claude Shannon announced the birth of information theory, an abstract technical analy-sis of messages and communication. Shannon's exacting description of information, initially embraced by scientists and engineers, planted the seeds of the concept's later flowering. The theoretical tools that Shannon created apply to any scenario in which a message is passed from a sender to a receiver along a communication channel—in principle, they can describe a conversation in a barroom, the replication of genetic mater-ial, or an episode of *Baywatch* bounced off a wheezy satellite into mil-lions of TV sets across the land. For the heroic message to reach its goal, it must survive the onslaught of "noise"—the chance fluctuations, inter-ference, and transmission errors that inevitably degrade signals as they make their way through an error-ridden and analog world. The popular kids' game of telephone—where a whispered phrase is passed person-to-person through a circle of people, a process that inevitably mutates the message—provides a good playground image for the semantic drift of such signal degradation; the bursts of static that mangle many a cellular phone call furnish a more visceral taste of noise in all its cranky glory.

In the face of this formidable foe, Shannon's celebrated second theo-rem proved that any message can be coded in such a way that it can be guaranteed to survive its journey through the valley of noise. The only limitation that needs to be factored into the equation is the natural carrying capacity of the channel—that is, its bandwidth. Shannon did not provide the "ideal code" of his second theorem—dubbed the holy grail of information theory—but he did show that such perfect communication was technically possible. More generally, his theory showed that the integrity of messages can be maintained by translating them into digital codes of varying degrees of complexity, redundancy, and bandwidth-sapping accuracy. Messages are not sent unalloyed but are embedded within additional information—the equivalent of decoder rings, say, or data that allow the recipient to know that the message received is really the proper one. This additional, or "meta," information relies heavily on redundancy, a kind of repetition that ensures that the message will prevail even if noise takes a meaty bite out of it along the way.

All this was great news for Shannon's employers, who were fruitfully multiplying telephone lines across the land and applying wartime communications know-how to civilian life. But like the sciences of complexity and chaos theory today, information theory also became a Big Idea, one that people in many disciplines hoped would revise and clarify the known world. Once information received an abstract and universal form, it somehow became more *real*—not just a turn of phrase or a squiggle on some Bell Labs blackboard, but a force in the world, an objective yet essentially mindlike material that could help explicate any number of seemingly unrelated phenomena by boiling them down to the crisp binary unit of the bit.

So in the 1950s and 1960s, social scientists, psychologists, biologists, corporate managers, and media organizations began reimagining and reorganizing their fields of expertise with information theory in mind. Shannon's nuts-and-bolts picture of signal and noise, sender and receiver, started shaping the culture at large. The paradigm of information began to invade humanist discourses, promising to efficiently clean up all sorts of messy problems concerning communication, learning, thought, and social behavior—all of which could now be seen as depending on more or less efficient systems of information processing. The budding technocracy of postwar society seemed to have found its *lingua franca:* an objective, utilitarian, and computational language of control with which to master the carnival of human being.

All of this set information on a collision course with *meaning*—that signifying magic that, for all the analyses of linguists, sociologists, and cognitive scientists, remains one of the trickiest, most seductive, and most consternating glyphs in the human equation. Meaning is at once the mundane foundation of the mind's trivial pursuits and the inspiration for our most intimate, creative, and spiritual quests. But meaning, even strictly linguistic meaning, is notoriously slippery stuff. Though the attempt to reconceive meaning under the abstract sign of information is vital for the technology of communication, the absolute dominance of the information model may well exact a withering cost. Information theory is fine and good if you are talking about radio transponders, telephone lines, and drive-through kiosks at Taco Bell, but its universal application saps the marrow from the rich lifeworld of meanings that humans actually inhabit—a world whose nuanced ambiguities are better captured by, say, Shakespeare's soliloquies and Yoruban myth than by statistical algorithms. As the neo-Luddite critic Theodore Roszak puts it, "for the information theorist, it does not matter if we are transmitting a fact, a judgment, a shallow cliché, a deep teaching, a sublime truth, or a nasty obscenity."[69] But today many people confuse information and meaning, which leads to a rather disturbing paradox: Our society has come to place an enormous value on information even though information itself can tell us nothing about value.

But let's be fair. If you have had the pleasure of downloading crystal-clear images of Martian real estate through little copper wires into your home computer, you probably recognize that dodging the briar patch of value judgment and semantic ambiguity has its technical advantages. Besides, the information paradigm does provide a number of powerful ways to think about what we mean by meaning. To start with, information seems to have something to do with novelty. For you to provide me with genuine information, you must tell me something *new*. That is, information requires an amount of uncertainty on the part of the receiver. If you are so predictable that nothing you tell me is a surprise, then nothing you say is really information, even if the signal is crystal clear. On the other hand, for me to understand you in the first place, you need to be *somewhat* predictable—which is why loads of the language we blurt out or write is made up of redundancy, a thick wad of repeated cues and familiar syntactical rules which themselves signify little at all. This structural redundancy ensures that not *too* much novelty occurs, because such wide degrees of freedom might lead us into the chaos of a schizophrenic's word salad, or the interminable ambiguities and connotations of *Finnegans Wake*.

Communicating information is not simply a matter of cramming data into an envelope and sending it off; information is also something con-structed by the receiver. In this sense, an element of "subjectivity" even-tually enters into any communications circuit, because the question of how much information is received depends in part on how the receiver (which may be purely mechanical) is primed to parse the incoming mes-sage and code. To explain the role that receivers play in processing infor-mation, the science writer Jeremy Campbell uses the example of three students listening to an economics professor, only two of whom know English, and only one of whom actually studies economics. For the non-English speaker, the noises spilling out of the old fellow's mouth are so uncertain, so unpredictable, that no information gets through. By virtue of shared language alone, the English speakers both receive more infor-mation, but the future mutual fund manager reaps the most, because his foreknowledge of economics concepts and jargon makes the professor's data-dump even more predictable, but still surprising enough to gener-ate novel differences.

At the heart of information theory, then, is probability, which is the measure of the likelihood of one specific result (the word *the* or the Jack of spades) out of an open-ended field of possible messages (the English language or a shuffled poker deck). Probability plays a powerful role in the predictions that scientists are wont to make about the world, but even as a no-nonsense statistical science, it is something of a trickster. Probability slips between objectivity and subjectivity, randomness and order, the mind's knowledge and the hidden patterns of the world—a conceptually hairy zone that the mathematician James R. Newman called "a nest of subtleties and traps." The sharp diagrams of informa-tion theory are etched on shiftier sands than at first appear.

Claude Shannon opened up an even weirder can of worms when he boiled down his theory to a basic equation and found that his abstract technical description of information took exactly the same form as the equation for thermodynamic entropy that the physicist Ludwig Boltz-man came up with at the height of the earlier steam age. As any Thomas Pynchon fan knows, entropy is a heavy trip, a metaphysical and exis-tential conundrum as well as an irrevocable law of the cosmos. Accord-ing to Maxwell's famous second law, entropy ultimately wins the field: However ordered and energetic a closed system may be, its energy will, while being conserved, inevitably become useless, and its form will go to seed. Toss a few ice cubes in a hot bath and you'll see a bit of entropy at work, as the crystal lattices of frozen water molecules melt into the uniform and random soup of stray H_2O. Though we rarely encounter genuine closed systems in real life—babies and wetlands and the Internet are all resolutely open systems—the second law does seem to condemn all the interesting things in the universe to tread water for a while before they get sucked downstream into a cold amorphous sea of bland disorder. More than any other force in physics, entropy strikes the mind like some dark and ancient doom etched into natural law.

At first glance, the fact that Shannon's description of information matches such a significant material process seems like a synchronicity forged in cosmic coincidence control. The exact reasons for this remarkably tight fit are rather tricky, but the trick revolves around probability. On the one hand, we can say that the more unpredictable a system of potential messages is—that is, the more it takes on the characteristics of random noise—the more entropy the system possesses; in this sense, it resembles the bathwater after the ice cubes have melted. On the other hand, we could just as reasonably say that highly unpredictable systems are actually *rich* with information, since any individual message we receive is likely to be surprising. The ambiguity between these two positions accounts for the fact that while Shannon described information as entropy, the mathematician and cybernetics honcho Norbert Wiener opposed the two terms, arguing that information is a measure of organization—pattern, form, coherence—while entropy measures a system's degree of randomness and disorganization.

Technically, the difference does not amount to much (a plus or minus sign in an equation), but for reasons perhaps more poetic than technical, Wiener's definition of information entropy won the day. In both the popular and the technocratic imagination, information and its technologies began to take on an almost redemptive character as they battled noise and error—the communications equivalent of dissipation and decay. Such heroism helped pave the way for the mythinformation that currently rules the wires: the notion that communication systems, databases, software, and complex technical organizations are in themselves avatars of the Good, actively keeping chaos and entropy at bay. In his popular 1954 book *The Human Use of Human Beings,* Wiener directly pits information against the dark force of the second law, a force that for him manifests itself not only as physical rot and garbled FM signals, but as *meaninglessness.* "In control and communication we are always fighting nature's tendency to degrade the organized and to destroy the meaningful."[70] Here and throughout his book, Wiener strays beyond the dispassionate scientific measure of bits and provocatively links the behavior of information systems to meaning, value, and life itself. Wiener even suggests that the order- and form-generating power of information systems is basically analogous to what some people call God.

Such information mystique got a major boost from biology in the 1950s, when scientists discovered the double helix structure of DNA and started unscrambling the genetic code. Before you could say "paradigm shift," DNA was cast as an information system, with a sender–message–receiver form. More specifically, DNA was described as a kind of alphabetic *writing*, a culturally specific media metaphor that nonetheless seems tough to avoid. DNA consists of four different nucleotides that array themselves in myriad combinations along the linear strand of the double helix. The arrangement of these four "letters" (AGCT) produces "words," called codons, that combine into genetic instructions for the cell. After copying some particular subset of instructions, DNA offloads them to messenger RNA, which delivers them to "factories" in the cell. There, the RNA code is copied into a linear sequence of amino acids that literally folds into three-dimensional proteins—the building blocks for life on this planet, which is all the life we know.

Though the DNA scribe obviously plays an enormous role in the development and maintenance of living bodies, genetic processes are also influenced by a variety of environmental and intercellular factors that are far from being understood. But DNA continues to be characterized as the only driver in the cockpit of creation. This singular focus on the "code of life," as well as the exuberant embrace of genetic engineering and the ideology of the "selfish gene," reflects a society still in thrall to scientific reductionism and obsessed with production and control through information. But DNA's aura of authority also reflects the religious heritage of the West, which features a cosmic maker who creates the world through divine language. Generally, this word is spoken, but sometimes it is written as well, as in the medieval "book of nature." Some mystical Jewish accounts of creation also foreshadow DNA in an almost eerie manner. In ancient days, Torah scrolls were written without punctuation or spaces between the letters (like DNA), and some later Jews argued that this artifact of the writing machine alluded to a cosmic Torah that preceded the one handed down at Sinai. This original Torah was a living text of infinite potential woven from the letters of the tetragrammaton—YHVH, the four-lettered name of God. This blueprint of creation was also described as a heap of scrambled letters, which one text calls "the concentrated, not yet unfolded Torah." Once God arranged these letters into words, the Torah "unfolded" into the manifold shapes of the created world. Far more pleasant worlds than ours were possible, but Adam's poor behavior selected the words, and the world, we got. Still, Kabbalists looked forward to the messianic age, when God would perform a kind of cosmic genetic engineering, rearranging the letters of the Torah to spell out paradise.

To this day, molecular biologists and genetic engineers regularly invoke metaphors of the Bible and the Book of Life when discussing their work—and not just when they are speaking to the lay public. Many prominent genetic engineers are born-again Christians, including Francis Collins, the director of the Human Genome Project and a member of an evangelical Christian organization of scientists whose members identify themselves as "stewards of God's creation." In their book *The DNA Mystique,* scholars Dorothy Nelkin and M. Susan Lindee also point out that genetic essentialism—the currently popular notion that you "are" your genes, that everything from your bad back to your mood swings is programmed by DNA—has a religious character. At a time when human identity is up for grabs, DNA takes on some of the social and cultural functions previously possessed by the soul. At once embodied and incorporeal, the genetic code grounds identity in a deathless essence. Indeed, for hard-core genetic reductionists like Richard Dawkins, DNA *is* the only essential part of ourselves; our bodies and our passions are just expendable machinery for the immortal propagation of the spiral molecule. But as Nelkin and Lindee point out, Dawkins's extreme reductionism, in which DNA achieves eternal life at the expense of the individual body, "is in many ways a theological narrative, resembling the belief that the things of this world (the body) do not matter, while the soul (DNA) lasts forever."[71]

Geneticists were not the first scientists to popularize the view of living beings as information-processing machines. In the 1940s, Norbert Wiener was already arguing that biological, communicational, and technological "systems" could all be analyzed with formalized descriptions of how such systems processed and stored messages, memories, and incoming sensory data. He dubbed this science of "control and communication" *cybernetics,* so if you are sick of cybersex and cyberspace and cyberdrool, you have Wiener to blame. Cybernetics placed particular emphasis on "feedback" loops, in which some of a system's output—or information about that output—is reintroduced into that system as new input. Cybernetic circuits constantly adjust themselves to the effects of their own actions and to the incoming flux of information. Curiously, Gnostic and hermetic lore furnishes us with an amazing image of such feedback loops: the Ouroboros, a serpent who eats its own tail and thus symbolizes the self-sufficient cyclicity of nature. In the hands of modern engineers, this dynamic and self-reflexive snake has helped design every-thing from antiaircraft guns to robots, and has also provided a rigorous model for understanding how machines and computer programs can "learn" about the world, updating and improving their output to opti-mize programmed goals. But this vision of feedback, learning loops, and constant interaction with the outside world also provided a new way to think about biological organisms. Wiener suggested that living creatures could be seen as systems that resist the evil deathlord of entropy through information, communication, and feedback. In due course, DNA would be assimilated to this model, its constant stream of dictated messages acting as an internal governor of system efficiency.

Cybernetics is thus a science of control, which explains the etymo-logical root of the term: *kubernetes,* the Greek word for steersman, and the source as well for our word "governor." The term *cybernetics* was first used by the nineteenth-century French physicist André-Marie Ampère, who developed an influential theory of electromagnetism, but the philosophical image of the *kubernetes* can be traced back to the great Neoplatonist Plotinus, who lived in Alexandria and Rome in the third century C.E. In the third section of his *Enneads,* the philosopher describes the intellectual soul as the steersman of the body—a rela-tionship that Plotinus, as a Platonist, found potentially disastrous. Sometimes, he warns, "the steersman of a storm-tossed ship is so intent on saving it that he forgets his own interest and never thinks that he is recurrently in peril of being dragged down with the vessel." The anal-ogy is clear: The incorporeal soul is in charge of governing the body, but must not be afraid of abandoning ship. That is, the soul's mystical goal of transcendence cannot be achieved by following the ways of the flesh and becoming "gripped and held by [its] concern for the realm of Nature."[72]

As a modern science exclusively concerned with the realm of nature, cybernetics obviously had no room for such mystical dualism. In con-trast to Plotinus, who was drawn to a world of changeless ideal forms, Wiener rejected the Greek language of form and substance for a vision of feedback-looping flux. At the same time, however, Wiener's cybernetic emphasis on process over matter did provide a new "scientific" image of the incorporeal self, one that rewrote identity as a *pattern of information*. As Wiener argued:

> The physical identity of an individual does not consist in the matter of which it is made. . . . The biological individuality in an organism seems to lie in a certain continuity of process, and in the memory by the organism of the effects of its past development. This appears to hold also of its mental development. In terms of the computing machine, the individuality of a mind lies in the retention of its earlier tapings and memories.[73]

By reconceiving the "individuality of mind" along the incorporeal lines of messages, memories, and patterns of information, cybernetics unconsciously introduced a subtle spirit into the scientific image of human being. The inner steersman is neither an eternal substance nor a figment of the teeming brain, but a fluctuating pattern in an endless cybernetic play. As Wiener poetically put it, human identity is more like a flame than a stone.

With its systematic language of patterns and process, cybernetics eroded many traditional distinctions between mind and machine, organic and mechanical, natural and artificial. In so doing, it anticipated (and helped generate) many of the conundrums we face today. Though the term *cybernetics* has now left the stage, in reality the science has simply mutated into a wide variety of disciplines: complexity theory, artificial life, network dynamics, cognitive science, robotics. Searching for an umbrella term to cover all these disparate sciences, many have settled on "systems theory." Simply put, systems theory attempts to complement or even supplant the reductionist orientation of classical science with a perspective based on fluxes, emergent behaviors, feedback loops, and unified but dynamic wholes. The systems paradigm argues that similar patterns of process underlie widely different dimensions of the real, from gadgets to galaxy clusters to games people play. In seeking to pin down this "pattern that connects," systems thinking has also seduced many nonscientists restlessly seeking a new frame for the Big Picture; as we will see in later chapters, the flowers of West Coast "holistic thought" in many ways sprouted from this cybernetic matrix.

Like most scientists, Wiener was also drawn to the pattern that connects—an attraction toward the universal that has more to do with traditional Western religious drives than most scientists are willing to admit. In *The Human Use of Human Beings,* Wiener describes science as a game whose goal is the discovery of the order of the cosmos. But Wiener warns that the scientist faces an adversary in the game, an "arch enemy" that he identifies with confusion and disorganization, the noise that obscures the order of the universe. "Is this devil Manichean or Augustinian?" Wiener asks. "Is it a contrary force opposed to order or is it the very absence of order itself?" Though Wiener appears to be talking about the force that frustrates scientists in their intellectual game, he really seems to be asking about the existence of disorder itself—not just confusion and ignorance, but noise and entropy, the all-swallowing rot of things and meanings. In that form, his passionate query is as old as the hills: Is evil separate from God, or a part of God?

The ancient Manicheans definitely thought they had the answer: The universe was a mixture of two primordial and active forces, Light and Darkness. All is not one; all is two. For the prophet Mani and his many followers, redemption lay only in rejecting the Darkness, which he identified with the corrupt world of matter. Salvation lay in gnosis, in gathering and awakening the divine spark that connects us to a pure and transcendent world of Light. Saint Augustine's answer to Wiener's question took a different tack. Though he spent his salad days as a Manichean, Augustine eventually came around to the orthodox Christian position that God holds all the cards, and that Manichean dualism is a heretical affront to the one creator. Evil is the absence of God, not his active enemy.

In *The Human Use of Human Beings,* Wiener convincingly argues that science—and by extension, modern thought—is Augustinian. The devil the scientist fights is simply confusion, the lack of information, and not an organized resistance waged by some dark trickster. "Nature offers resistance to decoding, but it does not show ingenuity in finding new and undecipherable methods for jamming our communication with the outer world."[74] The enemy is dumb and blind, Wiener says, "defeated by our intelligence as thoroughly as by a sprinkle of holy water."[75] Wiener's disavowal of Manichean thought was also motivated by the political conditions of the postwar world. As we use the word today, "Manichean" means the tendency to view conflicts as holy crusades between Good and

Evil, Crusaders and Saracens, white hats and black. Writing at the dawn of the cold war, Wiener hoped that the postwar world would walk another road, and that by emulating scientists in their Augustinian game with ignorance and entropy, humanity could resolve its problems through free communication flows, the open exchange of information, and a commitment to reason—all axioms of liberal economics and the "open society" that many continue to embrace as the only path to peace and prosperity.

At the same time, Wiener ominously hints that the Augustinian optimism of the scientist "tends to make him the dupe of unprincipled people in war and in politics."[76] Civil and military institutions are often founded in opposition to perceived enemies, both inside and outside society, and they are stuffed with cunning and often malicious manipulators—which Wiener hints resemble the dark rulers of Manichean myth. Despite the enormous role that Wiener played in promoting the computerization of postwar technocratic society, he was well aware of the insidious side of the cybernetic equation: totalitarian secrecy, covert forms of social control, the technocratic manipulation of human minds and bodies. Cybernetics suggested that the human individual is merely a momentary whirlpool within larger systems of information flow; thus the steersman himself was subject to control. Fearful of this, Wiener criticized the "machines of flesh and blood" that absorb autonomous human souls into bureaucracies, armies, laboratories, and corporations. But he was particularly worried about the ultimate issue of cybernetic thought: genuinely intelligent and autonomous machines. Warning that the hour was very late (and this was in the 1950s), Wiener compared such intelligent agents to the genies from *The Thousand and One Nights:* Once out of the bottle, there was no way to assure that their supposedly "brainy" actions would not unleash a nightmare of unintended consequences.

Wiener's words remind us that though the information age can be considered as a major leg up in the Augustinian battle with entropy and ignorance, we cannot ignore the Manichean element of the real world, the bloodred darkness mixed into virtual light. Wiener would like to believe that the enemy is dumb and blind, but he cannot shake the malevolent genies from his mind nor ignore the nasty games that our information machines—and the forces that control them—can play with the masses of humanity. Even a scientific and essentially optimistic humanist like Wiener could not ignore the dark gnostic mythos that saturates the postwar world, a mythos that, as we will see, insists upon the vital difference between the knowledge that frees and the delusions that reduce us to programmed machines.

Priming the Spark

Gnosticism is such a fragmentary and suggestive patchwork of texts, hearsay, myth, and rumor that you can label almost any contemporary phenomenon "gnostic" and get away with it. Existentialism, William S. Burroughs, Jungian psychology, Marxism, Thomas Pynchon, psychedelics, American religion, the European banking elite, even the Sex Pistols—all have been saddled at one time or another with the gnostic name. I admit that by teasing out the gnostic threads from the webwork of technoculture, I am perhaps only making a further mess of things, and it seems best to remind the reader that we are dealing with psychological patterns and archetypal echoes, not some secret lore handed down through the ages. For this reason, I will reserve the capital-G term *Gnostic* for those religious groups and texts of antiquity that most scholars recognize as such.

Not that old-timey Gnosticism was significantly more coherent than its supposed contemporary manifestations. The Nag Hammadi codexes, for one, scrape together quite a heterogeneous collection of writings. There are mystical instruction manuals, chunks of Plato, bits of the *Corpus Hermeticum,* Christian texts canonical and not, and wild-eyed space opera cosmologies. The authors of these texts were "heretics" according to their institutional rivals; as far as the authors themselves were concerned, they were for all intents and purposes Christian. Some may have adhered to esoteric cults along the lines of mystery religions, while others may have been philosophical types belonging to a small intellectual elite. Gnostic notions also fed directly into Manichaeism, which spread as far as Eastern China and at one point rivaled the broadcast power of the Roman Church. Given all these divergent and fragmentary religious forms, some scholars have come to use the word *Gnostic* as a description of certain philosophical and spiritual tendencies found throughout late antiquity, rather than a term referring to a particular sectarian movement.

One of the most essential Gnostic characteristics was a hard-core Platonism that amplified the otherworldliness of the old Greek metaphysician into a severe dualism that pitted the spirit against flesh and the world. Taking the widespread human intuition that *something is amiss* to new levels of cosmic crankiness, the Gnostics insisted that life on our heavy ball of sex and death was not just an unmitigated disaster—it was a cosmic trap. The central myth of Gnosticism's byzantine cosmologies held that the creator of this world is not the true god, but an inferior demiurge who ignorantly botched the job. Plato also spoke of a worldly demiurge in the *Timaeus,* though he characterized this craftsman as a basically benevolent fellow. The Gnostic demiurge is not necessarily evil, but he and his ministers (known as *archons,* or rulers) are at the very least arrogant blowhards who mistakenly consider themselves to be lords of the universe. Humans are imprisoned in the material universe of fate that they control, though we carry within ourselves the leftover sparks of the divine and precosmic Pleroma (Fullness) that existed before the demiurgic construction company plastered everything over. Human beings are thus, in essence, absolutely superior to the ecosystem—not stewards or even masters, but strangers in a strange land.

In contrast to orthodox Christianity, with its guilt-ridden doctrine of original sin, the Gnostics held that the sorry state of the world is not our fault. The error lies in the structure of the universe, not withinour essential selves. We don't need to expiate any crimes, but simply to discover or recall the way back home—a way out that is also, mystically speaking, the way inside. Unlike the Church, which encased the spiritual autonomy of the individual believer within an elaborate corporate hierarchy founded on the ruins of the Roman state and the magical transmission of apostolic authority, the Gnostics recognized instead the supreme authority of esoteric gnosis: a mystical breakthrough of total liberation, an influx of knowing oneself to be part of the genuine godhead, of knowing oneself to be free. In one of his few surviving fragments, the great Alexandrian Valentinus—a second-century Gnostic Christian who was once in the running for Bishop of Rome—wrote:

> What liberates is the knowledge of who we were, what we became; where we were, whereinto we have been thrown; whereto we speed, where from we are redeemed; what birth is and what rebirth.[77]

The primary polarity of Gnostic psychology is not sin and redemption, but ignorance and gnosis, forgetting and memory, sleep and the awakening of knowledge. The Gnostic sought the pure signal that overrides the noise and corrosive babel of the world—an ineffable rush tinged with the Platonic exaltation of mind, a first-person encounter with the Logos etched into the heart of the divine self within.

From another angle, however, gnosis appears less like a mystical moment of satori than an occult rite of passage. The Gnostics were accused of believing that Jesus passed on secret truths to an esoteric elite, and this more encrypted and fetishized form of knowledge influenced their vision of transcendent awakening. Like the Freemasons and other later secret societies, some Gnostics were apparently fond of doling out mysterious words, strange sigils, and mysterious hand gestures—information that the soul would need in its journey through the afterlife, which the Gnostics imagined as a kind of multileveled computer game inhabited by demonic gatekeepers and treacherous landscapes.

This more magical and alchemical approach to gnosis particularly informs the pagan *Corpus Hermeticum*, a portion of which made it into the Nag Hammadi library. In the eleventh treatise of the *Hermetica*, Mind—one of the grand old pontificators in the Neoplatonic playhouse—makes an extraordinary suggestion to Hermes Trismegistus, whom he addresses not as a mortal man but as a virtual being whose "incorporeal imagination" gives him the keys to the universe:

> Having conceived that nothing is impossible to you, consider yourself immortal and able to understand everything, all art, all learning, the temper of every living thing. . . . Collect in yourself all the sensations of what has been made, of fire and water, dry and wet; and be everywhere at once, on land, in the sea, in heaven; be not yet born, be in the womb, be young, old, dead, beyond death. And when you have understood all these at once—times, places, things, qualities, quantities—then you can understand god.[78]

On one level, this illumination penetrates to the subtlest spheres of consciousness—the call to "be not yet born" recalls the Zen koan that asks the practitioner to recall her original face, the face "before you were born." But unlike the Zen quest, which proceeds largely by emptying the mind of its obsession with mental bric-a-brac, the budding Promethean Gnostic is here encouraged just to keep loading it up. Hermes is not told to merge with the great ineffable Oneness, but to expand the conceptual and empirical mind, the mind that knows and understands the things of this world, quantities as well as qualities, information as well as wisdom. Gnosis enables the mystic not only to know God, but to know what God knows. Even more important, this cognitive ecstasy is not characterized as something that happens to the aspirant through God's infinite grace, but as a feat that the aspirant produces through his own mystical, magical, and intellectual labor—in a word, self-divinization.

The *Corpus Hermeticum*'s mystic hymn to information overload should serve as a reminder to contemporary infonauts that they are hardly the first humans to fall in love with the prospect of having all the data of the earth at their fingertips. Indeed, I would wager that part of the millennialist intensity of our technologies, part of what's driving our hardwired ecstasy of communication, is the subliminal hunch that our increasingly incorporeal information machines may be altering and expanding consciousness itself. We complain about information overload, and yet we also get an almost eschatological thrill from the glittering glut, as if the acceleration of communication and the bandwidth-bursting density of the datastream can somehow amplify the self and its capacities. As the literary and religious critic Harold Bloom reflects in *The American Religion,* "Gnosticism was (and is) a kind of information theory. Matter and energy are rejected, or at least placed under the sign of negation. Information becomes the emblem of salvation; the false Creation-Fall concerned matter and energy, but the Pleroma, or Fullness, the original Abyss, is all information."[79]

Though Bloom is being somewhat ironic here, he's also onto something. The ancient "Hymn of the Pearl," one of the most beautiful and paradigmatic Gnostic texts, is all about the saving power of incorporeal communications, and it may aid our techgnostic quest to read the tale, also somewhat playfully, through the eyes of information. In the beginning of the story, an unnamed prince, who is often identified with Mani, is told by his royal parents that he must journey to Egypt to retrieve a pearl from the clutches of a serpent. The prince chooses to accept the mission and soon finds himself in a tavern in Egypt, where he encounters a fellow "anointed one." The two high and holy confidants whisper about the mission and the nefarious ways of the Egyptians, and the prince grows so afraid of the locals that he dons an Egyptian cloak to disguise himself. "But somehow [the Egyptians] learned / I was not their countryman, / and they dealt with me cunningly / and gave me their food to eat." Drugged by the meal, the prince falls into the sleep of ignorance, and forgets both his mission and his true identity.

Aware of this turn of events, the prince's father and mother send him a letter, sealed against "the evil ones, the children of Babel." The missive flies to the prince in the form of an eagle; arriving, it "became speech."

> At its voice and the sound of its rustling
>   I awoke and rose from my sleep.
> I took it, kissed it,
>   broke its seal and read.
> And the words written on my heart
>   were in the letter for me to read.
> I remembered that I was a son of Kings
>   and my free soul longed for its own kind.[80]

Besides shaking the prince out of his stupor, the letter also provides him with the magic data—the true names of his father and mother—which he uses to spellbind the serpent while he plucks the pearl from its scaly grasp. Wandering east toward home, the prince finds the same letter lying in the road. "And as it had awakened me with its voice / So it guided me with its light." Guided by the radiating text, the hero returns home; there he changes into a stunning robe that "quiver[s] all over / with the movements of gnosis." Draped with the living texture of spiritual knowledge, he ascends to greet the king.

Though ostensibly an action-packed tale of serpents and treasure, the "Hymn" is really a story about messages and communication; the hero's information processing takes up far more lines than the battle with the beast or the description of the prized pearl. Information is exchanged in the bar, ruses are hatched, and conversation is overheard. Memory loss sets in until a letter arrives, a piece of writing that unleashes all the consciousness-bending powers of the alphabet. The letter transforms into a speaking voice; along with a noisy bit of rustling (whether of the papyrus or the bird's wings remains unclear), this voice awakens the hero. Then the letter triggers the knowledge already written in the heart of our hero—a classic media metaphor for the Platonic recollection of true origins and true destiny.

Expanding on Bloom's ironic comment, we might note that in this allegory of the soul's fall into matter and subsequent redemption, the internal spark behaves like one of those radio transponders found on satellites, instruments that lie dormant until they receive a specific transmission that activates them. Gnosticism is full of such signals. As one

Mandean Gnostic text puts it, "One call comes and instructs about all calls"; the second level of the Manichean hierarchy was known as "Listeners."[81] The Gnostic signal must penetrate the thick interference of the world, a world that is not only flawed but ruled by a conspiracy of ignorance—of noise. When the prince disguises himself, he takes on the flesh and its hungers; when the thugs slip him a Mickey, the worldly archons overwrite his memory, drowning his cosmic identity in the sleep of matter and the trance of "consensus reality." The Logos that saves the prince is an informing light embodied in a technology of communication, and its transmission echoes the archetypal scenario of information theory: a sender, a receiver, and a message that must protect itself from the demon of noise—the "children of Babel" against which the king's letter is sealed.

Gnosis always depends on the transmission of secrets, and the clandestine battle of messages and hidden doings runs throughout Gnostic lore. Some Gnostic creation myths tell us that agents of the Pleroma, working behind the scenes, trick the archons into unknowingly building a spiritual escape hatch into their false creation. According to Hans Jonas, the German scholar who found in Gnosticism an anticipation of existentialism:

> Through [the Demiurge's] unknowing agency the spiritual seed was implanted in the human soul and body, to be carried there as if in a womb until it had grown sufficiently to receive the Logos. The pneuma sojourns in the world in order to be pre-formed there for the final "information" through the gnosis.[82]

As the embodiment of universal order and mystic knowledge, the Gnostic Logos obviously means much more than mere "information." And yet this Logos sometimes appears in the quivering form of an informational signal, giving the Call an almost viral quality that allows it to penetrate an occluded world.

As the winged letter in the "Hymn" suggests, Gnostic mysticism must also be viewed within the context of the writing machine. The singular self-knowledge sought by the Gnostic, which reveals the self to belong to a transcendent order estranged from the mundane world, can be seen partly as a Platonic by-product of the phenomenology of alphabetic reading, whose artificial shapes are essentially alien to the natural order.

For the mystically inclined, the voice of the alphabet may act as an analogy of the far more otherworldly wisdom that sometimes arises from the core of consciousness. The Gnostics also got a lot of mileage out of exploiting the necessary ambiguity of text. By somewhat cantankerously *rereading* texts that already held some spiritual authority, they allegorized them to fit their own needs. As Ioan Couliano writes, "Gnosticism is Platonic hermeneutics so suspicious of tradition that it is willing to break through the borders of tradition, any tradition, including its own."[83]

This hermeneutics of suspicion, which restlessly seeks the cracks in every story, reaches its most audacious peak with certain Gnostic interpretations of the story of Adam and Eve. As everyone knows, God gives the newborn couple the run of the place, insisting only that they refrain from munching the famous fruit—a treat popularly imagined as an apple but which medieval art sometimes portrayed, perhaps tellingly, as a mushroom. Surprising no human parent then or now, Adam and Eve disobey, with a little prompting from a serpentine trickster who promises Eve that she and her beau will "be as gods, knowing good and evil." Once God discovers their trespass, he hands down a sentence that seems a touch on the harsh side: death, toil, and suffering for them and their entire progeny until the end of time. Conventionally interpreted, the tale implies that in our willful rebellion against the commandments of the Lord, we literally dug our own graves. We are at fault for our faulty world.

The Gnostics were having none of this. Concocting the world's first metaphysical conspiracy theory, the anonymous authors behind Nag Hammadi's "Secret Book of John" read Genesis against the grain, arguing that Eden was actually a low-rent reality fabricated by an incompetent and ignorant tyrant. In one of Gnosticism's most startling revisions, Christ (a.k.a. the Logos) secretly enters the garden disguised as the serpent, and thus manages to unload some redemptive knowledge on the original hoodwinked couple. The knowledge is basically what the snake promised: knowledge that wakes us up to our own divine essence, and that liberates us from the chains of ignorance. As such, the quest to know, and through knowing to become "as gods," becomes a leitmotif of Gnosticism. As we will see in the next chapter, the urge to overcome the natural limits of body through a divinized or omniscient mind remains one of the most characteristic "gnostic" traits, one that plays itself out today in strongly technocultural terms.

For the Gnostics, Eden was not a lost paradise but an allegory of the material world, a world many of them rejected with a dualist hostility that makes the Catholic Mass seem like a Dionysian keg party. Some Gnostics referred to our planet as an "abortion of matter," composed of pain and suffering; the Manicheans held the particularly sword-and-sorcery notion that the cosmos was built from the rotting corpses of demons. Not surprisingly, your typical Gnostic's body image was not what we would now consider healthy. Marcion believed that we were made in the image of the evil demiurge, and that this "flesh stuffed with excrement" was so repugnant that procreation could not be justified on any account.

Though the Gnostics certainly sipped from the same pool of Platonic body-loathing that came to characterize much of Christianity, their hostility to the material world and its archons cannot be reduced to a bad case of ascetic *ressentiment* against the ravages of time. They abhorred the world partly because they abhorred those powers—physical, institutional, or psychological—that prevented the self from realizing its potential, a potential they associated with liberation, with the dropping of all shackles. Embedded within their almost paranoid hostility to the ecosystem lay an incandescent yearning for freedom, and though this yearning may have gotten out of hand, then as now, its essence speaks to the new sense of autonomy that came to define the self in late antiquity just as it came to define the individual subject of the modern world. This self fancies itself as free, a knowing spark that struggles against external forces of limit and oppression. For all their paganish occultism, many Gnostics also ranted against the astrological archons who were almost universally believed to hold the fate of men and nations in their sidereal hands. Instead of accepting the Zodiac's rule of fate, the Gnostics insisted on the mind's ability to overcome such strictures through psychological depth, intelligence, and mystical will. In a word, the Gnostic struggle is libertarian.

By grounding the locus of spiritual authority in the self, the Gnostics also threatened to erode the rock of authority that the institutional structure of the Roman Church rested upon. It was partly to control such ideological truancy that the Church invented the whole notion of "heresy"—the perversion or subversion of orthodox truth, a concept that trickles down to us today in the notion of thought crime. In this sense, the Gnostics were accused of a literally *outlaw* spirituality, a challenge to conventional rule that at its most extreme led to antinomians

like the Carpocratians, who apparently took it upon themselves person-
ally to "despise and transgress all laws" fashioned by the (false) biblical
Creator God. According to their enemies, the Carpocratians were particularly fond of swapping sexual partners, foreshadowing the "free
love" of so many latter-day utopian collectives and liberatory countercultures.

By the dawn of the Dark Ages, the Church had basically stamped out
the embers of old school Gnosticism. But Gnostic ideas and imagery did
not disappear from Western thought and experience, although we
should now leave the uppercase G in the dustbin. Various heretical
strains of Manichean dualism and spiritual anarchy flared up throughout Christian history, and even orthodox Christianity, with its violent
hatred of Saracens, witches, Jews, and Satanists, often behaved in a more
Manichean fashion than it might care to admit. Gnosticism's elite Platonic dreams of transcendent liberty and self-divinization also streamed
into Europe's esoteric, hermetic, and alchemical underground, which
etched its archetypes far more deeply into the technological unconscious
than may at first appear.

As with all archetypes, the mythic patterns associated with gnosis are
ambiguous, multivalent, and contradictory. Today's techgnostics find
themselves, consciously or not, surrounded by a complex set of ideas
and images: transcendence through technology, a thirst for the ecstasy of
information, a drive to engineer and perfect the incorporeal spark of the
self. As we will see in later chapters, techgnostic myth also resurrects the
dark figures of the demiurge and his archons, who reemerge in the popular imagination as those vast technocratic cabals who deploy ersatz
spectacles, surveillance technologies, and an invisible calculus of media
manipulation in order to control society and keep individuals asleep.
These imaginings can lead into the black holes of paranoia, but given
how often twentieth-century history has justified such fears, a certain
gnostic distrust of worldly powers remains a healthy component of any
contemporary worldview. So we should not be Manichean about the
gnostic impulse that manifests itself in modern technoculture. Techgnosis is the esoteric side of the postwar world's new "information self," and
like all such secret psychologies, its faces are carved with both shadows
and light.

techgnosis, american-style

The American self is a gnostic self, because it believes, on a deep and abiding level, that authenticity arises from independence, an independence that is at once natural, sovereign, and solitary. When Thomas Jefferson wrote that he had "sworn on the altar of God Almighty eternal hostility against all forms of tyranny over the minds of men," he was articulating the structure of feeling and belief that informs the American self. This structure was enshrined in the Declaration of Independence and the Bill of Rights, and though these documents are secular and political, their rhetoric does not derive solely from Enlightenment notions about the inalienable rights of man. America's political embrace of the modern individual was also motivated by the land's curious spiritual temperament—a temperament that, in its quest to discover a motive ground outside of governments and established religious institutions, appears to be the very antithesis of religion as we usually conceive it.

We should take seriously Harold Bloom's willfully heretical argument that the "American Religion" is not Christian, at least in the way that Europe was Christian, but is, rather, Gnostic. Whether finding his evidence in Mormonism, the Baptist Church, or the poetry of Emerson, Bloom describes the core of the American religion as the unshakable conviction that there is something in the self that *precedes* creation, and that, for all our Whitmanesque desire to merge with groups, we can never fully trust external social institutions to care for the aboriginal freedom of this solitary spark, with its "personal relationship" to nature or a gnostic Jesus. In a crucial passage, Bloom writes that the American religion

> does not believe or trust, it *knows,* though it wants always to know yet more. The American Religion manifests itself as an information anxiety, but that seems to me a better definition of nearly all religion than the attempts to see faith as a compulsive neurosis or as a drug. It is neither obsessive nor intoxicating to ask, "Where were we?" and "Where are we journeying?"; or best of all, "What makes us free?"

The American Religion always has asked "What makes us free?"; but political freedom has little to do with that question.[84]

There is a great deal of value in this passage, especially in the unexpected light Bloom throws on the strangely American coupling of information and freedom that will beckon us throughout this chapter. But as we'll see, this gnostic consciousness, itself a frazzled patchwork of worldviews and contrasting camps, does not cleave to the clear divide Bloom draws between politics and spirit. While the political structures of the United States cannot encompass or satisfy the American self's will to freedom, the cornerstone of these structures was laid on gnostic soil.

There has always been an esoteric undercurrent to the United States. As Peter Lamborn Wilson has shown, pre-revolutionary America was flush with wandering alchemists, neopagan backsliders, and antinomian ranters. Within the occult imagination of some European colonialists, America's virgin land merged with the *prima materia* of the alchemists, the unformed chunk of primal chaos that forms the seed of the philosopher's stone and the potential foundation of a New Jerusalem. According to the contemporary gnostic writer Stephan Hoeller, this undercurrent gave rise to "Hermetic America," a national spiritual temperament that opposes the dominant religious narrative of Puritan America—that dour, God-fearing tale of witch hunters, prudes, and workaholics we all know so well. According to Hoeller, a number of the Founding Fathers explicitly intended the country to serve as a hermetic vessel, "an alchemical alembic in which the human soul could grow and transform with little or no interference from state, society, or religious establishments."[85]

To get a quick taste of hermetic America, simply take a dollar bill, flip it over, and try to stare down the glowing eye that tops the pyramid of the great seal. Like the Byzantine icons of Eastern Orthodoxy, which can catalyze a flash of beatitude in the eyes of their viewers, so can this decidedly weird symbol of the *novus ordo seclorum* (a New Order of Things) conjure up the secret architecture of power tucked beneath the bright and shiny pragmatism of the United States' young federal government. And this architecture's name is Freemasonry.

Freemasonry was (and is) a loosely occult network of elite male societies whose various lodges played a crucial role in the development of modern Europe as well as the birth of the United States. Before the War of Independence, Masonic lodges formed perhaps the principal "intercolonial network" for revolutionary leaders; these societies also allowed the explosive ideas cranked out by European Enlightenment intellectuals like Locke, Hume, and Voltaire to trickle down through the ranks. Nearly every American general that rassled with the redcoats was a Mason, as was nearly every signator of the Declaration of Independence and nearly every major contributor to the Constitution. John Adams, George Washington, and Benjamin Franklin were all Masons (the jury is still out on Thomas Jefferson). Like Franklin, Washington was a particularly passionate and active Mason, a onetime Grand Master who was inaugurated as president decked out in full Masonic regalia.

Long a topic of febrile speculation, Freemasonry is hardly the insidious leviathan envisioned by some conspiracy buffs. On one level, Masonic lodges simply functioned as the old boy networks of the Age of Reason institutions where ambitious men would gather in order to propagate and hatch revolutionary new notions about reason, science, and the proper construction of civil society. The God they worshiped was the "Great Architect," a distant demiurge whose hand was glimpsed, not in scripture, but in the new revelations of natural science. But even as lodge members helped to imagine and construct our secular world, with its anticlerical embrace of science, technology, and individual liberties, Masonic societies also served as the main channel whereby the ideas and psychology of gnostic occultism flowed into the heart of modernity. For the freethinking men of the seventeenth and eighteenth centuries, Freemasonry offered a social structure that bridged rationalism and esoteric mysticism, folding Enlightenment ideals and Deistic science into a ritualistic and deeply hermetic solar cult.

Though redolent with Rosicrucian rumors and tales of Templar knights, the symbols and rituals of "the Craft" principally derive from the traditions and guild structure of medieval stonemasons, whose practical lore was spiritualized by seventeenth-century English aristocrats into "speculative," or mystical, Masonry. By tracing its origins to Hiram Abiff, the architect of Solomon's Temple, Masons placed the image of the hermetic engineer at the heart of their mythological worldview. Budding lodge members were required to master an elaborate hierarchical system of secret hand signs, ritual tools, esoteric doctrines, and gnostic dramas of self-illumination. As they clamored up this Neoplatonic (and rather corporate) pyramid of grades and degrees, their rising status indicated the increasing, almost geometrical perfection of their souls. Developing themselves into Masonic "sons of light," these self-illuminated ones transmuted the gnostic impulse from a mystical dream into a systematic social technology of Enlightenment.

Freemasonry based its cosmology on a new image of nature, one that combined old esoteric notions of cosmic order with the new empirical understanding of natural law. Like many scientists of the day, Masons subscribed to the philosophy of Deism, which held that God retired from his creation after constructing the vast machinery of the physical world, leaving men to tinker and improve the cosmic contraption on their own. As Hoeller writes of Deists, "theirs was the Alien God of the Hermeticists and Gnostics, also known at times as Deus Absconditus, 'the God who has gone away.' "[86] Though Masons worshiped their Great Architect as the Christian God, this absent engineer, whose creation is clearly less than perfect, also resembles the demiurge of Gnostic myth, whose flawed designs could be overcome only by human smarts.

With their perfectionist Prometheanism, Masonic lodges thus brought what the historian David Noble calls the "religion of technology" into the modern secular age. Noble traces the religion of technology to medieval monks who came to believe that human beings and societies can be brought into a paradisal state of Edenic perfection through the proper exploitation of the "useful arts." Translated into secular terms, which are still very much with us, this millennialist mythology holds that technological and scientific men have a duty to understand, conquer, and tweak the world of nature for the sake of human salvation, both spiritual and practical. As Noble shows, Masons played a disproportionate role in the construction of scientific culture. Lodge members basically founded the Royal Society, the first modern scientific institution, and the generally recognized leader of speculative Freemasonry, John Theophilus Desaguliers, was also an avid natural philosopher and engineer who experimented with electricity, invented the planetarium, and investigated steam power. In England, France, and America, Masons organized scientific lectures, hyped the useful arts, and pushed forward the new encyclopedias and their "diffusion of the light of knowledge." Through the development and dissemination of the technical arts and sciences, Masons believed that they were helping to build utopia.

As Noble shows, Masons also participated heavily in constructing the educational institutions that gave birth to the modern engineer. "Through Freemasonry, the apostles of the religion of technology passed their practical project of redemption on to the engineers, the new spiritual men, who subsequently forged their own millenarian myths, exclusive associations, and rites of passage."[87] In America, this technological evangelism was principally carried forward by Benjamin Franklin, an indefatigable promoter of science and technology and the onetime Grand Master of the French Loge des Neuf Soeurs. Like countless later American Masons, including Henry Ford, Charles Lindbergh, and the astronauts John Glenn and Buzz Aldrin, Franklin put into practice America's cult of the technological sublime. As the American religious scholar Catherine Albanese argues in her discussion of American Masonry, "if any genuinely *new* popular religion arose in New World America, it was a nature religion of radical empiricism, with the aim of that religion to conflate spirit and matter and, in the process, turn human beings into gods."[88]

Albanese argues that America's self-deifying nature religion was not based solely on empirical knowledge or Romanticism or Masonic politics; it also turned on the metaphysical notion of "natural" liberty, a notion which identified the essential freedom of the individual with the supposedly uncultivated wilderness of the new world. "Nature, in American nature religion, is a reference point with which to think history," Albanese writes. "Its sacrality masks—and often quite explicitly reveals—a passionate concern for place and mastery *in society*."[89] That is, nature's aboriginal freedom from human society in turn becomes a basis for a new understanding of society, one which emphasizes the naturally endowed sovereignty of the individual and his pursuits. This imaginative and political relationship to the *prima materia* of virgin territory also helps explain America's almost mystical obsession with the frontier, an obsession that, as we will see, plays directly into the early mythology of the Internet.

The American frontier is one of the great mythic mindscapes of the modern world. An El Dorado of literally golden opportunity, the Western territories were also a landscape of the solitary soul, virtual spaces where the American self could remake and rediscover its longed-for origins. The frontier was a liminal zone beyond the mundane boundaries of civil society, with its archons of politicians, lawyers, and established religious institutions. In the nineteenth century, the myth of the frontier was inscribed into the national consciousness with a fetishistic force that could barely conceal the tremendous violence and exploitation that marked actual Western expansion. Pulp novels, newspapers, and Wild West shows trumpeted the heroism and self-sufficiency of pioneers, gunslingers, and mountain men; at the same time, the Mormons, a visionary and hermetic cult steeped in gnostic dreams of self-divinization, reimagined the harsh and monumental landscape of the Southwest as an Old Testament desert where covenants could be restored and a new purchase made on a fallen world. The rhetoric of the frontier became an indelible component of America's peculiarly stubborn optimism, its worship of the free self and free enterprise, its utopian imagination and its incandescent greed.

When the geographic frontier closed at the end of the nineteenth century, America was forced to sublimate its obsession with wilderness. In the popular culture of the twentieth century, the West's sacred fusion of freedom, self-sufficiency, and wide open spaces would infect everything from the Boy Scouts to NASA to the ecology movement. But the most influential purveyor of the frontier myth was Hollywood, which churned out westerns at a mind-boggling clip for well over half a century. Into the dream medium of celluloid was etched America's supreme archetype of the free individual: the cowboy, a violent hybrid of Arthurian knight and ascetic nomad who stands apart from social laws in order to tame the wilderness within and without, and who thus tastes a kind of freedom and self-understanding that the communities he makes way for will never comprehend.

In the 1980s, with a former Hollywood wrangler ensconced in the Oval Office, the cowboy reappeared in a most unlikely terrain: the disembodied "space" of computer networks. When William Gibson chose to dub his cyberspace jockeys "cowboys" in 1984's *Neuromancer,* he intuited the psychological dynamism that would come to fuel the real culture of early cyberspace, a culture that at the time his book was written was still in the mountain man and fur trapper phase. Even by the early 1990s, the Internet was still a lawless place of sorts, and the rollicking experimental anarchy of its social structures, technical triumphs, and heretical conversations—as well as those of its sister bulletin boards—is now the bloated stuff of legend. Of course, a computer network of abstract dataflows, UNIX engines, and file transfer protocols can hardly be considered a "real" space at all. But spatial metaphors inevitably emerged, lending the medium an imaginary dimension that paradoxically made it more real. Perhaps the first person to apply Gibson's word *cyberspace* to real digital networks was the digital pundit John Perry Barlow, a Grateful Dead lyricist and denizen of the WELL, the Bay Area's legendary electronic bulletin board. An ex-rancher from

Wyoming, Barlow also played a role in propagating one of the first and most important mythic images to drape cyberspace: the *frontier*. Though the ensuing dominance of the "digital frontier" had as much to do with lazy journalists as with network proselytizers, it can nonetheless be traced to America's libertarian imagination, with its primal identification of wilderness and freedom. Given the independent-minded, mostly white male Americans who were probing the technical and social possibilities of networked computers—not to mention the gold rush flashbacks already hitting the Bay Area's blossoming computer industry—the "digital frontier" emerged from America's technological unconscious with all the predictability of a high-noon shoot-out.

Nowadays, when the binary outback has given way to the neon strip malls of the World Wide Web, the frontier metaphor resounds with the hollowness of a Roy Rogers piggy bank. Nonetheless, the image of the digital frontier contains more truth than even its early enthusiasts may have realized. The Western frontier was not a utopia of self-determinism, of course, but an anxious crossroads of conflicting powers that played out the young country's violent tension between self-sufficient individualism and the necessity of creating community out of mottled peoples without much shared history to fall back on. The anxiety and longing produced by this endless struggle, which continues to characterize American consciousness, helped create the background alienation that subtly drives so many cybernomads, and explains as well the interminable and often sentimental discussions about virtual community. One of the most fascinating aspects of the WELL, the electronic tavern where much of this frontier talk first got bandied about, was the fact that the BBS was composed of a bunch of die-hard, freethinking soloists who became obsessed with their own sense of being, in some historically unprecedented manner, a *group*.

The image of cyberspace as frontier also rings true because the myth contains its own disappearance, its own twilight decline. In the brooding and melancholic westerns that Hollywood started producing in the 1950s and 1960s, the Wild West is always already fading, its rebels sacrificed to the engines of progress, its wide open spaces farmed and fenced. In its own way, cyberspace restaged this imposition of existing social and political structures upon the uncharted territory encountered by its earliest pioneers. By the early 1990s, the independent code cowboys and hacker outlaws of the 1980s were being hired out as Pinkertons and ranch hands, while bankers, lawyers, Christian schoolmarms, and AOL greenhorns started logging in expecting Mainstreet USA. Communications conglomerates started carving up the network's backbone like robber barons, while businesses, state agencies, and subscriber Web sites started unrolling the barbed wire of firewalls and restricted access across the formerly free range of public space.

Unfortunately, only a few passionate netheads today actively resist the commercialization and privatization of cyberspace. But the meddlings of government archons continue to provoke storms of protest, especially in the United States. To preserve the Net's wide open spaces from state control, Barlow and other computer mavens founded the Electronic Frontier Foundation (EFF), a well-funded advocacy group devoted to anticensorship efforts, cyberrights, and encryption issues. Once sucked inside the D.C. beltway, the EFF mellowed its stance, although the foundation did put up quite a fight against the Communications Decency Act, the federal government's noxious 1996 attempt to censor cyberspace. Curiously, many netheads continue to believe that EFF stands for the Electronic *Freedom* Foundation, a confusion between freedom and frontier that is symptomatic of the deeply American conviction discussed above: the assumption that liberty equals nature, or rather the self in nature, unrestrained by state power and the collective demands of history and society.

Applied to the Internet, this conviction received its most rhetorically sublime peak in Barlow's "A Declaration of the Independence of Cyberspace." Barlow shot off this widely circulated online diatribe in February 1996, when governments from the United States to Germany to Singapore were attempting to impose various restrictions on the growing digital culture. Written with Barlow's characteristic verve and Wyoming sized spirit, the text interweaves so many of the themes we've been discussing—nature, self-determination, gnostic disembodiment, the borderless America of the mind—that it is worth citing at length:

> Governments of the Industrial World, you weary giants of flesh and steel, I come from Cyberspace, the new home of Mind. On behalf of the future, I ask you of the past to leave us alone. You are not welcome among us. You have no sovereignty where we gather.
>
> We have no elected government, nor are we likely to have one, so I address you with no greater authority than that with which liberty itself always speaks. I declare the global social space we are building to be naturally independent of the tyrannies you seek to impose on

us. . . . Cyberspace does not lie within your borders. Do not think that you can build it, as though it were a public construction project. You cannot. It is an act of nature and it grows itself through our collective actions.[90]

In Barlow's hands, cyberspace becomes both a terrain and an "act of nature," an essentially mythological concept that allows him to construct the Internet as a technological rerun of the borderless (though inhabited) continent that greeted America's early colonists. Once Barlow establishes this virtual ground, he then goes on to tell the bloated, bad-guy governments just how *unnatural* the digital environment actually is:

Cyberspace consists of transactions, relationships, and thought itself, arrayed like a standing wave in the web of our communications. Ours is a world that is both everywhere and nowhere, but it is not where bodies live. . . . Your legal concepts of property, expression, identity, movement, and context do not apply to us. They are based on matter. There is no matter here.[91]

With its Jeffersonian individualism and bodiless fulfillment, Barlow's vision of a "civilization of the Mind" clearly rests upon the core of American gnosis, a "here" that is nowhere on Earth. His Declaration also shows the degree to which the Internet has become, in the words of the German media critic Pit Schultz, a "collective hallucination of freedom."

One problem with this neo-gnostic, libertarian psychology is that it needs tyrannical archons to attack; otherwise, there is no ready explanation for the fact that life in human societies (and human bodies) is composed of limitations and constraints. In the most extreme cases, the search for archons leads to what the historian Richard Hofstadter famously named the "paranoid style" of American politics: a conspiracy-minded tendency to intensify ordinary power struggles into Manichean battles between good and evil. This is the suspicious and often puritanical mind frame that lurks behind the Salem witch trials, the Anti-Masonic Party of the nineteenth century, Senator Joe McCarthy, and today's right-wing narratives about European banking cabals and the Trilateral Commission. Tuning in to the rebel yells that choke AM radio and shortwave frequencies across the land, one hears the paranoia of crude neo-gnostic myth: loud and clear tales of free, God-fearing individuals who wage guerrilla warfare against creepy conspiracies whose various tentacles are stamped with federal insignia.

Barlow is no paranoid, but he definitely has his archons. The tyrannical actions that motivated him to rattle off the Declaration were the "hostile and colonial" attempts of governments to regulate cyberspace, power grabs that "place us [i.e., netizens] in the same position as those previous lovers of freedom and self-determination who had to reject the authorities of distant, uninformed powers." Notice that these "uninformed powers" are associated not only with ignorance, but also with the lower order of *matter*, and it is precisely this association with matter that is their downfall online. Because the rule of states is based on material borders and physical coercion, the archons have no power in bodiless cyberspace. Barlow implies that with these ignorant leviathans out of the way, Jefferson's dreams of liberty—which somehow did not so bountifully emerge from flesh-and-blood-and-steel America—will be realized. In cyberspace, all may immigrate and act without privilege or prejudice or force, all may speak their minds, and a form of governance will naturally emerge based on enlightened self-interest, the commonweal, and the ethics of the Golden Rule.

The gnostic dimension of Barlow's vision lies beneath the surface of his utopian technopolitics, but the link between gnosticism and libertarian sentiments is explicitly made by Stephan Hoeller, the Jungian writer mentioned earlier, who also acts as bishop of a Gnostic Church in Los Angeles. Like other contemporary esoteric practitioners, Hoeller derives much of his spiritual sustenance from the alchemical myths, hermetic practices, and gnostic notions of Western occultism. But unlike most twentieth-century proponents of the Mysteries, Hoeller has not adopted a reactionary antimodernism but instead embraces the same giddy libertarian politics that came to dominate the digital ether. Unlike most libertarians, who are by and large a rather rationalist and atheist lot, Hoeller grounds his politics in the spirit—the *pneuma* to be exact. In his book *Freedom: Alchemy for a Voluntary Society*, he defines the ancient Gnostics as spiritual libertarians, arguing that they "saw themselves as the vanguard of human freedom, struggling by the use of spiritual means against the ubiquitous forces of tyranny in the realms of nature and being."[92] As a Jungian, Hoeller underlines the psychological aspects of this struggle, arguing that the Gnostics were "technicians of individuation" who attempted to overcome the internal archons that rule our mundane, messed-up psyches. But Hoeller also sees the demiurgic hands of tyranny in all manner of mass movements, ecological ideologies, and architectures of state power. Arguing that "the work of social transformation must not be managed or organized externally," he envisions the sort of free and open society of self-engendering individuals trumpeted by *Wired* magazine or the utopian proponents of laissez-faire global capitalism.[93]

Though your average technolibertarian is more likely to wax mystical about Adam Smith's invisible hand than about mystical states of consciousness, Hoeller's ideas provide a kind of archetypal snapshot of the psychological dynamics that may motivate some American libertarians. "Human beings are not on earth to be citizens, or taxpayers or socially engineered pawns of other human beings; rather they are here in order to grow, to transform, to become their authentic selves."[94] Having fled Hungary as a young man, Hoeller certainly earned his hatred for social engineering, and only nihilists would argue with his core belief that the purpose of human life, such as it is, involves growth, transformation, and a striving for meaning and authenticity. But with their strange brew of free speech monomania, capitalist Prometheanism, and intense antipathy toward regulation, libertarians take this core inspiration to often dangerous heights.

Countless blueprints for the libertarian great society are bandied about, but the guiding lines usually include ideas about the sovereignty of the individual; ferocious attacks on state mechanisms that constrain the productive force of market competition; loads of contract law; and the conviction that private property is at least as essential to genuine liberty as civil rights. Though libertarians share many economic notions with traditional conservatives, they are far more interested in freedom and experimentation than tradition; many would feel a lesbian leather fetishist's horror of being stuck in an elevator with the likes of William Bennett or Pat Robertson. In fact, about the only thing that libertarians might hold sacred is the First Amendment: the holy separation of Church and state, and the inviolable grace of free speech protection—a principle so heady and pure that in the heat of debate, it can hit the brain like pure oxygen.

For a taste of this mental rush, all you have to do is poke around the newsgroups and political Web sites of cyberspace, for libertarianism lives and thrives (and rants) on the Net like no other socioeconomic or ethical philosophy. In many ways, libertarianism seems perfectly designed for life in the nomad zones of the Internet. As Steven Levy shows in his great history *Hackers,* the hacker worldview was defined from its beginning in the 1960s by an antiauthoritarian love of open systems, experiment, and the free flow of information—sociocultural qualities that have been progressively incarnated into the technical structure of the Internet. Nonetheless, libertarianism became popular among America's programmers, engineers, and technological entrepreneurs long before the advent of cyberspace (a healthy chunk of the candidates that the Libertarian Party has been chucking at California voters for decades earned their keep from computer-related fields). This popularity makes sense: Libertarian arguments usually appeal to that chunk of your brain that cherishes self-evident truths, common sense, and the clear dictates of reason—and that finds rhetorical appeals to compassion, traditional morals, and social responsibility murky, suspicious, and unpleasantly religious in tone. For evident reasons (and admittedly overgeneralized ones as well), this cool, masculine, and somewhat emotionally hamstrung "style" resonates with the stereotypical mind-set of many hackers and engineers, especially given their appreciation for clarity, systematic efficiency, and logical pragmatism.

Which is not to say that libertarians or engineers are devoid of imagination. Far from it—visionaries from both groups are in love with possibility and novelty, and embrace the hard imaginative work that goes into designing untried scenarios that other people can barely wrap their brains around. It's no accident that both camps have also played a significant role in the production and consumption of science fiction, the twentieth century's most ardent, visionary, and technologically savvy literature of ideas. Besides exploring many different libertarian possibilities in their fabulations, SF writers like Vernor Vinge, Robert Heinlein, and Robert Anton Wilson have penned a number of texts central to American libertarian thought.

All these overlapping sympathies help lend cyberlibertarianism its distinct flavor—a kind of synthetic, vitamin-rich tang. But *libertarianism* is really just Yankee slang for anarchism, whose nineteenth-century European proponents were committed to the dream embedded in the very etymology of their cause: *an-arkhos,* without rules, and especially without those archons who maintain rules by force. Some anarchists were radical individualists, while others shared many of the collective goals of socialism. Refusing to accept the coercive and cynical violence of state power or the mentality of the herd, anarchists dared to imagine a world that respected the autonomous strivings, desires, and voluntary commitments of individuals and small, self-organized communities.

Significantly, many of the utopias envisioned by nineteenth- and twentieth-century anarchists were foreshadowed in the religious visions of radical sectarians who bedeviled the medieval Church and helped turn the Protestant Reformation into a carnival of dissidents, revolutionaries, and apocalyptic sects. For groups like the Anabaptists, the Diggers, and the followers of the Free Spirit (all spiritual radicals marked with many shades of gnostic enthusiasm), worldly institutions stood in the way of God's free grace, the spontaneous promptings of the spirit, and the wisdom of the individual mind. This convulsive tradition of spiritual anarchism is not dead. In his 1985 polemical tract *T.A.Z.*, the anarcho-Sufi ranter Hakim Bey invokes the "temporary autonomous zone," a nomadic slice of space-time where desires are liberated from commodity consumption and social forms follow the chaotic logic of the Tao. Though Bey is critical of cyberhype, his political and poetic vision of the T.A.Z. became a highly influential conceptual fetish for the digital underground.

Modern anarchists dispensed with the deus ex machina of divine spiritual grace, but they still needed to imagine some positive and productive force that would take up the slack once the state dissolved. Some turned to Nature, believing that human beings were instinctively drawn to cooperative social behavior, and that spontaneous human desire was inherently good. Others were captured by the utopian images of social organization that also inspired Marxists, images which implied that the dialectical engine of historical evolution was just about to turn a glorious corner. Bakunin predicted that "there will be a qualitative transformation, a new living, life-giving revelation, a new heaven and a new earth, a young and mighty world in which all our present dissonances will be resolved into a harmonious whole."[95] It was precisely this sort of secular millennialism that led the conservative historian Eric Voegelin to condemn all such apocalyptic social endeavors as gnostic heresies.

Today, many libertarians think another sort of New Jerusalem is just about to touch down upon our fragile globe: the total revolution of information capitalism. The "living, life-giving revelation" that today's cyberlibertarians will tell you about is the emergent neobiological properties of an unfettered free market seeded with databases, microwaves, and fiber-optic cables; the new heaven and new earth you'll find in their futurist scenarios is an entrepreneurial dream of floating tax-free islands, hog-tied governments, mind-boggling new technologies, and the eradication of "public space" and "social responsibility" from the imaginations of men. The reason that so many of today's libertarians love the Net is that its very structure—decentralized, efficient, unregulated, rich with opportunity—incarnates a libertarian ideal, or, at the very least, technologically resists centralized control. As the cypherpunk John Gilmore put it, the Net recognizes attempts at censorship as damage and routes around them. The Net has thus become a simulacrum of a possible libertarian world: an unregulated plenitude where technological wizardry and a clean hack can overcome the inertia of embodied history, where ossified political and economic structures will melt down into the liquid flow of bits, and where the New Atlantis of liberty appears as an evolutionary wave of digicash you either surf or suffer through.

The animating archetype of the information economy, its psychological spunk, lies in a gnostic flight from the heaviness and torpor of the material earth, a transition from the laboring body into the symbol-processing mind. Writing of the "liberating force" of high tech, Bishop Hoeller notes that

> the resources marketed in high technology are less about matter and more about mind. Under the impact of high technology, the world is moving increasingly from a physical economy into what might be called a "metaphysical economy." We are in the process of recognizing that consciousness rather than raw materials or physical resources constitutes wealth.[96]

Almost everywhere one turns these days, one finds signs of this "metaphysical economy," the parodic mirror image of Marx's insistence on the ultimately material basis of wealth and value. The pleroma returns as the world's financial markets, where money ascends into angelic orbit, magically multiplying itself in a weightless casino of light pulses and symbolic manipulations. As corporations, cabals, and networks of trade and dataflow overlay the territorial and social borders of nations, some thinkers believe that the information economy actually *transcends*, rather than simply extending, the previous material economies of industry and agriculture. As the technology futurist George Gilder put it, "The central event of the twentieth century is the overthrow of matter. . . . The powers of mind are everywhere ascendant over the brute force of things."⁹⁷ This technological dualism is perhaps most starkly reflected in the world economy's myopic and cavalier relationship toward the biosphere itself, the material matrix of trees, water, wetlands, critters, and toxins within which our bodies remain inextricably embedded.

As Hakim Bey notes in a scathing attack on Hoeller and the gnostic roots of information ideology, "In his enthusiasm for a truly religious economy, [Bishop Hoeller] forgets that one cannot eat 'information.' "⁹⁸ For Bey, the "metaphysical economy" depends on the alienation between mind and bodily experience, an alienation that receives its most intense religious form in gnosticism. Though our "materialistic" culture has abandoned such mystical mumbo jumbo, Bey argues that mass media and information technology actually deepen the mind-body split by fixating our flow of attention on alienated information rather than the direct, face-to-face, and embodied experiences of material human life, experiences that he believes form the core of any genuine spiritual freedom:

> In this sense the Media serves a religious or priestly role, appearing to offer us a way out of the body by re-defining spirit as information. . . . Consciousness becomes something which can be "downloaded," excised from the matrix of animality and immortalized as information. No longer "ghost-in-the-machine," but machine-as-ghost, machine as Holy Ghost, ultimate mediator, which will translate us from our mayfly-corpses to a pleroma of Light.⁹⁹

Like the Holy Ghost, an invisible medium that allows us to plug into the spirit of God, the incorporeal machineries of media and information offer to port our data-souls out of the body and into a virtual otherworld. William Gibson inscribed this dualism into the mythos of cyberculture when a virus destroys the console cowboy Case's ability to interface with cyberspace. Falling into "the prison of his own flesh," Case experiences "the Fall"—a Fall we now can see is more gnostic than Christian. Nor is this dualistic mythos restricted to cyberpunk science fiction. As the culture critic Mark Dery shows in *Escape Velocity*, one of cyberculture's defining tensions is the opposition between "the dead, heavy flesh ('meat,' in compu-slang) and the ethereal body of information"—an opposition that is "resolved" by the reduction of consciousness to pure mind. Combing through the worldviews of obsessive programmers, hackers, and video game junkies, Dery repeatedly came across the rather startling belief that "the body is a vestigial appendage no longer needed by late-twentieth-century Homo sapiens— Homo Cyber."[100]

Perhaps the most zealous shock troops for this new band of Homo Cyber are the brain-boosting transhumanists and cyberlibertarians known as the Extropians. As we'll see in the next section, the Extropians spend a lot of time plotting out neo-Darwinian future scenarios dominated by artificial intelligence, nanotechnology, smart drugs, weird physics, and massive government deregulation. But in doing so, they resurrect patterns of identity and desire that resemble the most transcendental of mysticisms, and it's their simultaneous commitment to cold hard reason and speculative fancy that makes their techgnosticism more compelling than most varieties found in the digital wing of the New Age. With the brash enthusiasm of a geek *Übermensch* whose steroid-fed muscles are bursting his "Beam Me Up Scotty" T-shirt, the Extropians are meticulously planning for the day when technology will form the ultimate escape hatch, and machines will free us forever from the clutches of the earth, the body, and death itself.

Extropy, Ho!

Of all the bummers lurking in the laws of physics, entropy is the heaviest. For if it is indeed the case that entropy holds all the trump cards— and Maxwell's second law of thermodynamics suggests that it does—then everything we stumble across that's ordered, interesting, or energetic enough to catch our eye is doomed to decay into a cold, tasteless Jell-O of meandering, know-nothing particles. As we saw earlier, Maxwell's second law only applies to closed systems, which by definition are sealed off from the world at large. But this technicality has not done much to curtail the rather gloomy suspicion that the law of entropy is inked into the charter of our lives, our creations, our civilizations— even the cosmos itself. Sculptures rust, cultures corrode, and the rose bouquet of being fades to putrid mulch. The slap-happy nihilism of Thomas Pynchon's *Gravity's Rainbow*, a visionary hymn to postwar entropy, seems motivated in part by the sense that the bulk of human endeavor boils down to a Sisyphian uphill jog on the slippery slope of the second law.

However doomed we are, though, we certainly do not emerge from our mothers' wombs as rotting corpses, which makes one wonder what cosmic force allows us and everything else to resist the swampy clutches of entropy, if only for a time. Some form-giving fluke of the universe wrestles down the second law, allowing babies and blueprints and bio- spheres to flourish, far from the entropic equilibrium that to living things spells death. This creative force has gone by many names over the centuries, from the spirit of God to the élan vital to the notion of infor- mation itself; recently we have been inclined to speak of novelty, self- organization, and emergence. But the snappiest buzzword of all may be *extropy.*

According to the Extropians, an L.A.-based crew of futurists and philosophers hopped up on megavitamins and cognitive enhancement technologies, extropy is the universe's way of strapping a booster rocket onto the wayward course of evolution and making it *go.* Giving rise to redwood trees and Gothic cathedrals alike, the force of extropy gener- ates novelty, breeds complexity, produces information, and thrusts us onward and upward. It is the opportunistic punch that surges through the more redundant and cyclic laws of matter and energy, and it mani- fests itself in human lives as reason, science, technology, and whatever evolutionary compulsion compels some human beings to learn new stuff, overcome physical and psychological limits, amplify intelligence, build weird contraptions, and dream of future possibilities. All of which just happens to be the kind of stuff that Extropians like to spend their days doing.

Incarnating the Promethean archetype with a high-tech salesman's edge, the Extropians set their sights on various technofuturistic scenar- ios that have been floating around science fiction and the science fringe for decades. Leafing through their magazines and plunging through their Web pages, you'll find upbeat prognostications about offworld space colonies, advanced robotics, artificial intelligence, and life extension. The Extropians keep the cold flame of cryogenics alive, and they hear- ken as well to the clarion calls of nanotechnology, a still rather specula- tive branch of engineering that seeks to build molecular machines theoretically capable of fashioning everything from space shuttles to T- bone steaks. Along with their Tom Mix will to power, the Extropians also hew to a skeptical empiricism that violently opposes "dogmas" in any form, even as it remains blissfully ignorant of the often naive assumptions that lie beneath its own, almost adolescent enthusiasms.

With their incandescent optimism and entrepreneurial hostility to voices of caution and restraint, the Extropians have become some of the most brash and notorious proselytizers of the libertarian cause in cyberculture. As they see it, social programs, legislatures, tax-hungry politicians, and environmental regulations all dampen the evolutionary force of extropy, preventing us from enjoying a veritable Cambrian explosion of diverse goods and giddy opportunities for economic growth. But their hostility to the state also derives from a bright-eyed and bushy-tailed techgnosticism, a passionate commitment to the transformative potential of the engineered self and a corresponding snarliness toward all external forces that inhibit that potential. In his "Extropian Principles 2.5," Max More, the iron-pumping president of the Extropy Institute, not only trumpets the anarcho-utopian assertion that no "natural" limits are written in stone, but emphatically calls for "the removal of political, cultural, biological, and psychological limits to self-actualization and self-realization."

At first, coming across a bit of New Age jargon like "self-realization" in the midst of an Extropian rant is like catching a whiff of Nag Champa incense in a Wall Street cigar bar. But along with exploiting all that reason and commerce have to offer, the Extropians also extol a new strain of technological perfectionism, one that comes across as a brain-jacked, hardheaded revision of the human potential movement. In his electronic text, More explains:

> Shrugging off the limits imposed on us by our natural heritage, we apply the evolutionary gift of our rational, empirical intelligence to surpass the confines of our humanity, crossing the threshold into the transhuman and posthuman stages that await us.[101]

According to the Extropians, Nietzsche was not just having a bad case of indigestion when he proclaimed that "Man is something that should be overcome." At the same time, their stance can also be seen as old school humanism with the volume turned up. Like the Renaissance Kabbalist Pico della Mirandola, the Extropians have elected themselves "free and proud masters" of their own mutation.

Along with a host of New Age perfectionists and technolibertarians, the Extropians justify their transhumanist goals by hooking them onto the engine of evolution. Just as natural selection honed the human race over millennia, so too must we continue to transform ourselves on an individual basis by constantly learning, improving, and sharpening the self. So while the Extropians reject the pastel visions of the New Age, they embrace similar "technologies of transformation": brain machines and visualization techniques, meditation regimes and cognitive enhancement drugs, computer networks and Neuro-Linguistic Programming. Moreover, Max More acknowledges that Extropianism's positive-thinking, "onwards and upwards" commitment to personal evolution can fill the existential gap left by the collapse of traditional religious narratives. More argues that, unlike most twentieth-century thought, Extropian philosophy provides meaning, direction, and purpose to human life; at the same time, it does not seek, as many religions have done, to suppress intelligence, stifle progress, or crush "the boundless search for improvement."

Like any spiritual leader worth his salt, More also emphasizes that his principles are not abstract ideas but ethical points that should be practiced and integrated into lived experience. Once successfully brought into the orbit of our lives and habits, Extropian principles allow us to overleap the ordinary run of the murky human mind. They will encourage us not just to think or believe differently, but to actually *become* transhuman—smarter, stronger, more masterful. But what happens to all those messy emotions that so vex the human animal, muddying all our best-made plans? In general, the Extropians have scant praise for the feelings and intuitions that haunt our sinews. Many want to transcend emotions altogether, though Max More—revealing more than he knows—insists Extropians simply want to make them more "efficient."

Once we've shed our doubts and fears, and hopped on the transhuman express, we will not just reap rewards in the here and now. Like saints awaiting the final trump, we will also be actively preparing ourselves for the moment when machines make a quantum leap beyond all science fictions and *everything changes*. Here is More's prophecy:

> When technology allows us to reconstitute ourselves physiologically, genetically, and neurologically, we who have become transhuman will be primed to transform ourselves into posthumans—persons of unprecedented physical, intellectual, and psychological capacity, self-programming, potentially immortal, unlimited individuals.[102]

Extropians spew a lot of pixels and ink plotting these great technological advances, but for all their hard science-fiction rigor, the group's technological speculations ultimately rest on the patterns of the apocalyptic imagination. The asymptotic, metahistorical moment they look forward to is so awesome and triumphant that some Extropians call it the

Singularity, a term poached from the science of nonlinear dynamics and injected with millennialist yearning.

No Extropian desire is more audaciously transcendental than their hope of overcoming entropy's most degrading insult: death. As aspiring Immortalists, many Extropians gobble brain pills and antiaging formulas; they scour technical journals and Web sites for signs that DNA's planned obsolescence may be forestalled; they open installment plans with cryogenics outfits that will one day freeze their biological hardware into Popsicles. But just in case the flesh will always remain an albatross of doom, the Extropians have an even more mind-boggling trick up their sleeves: uploading their consciousness—their mind, their *self*—into a computer.

The dream of uploading can be traced to the first decades of the computer age, when cybernetics, artificial intelligence, and communications theory hinted that the mechanistic philosophy of modern science might finally colonize the most incorporeal of territories: the human mind. Though the body has been considered a meat machine for centuries, and nineteenth-century psychology embraced the image of the "teeming brain," these new approaches to complex information systems suggested that the mind might finally be described as a nervous contraption that churned through feedback loops of symbols and percepts, and somehow produced the self in the process. For artificial intelligence Mephistos like Marvin Minsky and the Churchlands, a reductionist cogsci husband-and-wife team, the mind is no less a machine than anything else you can point to—that is, the mind is an essentially physical system that we can understand, describe, and, in theory, replicate. Every wistful memory, every crafty gambit, every tasty nibble of a chocolate éclair remains a product of the brain, and if we can figure out how the brain works, or even simulate its underlying network of nodes and linkages and chemical triggers (all major ifs), then we should be able to conjure up a mind inside the only machine that theoretically can simulate any other machine: the computer.

As the science writer Ed Regis points out in *Great Mambo Chicken and the Transhuman Condition,* a study of hard-core fringe science, the possibilities of uploading are implicit in information theory, which holds that *any* information can be reduced to controlled bursts of electrical energy. Since the brain is already alive with electrical activity, it's not that tough to reimagine ourselves and our experiences as patterns of information crackling beneath the skullcap like an endless fireworks show. As Regis points out, "Everything hinge[s] on the fact that the human personality was, in essence, *information.*"[103] Needless to say, this "fact" precariously rests atop a number of rickety assumptions about the nature of human consciousness, the role of the body in modulating thought, and the power of machine "intelligence." But if our minds and personalities do indeed boil down to patterns of information humming in the peculiar hardwiring of our nervous systems, then it's really not *too* much of a leap to imagine replicating that unique architecture inside the bowels of some machine—and thus digitally restuffing the seat of the soul.

No one follows this postbiological line of speculation with the mechanist abandon of the Carnegie-Mellon robotics wiz Hans Moravec. In his book *Mind Children,* an Extropian classic so full-on that it's sometimes tough to believe the author is serious, Moravec makes the case that not only will we be able to transfer our minds to machines, nothing should please us more. In one particularly bracing scene, he describes in pulp detail how this digital metempsychosis may occur. First, a robot surgeon lops off the top of your skull and begins probing your gray matter with high-tech nano-fingers that take minute magnetic resonance measurements. The robot doc then programs a high-resolution simulacrum of your brain inside a computer, a model so accurate that "you" suddenly find yourself popping up inside the machine. And away you go.

This is outrageous stuff, but if you are willing to cast a cold eye on the self, Moravec's logic remains devilishly compelling. To start with, we already live inside a virtual reality of sorts; sights, sounds, textures, and flavors are all ghosts in the brain, woven out of preexisting conceptual patterns and the incoming signals we receive from senses that shape those signals on the fly. These signals do not carry the things themselves, but only information about how we are prepared to relate to those things. In this view, the experience of "me" is a kind of cream that forms atop a swirling stew of memory, perception, and various cognitive recursion loops. And since there is nothing magical about the process that coaxes the mind from our neural networks, then nothing in theory should prevent the train of thought from laying its virtual tracks straight into a sufficiently high-resolution copy. In fact, such translation might improve things considerably. There we will sit, gazing out at a now brainless corpse flopping about in its final spasms, looking at our former body like astral travelers with cyborg eyes.

Of course, Moravec's macabre flight of fancy instantly triggers count-less questions. At a time when theme parks and edutainment replace his-tory, and when electronic and computer gadgetry increasingly supplant embodied experience, Moravec's investment in the ontological power of simulation seems part and parcel of a wholesale abandonment of the claims of the physical world. Can we so easily uncouple the mind from its embedded, carnal context, or identify reality with the ability to pro-duce the perception of reality? How can we so confidently identify the self with cognition alone and ignore the emotional and transpersonal ele-ments of the mind? Moreover, psycho-neuro-immunologists argue that the body thinks as a whole, that cognition is not limited to the brain but emerges from the entire "ecosystem" of the flesh. Other neurologists argue that emotions—the bugaboo of Extropian psychology—play a fundamentally constructive role in human thought. Moreover, medita-tors and mystics the world over agree that many different levels of con-sciousness are discoverable through contemplative introspection, states that, while possibly measurable, cannot simply be identified with the chattering conceptual activity that cognitive science fixates upon and Moravec wants to simulate.

Here then is the real wonder: that information technology allows even the most hard-core materialists to ruminate once again on the ancient dream of slipping the incorporeal spark of the self through the jaws of death unscathed. In the introduction to his book, Moravec pro-claims that it is no longer necessary to adopt "a mystical or religious stance" in order to imagine liberating our thought process from "bondage to a mortal body." Moravec also tells Regis that his upload-ing dream "really is a sort of Christian fantasy: this is how to become pure spirit."[104]

This claim demands a bit of theological bracketing. For all its other-worldly denigration of the flesh, the orthodox Christian "fantasy" embraces the total physical reality of the created world and insists that the saved will wear flesh again in the perfect world that follows Judg-ment Day. More important, the linchpin of all Christian creeds is Christ's incarnation in a human body that suffers, dies, and resurrects; in the Roman communion, the body of Jesus literally manifests itself as foodstuff through the miracle of transubstantiation. According to the patristic heretic patrol, many Gnostics rejected this image of the physi-cally suffering savior. According to the not entirely dependable Saint Augustine, some Gnostics claimed that Christ "did not really exist in the flesh, but in mockery of the human senses proffered the simulated appearance of fleshly form, and thereby also produced the illusion not only of death, but also of resurrection."[105] Even the ex-Manichean Augustine, who was no great fan of the horny bag of piss and pile we all carry around, berates the Gnostics for their docetist belief in Christos Simulacrum.

This curious doctrine, which supplants the entropic reality of the body with an incorporeal simulation, shows Moravec's fantasy to be less Christian than gnostic—and, it must be added, a mighty simpleminded gnosticism at that. As William Irwin Thompson notes in *The American Replacement of Nature,* "With its detestation of the imprisonment of the soul in matter, its imagery of mind as light, male, and informational, a *logos spermaticos,* and the flesh as dark, female, and entrapping, Gnosticism is a basin of attraction that awaits those naive technologists who step outside modern society's conventional worldview."[106] Thompson's point is astute: As modern Prometheans pursue the "rational" possibilities of science and technology, it becomes increasingly difficult for them to maintain the commonsensical perspective of the man on the street. Instead, such thinkers and tinkerers are loosed in a world of possibility whose profound metaphysical and religious dimensions they are often incapable of handling, let alone recognizing; as such, they find themselves unconsciously drawn to the soul's most adolescent fantasies of transcendence and immortality.

Moravec's gnostic inclinations are also boosted by the trace elements of Platonism that course through his rationalist bloodstream. According to the allegory of the cave, Plato held that we are so dulled by the restless swamp of ordinary sensual perceptions and feelings that the pure and eternal world of transcendental forms appears to us only as shadows flickering on a womblike dungeon wall. Similarly, Moravec and his Extropian fans drive an ontological wedge between our fallible and decaying bodies and the abstract process of cognition itself. On the one side lies our half-assed perceptual, emotional, and logical wetware; on the other lies the conceptual perfection of disembodied intelligence, an informational array of codes, rules, and algorithms they identify with the potentially immortal self and its infinite computational abilities.

For Plato, the art of geometry offered a window into the world of forms, the crisp perfection of its laws and figures describing a rational world that our material one, with its chaotic undulations and crumbling materials, can only approximately embody. Similarly, Moravec and crew also attempt to transcend our cheap evolutionary baggage through the distant descendants of Plato's ideal forms: binary logic, information theory, and mathematics. Though nearly all mathematicians, computer scientists, and engineers have long ago abandoned the Platonic view that numbers refer to a real world more substantial and perfect than our own, they do not always so easily shed the *psychological* dynamics of Platonic thought, with its inherent love of abstract perfection, and its hope that the hidden patterns of the universe boil down to simple equations. "It is curious how, at times in the most unpredictable way, something of the old Platonic spirit surfaces in the world of computer science," Theodore Roszak notes. "As tough-minded as most scientists might be (or wish to appear to be) in their response to the old mathematical magic, that Platonic dream survives, and no place more vividly than in the cult of information."[107]

The temple of this cult is of course the computer, which, as Jay David Bolter explains, embodies the world as logicians would like it to be. Bolter argues that computers hearken back to the universe of a Greek cosmologist; though the logic of Aristotle has long since been abandoned, the contrast between "order within and chaos without" remains.[108] Moreover, given the explosive power of digital number-crunching, complex predictive modeling, and data visualization, the logical operations of the computer are coming to assert their existence in an increasingly substantial yet incorporeal world of information that exists on the other side of the looking glass. As this world grows in complexity and representational power, it seems to parallel ours—even, in its binary perfection, to exceed it. Gazing onto a data-dense graphic rendering of global weather patterns or the factual reproduction of a high-rez leaf, we slip unconsciously into the worldview of Pythagoras, a mystical predecessor of Plato who held that the universe not only obeyed mathematical laws but was actually *composed* of numbers—numbers that he identified with geometric shapes. In the *Timaeus,* Plato revamped this notion, claiming that the four elements that compose the visible world are in essence four regular solid polyhedrons, rather like the two-dimensional graphic polygons that build the virtual surfaces of Zelda and Quake.

Perhaps the most brazenly metaphysical manifestation of this "old Platonic spirit" occurs in the mind of Edward Fredkin, a brilliant and eccentric computer scientist whose autodidacticism and lack of published papers did not prevent him from becoming an MIT professor and an important figure in some scientific circles. Fredkin believes that the universe is a computer—*literally*. Beneath the smallest subatomic dandelion tuft recognized by today's physicists lies a bunch of bits, a pattern of information reproducing itself according to basic algorithms. Espousing a kind of digital pantheism, Fredkin imagines the universe as a great cellular automata—one of those computer programs that consist of simple elements and basic rules, but which eventually breed into complex cybernetic ecologies. Fredkin's fascinating, if loopy, theory shows the full cosmological extent of the digital paradigm. And once you conceive the universe itself to be an immense logical matrix of information algorithms, then the activity of earthly computers may well assume a metaphysical, almost demiurgic power. The universal machine becomes a machine that builds universes.

Unfortunately, the siren call of the information pleroma also tends to suck human beings into the more troubling aspects of Platonic psychology. Once you fixate on the logical perfection of the computer's looking-glass world, then you may have a particularly tough time accepting the dying animal that you are. One does not have to look far to find a deep strain of body loathing in the engineering imaginary favored by Moravec and many Extropians, but unlike the old desert anchorite's horror of lusts, excrement, and bile, this loathing arises from a tinkerer's distaste for lousy design. As the futurist Bob Truax put it in his book *The Conquest of Death*, "What right-minded engineer would try to build any machine out of lime and jelly? Bone and protoplasm are extremely poor structural materials."[109] The Extropian hero Bob Ettenger, whose 1962 book *The Prospect of Immortality* launched the cryogenics movement, proposed that one of the first operations we should perform on our new transhuman bodies is to make the things clean and shit free. Hearing such plans, one almost automatically envisions the stereotype of the awkward and ungainly hacker, complaining about having to fuel, discharge, and occasionally even bathe his ever-decaying meat machine.

Hans Moravec wonders why we don't just go all the way and literally *become* machines. Moravec cannot fathom why the android Data on *Star Trek: The Next Generation* wants to be human; as he sees it, siphoning our minds into circuitry will allow us not only to dodge the grim reaper but to leap over our hardwired human limitations with a single bound. Once we are posthuman cyborgs, all the knobs can be twisted to the demigod settings: memory, information intake, perceptual acuity, processing power. Even the sky's no longer the limit, since our ability to siphon our minds into any number of possible machines will allow us to explore deep space, colonize other planets, and mine wealth from the raw stuff of the solar system.

Curiously, the imagery of the cyborg, which undergirds many Extropian speculations, is bound up from the beginning with extraterrestrial flight. The term itself was coined in the early 1960s by two scientists, Manfred Clynes and Nathan Kline, who wanted to tweak the bodies of astronauts technologically and pharmacologically until our boys could feel at home in outer space. In this sense, the cyborg interpenetration of technology and humanity is part and parcel of the heroic, otherworldly dream to leave the planet, a dream that sums up the transcendental materialism exemplified by Moravec, the Extropians, and other technophilic mutants. Later we will see how the Heaven's Gate cult swallowed this dream hook, line, and sinker, but offworld religious exuberance is hardly limited to UFO fanatics. As David Noble shows in *The Religion of Technology,* the American space program has been touched by the spirit since the rocket-man Wernher von Braun, freshly arrived from post-Nazi Germany, converted to fundamentalist Christianity in the 1950s. Indeed, with all the Bibles and communion wafers that astronauts have trucked back and forth to the moon, and with all the Mormons and born-agains running the show at home, it is hardly surprising that General Motors, one of the fathers of the U.S. space program, attempted to build a Chapel of the Astronauts near the Kennedy Space Center in the early 1970s.

Space technologies do not just materialize the offworld yearnings of those desperate to flee the grave fate of earthly life. They also literalize the cosmic homesickness that vibrates in so many human hearts, a longing for a transcendental level of authenticity, vision, and being reflected in the heavens. Many thoughtful moderns, religious and not, believe that this sense of estrangement cannot really be assuaged; instead one gains authenticity by throwing oneself into the existential conditions of real life, with all its limitations, sufferings, and insecurity. Others find this cosmic longing satisfied by the realization that earthly life is already composed of stardust, and that the patterns of distant galaxies are reflected in palm fronds, tidepools, and the iris in a lover's eye. But such intimations are not always enough to quench the gnostic suspicion that there is more to us than nature allows. As Bishop Hoeller proclaims, "The exoteric and esoteric traditions declare that earth is not the only home for human beings, that we did not grow like weeds from the soil.

While our bodies indeed may have originated on this earth, our inner essence did not."[110]

Needless to say, the bishop, like most libertarians and techno-utopians, has a pretty short fuse when it comes to environmentalists. On a political level, environmentalists represent tyranny because they proclaim the reality of limitation. They argue that we are reaching the natural limits of the biosphere, that regulatory agencies should impose limits on private citizens and corporations, and that technology is severely limited in its ability to clean up the mess it's already made. On a spiritual plane, many tree huggers, New Agers, and deep ecologists reject Hoeller's sense of offworld estrangement as pathological, embracing instead an almost pagan identification with nature and its healing powers. The philosophers and poets of a blooming earth have little fondness for the Platonic tradition of denigrating material life in the name of abstract ideals, or for the anthropocentric legacy of a triumphant and restless humanism. Nor are they particularly fond of Descartes's mechanistic philosophy, which cleaved the mind from the body and sapped enchantment from nature until nothing remained but a machine to hack.

Putting the pedal to the metal of the West, the Extropians bring all these anti-ecological trends to a feverish pitch, distilling what Mark Dery mordantly pegs the "theology of the ejector seat." In the Extropian utopia, the mind abandons the body, technology rewrites the laws of nature, and libertarian superbrights leave Terra's polluted and impoverished nest for a cyborg life in space. Certainly these dreams can be seen as symptoms of an arrogant and deadly rift with nature, or a hubristic refusal to acknowledge the grip of necessity, or a naive and callous disregard for the social and ecological networks that continue to bind us in the here and now. But the Extropians' technological drive toward transcendence must also be seen as a science-fiction mask of a psychospiritual intuition that's been tugging on humans for millennia. The intuition is alchemical: Buried in the murk of the human self lies an unformed golden core, and with technology, in both the metaphoric sense of techniques and the literal sense of tools, we can tap and transform this potential. We are already cyborgs, an Extropian might say, and we might as well set our sights on the stars.

V

the spiritual cyborg

If human history is the story of a creature who molts from ape to angel—or, as Nietzsche claimed, from beast to Superman—then somewhere along the way it seems that we must become machines. This destiny is rooted in our recent historical evolution. For as the engines of civilization pulled us farther and farther away from the unpredictable and often spiteful dance of nature, we withdrew from the animistic imagination that once immersed us in a living network of material forces and ruling intelligences. We started dreaming of transcending the old gods, of controlling our "animal souls," of building an urban heaven on a mastered earth. We became moderns. Though technology was by no means the only way that humans expressed or inculcated their experience of standing apart from nature, it certainly became the Western way. The modern West could even be said to have made a pact with machines—those systematic assemblages of working parts and potentials which by definition lack a vital spirit, a soul grounded in the metaphysical order of things. And so today, now that we have technologized our environment and isolated the self within a scientific frame of mind, we no longer turn to nature to echo our state. Now we catch our reflections, even our spirits, in the movements and mentations of machines.

This imaginal relationship between man and machine was a long time coming. The ground was laid by the mechanistic cosmologists of ancient Greece, and it seized the imagination when tinkerers like Heron started building those fanciful protorobots we call automata—mechanical gods, dolls, and birds that fascinated ancient and medieval folks as much as they fascinate kids at Disneyland today. The elaborate clocks that decorated medieval churches were often outfitted with mechanical figures representing sinners, saints, grim reapers, and beasts, all mimicking our passage through time. The notion of a mechanistic cosmos, which these clocks helped engender, eventually landed us at the philosophical doorstep of Descartes, who adopted the revolutionary notion that bodies were not animated by spirits of any kind. The difference between a living being and a corpse was nothing more than the difference between a wound-up watch and a spent automata. The Catholic Church recognized the threat to religion that Descartes's new mechanistic philosophy posed but was satisfied with the philosopher's dualistic solution: Simply divide the res cogitans, the realm of the mind, from the res extensa, the spatial world of bodies and objects, and insist that never the twain shall meet.

The enormously productive power of Cartesian philosophy ensured that bone-cold mechanism would come to dominate the Western worldview—so much so that today the flimsy wall that Descartes erected to protect the thinking subject has broken down. Neuroscientists, psychopharmacologists, and geneticists are now offroading into the wilderness of the human mind, mapping every step of the way. The most cherished images and experiences of the self are being colonized by authoritative scientific languages that threaten to reduce our minds and personalities to complex mechanisms—Rube Goldberg assemblages of genetic codes, mammalian habits, and bubbling vats of neurochemicals. Modern psychology can barely keep its hoary old tales alive; as *Time* magazine recently opined, even the Oedipus complex, that grand drama of human personality, has been reduced to a matter of molecules.

As we come to know more about the nuts and bolts of human life, we inevitably come to suspect that our actions, thoughts, and experiences, which seem so spontaneous and free, are programmed into our bodyminds with the mercilessness of clockwork. Speaking before the congressional committee that funded the Human Genome Project, which plans to map the entire human genetic code, the Nobel laureate James Watson said, "We used to think that our fate was in the stars. Now we know that, in large measure, our fate is in our genes."[111] As if such genetic determinism wasn't enough, sociologists and psychologists have also amassed a load of evidence that points to the profoundly automatic patterns of much of our social and cultural life—patterns that arise not only from our animal instincts but from institutions, family dramas, and cultural conditioning. Common sense may not be so common after all; our understanding of what constitutes normal reality may simply represent the power of what the psychologist Charles Tart calls "consensus trance."

With the recent decline of overtly authoritarian political regimes, we now believe ourselves more "free," but the power of consensus trance may actually be waxing in our highly networked and hypermediated age. As the hairsplitting scientific management of the Taylorist factory

proved, capitalism has a long and exuberant history of embracing whatever technologies and institutional frameworks allow it to fit human
beings into vast and efficient megamachines of production and consumption. The footloose "postindustrial" economy is supposed to have
left such soulless mechanisms of control behind, but in reality the megamachine has simply fragmented and mutated. While handing off its
primitive assembly lines to developing countries or illegal sweatshops, it
"spiritualizes" its routines into immaterial cybernetic meshes of information labor or the sophisticated marketing games appropriate to a society based on compulsive consumption. Charlie Chaplin's little tramp,
enmeshed in the cogs of *Modern Times,* has gone virtual, becoming at
once the home-shopping networker and the electronic sweatshop worker
whose every key tap and bathroom break is micromanaged down to the
nanosecond.

As Marshall McLuhan noted in the early 1970s, "we are all robots
when uncritically involved with our technologies."[112] Today there are far
more technologies to get involved with, far more cybernetic loops
demanding that we plug in and turn on. With the continued ideological
dominance of reductionist science and the sociocultural dominance of its
technological spawn, the once glorious isle of humanism is melting into
a silicon sea. We find ourselves trapped on a cyborg sandbank, caught
between the old, smoldering campfire stories and the new networks of
programming and control. As we lose our faith in free will or the coherence of personality, we glimpse androids in the bathroom mirror, their
eyes black with nihilism—the meaningless void that Nietzsche pegged
over a century ago as the Achilles' heel of modern civilization.

Needless to say, the loss of the motive soul unnerves a lot of people.
Most of the spiritual, New Age, and religious activity of the moment is
committed on one level or another to either trashing or supplanting the
reductionist and mechanistic imaginary. Fundamentalist Christians and
Native American animists alike attack Darwin's theory of natural selection, while acupuncturists and holistic healers rekindle the magical life
force of vitalism. Archetypal psychologists try to recover the timeless
images of the soul, while ecological mystics call for a "reenchantment of
the earth" and a rejection of the world of malls and virtual media zones.
Even liberal humanists scrabble about for values, for a "politics of
meaning" that can resist the steady encroachment of technological
thinking.

But can we ever turn back the clock, especially to the time before there were clocks? Perhaps the image of man as a machine holds more promise than its detractors admit, especially if the image is not allowed to totally dominate our vision. For a certain breed of twentieth-century seeker, in fact, the ancient goal of awakening is not served by a retreat into romanticism, religious orthodoxy, or magical incantations. Instead of denying the mechanistic or automatic aspects of human being, these seekers aim the psychospiritual quest *through* the image of the machine, using the mechanism, as it were, to trigger its own wake-up alarm. To paraphrase the Sufi mystic Hazrat Inayat Khan: One aspect of our being is like a machine, and the other aspect is like an engineer. In this view, the first step toward waking up is to recognize how zonked out and automatic we already are; such dispassionate and reductive observations help dispel delusions, reveal genuine possibilities, and thus paradoxically enable us to cultivate some of the most deeply human aspects of being. The machine thus comes to serve as an interactive mirror, an ambiguous Other we both recognize ourselves in and measure ourselves against. This is the path of the spiritual cyborg, a path whose buzzing circuits and command overrides represent both the perils and promise of techgnosis.

Meetings with Remarkable Machines

Loosely speaking, the first spiritual cyborgs were probably the shamans, those ecstatic technicians of the sacred. But the first modern spiritual teacher to productively exploit the language of mechanism was G. I. Gurdjieff, a Greek-Armenian teacher known for his harsh wisdom, hypnotic charisma, and very large mustache. According to his own writings, Gurdjieff spent the turn of the century cruising the monasteries, yogi shacks, and mystic schools of the Middle East and Asia—though it is difficult entirely to believe a man who once packed up and fled a hamlet after a rainstorm threatened to wash the yellow paint off the "parakeets" he was selling about town. But though some skeptics and spiritual leaders continue to write Gurdjieff off as a metaphysical flimflam man, a close reading of the most important Gurdjieff texts makes it clear that the master not only synthesized a variety of teachings and techniques into an eminently practical form of esoteric work, but he creatively integrated a number of modern psychological and scientific ideas into the ancient goal of gnosis.

Gurdjieff died in 1949, and throughout his life, he had little but scorn for European civilization and its rejection of the great spiritual traditions of old. But in other ways, he was very much a modern man. He mocked Spiritualism, ignored the gods, enjoyed working with machines, and embraced the seemingly reductionist notion that "all psychic processes are material." Like the Theosophists, he adopted a loosely evolutionary notion of cosmic history, though he balanced the external course of material evolution with the corresponding necessity of involution—the retreat from the multiple laws that govern material phenomena and the turn toward the liberating cosmic All. Many aspects of Gurdjieff's cosmological system, at least as they appear in P. D. Ouspensky's *In Search of the Miraculous,* were grade A mystical pseudoscience. Ouspensky's text is chock-full of curious psychogeometric laws, charts of "higher hydrogens," and descriptions of cosmic chains of command, the latter of which culminated in the amazing notion that the ordinary purpose of humanity's energetic life was to provide "food for the moon."

Gurdjieff was a trickster, however, and both his eccentric teaching style and eyebrow-raising cosmology seem designed to keep his students and followers on their toes. The same holds true for Gurdjieff's withering assessment of human psychology, a vision that basically boils down to the most repellent of axioms: "Man is a machine." In our ordinary state, Gurdjieff argued, we are just like motorcars or typewriters or gramophones—mechanically pushed and pulled by external chance or internal habits, never genuinely *doing* or *realizing* anything ourselves. We always react, and never cause. Though he implied that our zombiedom was written into the human condition, he also believed that modern industrial life perpetuated and reinforced this trance. "Contemporary culture requires automatons," he said.

Having diagnosed this condition, Gurdjieff made a pretty good case that the only intelligent thing to do in our predicament is to *escape*—an escape that was synonymous with awakening to our nonmechanical essence. Only by upgrading our ordinary, everyday awareness can we genuinely hope to govern and take responsibility for our actions and our desires. As an alchemical modernist, Gurdjieff conceived of this development as an "artificially cultivated" process. Our soul, our nonmechanical essence, is not born with us; it is *made,* and this soul-making runs counter to the course of things. "The law for man is existence in the circle of mechanical influences, the state of the 'man-machine.' The way of the development of hidden possibilities is a way *against nature, against God.*"[113] Rather than embracing Gaia's élan vital, the carnal rhythms and imaginative powers beloved by Romantic animists and nature-worshipers past and present, the awakening human goes against the grain, shifting control from mechanical forces to the awakening "I." Gurdjieff was a gnostic Promethean, seeking to realize the self in an *opus contra naturam* divorced from any myths of divine intervention. For all his traditionalism, he was the spiritual godfather of the Extropians.

Unlike the Extropians, however, Gurdjieff believed that modern people were so hypnotized by technologies, intellectual concepts, and the mounting waves of information churned out by journalists and scientists that they had lost their potential for recognizing and realizing the deeper levels of consciousness. As Jacob Needleman argues, Gurdjieff was the first esoteric thinker to describe the object of spiritual work as "consciousness," though he did not romanticize consciousness like so many New Agers today. Instead, he treated it as a basically material force that could be shaped and transmuted by psychospiritual *techne*—what students call "the Work."

The Work begins with ruthless self-observation, a coldhearted analysis of "our machine." Somewhat like the Theravadan Buddhist practitioners of vipassana, or mindfulness, the budding Worker is encouraged to notice and register her own thoughts, emotions, and behaviors—an objective process of discrimination that Gurdjieff describes as "recording." This is not the recording of the ancient scribes, but the unforgiving recording of the camera or the research scientist, gazing through a microscope at a wiggling germ. After recording ourselves for a while, one of the first things we realize is that we have no permanent and unchangeable "I." As Gurdjieff explained, "Each minute, each moment, man is saying or thinking 'I.' And each time his I is different. Just now it was a thought, now it is a desire, now a sensation, now another thought, and so on, endlessly. *Man is a plurality.* Man's name is legion."[114] Here lies our fundamental inauthenticity—the I that makes one promise is not the I that breaks it. Needless to say, the notion that we have "hundreds of thousands of separate small I's," oftentimes ignorant of and in conflict with one another, runs counter to our existential sense of a stable self. But Gurdjieff argued that if we committed ourselves to ruthless self-observation, we would come to realize that this ordinary sense of unified being is a sham.

Gurdjieff's psychological vision owed much to his metaphor of the "man-machine," for the principle of the machine is the assemblage, the soulless conglomeration of subsystems, working parts, and shifting points of energy and production. Many decades later, the hardheaded mechanists working on the problem of human cognition would bring this "assemblage" model of the mind into popular consciousness. Though possessing considerable variety, most of the models in cognitive science imagine the mind as a construction created through the struggles and alliances of myriad small and densely interconnected symbolic subsystems and agents, a vision that the artificial intelligence wizard Marvin Minsky calls the "society of mind." More recently, other cognitive scientists have served up less hierarchical or symbolically dependent models; these picture the mind as the product of even more primitive and "asocial" mechanisms of sensation, perception, and memory. The ego, the self, the conscious sense of "me," is seen as an "emergent property," a vaporous afterimage of the complex machinations of glandular data gates, neurochemical sparks, and the perceptual structures that whir and buzz beneath the surface of thought.

Gurdjieff was hardly the only spiritual thinker to anticipate what seems at first to be a uniquely modern, technological deconstruction of the self. Buddhist psychology also holds that there is no core essence, no *atman*, no singular I. Instead, traditional Buddhists divide the self into a number of "heaps" *(skandas)* that are composed of a shifting array of objects, perceptions, judgments, mental categories, and states of awareness. The material in these heaps is pushed and pulled by habit, desire, and the constantly changing causes and conditions of the world of karma. Because this groundless flow terrifies us, Buddhist shrinks reasoned, we build castles out of the shifting sands of consciousness and proclaim them stable, real, and eternal. Within our minds, we reify an essential self, whose inability to respond spontaneously to the flux of things, or to recognize its own insubstantial nature, generates the delusions and sufferings of samsara.

Indeed, Gurdjieff sounds a bit like a dour Buddhist when he says that "to awaken means to realize one's nothingness, that is, to realize one's complete and absolute mechanicalness and one's complete and absolute helplessness." But even this depressing analysis contains the seed of hope, a seed that Gurdjieff believed lay in our very capacity for realization and awareness. By paying attention to our own mechanical routines, we cease to identify with them, and this de-identification shifts our attention toward the higher I that observes its own process and directs, as best it can, its own inner growth. This transcendence-through-feedback separates the essential self from the automatism of the machine and creates a crystal of consciousness capable not only of genuinely directing its own activity, but of actually surviving death.

That's the plan anyway. In a sense, the Gurdjieffean Work can be seen as an explicitly spiritual analog of the Extropians' brash commitment to master the sluggish body, control the emotions, and reprogram themselves for immortality and self-realization. Like the Extropians, the Gurdjieff Work can also be accused of being elitist, antinomian, and pretty thin on universal compassion and those other "myths" that remind us of our indissoluble links to the human community and the physical biosphere. At the same time, the Work possesses a psychospiritual sophistication rather lacking among the gonzo Extropians, and its transcendental thrust is tempered by Gurdjieff's insistence on a pragmatic engagement with ordinary life. Students are encouraged to live and work in the everyday world, and to refine, expand, and integrate the levels of consciousness associated with the body and emotions—not to leave these "lower" apparatuses rusting in a Darwinian trash heap.

But one of the principal dangers of the Work is not shared by the fiercely individualistic Extropians. Gurdjieff insisted that only an awakened teacher can help students snap out of their most intractable hypnotic habits, and that serious Work thus requires strict fidelity to an external master. As the history of new religious and esoteric movements demonstrates all too well, such situations regularly degenerate into those dangerously authoritarian patterns of behavior we associate with cults. A number of the groups that picked up the Work after Gurdjieff's death did not escape the clutches of this kind of tyranny. On the other hand, one person's cult is sometimes another person's community of awakening. In one passage of *In Search of the Miraculous*, a group of students tell Gurdjieff that their old friends believe that they have become colorless and boring, nothing more than parrots of Gurdjieff, veritable "machines." (Today we would say that they were "brainwashed.") Gurdjieff laughs enigmatically: "There is worse to come."

Gurdjieff's chuckle arises from the fact that when you are dealing with religious countercultures, which call into question the assumptions of conventional society, awakening and hypnosis often appear as two sides of the same coin—and it's not always easy to tell which side you're on. "Liberating" your outlook and behavior through psychospiritual means does not erase the problem of power and control; disrupting the troubled sleep of ordinary delusion, one runs the risk of simply swapping the old familiar archons for obscure and potentially more maniacal ones. At the same time, if the consensus reality world we work in daily (and tune in to nightly) does indeed generate the kind of mechanical trance Gurdjieff describes, then awakening from this condition might make one *more* aware of, and even obsessed with, the subliminal forces of control. Suddenly, the whole social and symbolic arena of social reality, that rather haphazard carnival of soapbox cranks, snake-oil salesmen, and apparently reasonable discourse, takes on the appearance of a vast, if unconscious, conspiracy. Such paranoid specters often dog subcultures that self-consciously slip outside the mainstream, but they can be particularly vexing for those spiritual cyborgs who integrate modern ideas about thought programming, Pavlovian trigger signals, and hypnotic trances into their worldview.

Ideally, the sort of "self-remembering" techniques Gurdjieff described would enable one to evade the lures of paranoia and esoteric authoritarianism, but some psychospiritual sects that engage the mechanistic imaginary have impaled themselves on these two flesh-gripping prongs. Take Scientology, whose far cruder attempt to spiritualize the man-machine has made it the world's first corporate cybernetic mystery cult. In the 1940s, L. Ron Hubbard was a regular contributor to John Campbell, Jr.'s *Astounding Science Fiction*, where he wrote stories about paranormal and rather fascist supermen who conquered worlds and wielded amazing psychokinetic powers; he also wrote *Fear*, one of the meatiest paranoia stories in pulp SF. After being hyped by Campbell, Hubbard's article on Dianetics appeared in the May 1950 edition to great acclaim; its subsequent book form, *Dianetics: The Modern Science of Mental Health*, sold 150,000 copies in a year. Offering a hands-on, straightforward approach to the problems that beset the human mind, Dianetics presented simple and sensible techniques that could clear people of the psychological problems and psychosomatic ills that Hubbard claimed constituted most ailments. As an added bonus, Hubbard hinted that these tricks could potentially unveil the same latent psychic powers that drew readers to his tales.

Less a science of mind than an engineering manual of mind, *Dianetics* began with a bold and now familiar assertion: The mind is a computer. In its optimum state, our "active mind" recalls all data, responds rationally, and solves all possible problems. But our active mind is obstructed by our "reactive mind," a "memory bank" that corresponds loosely with Freud's concept of the unconscious. Here lie "aberrative circuits," dysfunctional habits that Hubbard labeled "engrams": multi-sensory records of unpleasant experiences that can resurface in our lives as moments of fear, pain, or unconsciousness. For example, let's say I was once bitten by a dog in a rainstorm; the sound of falling water and a barking Chihuahua would then restimulate the engram and ruin my day. By "auditing" such engrams—which means bringing them to consciousness and "processing" them through Dianetic techniques—one can step toward the optimum state of "Clear."

Today the belief that the mind behaves like a computer barely raises an eyebrow, and for decades has almost constituted a guild oath for reductionist cognitive scientists. But in 1950, the world's first electronic computer (ENIAC) was only four years old, and Hubbard's transistorized Freud packed a healthy punch among people feeling the first stirrings of the digital revolution. His "modern scientific methodology" particularly appealed to *ASF* readers and their intellectual ilk, who evidenced much of the pragmatic rationalism and Promethean dreams that would later breed technological enthusiasts like the Extropians. These were the kind of people who were tickled pink about mainframe computers and the promises of cybernetics, Norbert Wiener's new science of communication and control.

Hubbard became one of the first people to hawk the new paradigm to an American market notoriously attracted to self-help scams and quick-fix gadgets. By employing a cybernetic language of "circuits," "process," and "memory banks," Hubbard seemed to offer his readers technical control over their own minds, giving them an effective therapeutic system they could use to improve themselves in the comfort of their own homes, and without the expensive intervention of meddling psychoanalytical witch doctors. Hubbard was also reacting to the dominant psychological theory of behaviorism, which conceived of human beings as "black boxes"—organic stimulus-response machines whose behavior could be understood and treated on an essentially mechanical basis that paid no attention at all to subjective experience. Hubbard did not so much reject this paradigm as give it a comic-book, Gurdjieffean twist: Our bodies and ordinary minds may be programmable contraptions, but our essential selves are capable of programming and debugging these machines.

In the early 1950s, Dianetics groups started spontaneously popping up across the land, and Hubbard may have felt that he was losing control of his do-it-yourself, self-help program. In any case, his initially secular techniques were soon absorbed into the "spiritual" philosophy (and hierarchy) of Scientology, which incorporated its first church in 1954. To the Freudian circuit diagrams of Dianetics, Hubbard added ungainly chunks of Buddhist psychology, New Thought, and probably elements of Aleister Crowley's Nietzschean brand of modern occult "magick." Early in their spiritual career, budding Scientologists learned to break down ingrained patterns of social behavior and to generate altered states of consciousness (one training routine consisted of staring blankly into another person's eyes for hours without reacting). These palpable shifts in perception and awareness were then reframed according to Scientology doctrine, a process that led students deeper into Hubbard's off-the-wall cosmology and the authoritarian structure of his church. Bureaucratic and technological efficiency reigned supreme as metaphors of spiritual progress. Scientologists still refer to Hubbard's elaborate and byzantine system of training routines, audiotapes, and texts as the "tech." And the tech, they say, always works.

Hubbard also pushed a new cyborg technology, a strange and intriguing box originally demonstrated to him in 1952 by a New Jersey Dianeticist named Volney Mathison. The "electropsychometer," or E-meter, is equipped with dials and two attachments that resemble tin cans. Somewhat like lie detectors, the E-meter registers changes in galvanic skin response—roughly speaking, the flow of electricity through the body. Budding Scientologists hold the cans while an auditor asks them questions (or attempts to "push their buttons"); eventually, the dials register a charge that indicates the presence of an engram. Hubbard's idea was that thought has mass, and that the neurotic "heaviness" of engrams creates resistance to electrical flow. Once the imprints are cleared through Dianetic techniques, the E-meter needle "floats," and the subject is one step closer to enlightenment. The E-meter is like God in a box—as one operator's manual put it, "It sees all, knows all. It is never wrong."[115]

Such claims did not cut it with the FDA, who teamed up with some U.S. marshals and stormed Scientology's Washington, D.C., headquarters in 1963, seizing truckloads of E-meters and manuals. In a protracted court battle, the Church of Scientology contended that auditing was akin to Catholic confession, that the E-meter was a "religious artifact," and that Scientologists didn't have to prove its efficacy any more than the

Vatican had to run tests on wafers and holy water. The argument was ingenious: Rather than attempting to prove the scientific validity of the E-meter—a challenging task to say the least—they simply hid behind the cloak of religious mystery. But they also unwittingly underscored the fact that technologies sometimes derive their power from symbolic and ritual performance rather than mechanical effects. Attempting to clarify the distinction between these two overlapping dimensions of technological efficacy, a federal judge banned the E-meter for "secular" diagnosis and treatment but allowed its continued use for "religious" counseling.

In a history of Scientology entitled *Religion Inc.,* the British journalist Stewart Lamont noted that for Scientologists, "spiritual progress could actually be measured and practiced without recourse to providential grace from God. It could be assured by performing the correct techniques and by following a manual. . . . It was the age-old heresy of gnosticism repackaged in a way to appeal to twentieth-century scientific man."[116] Though Lamont's conception of gnosticism reflects orthodox propaganda more than the phenomenon itself, he is right to note the gnostic current that gives Hubbard's tech its peculiar zap. Sounding like an Extropian battle plan, Scientology claims "to increase spiritual freedom, intelligence, ability, and to produce immortality." Once the E-meter has erased all the instincts, memories, and pains that define our personalities, we are left with what Hubbard calls the "thetan," an immortal essence that he defines as the incorporeal part of us that is "aware of being aware." Taking Cartesian dualism into the stratosphere, Hubbard imagined an alien spiritual entity that distinctly resembles the "spark" described by the Gnostics of yore.

In fact, Hubbard's cosmology reads like "The Hymn of the Pearl" as filtered through Darwin and paranoid science fiction. In his brain-bending book *Scientology: A History of Man,* which purports to be nothing less than a "a cold-blooded and factual account of your last sixty trillion years," we learn that long ago a bunch of bored thetans decided to amuse themselves by creating and destroying universes. To make the game more interesting, they relinquished some of their super-powers, voluntarily entering the universe of MEST—Matter, Energy, Space, and Time. Our universe. Falling into MEST in a "dwindling spiral," they became so hopelessly ensnared in physical space that they wound up forgetting their true origins. Reduced to "pre-clears," these thetans were condemned to pass from one lifetime to the next, accumulating karmic banks of engrams that only Dianetics could clear. Once freed of the vegetable body and its psychic crud, the thetan would be fully operational again, able to simulate "facsimiles" of a body, and manipulate the virtual reality of MEST at will.

Thetans are not the only forces in the cosmos, however. After arriving on Earth and transforming mindless apes into *homo sapiens,* the body-snatching thetans encountered the Martian "Fourth Invader Force." These sinister legions trapped and enslaved the thetans using a variety of psychological and electronic torture devices, including the dread "Jack-in-the-Box" and the horrifying "Coffee-Grinder." When we die, our inner thetan goes to a report station where Martians erase its memories using a "forgetting implant" that resembles a satanic wheel of television sets.

Beneath their "hoods and goggles," the Fourth Invaders clearly recall the Gnostic archons of old. But with their battery of bizarre electronic machines, these archons also represent Hubbard's feverish pulp spin on psychiatry. Hubbard hated the mental health establishment, and particularly loathed the widespread use of electroconvulsive therapy. (Hubbard's *A History of Man* includes extended rants about how "electronics alone can make a truly slave society.") In the 1950s and 1960s, he fanatically and publicly opposed ECT, lobotomies, the deplorable conditions of mental institutions, and the authority granted to psychiatrists by the law. He also became one of the first to accuse the CIA of performing mind-control experiments, accusations that later revelations about MK-ULTRA proved perfectly true. In his own paranoid and self-serving way, Hubbard suggested the position that Michel Foucault would later articulate in *Madness and Civilization:* that institutional psychiatry is as much a form of social control as a form of healing.

Like many heretical and authoritarian organizations, however, the Church of Scientology was also capable of reproducing and far exceeding the most manipulative, totalitarian, and fanatical elements of the social institutions it opposed. As exposés like Jon Atack's *A Piece of Blue Sky* document in chilling detail, the church hierarchy became quite paranoid in the late 1960s and early 1970s, and used a variety of dirty tricks to undermine "suppressive persons" deemed hostile to the organization. Inside the church, Hubbard increasingly put communications in the service of control. Fleeing from the authorities to the high seas, Hubbard maintained tight control over his "Orgs" through an elaborate telex network. He also churned out tens of thousands of pages of Scientology material, an endless stream of books, pamphlets, directives, memos, and policy letters that unconsciously parodied the most absurd excesses of print-based bureaucracy. Audiotapes of Hubbard's mesmerizing, rambling, and vaguely amusing lectures were also used extensively during Scientology training, perhaps fostering the "deep tribal involvement" that Marshall McLuhan claimed allowed demagogues like Hitler to sway the masses through the radio.

Needless to say, the most advanced levels of Scientology did not always deliver the promised superpowers, and Hubbard was forced to constantly upgrade his increasingly expensive tech. Atack describes the scenario in terms all too familiar in these wired days: "Each new rundown [or upgrade] would be launched amid a fanfare of publicity, and claims of miraculous results. One critic . . . complained of 'auditing junkies,' forever waiting for the next 'level' to resolve their chronic problems."[117] Drawn ever deeper into a worldview rigidly enforced by insiders and well-nigh incomprehensible to the rest of us, many Scientologists found themselves locked in a paradigm without exit doors. As Margery Wakefield explains in her survivor text "The Road to Xenu," which floats about the Internet's myriad anti-Scientology sites, Scientology's attempt to overcome cultural and psychological programming paradoxically drew its acolytes into vicious cybernetic loops. Wakefield's tale culminates when, after twelve years in the organization, she reaches the level of OT3 and its extremely esoteric texts. She learns that many moons ago, Xenu, the head of the Galactic Federation, solved a cosmic overpopulation problem by sending thetans to Earth and then blowing them up with nuclear weapons hidden in volcanoes. Reading this seriously baked tale, Wakefield experiences a kind of cognitive dissonance:

> I was feeling very strange. I had been programmed under hypnosis for ten years to accept as gospel everything said or written by Hubbard. . . . But the materials were too absurd to be believed. The result was that my mind, like a computer which has come upon data impossible to analyze, simply refused to compute. . . . Hubbard had jammed my mind. And from that point I became a total pawn. Not able to think, I was a completely programmable stimulus-response machine. I had become a robot. Or, to use the phrase now popular among ex-Scientologists, a "Rondroid."[118]

Wakefield's knotted mix of technological metaphors is fascinating, not least of all because it shows how a therapeutic "technology" based on liberating the mental computer could produce in some of its followers a sense of robotic stimulus-and-response reminiscent of the evil Borgs (Orgs?) on *Star Trek: The Next Generation*. But while one one can hardly fault Wakefield for considering herself a Rondroid, her technological language also obscures as much as it reveals. As the psychologist Lowell Streiker points out, the tactics of persuasion used by Scientology and other cults "are not so much a 'technology of mind control' or hallmarks of brainwashing as they are . . . common techniques by which groups break down personal resistance and establish their influence."[119] But to acknowledge this is to acknowledge the possibility that every day we swim in a sea of brainwash, albeit a diluted one. Every time we rally around a flag or a logo, or pop a Prozac, or accept a marketing campaign into our lives, we are dancing with the forces of control, or at least with the "consensus trance" that unconsciously seeks to keep us, for all intents and purposes, dazed and confused.

Gurdjieff's Work suggests that the "man-machine" can wake up and free itself from its own automatic and socially imposed behavior, and that the spiritual cyborg can move toward higher consciousness by first getting in touch with his or her inner machine. Scientology exemplifies the creepy cultic hazards that lurk along this road and reminds us that liberating the self from some programs may simply free up blank tape for new and far more debilitating trances. In any case, and despite Hubbard's resoundingly bad example, computers, cybernetics, and information technology now provide curiously useful mirrors and metaphors along the trail of self-development. For people drawn to psychospiritual transformation but repelled by the old fairy tales, the notion of "technologies of the self" does not dehumanize so much as empower. Besides satisfying the gadget-happy temperament of modern people, it carves out room for a pragmatic experimentation that is freed, at least in principle, from any dogma.

At the same time, the increasingly popular image of the programmable self also reflects the steady bureaucratization and technologizing of society that took place throughout the twentieth century, a process that brought with it an order of social control impossible to jibe with the genuine exploration of human potential. For this reason, many of the countercultural spiritual movements of the postwar Western world violently rejected the mechanistic imaginary, strongly opposing electronic

Babylon and the dehumanizing effects of technocracy, with its abstract, institutional calculus of the organized man-machine. But as we will see, beneath their buckskin vests and Japanese robes, the spiritual rebels of the postwar counterculture were far more intimate with the logic of technique than they initially let on.

Freak Technique

In his 1954 book *The Technological Society,* the French theologian Jacques Ellul proclaimed that the forces of "technique" had begun to run amok, invading and transforming all spheres of human activity. For Ellul, *technique* referred not just to machines, but to the logic of manipulation and gain that lay behind machines. Sociologically, technique described the procedures, languages, and social conditions generated by the "rationality" of modern institutions, bureaucracies, and technocratic organizations. Following World War II, these organizations made an ever deeper pact with technique when they began to computerize themselves and to incorporate the cybernetic logic of control, with its feedback loops and information flows, into their management structures. The System, as it was known to its later foes, began to hit its stride.

At the same time that computer scientists began to consider the possibility of artificially intelligent machines, Ellul argued that *technique* had already taken on a life of its own. The System was, in essence, out of control. In its ceaseless drive for efficiency and productive power, this hell-bent technoeconomic Frankenstein was squeezing the life out of individuals, cultures, and the natural world, reducing everything to what Heidegger described as a standing reserve of raw material. Like Heidegger, Ellul rejected the humanist notion that technology was simply a tool we use to implement human goals. Instead, technology installs a new and invisible framework around the world we live in, a potentially catastrophic structure of knowing and being that swallows us up whether we like it or not.

The rather Manichean portrait that Ellul painted proved enormously influential among the postwar generation destined to stage the blazing freak show known as "the sixties." An uneasy alliance of political radicals and bohemians, violent revolutionaries and anarchic acidheads, the young men and women of the 1960s counterculture were united in their hatred of the System. They dreamed of a millennial world that would replace the dehumanizing megamachine of technocratic society and its military-industrial complex; whether expressed in Marxist, mystical, or hedonistic terms, this new age would usher in a redeemed society of justice, human potential, and organic freedom. In the counterculture's eyes, technology symbolized the System, with its heartless yen for domination and its fetish for rational control.

At the same time, revolutionaries like the Students for a Democratic Society or the Weathermen were more than willing to use the master's tools against him, whether they be bullhorns or guns, bombs or radios. For the more apolitical hippies, however, who believed that changing consciousness would itself change the world, modern technology radiated seriously bad vibes. Many opted for a more "organic" lifestyle based on bean sprouts, moon charts, scruffy hair, and rural Rousseauism. Nonetheless, the freak scene would never have spread without technology: FM radio, underground newspapers, powerful stereos, television news, the pill, the electric guitar. Especially the electric guitar. By the midsixties, the rock concert had become the hedonic agora of the counterculture; musicians dove headfirst into the electromagnetic imaginary, transforming previously "extraneous" electrical effects like feedback and distortion into ferocious transcendental chaos. Combined with the flashing goo of light shows and the LSD that had migrated out of elite psychological circles and military experiments, these kundalini-tweaking soundstorms staged electrified Eleusinian mysteries whose power, as Theodore Roszak notes, was "borrowed from the apparatus"—that is, from the very System the freaks sought to supplant.

Alongside their embrace of certain select technologies, the hippies must also be seen as revising, rather than rejecting, the dreams of technique. Freaks created an entire mythos around self-empowering tools and instrumental skills, an organic and imaginative transformation of technical manipulation that is nowhere more evident than in the generation's powerfully innovative spirituality. Rejecting the arid and authoritarian religious institutions of the West, the freaks decided to get their mystical hands dirty, to pry open the human sensorium and uncover whatever was inside. Which is why, from yoga to psychedelics, from the *Kama Sutra* to the *I Ching*, countercultural spirituality is characterized by nothing so much as techniques, especially what Mircea Eliade called "techniques of ecstasy." This grab bag of mystic methods and psychological tools, plucked out of their original cultural context or invented anew, allowed individual seekers to probe and expand their own bodyminds while avoiding the dogmatic traps of orthodoxy.

Gurus and demagogues waited in the wings, of course, as demonstrated by the later explosion of authoritarian fringe religions like the Hare Krishnas, the Unification Church, and the Children of God. But at its most self-aware, the counterculture gave birth to a new kind of pilgrim, a postmodern seeker who embodied a radically democratic and experimental relationship to the myriad domains of the human spirit. At their best, these spiritual tinkerers were (and are) dynamic and pragmatic, open to the protean possibilities of creative magic and deeply suspicious of the "one-size-fits-all" approach of more traditional and absolutist religions. Though running the risk of aimless dabbling, the eclecticism of what would eventually be called "New Age" was also a prescient religious response to a shrinking globe. Recalling the metaphysical melting pot of ancient Alexandria, it seems that polyglot times demand that religion be not just rekindled, but reinvented.

And as any dweeb with a pocket protector will tell you, invention proceeds by *bricolage,* the creative and experimental assemblage of ad hoc techniques. For all its purple haze, freak spirituality implied a curiously empirical interpretation of *homo religiosus.* Visionary and sacred experiences were facts of human existence, but they were also products of human endeavor, and could be catalyzed and tweaked through a wide variety of psychophysiological means. For meditators, mystics, and Caucasian shamans, the only legitimate course into the blazing dawn of enlightenment was to cobble together experimental protocols from a wide range of traditions. As the "Cookbook for a Sacred Life" that closes Ram Dass's freak classic *Be Here Now* explains, "This manual contains a wide variety of techniques. Everyone's needs are different and everyone is at a different stage along the path. But, as with any recipe book, you choose what suits you."[120]

As the glossy mail-order catalogs of the New Age would later demonstrate, the sacred cookbook is only one step away from the spiritual supermarket, where Zen clocks, Navajo dream pillows, and plastic rune stones repackage the same old magic of the commodity. But the counterculture's fetish for "consciousness tools" cannot be written off simply as esoteric consumerism. After all, the baby boomers were the lab rats of the information age, the first human beings weaned on television, transistor radios, and the other consumer technologies that flooded American society following World War II. Even when they turned their backs on the mechanistic West, they could hardly shake their birthright as children of technique. So while freak seekers may have been naive in believing that tantric sex, mescaline trips, or yoga asanas would patch their souls straight into the cosmic motherboard, they were perfectly reasonable in recognizing that such "technologies of transformation" catalyze powerful and potentially meaningful psychospiritual experiences.

Some sacred technologies even offered *information,* which is why Tarot cards and astrological manuals rocketed to the top of the occult charts. Perhaps the most sublime of these oracular media was the *I Ching,* the ancient Chinese Classic of Changes whose English translations were embraced by Jungians and beatnik poets in the 1950s. The text itself is a profound but often puzzling brew of shamanic Taoism, nature symbolism, and Confucian legalese. The roots of the system are the polar forces of yin and yang, the creative and the receptive, whose statistical permutations are organized into sixty four hexagrams—a binary system impressive enough to have fascinated Gottfried Leibniz, the seventeenth-century Rationalist metaphysician whose innovations in logic helped lay the foundations of computer science. By tossing coins or dividing piles of yarrow sticks, the user derives the hexagrams appropriate to his or her situation. The *I Ching* thus functioned as a kind of personal countercomputer: a binary book of organic symbols that could challenge a System raging against the Tao. But even as it tapped into the analog patterns of the soul, the *I Ching* was at root a *digital* system, its underlying numerical patterns familiar to any hacker.

But of all the consciousness tools embraced by hippies, the most potent was certainly LSD, a gnostic molecule first synthesized and ingested in 1943 at the Sandoz chemical labs in Switzerland. An artificial product of laboratory technique, LSD is a synthetic molecular apparatus that catalyzes its *mysterium tremendum* with mechanistic predictability. At the same time, LSD catapults the user into a world whose workings utterly defy the causal logic of modern science. As Terence McKenna writes, psychedelics open up

> an invisible realm in which the causality of the ordinary world is replaced with the rationale of natural magic. In this realm, language, ideas, and meaning have greater power than cause and effect. Sympathies, resonances, intentions, and personal will are linguistically magnified through poetic rhetoric. The imagination is evoked and sometimes its forms are beheld visibly.[121]

By delivering such fantastic and occult perceptions in a cluster of synthetic chemicals, LSD subliminally and paradoxically expressed the cultural logic of the information age, when technique invades and rewires, not just the mind, but the imagination. In this sense, psychedelics are perhaps best seen as *media,* apparatuses of communication that channel "information" into the mind while shaping that information into dreamtime. In his vastly influential 1954 book *The Doors of Perception* (whose title was snatched from William Blake's visionary snippet: "If the doors of perception were cleansed, everything will appear to man as it is—infinite"), Aldous Huxley argued that in its ordinary state the mind acts as a "reducing valve," filtering out the chaos of sensations and subconscious processes. Hallucinogens blow open the valve, letting the "Mind at Large" gush in with visions, insights, and swelling emotions. Though many people interpret this gnostic rush mystically, it also sounds a lot like information overload. The profound connections and giggling synchronicities that visit the psychedelic traveler may signify nothing more than the mind's exuberantly creative but ultimately doomed attempt to organize a multidimensional spew of incoming data.

Thinking along similar lines, Marshall McLuhan described psychedelics as "chemical simulations of our electric environment"; as such, they allowed users to "achieve empathy" with the archaic echo chamber of the electronic media. More soberly, the Zen writer Alan Watts pointed out that "psychedelic drugs are simply instruments, like microscopes, telescopes, and telephones."[122] Or televisions, one might add, noting that the image of the boob tube sneaks into *The Psychedelic Experience,* a self-consciously spiritual workbook written by the trippy Ph.D.s Timothy Leary, Ralph Metzner, and Richard Alpert before they dropped out of the straight world. Mapping the LSD trip onto the afterlife dramas described in the *Bardo Thödol,* the so-called *Tibetan Book of the Dead,* the authors describe a stage where the tripper realizes that all sensation and perception are based on wave vibrations, and that "he is involved in a cosmic television show which has no more substantiality than the images on his TV picture tube."[123] Nearly everyone took it for granted that, if tuned in to the proper set and setting, the psychedelic voyager would transcend the world of information and taste states of unitive consciousness similar to those glimpsed by the yogis and alchemists. But not everyone agreed about the ultimate value of such pinhole visions, especially given their ultimately technological basis. Watts coolly concluded that "When you get the message, hang up the phone."

Ken Kesey didn't want to hang up the phone—he wanted a party line. In the early 1960s, Kesey and his Merry Pranksters began throwing experimental fetes that were destined to bring the acid gospel to the masses. During these electric Kool-Aid acid tests, LSD was only one component of a storm of media frenzy that did not so much cleanse the doors of perception as coat them with experimental movies, Day-Glo glyphs, and dripping light projections. The house band was the Warlocks, later to transmogrify into the Grateful Dead. For Jerry Garcia, Kesey's acid tests conjured up nothing less than electromagnetic magic:

> They had film and endless kinds of weird tape recorder hookups and mystery speaker trips. . . . It always seemed as though the equipment was able to respond in its own way. I mean . . . there were always magical things happening. Voices coming out of things that weren't plugged in . . .[124]

From most accounts, the acid tests certainly got their mojo working. But unlike the serious psychological researchers who preceded them, the Pranksters and many of the freaks that followed generally failed to construct anything like the *contexts of meaning* that traditional shamanic or religious cultures have always used to integrate cognitive ecstasy (and its metaphysical morning-afters) into ordinary life. Once you hopped on the magic bus, all road maps became suspect; all you had were the knobs and dials.

That's why Uncle Tim's famous sound bite calls to "tune in" and "turn on" were metaphors of media, not of message. Trust in the psychedelic apparatus, the televised pied piper said with a grin, because with it in hand you can "storm the gates of heaven." For all its creative magic, this quintessential Promethean dream also reflected the instrumental hubris that already inflamed postwar society. In many ways, freak spirituality simply reproduced industrial society's belief in quick-fix technological solutions. As Mark Dery writes in *Escape Velocity*:

> The inhabitants of the sixties counterculture exemplified by Kesey and his Pranksters may have dreamed of enlightenment, but theirs was the "plug-and-play" nirvana of the "gadget-happy American"— cosmic consciousness on demand, attained not through long years of Siddharthalike questing but instantaneously, by chemical means, amidst the sensory assault of a high-tech happening.[125]

Dery suggests that when the acidheads tweaked a DuPont Corporation slogan into the rallying cry of "Better Living Through Chemistry," they were being less ironic than they supposed.

On the other hand, by poaching drugs and technologies from the military-industrial-media complex, the sixties consciousness brigade can also be seen as imaginative pragmatists, reenchanting the world by any means necessary. Humans have gobbled visionary drugs throughout history, and the fact that the most influential psychedelic of the twentieth century came in a twentieth-century package says nothing about its power to, at the very least, *simulate* the exalted states that bug-eyed visionaries and shape-shifting shamans have reported throughout the ages. Once through the neon Paisley gates, many a freak grew weary of acid's metaphysical shell game, hung up the phone, and hit the meditation mat. Many logged "long years" tracking Siddhartha's faded footsteps, recognizing a glimmer of themselves in the Buddha's relentless empirical self-exploration.

Others fled to the Esalen Institute, perched on the edge of California's arcadian Big Sur coast, dangling on the literal edge of the West. There they found psychotherapeutic frameworks for their explorations and, occasionally, a more systematic philosophy to boot. Founded by Michael Murphy and Richard Price, two intellectuals committed to radical psychological development, Esalen helped spawn and nurture what came to be called the human potential movement, an eclectic blend of spiritual practices and psychological therapies that heavily influenced the later New Age scene. Just as the sixties' occult revival reintroduced magical practices and archetypal imagery into popular culture, so did the human potential movement pry open the iron gates of Western psychology to make way for states of consciousness previously ignored or written off as gibberish or madness. Meditators, psychedelic visionaries, yoga freaks, group gropers, Gestalt therapists—all had a place at Esalen. Inspired by Abraham Maslow's emphasis on "peak experiences," those flashes of godlike or transpersonal capacities far above the muddy ruts of the mundane mind, the intellectuals and therapists behind Esalen pushed the envelope of consciousness without entirely abandoning the positivist sensibilities of their university peers.

As any of Esalen's original "psychonauts" could tell you, the center's commitment to the exploration of transpersonal states of consciousness often paled beside its celebration of the liberated flesh. For Harold Bloom, Esalen hosted the rebirth of gnostic Orphism, with its doctrine that the redeemed self lives in perpetual intoxication. But amidst all the body oil, drug trips, and nude hot tub comminglings, the headier characters at Esalen also helped refashion the paradigm of cybernetics and information theory into a pragmatic, hands-on, and dispassionate approach to the new mutations of the bodymind that characterized the Esalen experience. While criticizing the modern cult of instrumental reason, they yanked the old alchemical quest into the information age.

One key figure in this reconstruction was Gregory Bateson. An anthropologist by training, Bateson had participated in the pivotal Macy Conferences of the 1950s, gatherings that hammered down the social and scientific implication of cybernetics. But for all his links to the technocratic and scientific elite, Bateson later bloomed into the quintessential California philosopher, a resident of Esalen and patron saint of the *Whole Earth Catalog*. Calling cybernetics "the biggest bite out of the Tree of Knowledge that mankind has taken in the last 2,000 years," Bateson argued that the science provided nothing less than a philosophical paradigm shift, one that would enable us to understand nature, social behavior, communication, and consciousness as holistic elements interacting within an even broader living system that folded together mind and matter. Suitably popified, Bateson's antireductionist, deeply ecological take on cybernetics would eventually trickle down through the popular counterculture as holistic thought.

Studying everything from Balinese art to schizophrenia to the dolphin researches of John Lilly, Bateson helped give birth to a cybernetic model of the self. For Bateson, the self is an information-processing pattern inextricably linked through feedback loops to the body and the environment. Mind is not a transcendent blip of Cartesian awareness, but an immanent pattern that links the knower with the known in a larger "ecology of mind." For Bateson, the gnostic escape hatch is inconceivable, because there is no separate soul or self that can escape this larger ecology. In his article "The Cybernetics of 'Self,' " Bateson clarified his notions using the example of a man chopping down a tree. The process of constantly adjusting the swing of the ax to the shape of the cut face— an action that Bateson identified as a "mental" process—is not something just whirring around inside the man's skull. Instead, it is brought about by the whole system of "tree-eyes-brain-muscles-ax-stroke-tree." Information, which Bateson memorably defined as "a difference that makes a difference," flows through the total system, and this larger pattern of information has the "characteristics of immanent mind." This immanent mind is an ecology of information that permeates the material world, an intelligence much greater than the trivial thoughts zipping about the lumberjack's brain. Presumably, if our sweaty gentleman could cut out his internal chatter, he might be blessed with a visceral, intuitive perception of this larger networked intelligence.

If all this strikes you rather like cybernetic Zen, you have definitely been keeping your eye on the ball. Taoism and Zen, at least as the counterculture perceived them, offered a worldview based on natural flux, nondual awareness, and the spontaneous and transpersonal creativity that arises when the ordinary ego gets out of the way. Bateson himself gestured toward tenets of Eastern philosophy, as did the systems theory buff Fritjof Capra in his 1975 freak best-seller *The Tao of Physics*. Though Capra was criticized for his metaphysical leaps, the connection between systems theory and Eastern thought is no joke. As the scholar and ecological activist Joanna Macy later argued in her book *Mutual Causality in Buddhism and General Systems Theory,* both cybernetics and early Buddhist philosophy can be said to characterize the world as a nonlinear dance of mutually adjusting feedback loops. Macy points out that early Buddhists described the self as a product of twelve constantly interacting subcomponents, including sensation, desire, physical contact, and mental grasping. As in a cybernetic circuit, there is no single control center or stable point of agency; instead, the self emerges from a dynamic and interdependent ecology of mind and being.

Though the school of "humanist psychology" that Esalen helped bring to life rejected the grim determinism of behaviorism, it did not entirely *abandon* the model of the human-machine that still dominated more conventional psychological discourses. Instead, the Esalen crew attempted to cultivate the human-machine's cybernetic intelligence, amplifying its embodied awareness and psychological potential, and helping it get a handle on the various "programs" the self habitually and instinctively cycles through. The most hardwired manifestation of this dynamic cybernetic alchemy was biofeedback, first pioneered and popularized by Elmer Green. A relatively simple technological process, biofeedback allows human subjects to directly monitor their own brain waves (or other "invisible" physiological functions) in real time. With practice, one can extend one's volition and begin to consciously modulate and regulate these previously unconscious somatic functions. In essence, one learns to cyborg the self, managing stress levels or any number of physiological functions.

Of course, yogis had been regulating their heart rates and internal sphincters for thousands of years; in this sense, Hinduism's more physiological techniques of ecstasy formed a kind of old school cybernetics. Inevitably, Green and others came to suspect that biofeedback might serve as a handy pogo stick to help people reach the transpersonal states of consciousness that yogis and Zen monks took decades to cultivate—states that various EEG studies showed were tied to distinct patterns of brain wave activity. Green started hooking electrodes up to yogis, while the behaviorist Joe Kamiya proved that one could train oneself to alter brain wave states through biofeedback. As Green explained recently, "the average person, without having to subscribe to a religion, or to a dogma, or to a meditation system, could learn to move into the state of consciousness in which the seemingly infallible Source of Creativity could be invoked for the solution of problems."[126] Though the correlation of brain waves to specific states of consciousness was hardly an exact science, then or now, seekers inevitably started clamoring about "instant Zen."

Unfortunately, the brain wavers soon found that biofeedback was by no means a plug-and-play avenue to satori. Even at the time, Green argued that biofeedback training could only open the transpersonal gates when coupled with other techniques of consciousness expansion. "The True Self," he wrote, "can be quickly approached if the personality is made silent through theta EEG feedback and at the same time we focus detached attention 'upward.' "[127] For some, such cyberspiritual regimes worked, but such success only begged a larger set of questions: Does the True Self catalyzed by electronic gear wear the same face it does for Christian mystics who meet the midnight sun, or for Zen monks who discipline themselves with decades of subtle effort? If higher states of consciousness "de-automatize" the self from its habitual ruts, as many human potential advocates held, can they be made to do so automatically?

The experiences of Green and many others prove that cybernetic technologies can certainly be integrated into an intelligent pursuit of whatever quintessence lurks beneath our mundane masks. But the techno-idolatry that underlies a portion of the later New Age amply demonstrates how naive and vacuous this instrumentalist approach to spiritual self-improvement can become, especially when it gets mixed up with commodity culture and the old electromagnetic imaginary. Regardless of whatever psychospiritual phenomena they help trigger, consciousness gear like MindsEye Synergizers, neurosonic tapes, and polysynch MindLab light-and-sound machines amplify two questionable trends that already dominate the information age: an escapist desire for vivid and entertaining trances, and a utilitarian desire to reorganize the self according to the productive and efficient logic of the machine. Skimming through books like Michael Hutchison's *Megabrain Power* or New Age catalogs like *Tools for Exploration,* one realizes that the idea of "technologies of transformation" fits into our gadget-happy, Promethean land like a three-pronged plug with the ground ripped off.

The electronic wings of the New Age represent a quintessentially American blend of positive thinking and technological fetishism, but this tendency is hardly "New." In the mid–nineteenth century, for example, the ex-revivalist and mesmerist John Dods started hyping "electrical psychology," a set of practical techniques that he believed would ride the "glorious chariot of science with its ever increasing power, magnificence, and glory."[128] For Dods, "electricity" acted as God's invisible spiritual agency, and was thus the medium that God used to directly change the material world. Drawing inspiration from one of the new media of his day, Dods argued that by cultivating the electrical powers available in the mesmeric trance, we can make ourselves and our lives a "visible daguerreotype" of God's electrical emanations. That is, just as the daguerreotype—an early form of photography—captured the visible reality of light on the blank surface of silver-coated metallic plate, so could the mind use the electric vibrations of mesmerism to overcome external limitations and impress new visions onto the world itself.

By the end of the nineteenth century, this dream of mind over matter would mutate into the American cult of positive thinking. According to the mesmerist and healer Phineas Quimby, one of the early ideologues of this new school, sickness and disease were the result of negative thoughts that blocked the nurturing flows of animal magnetism. As one of the first self-helpers, Quimby had little interest in the theoretical or mystical questions that dominated the minds of many earlier mesmerists. By putting his patients in direct contact with "a higher source," Quimby simply wanted to improve their outlook on life, a positive attitude that he believed would directly restore their health and well-being. With his "Mind Cure Science," Quimby helped set the stage for the rise of Christian Science and the New Thought movement, whose affirmations live on today in the New Age mantra that "you create your own reality."

Without a doubt, positive thinking can work wonders. But for Mind Scientists and New Agers alike, this hands-on "science" of consciousness improvement became infected with America's uncritical faith in scientific and technological progress. Detached from a deep questioning of both social and spiritual life, such instrumental approaches to the power of the mind can rapidly lead their users into a rather infantile self-obsession. Hard-core devotees of positive thinking often find themselves reproducing the mythic scenario that Marshall McLuhan argued was the archetypal scene of all technology: Narcissus gazing into the pool, mesmerized by his own reflection.

As its name indicates, the New Age rests on a social vision of utopia as well as a vision of individual psychic revolution. One's own self-realization contributes to a creative and healing culture; by programming a better reality, one helps actualize a "paradigm shift" that collectively brings together mind and body, earth and culture, science and spirit. And yet in practice, New Agers often aim for goals barely distinguishable from the dominant logic of success that drives commercial culture—goals like efficiency, satisfaction, productivity, performance, and control, not to mention the prosperity gospel that holds that the self is actualized through money. Though these Extropian values certainly have their place, they often run directly counter to the far less quantifiable collective concerns and mystical passions traditionally associated with the taxing dance of spiritual growth, or with the loving and mysterious influx of the sacred. Without a larger ethical, aesthetic, or religious cosmology, engineered states of consciousness can easily become new power tools for the same old clutching ego.

Once its emphasis on transpersonal unity loses any genuine transcendent ground, New Age logic slides with unsettling ease into corporate management jargon and business success seminars. In the 1970s, one of the most popular and influential New Age self-improvement regimes was est, an instrumentalist and thoroughly secular mishmash of Scientology, Gestalt-styled psychotherapies, and American Zen. Providing new "data" about reality, and leading people through various "processes" over long and arduous weekends, est sought to break down people's self-limiting beliefs. Enlightenment, they would learn, is knowing that you are a machine, and thus taking control of your own programs and conditioning. But as many concerned observers noted, the est organization also did plenty of its own psychological programming along the way. Though est graduates were hardly the authoritarian robot army that some of the movement's detractors claimed, the organization did function as what the sociologist Steven Tipton called a "boot camp for bureaucracy."

Today one of the slickest New Age corporate cheerleaders is the big-bucks motivational counselor Anthony Robbins, a charismatic but eerily synthetic Schwarzenegger lookalike often found hawking his wares on television infomercials. To help his customers achieve happiness and satisfaction, Robbins digs through the human potential toolkit, showing how self-affirmations, psychological discipline, spiritual workouts, and the inevitable battery of Personal Power tapes can help people "achieve their goals." But Robbins never makes the spiritual move, which is to question the goals themselves. For it may be the case that these goals, embraced by an anxious ego with immortalist fantasies or picked up like the flu from the smiling happy people on TV, are the very source of the sense of failure, misery, and bondage that Robbins promises to banish.

Altered Solid States

The popular New Age image of "sacred technologies" suggests that Ellul was right, and that the empirical and instrumentalist logic of technique has colonized the human spirit. But though this tinkerer's logic erodes traditional theological foundations like faith, grace, and divine agency, it also embodies a pragmatic and demystifying bent that may go a long way toward correcting the ideological absolutism, violent shenanigans, and parochial folklore that characterize so much religious history. As Gurdjieff hinted, the dispassionate and pragmatic mind-set of the modern world, a mind-set at home with machines, science, and instrumental techniques, can be a boon to twentieth-century seekers, steering them away from sticky old myths or contemporary delusions while engendering a discriminating, objective, and self-critical perspective that keeps them always on their toes.

Not surprisingly, many of the human potential movement's cybernetic gurus owe much to Gurdjieff and his spirit of dispassionate self-observation. Take the work of the psychologist Charles Tart, who now teaches at the University of California at Davis. After decades of research and writing, Tart is still best known for *Altered States of Consciousness,* a landmark collection he edited in 1969. In the book, Tart and many other contributors turned their laboratory-bred eyes toward the same inner world that mesmerists began charting over a century before. They investigated hypnosis, trance, hypnogogia, and dreams, while also exploring more with-it topics like Zen meditation, psychedelic drugs, and brain wave biofeedback. Without closing the door on the more exalted and even spiritual potentials of the self, Tart and company soberly analyzed these "states," treating them as cybernetic systems of awareness that stabilize themselves by establishing feedback loops between different mechanisms of perception and cognition. Tart and his colleagues also suggested that these cognitive states not only drastically change the world we perceive, but can be cultivated as well, as both Hindu yogis and exceptional Western psychonauts prove.

Eventually, Tart came to interrogate our "normal" state of consciousness as well. He concluded that the mundane world we ordinarily perceive, relate to, and understand with our "common sense" is both physiologically and psychologically a *simulation,* a determined product of essentially arbitrary perceptual filters, culturally conditioned reflexes, and habitual ways of reading the world rooted in our biological past. Tart was no postmodern relativist: He believed that some simulations fit the outside world better than others. But in analyzing ordinary consciousness, Tart came to believe that our day-to-day simulations of the world were usually mucked up with unconscious assumptions, projections, delusions, and cultural myths.

In 1986, Tart published *Waking Up,* a "nuts-and-bolts" self-help book heavily indebted to his years studying the Gurdjieff Work with teachers at Esalen and elsewhere. In the book, Tart chalks up the bulk of our daily thoughts and behaviors to "consensus trance"—the particular social construction of reality we have been hypnotically conditioned to perceive and maintain since birth. Using a well-crafted analogy of a computer-driven robot-crane, Tart argues that most of our precious human traits are basically automatic, "programmed," as it were, by evolutionary habits and social mechanisms. Despite this rather withering and mechanistic exposure of the myth of self-consciousness, Tart remains cautiously upbeat. In order for our human potential to begin to bloom, he argues, we first need to get in touch with our inner machine. "By studying machines, we can learn about ourselves," he writes. "By fully recognizing and studying our machinelike qualities, . . . it is possible to take a step no other machine can take: we can become genuinely human and transcend our machinelike qualities and destiny."[129] This transcendence occurs through the cybernetic development of the higher control center—Gurdjieff's elusive I—which in turn allows us to extend the capacities of our bodies, emotions, and intellects.

Unlike so many psychospiritual teachers attracted to this line of thought, Tart also recognized the dangers of the spiritual cyborg. Even practices as different as the Gurdjieff Work, est, Scientology, and Extropianism show a strong tendency toward a certain heartlessness, an elitist rigor that places the gnostic salvation of the individual and the in-group far beyond the problems of humanity as a whole. In sharp contrast, Tart insisted that compassion was not only a necessary complement to dispassionate wisdom, but that it serves as one of the most highly evolved and intelligent components of human consciousness—a notion Tart partly derived from Mahayana Buddhism and its image of the bodhisattva, who refuses to enter nirvana until all sentient beings are awakened.

Though his research into parapsychology has raised many an eyebrow, Tart remains a paragon of grounded and pragmatic cybernetic spirituality. Other altered states pioneers, however, got pretty bent out of shape on their climb to the higher control centers. One of the most fascinating of these characters is John Lilly, a neuroscientist, psychonaut, and Esalen workshop leader who clung to the dispassionate style of objective science even as he plumbed the iridescent fractal maw of psychedelic hyperspace. In the 1950s, Lilly had all the markings of a high priest of the hard sciences: a Cal Tech degree, an M.S. in neuroscience, and a gig at the National Institutes of Health studying the interface between mind and brain. Schooled as a reductionist, Lilly wanted to prove empirically that the mind was indeed contained inside the "biocomputer" of the brain. So the good doctor would while away the hours sticking electrodes into monkey brains, proving how easy it is to stimulate terror and orgasms alike with electric current. Lilly's hardwired Pavlovian excursions into electromagnetic control soon drew the interest of Pentagon operatives, who showed up at his lab one day asking questions about certain hairless cousins of the monkey clan. The appearance of these sinister archons eventually convinced Lilly that he could not continue his research without becoming drawn into a sticky federal web of darkside behaviorism and electronic mind-control projects. So he quit the NIH and went off to study interspecies communication with dolphins, nifty work immortalized in the film *The Day of the Dolphin*.

In the 1950s, most members of the psychological establishment believed that external stimuli alone kept the mind humming and that the brain would promptly go to sleep if those incoming signals were squelched. To test this crudely materialist theory, Lilly built an isolation tank that muffled external sensory stimulation, and then clambered inside. After spending hours floating in his jet-black saltwater womb, Lilly discovered that mental phenomena were not simply reactive, but internally generated. Moreover, they were potentially mind-blowing as well. After an hour or so, Lilly found himself slipping into strange, relaxing, and sometimes visionary states of consciousness that lay far beyond the cartography of conventional psychiatric charts.

Once outside the orbit of the NIH, Lilly's isolation tank experiments put him on a collision course with LSD-25, then making the rounds among North America's more adventurous psychotherapists. After gobbling jaw-dropping doses of acid, Lilly would gaze upon the screen of his internal theater with the icy enthusiasm of a postdoc peering at a paramecium. After many such experiments, Lilly concluded that the "circuits" of the "human biocomputer" were not only wired by evolution but were constantly being programmed by the feedback loops established between the environment and that biocomputer's assumptions about the world. LSD not only laid bare the workings of these invisible circuits but allowed one to reprogram one's experience, "bootstrapping" new modes of consciousness and perception into experience. "As the theory [of the biocomputer] entered and reprogrammed my thinking-feeling machinery," Lilly wrote, "my life changed rapidly and radically. New inner spaces opened up; new understanding and humor appeared."[130] Lilly's mantra of "self-metaprogramming" became well known among spiritual cyborgs: "What one believes to be true, either is true or becomes true in one's mind, within limits to be determined experimentally and experientially. These limits are beliefs to be transcended."[131] In essence, the mind was seen as the ultimate universal computer, capable of simulating any reality under the sun.

Though Lilly heartily rejected theology, Eastern gurus, and psychedelic mumbo jumbo, he also logged serious time with Oscar Ichazo and his student Claudio Naranjo, both Gurdjieffean-styled esoteric teachers from Chile who were committed to the dispassionate work of self-observation and self-remembering. When Lilly himself gave workshops at Esalen and other human potential centers, he would demonstrate his ideas by using high-fidelity tape loops that repeated a single word over and over. He used these loops not to hypnotize his audience, but to demonstrate that the mind inevitably began "hearing" different words, and that these variations could be preprogrammed in advance. These cut-and-paste, tape-machine mutations paled before the psychedelic protocols Lilly designed for himself, especially once he discovered ketamine, an injectable tranquilizer that produces a disembodied state of deep-space psychedelia far more alien than LSD's fractal electronica. With the obsessive self-absorption of a late-night hacker, Lilly became addicted to "K," sometimes decoupling from consensus reality for weeks at a time. Even as his mind went overboard, Lilly's "scientific" reports back from the depths continued to express the crucial tension that lies at the heart of techgnosis: the tension between consciousness and the machine.

In one particularly knee-rattling revelation, Lilly experienced the universe as an utterly dispassionate and objective "cosmic computer," a vast and labyrinthine hierarchy of meaningless automata alternately programming and being programmed by other senseless mechanisms. In essence, Lilly entered Edward Fredkin's universal cellular automaton, and he experienced this intellectually compelling cosmology as an unmitigated and terrifying hell. Over time, Lilly also started channeling messages from the comet Kohoutek. He came to believe that a nonorganic, solid-state extraterrestrial civilization was controlling the spread of all technologies, communications systems, and control mechanisms on earth. This civilization was set on killing off organic life and replacing it with a Borg-like hive mind of hardwired consciousness.

Lilly was by no means the only countercultural cyberneticist to dream of galactic machines. During the 1960s, Timothy Leary was the archetypal egghead hippie, draping himself with guru flowers and delving into *The Tibetan Book of the Dead* for maps of the psychedelic funhouse. But by the mid-1970s, he had rejected the "sweet custard mush" of Eastern mysticism and embraced a proto-Extropian worldview that he dubbed S.M.I.²L.E., an acronym formed from his pet obsessions at the time: Space Migration, Intelligence Increase, Life Extension. In a number of turgid if influential books, Leary engineered transformational models of the self out of his mildly tongue-in-cheek blend of developmental psychology, cybernetic jargon, and tanked-up cosmic boosterism.

Sifting through the half-baked neologisms of 1977's *Exo-Psychology*—a work rather impishly subtitled "A Manual on the Use of the Human Nervous System According to the Instructions of the Manufacturers"—one discovers some surprisingly intriguing technomystical discussions of the only "robot designed to discover the circuitry which

programs its behavior." Leary outlines the development of human consciousness according to eight progressively "higher" circuits. When they
are locked into the first four "terrestrial" circuits, people are basically
asleep, robotically plugged into the fears and rewards of mammalian
psychology, consensus trance, and the insectoid hive mind of industrial
society. Drugs and metaprogramming tricks like yoga and isolation
tanks help trigger the next four circuits, which take us progressively further into nonordinary reality. Liberated from psychosocial repression,
the brain begins experiencing itself as an "electromagnetic transceiver"
of galactic information; at a later stage, we establish communication
with the genetic code itself, a cosmic database that contains the collective history of the species and the plans for its future.

While claiming that these higher circuits tune in to "mystical" levels
of reality, Leary always described them in the mechanistic language of
biochemicals, neural pathways, electromagnetic waves, and genes. No
"soul" emerges along the way. Like the Extropians, Leary looked to evolution as the true source of cosmic meaning and agency, as DNA
becomes the real hero beneath our thousand faces. In a cosmic clown
twist on Francis Crick's theory that DNA may have been seeded from the
stars, Leary argued that the double helix arrived on the planet with the
sole purpose of producing intelligent life that could one day return to its
sidereal palace. Literalizing the transcendent urge that animates gnostic
desire, Leary claimed that activating the four higher circuits of his model
would make us "post-terrestrial," preparing us for life in space.

In Leary's cybernetic parable, even the technological developments of
modern civilization are coded in DNA. Leary suggests that the massive
social changes that emerged from the watershed year of 1945 were programmed in advance, DNA-spawned triggers for a new phase of human
mutation. The baby boomers were the first crop of offworld superbrights, destined to turn on the higher circuits, go to the moon, build
space stations, get "high." With a brash optimism at once admirable and
terrifying, Leary assures us that if we keep our eyes on the big picture,
we have nothing to fear. "Billions of similar planets have suffered
through Hiroshimas, youth-drug cults, and prime-time television."[132]
Radioactivity, electromagnetic technologies, psychedelics, food addi-
tives, and even industrial toxins are all part of the plan, signals that
sound Darwin's final trump: wake up, mutate, and ascend. Echoing the
otherworldly framework of "The Hymn of the Pearl," Leary writes:

The brain is an extraterrestrial organ. The brain is an alien intelligence. The brain has no more concern for earthly affairs than the cultured, sympathetic traveler for the native village in which SHe [*sic*] spends the night.[133]

This is the voice of the technomystical elect, the cool Gurdjieffean aristocrat who has overcome his own programmed behavior and now views the ordinary human personality as "an ignorant, gross, uneducated, opinionated, irascible rural inn-keeper." As we saw with the Extropians, a bracing arrogance lurks beneath the posthuman and techgnostic rerun of Darwin's survival of the fittest.

At the same time, Leary's vibrant "science faction" remains a creative if delirious call to keep our hands on the rudder of the self, a necessary skill at a time when human consciousness is increasingly interwoven with electronic technologies and media networks. Without going as far as Leary, it does seem that we need to rethink our fundamental relationship to mechanism, both in ourselves and in the world. In a 1992 essay entitled "Remaking Social Practices," the French psychologist and philosopher Felix Guattari noted how virulently we continue to oppose the machine to the human spirit: "Certain philosophies hold that modern technology has blocked access to our ontological foundations, to primordial being." But, he asks, what if the contrary were true, and that "a revival of spirit and human values could be attendant upon a new alliance with machines"?[134] This is the intuition that drives the spiritual cyborg into such uncharted and treacherous seas.

In this sense, Leary's prescient plunge into personal computer evangelism in the 1980s was not simply a sign of his relentless and desperate need to constantly ride the cutting edge. As Leary noted in 1987, when he revised *Exo-Psychology* into *Info-Psychology*, the new digital devices were destined to reawaken the cybernetic freak dream of reprogramming one's states of consciousness. Etymologically speaking, after all, computers are literally *psychedelic;* that is, they manifest the mind. Many psychonauts recognized the potential of personal computers long before the rest of the culture caught on, and a few made fortunes off their iridescent intuitions. With his canny sociological radar, Leary also saw how much the offworld impulse toward outer space and higher planes would come to focus on the "inner," or cyber, space of the computer. For reasons we will track down in the next chapter, many of the counterculture's lingering dreams of self-determination and creative magic wound up migrating into the universe of digital code. With the spread of personal computers, the cyborg possibilities of the human-machine interface, spiritual and not, would fragment, decentralize, and begin to spin out of control. The System itself would begin to hallucinate, and the most popular technique of ecstasy would become the ecstasy of communication.

a most enchanting machine

In the 1960s, the utopian imaginary seized America more forcefully than
it had in living memory. For all the violence and waste the counterculture both encountered and engendered, it held out a furious hope for a
better society, and this fury took the form of a millennialist expectation
that ran deeper than reason. Freaks and radicals across the land felt in
their guts that, whether it was called the Revolution or the Aquarian
Age, a new and more perfect world was just dying to dawn, and this visceral sense of anticipation helped keep the movement's internal contradictions at bay long enough to confront the System with a loosely united
front. But when neither the hard rain nor the garden arrived, the counterculture's political radicalism and magical desires fragmented and dispersed. In the 1970s, they found new purchase among such balkanized
tribes as feminists, whale savers, religious cults, terrorist cells, liberal arts
professors, and the nomadic heads who tracked the Grateful Dead
through fields and parking lots across the land. But of all the cultural
zones that wound up hosting lingering freak dreams, undoubtedly the
most unexpected was the universe of digital code, a world tucked inside
miniaturized versions of the very machines that once epitomized blue-
suited technocracy and military command and control.

Today, the rhetoric that enchants personal computers and digital
communication networks continues to draw upon such sixties values as
radical democracy, personal empowerment, alternative community, and
a decentralized society of free-flowing data. For a few years there, even
Newt Gingrich sounded like an anarchist longhair with a megaphone as
he spouted techno-Republican visions of the information age. In other
circles, the computer radiates overtly cosmic vibrations, especially
within the mostly Northern Californian subculture that Mark Dery calls
"cyberdelia," a world of ravers, technopagan programmers, and high-
tech hedonists who attempt to reconcile "the transcendentalist impulses
of sixties counterculture with the infomania of the nineties."[135] But this
hopped-up crew, already long past its prime, is only the most extreme
example of a hallucinatory bitstream whose lava-lamp flows drip into

PC Computing ad copy, fractal screen savers, virtual reality, videogame design, and the layout of *Wired*.

On closer inspection, the digital remastering of the counterculture should not seem altogether surprising, for the utopia of the sixties was in many ways a utopia of liberated technique. With designer-prophets like Buckminster Fuller and Paolo Soleri at the visionary helm, one wing of freak technophiles sought to build a new helm for spaceship earth. Attempting to design a "people's technology" that would harmonize with the rhythms of organic life, these pioneers embodied the same spirit of self-sufficiency and social tinkering that lay behind the experimental religious communes that once dotted nineteenth-century America. Among these architects of community, the most popular almanac was without a doubt the *Whole Earth Catalog*, founded by the Merry Prankster Stewart Brand in 1968 as an "outlaw information service" that promised "Access to Tools." Most of the tools listed in the catalog were preindustrial marvels discarded in the hell-bent juggernaut of the twentieth century—woodburning stoves, teepees, techniques for organic horticulture and midwifery. But the *Whole Earth Catalog* was also cottage-published and typeset for a fraction of the cost of mainstream magazines, and its editors drooled over hands-on media technologies as well—cameras, synthesizers, stereos, and, most significant for our tale, computers.

In a landmark 1972 article for *Esquire,* Stewart Brand coined the term "personal computer." Much of Brand's fascination with the machines reflected his commitment to Gregory Bateson's version of cybernetic systems theory, which offered a novel, productive, and computer-friendly way of thinking about the ecology and technology of design. Some hippie holists nursed a fascination with *all* systems, circuit boards as well as tidepools. As Robert Pirsig put it in his 1974 best-seller *Zen and the Art of Motorcycle Maintenance,* "The Buddha, the God-head, resides quite as comfortably in the circuits of a digital computer or the gears of a cycle transmission as he does at the top of a mountain or in the petals of a flower."[136] Along with the poet Richard Brautigan, a few freaks imagined a "cybernetic ecology" where animals and humans lived in "mutually programming harmony . . . all watched over by machines of loving grace."[137]

Some members of the counterculture had more political reasons for embracing computers. In 1970, a loose affiliation of dropout computer scientists and radicalized programmers in Berkeley realized that computers offered a potential alternative to the top-down information control that typified technocratic institutions and the mass media. These populist geeks imagined a society driven by the "Hacker Ethics" that the author Steven Levy traces to the late-night computer labs of MIT: an anarchic blend of hands-on control, decentralized networks, and a fierce commitment to the free flow of information. In the early 1970s, a handful of these Berkeley computer buffs made a donated IBM mainframe called Resource One available to the public. Others created Community Memory, a network of terminals stuck in libraries and record shops that served as a primitive bulletin board system, and which soon featured a now familiar stew of data swaps, soft sells, graffiti, and weird personas.

Neither Resource One nor Community Memory lasted long, and the countercultural dream of bringing computers to the people would have to wait some years, until the scruffy hardware hobbyists at the Homebrew Computer Club near Stanford University started building their own micromachines. Homebrew was the kind of place where a slovenly mastermind like Steven Wozniak felt at home showing off his cleverly hacked gear. It was also the kind of place that attracted the acidhead and part-time Buddhist Steven Jobs, whose fruitarian diet may have partly inspired the name of the computer he started selling out of a garage with Woz: the Apple. With a name that hearkened back to Eden's fruit of knowledge (and an initial selling price of $666), the Apple proffered the Promethean dream of putting godly power in your hands. People didn't just bite the thing—they swallowed it whole. As it turned out, Jobs was not the only former psychedelic bum who made a fortune on the personal computer revolution; Mitch Kapor, the designer of the enormously successful spreadsheet software Lotus 1-2-3, once taught transcendental meditation and credited "recreational chemicals" with sharpening his business acumen.

As the eighties progressed, the dreams of the counterculture found a new home in the decentralized digital commons that computer networks had woven through the copper cables and routers of the telephone system. For years bulletin board systems had allowed mainframe UNIX jockeys to exchange technical tips, but it wasn't until people started logging on from personal computers that these computer-mediated conversations bloomed into the "virtual communities" and "grassroots group minds" described by Howard Rheingold. Rheingold knew whereof he spoke. He was an editor and contributor to the *Whole Earth Review*, and the granddaddy of these communal BBSes had its roots firmly planted in the Whole Earth. In 1985, Stewart Brand and a former member of Wavy Gravy's Hog Farm founded the WELL—the Whole Earth 'Lectronic Link. Signing up some veterans from the Farm, one of the longest-lived communes of the 1960s, Brand hoped to structure the WELL in a manner that would naturally breed community. The system would be an "open-ended universe," self-governing and self-designing—a cybernetic ecology of minds. And for the smart, white, and liberal Bay Area denizens who started posting to the WELL's various conferences, the experiment worked like a charm. By creating a place where the clever exchange of helpful information became what Rheingold calls a source for "social capital," the WELL played the role of the "superior man" described in the *I Ching* hexagram called the Well: "the superior man encourages the people at their work, / And exhorts them to help one another."

Early in its history, the WELL also became a way station for hardcore fans of the Grateful Dead, one of the hoariest institutions of Bay Area freakdom. By the mid-1980s, the Dead were one of the sole living links to sixties bacchanalia, their iridescent jams and creatively engineered sound systems stretching all the way back to Prankster days. Though superficially unsuited for a decade associated with yuppie cokeheads and glossy New Wave haircuts, the Dead actually exploded in popularity as the eighties wore on. And one of their greatest draws was the nomadic community that Deadheads had managed to carve out of the belly of commodity culture. With their earthy costumes, bumper sticker iconography, and revival-tent enthusiasm for ritualized ecstasy, Deadheads became the closest thing we'll probably ever see to devotees of a mass psychedelic religion. Alongside their commitment to spontaneous experience and live performance, many Deadheads were also collector freaks and compulsive infomaniacs. During shows, many would regularly pause in the midst of their ecstatic trance-dancing to scribble down the set list; others gathered in the bootleg section of the concert floor to record the performance with high-tech equipment and microscopic concentration. Outside the hall, tapes were hoarded and swapped like baseball cards, while the most devoted geeks compiled mountains of set list data into thick "DeadBases."

On top of their already rather virtual community, this infomania made the Deadhead transition to information space even more fruitful.

Deadheads soon became the WELL's single largest source of income and new members, and they created a community boisterous enough to attract the attention of John Perry Barlow, a prep school friend of Dead guitarist Bob Weir and the wordsmith behind a number of Dead songs. As we saw in the last chapter, Barlow went on to become one of the earliest and most colorful popular proponents of the information society, writing articulate pieces about hackers, hobnobbing with the budding digerati, and cofounding the Electronic Frontier Foundation with Mitch Kapor—an organization whose defense of cyberrights owed much of its early punch to the pioneer wing of the sixties counterculture.

The genteel ex-hippies who first dug the WELL were not the only cognitive dissidents to leave their swirly fingerprints on the blossoming computer culture of the late 1980s and early 1990s. Across the bay from the Sausalito houseboats that the Whole Earth folks called home, the freak machine was being savagely hacked anew by a mutant breed of weirdos lurking in the Berkeley hills. Led by a troll-like former Yippie named R. U. Sirius and a wealthy scion known as Queen Mu, this merrily posthumanist crew churned out *Mondo 2000*, a magazine that self-consciously spearheaded a slick new underground culture between its glossy, Photoshop-spawned pages. Infusing the Prankster psychedelia of the sixties with (over)doses of slacker irony and unrepentant techno-Prometheanism, *Mondo 2000* created the demimonde it reported, a kinky pop-up romper room of brain machines, teledildonics, virtual reality games, fetish fashions, electronic dance music, and new designer drugs. It was a rave on paper.

Mowing down the garden of flower power with cyberpunk glee, *Mondo* nonetheless perpetuated the freak dream by translating hedonism onto the perceptual plane (hence its fascination with virtual sex). As Mark Dery notes, the magazine had "one foot in the Aquarian age and the other in a Brave New World."[138] But though it served up smart non-New Agey assessments of mind-enhancing drugs and gadgets, the magazine's smorgasbord of brainware, neural boosters, and sound-and-light gizmos often seemed to be whirring and buzzing in the dark. In *Mondo*'s hands, consciousness-altering techniques became divorced from any broader notion of consciousness, social or spiritual. Everything was reduced to knobs and sliders on the control panel of the central nervous system. Compared with the flaky rhetoric of sixties utopians, *Mondo*'s brash attitude reflected a refreshing frankness about the technical dimension of our pleasures, visions, and ecstasies. But from another angle, the hopped-up, plugged-in superbrights of the *Mondo* world were little more than mindless instrumentalists, "users" in the most decadent sense of the term.

Perhaps the most curious property of *Mondo*'s digital Kool-Aid was how deeply it saturated the groundwater of Silicon Valley. R. U. Sirius reported that a "large portion" of *Mondo*'s audience were successful businesspeople in the information industry, while a brochure for potential advertisers boasted that 80 percent of readers were computerfolk with a median income of sixty-five thousand dollars. *Mondo*'s millennialist buzz and info-overloaded layout eventually made their way into the far more mainstream San Francisco magazine *Wired* (whose editorial vision was shaped in part by Kevin Kelly, another member of the Whole Earth gang). Though *Wired* shaved off *Mondo*'s hairier kinks and replaced its anarchist rants with corporate libertarianism, the *"Rolling Stone* of the Information Age" rode into town on *Mondo*'s fractal wave of cyberdelia, gadget fetishism, and sincere devotion to the fiercely creative edges of the digital community.

The computer industry's infatuation with the "New Edge" represented by *Mondo* and *Wired* also signifies a strange mutation in the halls of infotech's corporate culture. The British authors Richard Barbrook and Andy Cameron identify this new face of information capitalism as "the California ideology," an economic and political vision that "promiscuously combines the free-wheeling spirit of the hippies and the entrepreneurial zeal of the yuppies." While many Silicon Valley firms are straitlaced operations, others consciously design a wacky, freewheeling environment that encourages their employees to pour every ounce of their creative juices into new products and research—a trend that goes back at least to Xerox PARC in the 1970s, which serviced its brilliant Menlo Park researchers with beanbags and Frisbees.

By taking controlled sips of California's creative anarchy, its "go with the flow" Beat Taoism, the computer industry discovered new philosophies of management and productivity that were appropriate to the increasingly chaotic global market their products were helping to produce. Such philosophies are by no means limited to the computer industry, of course.

Faced with information overload, a spin-cycle marketplace, and the broiling seas of deregulation, businesspeople across the globe are now learning to "surf"—a supremely Californian image based on loosening top-down control and resiliently responding to the unpredictable flux of capital, data, and shifting demand. Management gurus speak an increasingly New Age lingo of "thriving on chaos," generating "dynamic synergy," and cultivating the Tao of the Dow. In *Out of Control,* his manifesto of cybernetic technocapitalist evolution, *Wired* editor Kevin Kelly even quotes Lao Tzu, whose wisdom could "be a motto for a gung-ho 21st century Silicon Valley startup."[139]

In 1968, Marshall McLuhan prophesied that "the computer is the LSD of the business world."[140] But in today's Silicon Valley and San Francisco's multimedia gulch, computers *plus* LSD sometimes seems like the formula for success. For years, Apple bought Grateful Dead tickets for employees at the end of the year, and the band's tie-dyed iconography could even be spotted at the NASA-Ames military research facility in Mountain View, a home for hard-core virtual reality research. In a 1991 *GQ* article, Walter Kirn reports on the industry's "no sweat attitude toward chemical recreation," noting that Intel and other major corporations apparently give employees plenty of advance warning for the urine tests they are required to take. Moreover, most psychedelics cannot be traced in such screenings—almost an argument-by-design for their use as R&D enhancers. Kirn points out that Silicon Valley's corporate heads didn't just come to accommodate the fact that many of their most brilliant employees liked to gobble weird drugs—they also realized that "weirdness can be an export commodity." Experienced and intelligent trippers are often characterized by a fluid sense of perception, a willingness to tinker with cognitive structures, and a sensitivity to what Gregory Bateson called "the pattern that connects"—just the kind of mental gymnastics that come in handy when you're crafting the giddy complexities of information space.

Corporate cyberdelia is only one indication of the integration of certain countercultural techniques of ecstasy into the fabric of West Coast information society. One of the great paranoid rumors of the 1960s was that the freaks were going to pour LSD into the water supply; it may turn out that digital devices and media machines wind up dosing the population, infusing an undeniably psychedelic mode of cognition into the culture at large. Modems pry open Huxley's mental "reducing valve" and let in the networked Mind at Large, while digital animation studios routinely reproduce the kaleidoscopic mandalas that wallpaper the acidhead's inner eye. Techno music and its various electronic offshoots generate sonic psychedelia with the precision of an EEG, while the hyperfast editing and explosive computer graphics of Hollywood blockbusters and TV toy ads reach a hallucinogenic pitch that would leave Wavy Gravy slack-jawed. Computers and electronic media are turning everyone on, and cyberspace is shaping up as the virtual, mutable landscape of the melting collective mind. The liberating energies of ecstasy, defined as the explosive expansion of the self outside its quotidian boundaries and lionized by the ideologues of the sixties counterculture, are now a technological fact.

According to Jacques Ellul, this technological ecstasy should neither surprise nor please us. In one of his sour and foreboding prophecies, made way back in 1954, Ellul wrote:

> We must conclude that it is far from accidental that ecstatic phenomena have developed to the greatest degree in the most technicized societies. And it is to be expected that these phenomena will continue to increase. This indicates nothing less than the subjection of mankind's new religious life to technique. . . . Ecstasy is subject to the world of technique and is its servant.[141]

Like Eliade, Ellul recognized the link between techniques and ecstasy, but the Frenchman saw this symbiosis operating on a societywide basis, with mass technology catalyzing dangerous and hyperkinetic mass emotions that swamped the stillness and sobriety of the moral individual's inner life. For Ellul, the freak embrace of consciousness technology was not a spiritual resistance to the dominant society, but a complete capitulation to it. In this sense, the re-emergence of so many motifs of the sixties counterculture within the rhetoric of information culture follows a distressingly predictable logic, as the System simply extends its technological tendrils ever deeper into the soul.

Ellul's critique is ultimately theological, and one senses a powerful odor of fire and brimstone wafting through his depiction of the autonomous and increasingly ferocious force of *technique*. Indeed, in *The Technological Society,* Ellul contrasts our fragmented, harried days with the social homogeneity and coherence of the theocratic Middle Ages, which, he claims, rejected technical development with "the moral judgment which Christians passed on all human activities."[142] It must be said that Ellul got his history of invention wrong; as the historian David Noble has convincingly shown, medieval monasteries spawned the perfectionist project of technology in the first place. Monasteries also exuberantly adopted one of the most psychologically constraining mechanisms of control found in the premodern world—the clock. But what's important here is that, beneath his penetrating political attacks on the inhuman engines of enterprise and control, Ellul shares orthodox Christianity's rather pessimistic assessment of humanity's Luciferic tendency to deny our fundamental foolishness and to rebel restlessly against the divine order by constantly trying to manipulate the world.

Throughout *The Technological Society,* as well as the doomy plaints of many later technology critics, one hears echoes of the tale of Faust, the hubristic wizard of folktales and high literature who signed on Mephisto's dotted line in exchange for knowledge, power, and worldly command. These echoes of magic are not anachronisms. As the lore of Hermes Trismegistus reminds us, technology operates as easily in a magical universe as a rational one; indeed, from the perspective of cultural narratives and political power, technology often functions *as* magic. In the next section, we will see that magic is one valid way of understanding the workings of propaganda, advertising, and mass media, those modern machineries of perceptual manipulation that often explicitly deploy the rhetoric of enchantment. In this sense, the liberatory and ecstatic techniques of the sixties counterculture should not be seen as an anomalous eruption of occult superstition into postwar society, but as a particularly vibrant battle in the twentieth century's immense war of social sorcery.

Social Imagineering

More than a century ago, when European anthropologists first started tracking down the dwellers of the jungles and outbacks of earth, they did not believe, as many white folks do today, that the magic and medicine of shamans and witch doctors might heal Western souls from the ravages of technology and modern science. Early anthropologists had no interest in guzzling brews or trying their hand at ancient ritual techniques; they were there, pen in hand, to classify, record, and analyze. Because their enterprise was self-consciously "scientific," field researchers and anthropological theorists were particularly obsessed with delineating the distinctions and, to a lesser extent, the continuities between native magic and modern science. According to the influential theories of old school

British thinkers like Sir Edward Tylor and Sir James Frazer, the magical practices that witch doctors wielded within animist societies functioned as proto- or pseudosciences. In this view, magic was not so much religious mumbo jumbo as the most stunted, larval stage of the empirical understanding of nature. By establishing this evolutionary link, anthropologists also constructed a universal narrative of intellectual progress that placed European civilization at the head of the pack. It was also, in many ways, true: Both traditional magic and modern science are concerned with empirically understanding and manipulating natural forces and hidden universal laws.

But by framing magic as nothing more than an ignorant pit stop along the glorious march toward objective rationality, early anthropologists tended to overlook the positive aspects of what gets lost in the transition from magic to science. And what gets lost is the resonating worldview that organically bound the perceptions and procedures of the magician to a holistic webwork of cosmic, animal, and ancestral forces. This worldview is the "anthropological matrix" we discussed in chapter 1: a living field of cultural practices and narratives that are inextricably woven into the world of objects and natural laws, and that therefore can never be entirely reduced to an underlying objective reality. One might argue that the early Western practitioners of the "human sciences" were themselves somewhat ignorant, for they believed that scientific procedures enabled them to transcend the anthropological matrix of their own cultures.

As the social and ecological psychiatrists of their societies, shamans and native healers did not separate magic as empirical science from magic as virtual theater, a theater where the magic-worker maintained the anthropological matrix by performing it into existence. So while magicians operated on the material level of stone, flame, and herb, they also aimed their beams at the human imagination, that primordial faculty of the mind that weaves its webs between perception, memory, and dream. Using language, costumes, gestures, song, and stagecraft, magicians applied *techne* to the social imagination, actively tweaking the images, desires, and stories that partly structure the collective psyche. Through this creative manipulation of phantasms, magicians conjured up perceptions, habits, and states of consciousness, which in turn impacted the construction of native reality as a whole. Not necromancy, but neuromancy.

If Bruno Latour is right, and the West never left the anthropological matrix, then what are the differences between the worlds that magicians and scientists construct? In his book *Magic, Science, Religion, and the Scope of Rationality,* the anthropologist Stanley Jeyaraja Tambiah argues for the existence of "multiple orderings of reality": different cultural frameworks of knowledge and experience that build, in essence, different kinds of worlds. Tambiah compares and contrasts two basic frameworks found in human culture, one based on *causality* and the other on *participation.* Causality boils down to the pragmatic rationalism of science: The detached individual ego divides and fragments the welter of the world according to objective and explanatory schemes based on neutrality and instrumental action. In contrast, the world of participation plunges the individual into a collective sea that erodes the barrier between human agency and the surrounding environment. In this world, which I am associating with the magical paradigm, language and ritual do not objectively delineate the world but help bring it into being; objects are organized according to symbolic resemblances and the rhetoric of dream rather than the dry and objective classifications that pack scientific texts or corporate reports.

All cultures and societies display different mixtures of these two orientations. The world of participation dominates archaic and oral cultures, while moderns inhabit an everyday world defined by the technoscientific logic of causality. But though our cosmology is scientific, our cultures, psyches, and collective rituals are not. The technological civilization that now blankets the globe is actually seething with myriad forms of participation: massive sports events, global pop music, networked video games, fashion fads. In fact, media technology may actually be amplifying the collective resonance that lies at the psychic heart of participation.

This was Marshall McLuhan's view anyway. McLuhan was convinced that electronic media were eroding the logical, linear, and sequential worldview that dominated the modern West. He believed that this "causal" worldview was itself the product of technology, especially alphanumeric characters, the printing press, and the techniques of Renaissance perspective drawing. But with the spread of new media technologies like the phonograph, radio, and television, the older paradigm of literacy and logic was breaking down. With its new bias toward image, orality, and simultaneous participation, the electronic environment was conjuring up the collective psyche of earlier oral cultures. "Civilization is entirely the product of phonetic literacy," he wrote, "and as it dissolves with the electronic revolution, we rediscover a tribal, integral awareness that manifests itself in a complete shift in our sensory lives."[143] McLuhan described the emerging electronic society as "a resonating world akin to the old tribal echo chamber where magic will live again."[144]

McLuhan often went overboard with his rhetorical bravura and sweeping sound bytes, but methodical scholars like Walter Ong have given more detailed and rigorous shape to McLuhan's vision of the "electric retribalization of the West." In his landmark book *Orality and Literacy,* Ong argues that electronic media are leading us into a time of "secondary orality," an era that, despite important differences, bears some striking similarities to the cultural logic of oral societies. In particular, Ong draws attention to the new power of participatory mystique, group identification, repetitive formulas, and the ethos of "living in the moment."

Given that human societies are mixtures of participation and causality, McLuhan's vision should probably be tempered with the notion that electronic media are simply shifting the relative balance between these two worlds, orality and literacy, participation and causality. In fact, it is the conscious *combination* of these two different modes that leads to some of the most important forms of modern technological magic. Television advertising, for example, uses seductive phantasms, participatory mystique, and repetitive mantras like "Just Do It" to impress Pavlovian buying habits into the minds of consumers, whose imaginations and desires have themselves been "scientifically" mapped through focus groups and market surveys. The faddish fascination with subliminal advertising in the 1970s only masked a deeper recognition: that advertisers don't want to inform us about new products, but to capture our attention and manipulate our imaginations. As the cultural theorist Raymond Williams writes, advertising is "a highly organized and professional system of magical inducements and satisfactions, functionally very similar to magical systems in simpler societies, but rather strangely coexistent with a highly developed scientific technology."[145]

Williams's analysis is spot-on, but the coexistence of magic and scientific technology should not strike us as particularly strange. After all, magic has always deployed the tools of media to work its wonders on the human mind. Williams's observations only seem odd if you accept the rather naive belief that advanced technologies should automatically engender skeptical reason in their users. The ancient arts of persuasion can hardly be expected to disappear at the very moment that the science of social engineering, which we now call marketing and "perception management," is sharpening and multiplying its techniques. As William A. Covino argues, advertising is only one example of the "arresting magic" of modern institutions, a sorcery of psychological control that he defines as the imposition of binding symbolic restraints on the many by the few. Arresting magic is utilized by autocratic teachers and governments, "and is practiced in some measure by the ostensible detractors of magic, voices of science who attempt to constitute official knowledge."[146]

The strongest example of arresting magic is the mass media, which many twentieth-century social critics have vociferously attacked for its technological and industrial domination of our psychic, aesthetic, and imaginal lives. The situationist Guy Debord bitterly deplored what he famously called the "society of the spectacle," a "permanent opium war" waged against society by the lords of capitalism, who seek to channel human dreams and desires into the passive consumption of mediated images and commodity fetishes. Ellul analyzed the society of the spectacle in terms of propaganda, while Theodor Adorno and other members of the so-called Frankfurt School critiqued what they called the "culture industry," an essentially economic apparatus which they believed destroyed the spiritual imagination, the organic social functions of popular culture, and the critical role of art. Though Adorno mourned the Enlightenment's reduction of the world to a dead object of instrumental control, he held out no hope for the restorative power of the magical imagination in the modern world. In fact, in his withering attacks on popular astrology, he argued that the occult had been thoroughly co-opted by commodity culture and the arresting magic of authoritarian institutions.

Today the fears of Debord, Adorno, and Ellul may seem musty and rather extreme, but it's important to remember that all these writers wrote with the necromantic specter of European fascism in mind. After all, Hitler used Olympian electric spectacles, occult symbols, sophisticated propaganda, and what McLuhan called "the tribal drum of radio" to drag a thoroughly industrialized nation into a Wagnerian horror show of barbaric proportions. While our current media climate seems far too open and tumultuous for such totalitarian horrors to arise, any visions of the inherently liberating and democratic power of the information age must wrestle with the fact that only a small handful of gargantuan corporations now dominate the bulk of media traffic across the planet. Though today's crew of spin doctors, marketeers, and corporate shills are not a particularly ideological lot, their rain dances do attempt to ensure the continued prosperity of the global business climate, often to the detriment of social, cultural, and ecological considerations. Some critics fear that we are being mesmerized by the media's increasingly powerful and pervasive specters at the very moment that the possibilities of real change are being sacrificed on the altar of the invisible hand.

Though the boundaries between marketplace and imaginal space have always been porous, America's culture industry has in many ways simply fused the two. Golden arches, Trump towers, Gotham cities, and Las Vegas pyramids now tower over the landscape of imaginative desire. Our collective symbols are forged in the multiplex, our archetypes trademarked, licensed, and sold. With unintended irony, Disney has dubbed its own industrial production of phantasms "imagineering"; others simply call it the corporate colonization of the unconscious. A baroque arcana of logos, brand names, and corporate sigils now pepper landscapes, goods, and our costumed bodies. A century ago, advertisements were almost exclusively textual, but today's marketing engines now saturate the social field with hieroglyphics to an extent never seen before in human history. Unlike the figures of Egyptian lore, our mnemonic icons no longer mediate the animist powers of nature or the social magic of kings, but the power of corporate identity and the commodity fetish. Many consumers, especially young people, cling to logos like Timberland and Stüssy as if they were clan totems, while some enthusiastic male Nike employees have gone so far as to tattoo the "swoosh" on their calves and upper thighs, etching into their flesh McLuhan's insight that the great corporations were the new tribal families.

Such tribal myths are hardly restricted to corporate culture or the logomania of fashion victims. Anthropologically speaking, many of the youth subcultures that have popped up like mushrooms across the landscape of the postwar West might well be considered tribes. Mods, rockers, hippies, punks, skinheads, street gangs, Deadheads, football hooligans, rap crews, and ravers—all of these grassroots subcultures use some hermetic combination of slang, music, body language, and insignia to define themselves as a tightly knit group whose unique rituals and frequently nomadic movements are set against the organized anomie of modern life. For some subcultures, the echoes of tribalism are explicitly part of the package: Rainbow families mimic Native American rituals, while "modern primitives" adorn themselves with Gothic pierces, African earplugs, and Maori tattoos.

Many such subcultures can also be defined as "media tribes." Hackers, DJ crews, and pirate radio posses bond over technology, while fan cultures actively splice up and reconfigure mass media in accordance with their own needs and desires. The enthusiastic and sometimes ecstatic musical "cults" that have formed around the Beatles, the Grateful Dead, Rastafarian reggae, heavy metal, and techno music are perhaps the epitome of this process. Sometimes the term is almost literal; for thousands of American Elvis fans, the cult of the King now satisfies devotional desires that an immortal Jesus once did. Though media companies actively attempt to stimulate such profitable fanaticism, the emotions and desires themselves run deeper than advertising, and can generate an authentic quality of folk culture. *Star Trek* and its various spin-offs function as modern mythologies not only because Paramount's scriptwriters dip into Joseph Campbell, but because Trekkers have lent the show resonance and depth by investing it with personal meanings, collective rituals, and a profound sense of play. Trekker conventions are not simply orgies of collector frenzy and star worship, but costumed carnivals of the postmodern imagination.

Following the work of the social historian Michel de Certeau, many cultural studies theorists describe these inventive attempts to reappropriate mass culture as "poaching." According to de Certeau, modern poachers recognize that they cannot defeat the massive social institutions that surround them, and so they pilfer symbols, practices, and commodities on the sly, using them for their own purposes. Praising the art of poaching, de Certeau suggests that people can resist the stifling frameworks of contemporary urban civilization through the imaginative tactics they deploy in their everyday lives.

> Increasingly constrained, yet less and less concerned with these vast frameworks, the individual detaches himself from them without being able to escape them and can henceforth only try to outwit them, to pull tricks on them, to rediscover, within an electronicized and computerized megalopolis, the "art" of the hunters and rural folk of earlier days.[147]

This art is magic, in the most broad and poetic sense of the term. But rather than the arresting magic of authoritarian social institutions, the poacher performs *creative* magic, a critical rebellion of the grassroots imagination against the symbolic and social frameworks of consensus reality. While arresting magicians disguise their spells as Apollonian truths, as reality pure and simple, creative magicians manifest the mischievous trickery of Hermes. They exploit the rich ambiguities of words, images, identities, commodities, and social practices in order to craft protean perspectives, to rupture business as usual, and to stir up new ways of seeing and being in a world striated with invisible grids of technocultural engineering.

Technopagans

Some of the most self-consciously creative magicians wielding spells today are found in the world of contemporary Paganism, an earthy and celebratory magical culture that attempts to reboot the rituals, myths, and gods of ancient polytheistic cultures. Pagans are far too anarchic to be lumped into a movement, and they come in many flavors—witches (they prefer *Wiccans*), fairies, druids, Goddess worshipers, ceremonial magicians, Discordians. They might worship trees, invoke the Horned God and the Great Goddess, toss rune stones, or dance around bonfires. But one thing that unites all Pagans is their sense of the imagination as a *craft*—at once an art, an instrumental practice, and a vessel for spirit.

Though some Pagans claim direct contact with hidden traditions centuries old, most trace Paganism's modern roots to the 1940s, when a civil servant and nudist named Gerald Gardner founded a witchcraft coven in the British Isles. From that point on, Pagans have cobbled together their rituals and cosmologies from existing occult traditions, their own imaginative needs, and fragments of lore found in dusty tomes of folktales and anthropology. Pagans have self-consciously invented their religion, making up their "ancient ways" as they go along. Highly aware of their outsider status, Pagans also set themselves in opposition to what they see as the patriarchal, authoritarian, and antiecological forms of spirituality that have dominated the Christian West. Women play an enormous role in practice and worship alike, and much of the Goddess feminism that now permeates the New Age and the fringes of liberal Christianity can be traced to pioneering Wiccan feminists like Z. Budapest and Starhawk. But though Pagans root through the New Age grab bag of positive thinking, healing meditations, and Gaian mysticism, they also embrace the embodied world, grounding the higher frequencies in what the Pagan writer Chas Clifton describes as "dirt and flowers, blood and running water, sex and sickness, spells and household tools." With passionate and often deliberately amusing verve, they insist on the sacredness of the body and the earth, and most believe that the active cultivation of magic can build a bridge back to the enchanted, but very concrete, world that most humans lived in before the Enlightenment reduced the *anima mundi* to a soulless machine.

In 1985, when the witch and NPR reporter Margot Adler was revising *Drawing Down the Moon,* her great social history of American Paganism, she conducted a survey of the community and discovered something that would surprise anyone teleported into the woolly Renaissance Faire atmosphere of your typical Pagan gathering: An "amazingly" high percentage of this willfully anachronistic bunch drew their paychecks from technical fields and the computer industry. In her 1989 study of modern witchcraft in England, the anthropologist T. M. Luhrmann also found that a significant number of her subjects were similarly involved with computers. Adler's respondents gave many reasons for this apparently paradoxical affinity—everything from the belief that "computers are elementals in disguise" to the simple fact that the computer industry provided jobs for the kind of smart, iconoclastic, and experimental types that Paganism attracts. But one suspects that most of these "technopagans" would also get behind the science-fiction writer Arthur C. Clarke's amply cited claim that "any sufficiently advanced technology is indistinguishable from magic"—a quip that deserves more scrutiny than it usually receives.

As a rationalist (if an often mystical one), Clarke cannot be accused of setting ICBMs and Deep Blue on the same shelf as love potions and mojo wads. What he seems to mean is that, in sociocultural terms, advanced technologies *appear* to be magical. For many people, condemned by lax education and uneven patterns of development to remain uninitiated into the logical world that undergirds our massive arrays of machinery, advanced technologies seem magical because they seem spontaneous and supernatural. Even among the well educated, people often know more about the warp coil converters on the USS *Enterprise* than they do about their CPUs or their local utility grid.

The situation is not likely to improve. In the old days, at least, you could see or even touch the latest machines as they made their way through the world, grinding up raw materials, assembling objects, blowing things up, and racing across the surface of the planet. It was easy to understand that these contraptions were mere machines, exploiting perfectly natural forces through clever arrangements of mechanical parts and guileless forces of energy. But today's digital technologies have reached the beachhead of the incorporeal, with the smallest components on some chips shrinking below the wavelength of visible light. Micro-technologies reorganize matter on the scale of silicon grains and genetic base pairs; they invade and inhabit the body; they sculpt vibrating streams of electrons into complex invisible architectures of logic and information. Twenty years ago, you had half a chance of fixing your car; these days, with computer chips and miniature sensors scattered through the vehicle like chunks of fudge in a tub of Ben & Jerry's, you need some serious tech just to hack the nature of a glitch. The logic of technology has become invisible—literally, *occult*. Without the code, you're mystified. And nobody has all the codes anymore.

Clarke's maxim can be interpreted more positively as well. Powerful new technologies are magical because they *function* as magic, opening up novel and protean spaces of possibility within social reality. They allow humans to impress their dreaming wills upon the stuff of the world, reshaping it, at least in part, according to the designs of the imagination. Of course, as we integrate new technologies into the workaday world, their pixie dust settles, and their glamour—in the old fairy-lore sense of a compelling spell—disappears. New inventions are also notorious for conjuring up situations, many of them decidedly unpleasant, that nobody could possibly have imagined in advance. But the mages in the R&D labs, possessed by what Teilhard de Chardin called the "demon of Research," show every sign of continuing to churn out phenomenal new technologies. Whether these machines and techniques do their tricks with digital or genetic code, they will, at the very least, produce the illusion of leading the mind ever closer to its longed-for mastery of matter. And if we remember that appearances compose our world as much as truths, then the ceaseless emergence of advanced technologies that define life on the flying crest of the twenty-first century may paradoxically draw us into a silicon wizard world.

Such paradoxes tantalize many a technopagan, but there are also some basic sociological reasons for the healthy number of folks that overlap computer culture and the occult fringe. One meeting ground is science fiction and fantasy fandom, a deeply imaginative subculture whose bookworm enthusiasm and geeky humor has bred many a Pagan. The Church of All Worlds, one of the more eclectic and long-lasting American magical groups (and the first to start calling themselves

Pagans), began when some undergraduate libertarians started practicing the polygamous Martian religion described in Robert Heinlein's *Stranger in a Strange Land*. Many Pagans inject their public rituals or personal cosmologies with self-consciously playful references to *Star Trek*, Tolkien, or comic books. Such pop culture "poachings" reach their giddiest peak in the satirical Church of the SubGenius, a mock fringe religion whose goofy devotion to flying saucers, thrift store kitsch, and a pipe-smoking Ward Cleaver-like god named Bob conceal rather profound explorations of America's magical mind.

Though many computer buffs don't go in for this kind of stuff, allusions to science fiction and fantasy fiction are staples of hacker culture, and the popularity of role-playing games like Dungeons & Dragons has, as we will see in the next chapter, unleashed occult phantasms inside the cultural circuitry of the digital age. One reason that hackers are attracted to these genres is that science-fiction and fantasy writers don't just tell tales—they build worlds. Though SF writers generally stick closer to scientific plausibility, the creators of both genres usually try to make their scenarios ring true by establishing certain axiomatic conditions (ecology, fantastic technologies, social stratification) and then developing narratives within those parameters. Hackers and witches also take to these genres because, as Luhrmann points out, "both magic and computer science involve creating a world defined by chosen rules, and playing within their limits."[148] With a certain interpretive license, we could say that this process describes all creative religious thought, although Pagans bring a peculiar self-awareness and playful tinkering to their sacred fabrications, rarely overlooking the role of the human operator in the process.

If you visit a contemporary Pagan festival like Starwood or Ancient Ways, you might see groups of suburbanites dressed like Morticia Addams and Ming the Merciless waving ceremonial knives at the moon and chanting to Pan in singsong rhymes. You might reasonably conclude that these folks had simply abandoned their heritage as modern people and reverted to the superstitions of the past. But a good number of Pagans don't adopt premodern belief systems so much as ignore the limitations imposed by the belief systems modern people already hold. The heaviest magic users often pride themselves on their skeptical relativism, deeply questioning all appearances and truth-claims—including, to be sure, the orthodox scientific accounts of the relationship between mind and matter. The canniest Pagans proceed empirically, using their "workings" to explore the possibilities inherent in the human bodymind on a pragmatic and subjective basis. The American druid Isaac Bonewits, author of an early and influential Pagan text entitled *Real Magic,* considers himself a materialist; as he told Margot Adler, "I just have a somewhat looser definition of matter than most people."[149] In constructing a premodern religion in a postmodern world, Pagans have thus learned to maneuver quite cannily between technoscientific categories and imaginative practice. And they have done so in part by replacing the religious question of belief with the hands-on exploration of embodied experience and altered states of consciousness. The notorious occultist Aleister Crowley captured the essence of this imaginative pragmatism when he wrote that magic speaks of

> spirits and conjurations, of gods, spheres, planes and many other things which may or may not exist. It is immaterial whether they exist or not. By doing certain things certain results follow.[150]

Whatever metaphysics Pagans hold, the proof of practice remains in the pudding—and the ingredients can always be tweaked. That's why occult shops stuff their shelves with herbs, potions, amulets, and ritual paraphernalia alongside countless manuals, almanacs, and ritual cookbooks. Pagans are tinkerers.

This experimental spiritual pragmatism has made it easy for Pagans to embrace new occult technologies: sophisticated astrological software, *I Ching* CD-ROMs, Tarot hypercard stacks. More important, it has led them to reimagine "technology" as both a metaphor and a tool for ritual. In a sense, the connection was there all along; as the anthropologist Ronald Grimes points out, magical rites are performances that refer to mystical powers in a technological manner, "and must not be definitionally separated from technology."[151] In the words of Sam Webster, an accomplished ceremonial magician and a Webmaster at Berkeley's Lawrence Livermore Labs, ritual is "the principal technology for programming the human organism." According to Webster, Pagan ritual serves as a kind of virtual theater that cultivates, or "programs," intentions and spiritual experiences in participants. With its dramatic language of gesture, symbol, and scent, ritual bypasses the intellect and stimulates psychological and perceptual aspects of the self that register on a more subliminal level; by cutting a pentagram into the air or dancing a wild spiral dance, the self submits to the designs of human and cosmic powers on a more visceral plane than philosophical conceptions or sermons allow.

Orthodox and Catholic Christians also recognize the extraordinary power of ritual, but they would describe the force of liturgy as arising from the spiritual authority of tradition. By rejecting such institutional claims, Pagans instead bring the question around to intent: What do we want to achieve with this ritual program? What powers—natural, emotional, social—do we want the self to engage? As Webster noted in an email interview, the metaphor of technology allows one to think about the transformative potential of ritual without lapsing into "fuzzyminded mysticism."

> By seeing what we are doing as tech, we can avoid seeing [it] as a sacred cow, and instead criticize it with accuracy and without attachment: is it doing what we intend? If so, can we improve on it? If not, how not: change or trash.[152]

Though at first it may seem as if the notion of "ritual technology" would sap rites of their psychospiritual efficacy, Paganism's creative and experimental approach to the sacred seems to actually profit from its self-conscious instrumentality. Of course, such technological thinking also brings along the familiar sorts of problems discussed earlier; Webster notes that many magic users get caught up with "the tech" for its own sake and pay much less attention to refining their spiritual goals.

The love that Pagans and other contemporary magic users have for tinkering and arcana may help explain the fact that they became one of the first religious subcultures to colonize cyberspace. These days, of course, even the most stick-in-the-mud religions have set up shrines along the information superhighway, and Net surfers can learn more than most want to know about Bahai, Byzantine monasticism, or the Vatican library. But Pagans were online, and in force, long before the World Wide Web, and the Net continues to house a disproportionate amount of information on occult subjects: ftp sites collect GIFs (graphic image files) of magical sigils and alchemical diagrams, Web sites offer numerology profiles and real-time astrological ephemera, and meta-lists like MaGI (the Mage's Guide to the Internet) act as the mystic portals to further arcana.

Such databases are a natural outgrowth of Pagandom's love of lore, but for many Pagans, the computer serves more vital religious purposes than simply downloading bit-mapped hieroglyphs or storing Crowley's pornographic poesy. Collective anarchy is the nature of Pagan community, an unstable social structure in which the loose exchange of information between far-flung and often cantankerous groups plays a binding role that dogmatic hierarchies play in orthodox religions. For decades, Pagans have poured enormous loads of time and effort into zines like *Green Egg* and *WomanSpirit*—frequently hand-stapled, low-budget communiqués sent through the post. Needless to say, computer bulletin boards (and later Web sites) fit this heterodox and talkative community like a leather glove. By the late 1980s, hundreds of electronic Pagan BBSes dotted the land, boasting names like the El Segundo Spiders Web, the Ft Lauderdale Summerland, and Ritual Magick Online! The anarchic environs of the Internet, with its chat lines and newsgroups, swelled with Wiccans and druids, and Usenet's alt.pagan and alt.magic hierarchies became flaming cauldrons of debate. Despite the fact that Pagans represent a tiny slice of religious America, alt.pagan consistently holds a place in the top five Usenet newsgroups related to religion and spirituality.

For the bulk of Pagans and magic users, online community plays second fiddle to spiritual experience. Paganism is an earth religion, after all, and its practitioners seek sacred communion on the material plane, in woods and deserts and black-lit basements, amidst unguents and drums and dancing flesh. This visionary materialism is worlds away from the incorporeal writing space of the Internet, and many Pagans, especially Goddess-oriented Wiccans, distrust the cyberspace obsessions of techno-pagans, fearing that the enthusiasm for cyberchat and virtual reality may simply reproduce the same disembodied and ecologically bankrupt tendencies of modern civilization that Pagandom otherwise so imaginatively resists.

But the antinomian mages who occupy the darker bands of the contemporary occult spectrum have few such qualms. Among this more sorcerous and satanic crew, many of whom reject the label of "Pagan" as too vanilla, the so-called chaos magicians have come to play a vital and vocal role, especially on the Internet. A soberly irreverent antitradition, chaos magic rejects the historical symbolic systems of the occult as arbitrary constructs devoid of any intrinsic "spiritual" power. For these postmodern magicians, the naive and crunchy romanticism of Paganism's "ancient ways" obscures the true source of magic: the mage's own will, making itself up in the existential emptiness of an impersonal and relativistic cosmos. Chaos magicians might accept the reality of paranormal events, but they are more apt to chalk them up to "fourth-dimensional exchanges of information" or the primal instincts of the human brain-stem than to gaseous specters from dead cultures. Even when they do invoke godforms, they are more likely to traffic with one of the eldritch creepies from H. P. Lovecraft's pulp fiction than with an old ham like Pan. As you might expect, chaos magicians also dig computers—as the magickal nethead behind MaGI put it, "Most Neopagans would connect [electronically] and say, let's get together and do a ritual, while chaos magicians would say, let's do the ritual online."[153]

The chthonic forces that chaos magicians call upon may seem like lit-tle more than an occult primal scream, but such forces can be put to crit-ical use. For members of the Temple ov Psychic Youth, a technopagan outgrowth of the British industrial musician Genesis P. Orridge's mideighties group Psychic TV, the dark and convulsive energies of chaos magic are a wake-up call. Loosely echoing the fears raised by Ellul, Adorno, and other critics of modern civilization, TOPY considers main-stream society as nothing more than a totalitarian system of social con-trol. Like de Certeau's poachers, they try to outwit and trick the society of the spectacle, breaking its ideological spell through atavistic magic, experimental media, and darkside sexuality. Along with reclaiming their bodies through the kind of tribal tattoos and novel piercings that would only later make it to the mall, TOPYites spent a lot of time communi-cating through alternative networks in which the information they passed around seemed less important than the manner in which it was swapped. When he still served as the movement's ideologue, Genesis P. Orridge also put great magical weight in the cut-and-paste techniques first developed by the Beat artists William S. Burroughs and Brion Gyson. Orridge argued that these disruptive and recombinant tactics could be deployed in music, visual media, and collage art in order to rup-ture social programming and consensus trance. But TOPY's most brazenly imaginative—if rather desperate—act of media poaching was the television magic described in Orridge's book *Esoterrorist*. Though deploring TV's use as a tool of mass indoctrination, Orridge also believed that, actively engaged, the tube could be a "modern alchemical weapon," an electromagnetic threshold into the primal goo of dreams. Some TOPYites used the TV as a scrying stone (or "crystal ball"). After tuning in to a dead channel, they would stare at the dancing static until strange patterns and images emerged.

This kind of occult pop art is an extreme example of the technopagan will to reenchant contemporary psychic tools along the lines of archaic ones. But as suggested earlier, modern electronic technologies have been enchanted to some degree all along, and technopagan magic must be seen in the larger and more ambivalent context of a widespread, if unacknowledged, technological animism. As the science-fiction writer Philip K. Dick noted in a 1972 speech:

> . . . our environment, and I mean our man-made world of machines, artificial constructs, computers, electronic systems, interlinking homeostatic components—all this is in fact beginning more and more to possess what the . . . primitive sees in his environment: animation. In a very real sense our environment is becoming alive, or at least quasi-alive. . . .[154]

The paradox that Dick describes is considerable. With their exacting and mechanized logic, computers are in some sense the farthest outpost yet reached on the West's technologically mediated flight from archaic animism. Along this journey, we reimagined the cosmos and ourselves through progressively more complex images of the machine: the loom, the potter's wheel, the clock, the steam engine. Scientific reductionism banished the spirits and intelligences of premodern cosmology from our perceptions of the physical world. And yet today an electronic parody of these powers has subtly come home to roost, not in the reenchanted Gaia worshiped by the Pagans, but in the media and mechanisms of the information age. For just as the timber conglomerates chase the last of the old ones from the ancient rain forests, our digital technologies appear to be acquiring mind.

The computer is the most animated and intelligent of machines, the most interactive, and by far the least "mechanical." Even if we insist upon their entirely mechanical nature, these cybernetic contraptions are now so resilient and complex that they provide us with technological reflections of thought itself, and even life. This potential explains why the electronic computers of the 1950s so quickly gave rise to the notion of artificial intelligence, and why some of today's computer scientists seriously discuss the possibility of breeding life forms made of digital code. Though wisecracking AIs have yet to see the light of day, the Internet has already become home to a variety of autonomous and rather parasitic programs—including viruses, Trojan horses, spiders, worms, smartshoppers, and bots—that trawl the Net, replicate themselves, perform various data-processing deeds (often on the sly), and return to their masters with information in tow—that is, if they have masters at all.

Philosophers and programmers may wrangle over the question of how "alive" these wild things really are, but the question of technological life cannot be decided solely with the analytic language of neural networks, Darwinian selection, and genetic algorithms. For all its technical prowess, such language tends to disguise the fact that our sense of agency, of the presence of life and intelligence, also depends on the narratives and emotions that structure our everyday experience of the world. Though the chess grand master Gary Kasparov knew that Deep Blue was devoid of desires and intuitions, he claimed to sense a thinking opponent, a perception that did not derive from the machine's data architecture but from his own embodied relationship with a social actor. Many computer users unconsciously treat their PCs as pesky if powerful imps, an animist relationship to the machine that is often encouraged by the design of user interfaces, games, and children's software. Millions of kids bought the Bandai Company's Tamagotchis—digital pets that inhabit handheld calculatorlike gadgets—because their feelings were engaged by a narrative construction of technological life. And if the designers of "intelligent agents" have their way, then even more explicitly lifelike digital critters will be loosed into the information jungle, bargaining for plane tickets, leading us through databases, and undoubtedly trying to make a buck from us as well.

Perhaps the phenomenon of techno-animism is nothing more than the latest upgrades from the society of the spectacle, infantilizing spells designed to crush whatever critical distance still allows some of us to question the technocapitalist domination of the world. On the other hand, a degree of animism can also be seen as a psychologically appropriate and imaginatively pragmatic response to the peculiar qualities of the information jungle. We associate intelligence with what reads and writes, and nowadays everything electronic reads and writes. For technopagans, the fallout from this is clear: The postmodern world of digital simulacra is ripe for the premodern skills of the witch and magician. To be sure, the "return of magic" may be just another story to while away the postindustrial night, but it is precisely through such stories that technologies gain their character, if not their lives. In this sense, the evil AIs, sexy androids, and cuddly robots that keep popping up in comic books, video games, movies, and television are not just pop culture effluvium, but narrative figures who are helping to thicken the plots we are weaving with very real, and very spunky, technologies. Magic too is a myth, but myths shape our machines into meanings. And nowhere is this metamorphosis more evident than with the most vivid and enchanting myth that computers have yet to conjure: the myth that they can act as portals to another world, another dimension of space itself.

cyberspace: the virtual craft

Like Trojan horses, buzzwords carry their own secret contents, hidden histories and meanings that many of their users hardly suspect. Most of us first heard the term *virtual reality* in the beginning of the 1990s, when a large and very clever dreadlocked gearhead named Jaron Lanier started showing off various goggles and gloves capable of launching the mind into three-dimensional worlds made of computer graphics. Hitting the mass brainstem like a rush of crack, the term rapidly took on the millennialist charge of all pop futurisms. Though the hype died down when the technology failed to deliver digital dreamtime, virtual reality remains a fundamental raison d'être of computer culture, a holy grail that keeps beckoning through the forest of tangled protocols and clunky hardware.

But *virtual reality* was not hatched in the hopped-up halls of Silicon Valley. Back in 1938, the French playwright, film actor, and state-declared madman Antonin Artaud dropped the phrase in one of the blazing manifestos collected in his magnum opus, *The Theater and Its Double*. Discussing the "mysterious identity of essence between alchemy and the theater," Artaud argued that the theater creates a virtual reality—*"la réalité virtuelle"*—in which characters, objects, and images take on the phantasmagoric force of alchemy's visionary internal dramas. For Artaud, theater is no more about representing ordinary life than alchemy is about the chemical transmutation of lead into gold. Instead, both of these symbolic rituals should catalyze the same psychological states once produced in the "archetypal, primitive theater" of the Eleusinian Mysteries and the shamanic Orphic cults of ancient Greece. Artaud argued that, at their essential core, these ancient ritual spectacles evoked "the passionate and decisive transfusion of matter by mind"—the ultimate gnostic transmutation of reality that alchemists symbolized with the fabled philosopher's stone.

Artaud wrote that the image of this spiritualized state of matter beckons to us from "the incandescent edges of the future," and that it is this brass ring that powerful art and theater are constantly striving to hook.

But today it is technology that restlessly plunges toward the incandescent edge of the future. As we'll see in this chapter, the techgnostic drive does not aim solely for the disembodied cognitive augmentation of the Extropians; it also sets its sights on a more hermetic world of magical iconography, mythic masks, and otherworldly journeys. The VR gear trumpeted by Lanier provided one snapshot of such an alchemical realm, but the astral plane of technoculture had already made its appearance in, of all places, a science-fiction novel.

Written on a Hermes 2000 manual typewriter and published in the prophetic year of 1984, William Gibson's *Neuromancer* hit the cultural cortex around the same time that personal computers invaded the home, and world financial markets launched into twenty-four-hour orbit. Though both Hollywood and recent history have made Gibson's dystopian vision of gritty data-hustlers, cutthroat corporations, and pervasive brand names as clichéd as the trench coats and femmes fatales of the *noir* thrillers that Gibson drew from, the novel's continued relevance (and resonance) can be boiled down to one single, religiously cited image:

> Cyberspace. A consensual hallucination. . . . A graphic representation of data abstracted from the banks of every computer in the human system. . . . Lines of light ranged in the non space of the mind.[155]

Like all great mythic images, cyberspace suggested more than it explained, and while it concealed ironies its many enthusiasts would miss, it also provided a conceptual handle for the emerging hyperspace of digital communication. By hinting that the "unthinkable complexity" of the world's networks and databases could be tamed by an interactive three-dimensional map you could "jack into" through a video game deck, Gibson's vision struck a deep chord, crystallizing the inchoate desires of everyone from hackers to journalists to psychedelic bohemians. By the end of the 1980s, cyberspace had become a cultural attractor, sucking an increasingly computerized society forward with the relentless force of a *Star Wars* tractor beam.

For megatrend watchers and hype masters, cyberspace came to serve as a shorthand for a variety of very different developments—virtual reality, computer games, the rapid growth of Internet traffic, and the electronic etherealization of commerce across the globe. John Perry Barlow simply defined cyberspace as the place where you are when you're on the phone. But for others, *Neuromancer*'s "consensual hallucination" appeared to be something much more. In her book *The Pearly Gates of Cyberspace,* the science writer Margaret Wertheim argues that by creating a space that follows the virtual laws of thought rather than the concrete laws of matter, cyberspace provides a cosmos where the psyche can once again live and breathe. "Strange though it may seem for a quintessentially twentieth-century technology, cyberspace brings the historical wheel full circle and returns us to an almost medieval position, to a two-tiered reality in which psyche and soma each have their own space of action."[156] Like novels or cinema or comic books, cyberspace gives us a place to suspend the usual scientific rules that constrain the physical reality where our bodies live. But unlike these media, cyberspace is a shared interactive environment, an electronic "soul-space" that beckons the postmodern psyche to both find and remake itself.

Many people working inside the computer industry recognized the possibilities of technological soul-space as well, including a particularly energetic computer geek named Mark Pesce. In the early 1990s, Pesce concluded that the best way to build real cyberspace was to "perceptualize the Internet." So over the next few years, he and a few cronies cooked up VRML, a "virtual reality mark-up language" that would add a graphic third dimension to the World Wide Web's tangled two-dimensional hypertext of pages, links, and endless URLs. For Pesce, as well as the legion of enthusiastic techheads infected by his charismatic trade show evangelism, VRML became the key to transforming the Web into a *world,* or rather a universe of worlds, each capable of nesting information within a kind of virtual theater: downtown Boston, a mock-up of Stonehenge, a blasted moonscape littered with Day-Glo monoliths.

Mark Pesce is also a technopagan, a goddess-worshiper, ritual magician, and occasional partaker of psychedelic sacraments. VRML was not just his day job, but a vital dimension of his occult work. As Pesce said in a 1994 interview with the author:

> Both cyberspace and magical space are purely manifest in the imagination. Both spaces are entirely constructed by your thoughts and beliefs. Korzybski says that the map is not the territory. Well, in magic, the map *is* the territory. And the same thing is true in cyberspace. There's nothing in that space you didn't bring in.

For Pesce, you don't need to anthropomorphize computers to give them a spiritual dimension. Computers can be sacred simply because human beings are sacred. Spiritual reality does not descend from on high; it is something we discover and make for ourselves, through our symbols and rituals and communicative interaction. Because cyberspace embodies and extends our symbol-making minds, it can mediate these sacred communications with each other, as well as "with the entities—the divine parts of ourselves—that we invoke in that space."

Loopy speculations about virtual reality and cyberspace are cocktail party chatter for West Coast cyberculture, but Pesce is the sort to put his notions into ritual practice. He and an ad hoc crew of sysops and programmers decided to give VRML a magical send-off with Cyber-Samhain, a technopagan ritual held in San Francisco just as the Internet was beginning to explode in the mass mind. In general, Pagan ceremonies set the stage by establishing a ritual circle through a combination of performance and creative visualization. At once laboratory and temple, these circles stand "between the worlds," carving out room for magic and the gods in the midst of mundane space-time. After casting the circle, Pagans usually invoke the powers that animate the four elements of ancient lore: earth, air, water, and fire. Often symbolized by colored candles or statues, these four "Watchtowers" are imagined to stand like sentinels in the cardinal directions of the circle. For Cyber-Samhain, the Watchtowers were symbolized by four 486 PCs networked through an Ethernet and linked to a SPARC station hooked to the Internet. Each monitor screen became a window into a three-dimensional ritual space, a VRML world whose pentagrams and colored polyhedrons mirrored the actual room's magic circle. The astral plane had been reconfigured in cyberspace.

Needless to say, CyberSamhain baffled many of the multimedia mavens and Silicon Valley operatives who had been invited to the rite. But Pesce's desire to enchant cyberspace with images was prompted by more than obscure technopagan dreams, and these practical considerations attempted to address a problem that besets everyone attempting to manage the information glut of the online world. Pesce figured that as the World Wide Web continued to explode (or, perhaps more accurately, implode), the Web's array of search engines, domain names, and haphazard links would reach a point of chaotic breakdown. By using VRML to create virtual environments that could organize online data, Pesce hoped to enable humans to exploit the spatial navigation skills they had honed over hundreds of thousands of years. In *Mona Lisa Overdrive,* Gibson had already suggested the organizational power of cyberspace's visual map:

> Put the trodes on and they were out there, all the data in the world stacked up like one big neon city, so that you could cruise around and have a kind of grip on it, visually anyway, because if you didn't, it was too complicated, trying to find your way to a particular piece of data you needed.[157]

Pesce was not alone in his intuition that Gibson's cyberspace fiction concealed a deeper truth about the potential power of visualizing and mapping digital data. In *The Axemaker's Gift,* a study of the entwined history of technology and consciousness, James Burke and Robert Ornstein argue that, from the very beginnings of human culture, "axemakers" have produced technologies that put selection pressures on the human brain, pressures that encouraged our minds to develop logical and analytic procedures that gradually alienated us from the matrix of nature. Acknowledging the devastating social and ecological costs of this great divide, the authors wind up their study arguing that the computer—the ultimate ax—may actually "take us back to what we were, mentally, before the axemaker's first gift changed the way our minds got developed and selected."[158] They hope that the icons, associative links, virtual spaces, and parallel processing of multimedia computing may resurrect the "arational thinking" of earlier days, a mode of consciousness based on intuition, imaginative leaps, and fuzzy rules-of-hand. "When much of the routine drudge-work of the mind is automated, the spatial, intuitive, 'navigational' talents may well be much better adapted to accessing knowledge that is structured more like the natural world rather than being reduced to alpha-numeric codes."[159]

Given its anarchic and constantly mutating complexity, the Internet lends itself to such cartographic desire about as easily as the Everglades or the traffic flows of downtown Tokyo. But considering the intuitive handiness of three-dimensional images, it's a good bet that Internet developers (and the marketeers salivating over their shoulders) will not cease their labors until people can slip into polygon costumes and cruise through some portion of data space the way we now stroll through a theme park, bookstore, or mall. In fact, many of the worlds we'll have the opportunity to jack into will more than likely resemble some unholy combination of theme park, bookstore, and mall. The banal fate of our culture may be to simulate the astral realms inside our machines, and then blanket them with Planet Hollywoods, Donkey Kong miniature-golf courses, and Lexis-Nexis fast-food data franchises.

Mark Pesce, Jaron Lanier, and other cyberhumanists share the hope that there will be room in this world for people to discover their own potential for creative magic, for socially improvising the language of soul. After all, if the Net does indeed unfold into a honeycomb of pop-up worlds, online exploration may encourage mythic thinking just by its very nature. We may become more and more like Gibson's cyberspace-jockey Case, who the science-fiction writer Norman Spinrad describes as a

> magician whose wizardry consists of directly interfacing . . . with . . . the computersphere, manipulating it imagistically (and being manip- ulated by it) much as more traditional shamans interact imagistically with more traditional mythic realms via drugs or trance states.[160]

Though we can't deny the enormous differences between our data-surfing selves and our premodern forebears, we shouldn't write off the archaic and occult metaphors that cluster around new technologies as being totally inconsequential to digital experience. If multimedia and networked computers are indeed inculcating the "arational" thinking that Burke and Ornstein describe, then such metaphors, lifted from folk-lore or science-fiction novels, are actually helping to map the infosphere. Such online mythologies will never dominate our view of cyberspace, of course, but they will never disappear either. The digital world that lies before us is a hybrid one, a crossroads of codes and masks, algorithms and archetypes, science and simulacra.

The explosive mythology of cyberspace is also a symptom of the dig-ital animism that is creeping into the technocultural border zones of the scientific paradigm. As we discussed at the end of the last chapter, various bots, spiders, and intelligent agents already inhabit the Internet, and these programs will more than likely be increasingly perceived, in the popular imagination as well as the scientific fringe, as autonomous entities. This move toward digital life inevitably registers on the mythic plane. Discussing the angels, demons, and Bosch-like mutant morphs that animate so many video games and online computer worlds,

Margaret Wertheim notes that "the population of soul-space is almost infinitely varied and mutable." That is, once the soul has made itself at home, that home inevitably fills up with fantastic critters. Wertheim compares today's digital populations to those that inhabit the colossal medieval soul-space found in Dante's *Commedia*. "From the dazzling six-winged 'thrones' who guard the set of God, to the six-bat-winged three-faced horror of Satan himself encased in ice at the center of hell, soul-space has always teemed with life on a cosmic scale."[161]

Gibson also recognized that the living fictions of the premodern imagination would inevitably populate the "vastness unutterable" of information space. As an old-time hacker in one of his novels admits:

> Yeah, there's things out there. Ghosts, voices. Why not? Oceans had mermaids, all that shit, and we had a sea of silicon, see? Sure, it's just a tailored hallucination we all agreed to have, cyberspace, but anybody who jacks in knows, fucking *knows,* it's a whole universe.[162]

While the dominant mystical images of cyberspace today stress its unity as a global electronic mind, Gibson cannily suggests that the dynamics of polytheism may be a more appropriate religious metaphor for the chaos of the new environment. At the end of *Neuromancer,* the artificial intelligence Wintermute achieves cybernetic godhead, but in *Count Zero,* the next novel in the series, we learn that this totalizing information entity fractured into various subroutines that somehow took on the behavior and personality of the gods, or *loa,* of Vodou—the Haitian spin on New World African religion. For Gibson, Vodou is not a figure of superstition but of technological savvy. *Count Zero*'s Vodou priest compares the religion's possession rites to "street tech," explaining that the *loa*'s "program" slots into the hardware of the human dancer—a nifty revision of the traditional Haitian metaphor of a horse and rider. As Gibson said in an interview, "The African religious impulse lends itself to a computer world much more than anything in the West. You cut deals with your favorite deity—it's like those religions already are dealing with artificial intelligences."[163]

By linking software programs and the gods who possess the dancing bodies of Vodou devotees, Gibson is not just playing cyberpunk games with Haitian religion. He's also suggesting something about the nature of the digital agents that may come to infest cyberspace. On a rational level, we will know that such computer programs are devoid of any animating substance; similarly, we might describe the *loa* as nothing more than culturally determined disassociative trance states catalyzed by Vodou's ritual technology. But as anyone who has attended a possession ritual can tell you, these entities quickly take on a life of their own. The skeptical question that we may find ourselves asking the AIs and software agents of the future—"How do I know if you are a sentient being and not just a simulation?"—could similarly be addressed to Vodou's wise and mischievous entities. And the answer might very well be that it doesn't really matter; by the time you reach the point of asking, "they" are already loosed into your world.

In the New World, most African-based religions—Vodou, Cuban Santería, Brazilian Candomblé—derive from the Yoruban religious culture that still thrives in present-day Nigeria. As Ed Morales writes in the *Village Voice*, "Yoruban religion is perhaps the most powerful aspect of African culture that survives, and actually thrives, in late-20th century postindustrial society."[164] One of the reasons behind this apparent paradox is that, for all its deeply spiritual import, the "African religious impulse" remains an eminently pragmatic practice thoroughly in tune with the push and pull of everyday life. In his novel, Gibson calls Vodou "a *street* religion"—a phrase that significantly echoes his most famous maxim: "the street finds its uses for things." For Gibson, the twists and turns that new technologies will take can never be programmed in advance, because the more marginal, crafty, and subversive elements of society ("the street") will always appropriate and reconfigure machines in new and unexpected ways. With his fanciful if rather pulpy image of technological Vodou, Gibson suggests that religious forces also possess such an unpredictable and volatile power when faced with new technologies.

In seeking to give mythological heft to his polytheistic intuitions, Gibson was psychologically savvy in fictionalizing such a pragmatic and syncretic practice as Vodou, even if the bulk of Haitians are precisely the sorts of folks who look to be structurally banished from the emerging information society. But if the author had wanted to scrounge up a premodern image of cyberspace itself—that is, of an information space constructed from virtual phantasms and data architectures—he could have poked through the dusty attic of Western consciousness, where, after digging around a bit, he eventually would have come across a most curious and ancient psychic technology: the art of memory.

The Palaces of Data

Imagine arriving at your local shopping center. Park the car, slip in through the whooshing automatic doors, and start exploring the place, picturing the stores and escalators and displays of goodies as clearly and distinctly as possible. Then imagine that this structure you've carved out of mindstuff is actually a database. Stick a mental Post-it note on the most striking objects you pass, associating each thing—a purple pair of Reeboks, a popcorn maker, a Tickle-Me Elmo doll—with some bit of pertinent minutia. Perhaps you organize your data by venue: business contacts at Brooks Brothers, mental snapshots of your travels in the multiethnic food court, lovers' birthdays and phone numbers in Victoria's Secret. But in any case, you should inscribe this virtual mall in your imagination so vividly that you can move through it as surely as you pad around your own home. And by mentally "clicking" on each storefront and commodity, you can also recover the information you stored there.

This, in a cheap American nutshell, is the *ars memoria:* the ancient mnemonic technique of building architectural databases inside your skull. A few Roman writers gave compelling technical descriptions of these "memory palaces," considering them a vital and practical aspect of the art of rhetoric (the rhetorical term *topic* derives from *topoi,* the "place" where one might lodge an argument or idea). Memory palaces could be based on real spaces or imaginary ones; some believed the best palaces combined the two modes, so that simulations of actual buildings were infused with impossible properties. Though it's tough to believe this rather baroque system worked very well, the prodigious memories of the classical world suggest otherwise. Seneca, we are told, could hear a list of two thousand names and spit them back in order, while Simplicius, a buddy of Augustine, got a kick out of reciting Virgil's *Aeneid* off the top of his head—backward.

We are as chipmunks to these mighty elephants of recall. Having externalized our memories, we squirrel facts away in written texts, hard discs, and Palm Pilots rather than swallow them whole. And yet with the immense honeycomb of cyberspace—the supreme amputation of memory—we spiral around again to the experience of memory as a *space of information,* a three-dimensional realm that's "outside" ourselves while simultaneously tucked "inside" an exploratory space that resembles the mind. From this perspective, Saint Augustine's paean to memory in the *Confessions* suggests not only the realms of the artificial memory but also the evanescent grids of cyberspace: "Behold the plains, and caves, and caverns of my memory, innumerable and innumerably full of innumerable kinds of things." Augustine calls this an "inner place, which is as yet no place," piled high with images, information, emotions, and experiences. "Over all these do I run, I fly," he writes, sounding like one of Gibson's console cowboys. "I dive on this side and that, as far as I can, and there is no end."[165]

The closest that today's online spelunkers come to these endless associational flights of recall is surfing the World Wide Web—a technology that was invented because of an irritating quirk of one man's memory. As a visiting scholar at CERN, Tim Berners-Lee had to master the European physics laboratory's labyrinthine information system, but he wasn't particularly hot at recalling what he terms "random connections." So he whipped up a personal memory substitute called Enquire, basically a hypertext system that allowed him to drop words into documents that acted as specific links to other documents. To share the system with other researchers on the network, Berners-Lee cranked out and distributed the expanded protocols for what he came to call the World Wide Web. The rest, as they say, is history. In a 1997 *Time* interview that took place at MIT's computer science lab, Berners-Lee describes the intuitive, neural structure of the Web's hypertext by referring to his cup of coffee. "If instead of coffee I'd brought in lilac," he says to the interviewer, "you'd have a strong association between the laboratory for computer science and lilac. You could walk by a lilac bush and be brought back to the laboratory."[166] The icons and hyperlinks of the Web thus simulate the associational habits of memory, habits that lend the imagination its intuitive capacity for leaps and analogies.

This is not to say that Augustine would confuse a few hours of Web grazing with the rich and penetrating introspection that he believed brought one closer to God. On the other hand, if he *had* been an adept of the *ars memoria,* he would also have regarded the art as a perfectly pragmatic intellectual tool, a *techne* that transforms the imagination into a psychic file cabinet as functional as any desktop metaphor. In fact, the orator Cicero's technical specs for memory palaces seem almost tailor-made for Java jockeys toiling over corporate Web sites:

One must employ a large number of places which must be well-lighted, clearly set out in order, at moderate intervals apart; and images which are active, sharply defined, unusual, and which have the power of speedily encountering and penetrating the psyche.[167]

Using the media metaphors of his day, Cicero wrote that "we shall employ the places and images respectively as a wax writing-tablet and the letters written on it."[168] For Cicero, these "images," or *simulacra*, functioned similarly to the icons of today's Web—compressed graphics that open up a store of data and that supplement, without replacing, the more abstract inscriptions of text. Though simple icons like anchors and swords were apparently employed, the anonymous author of *Ad Herennium* insisted that the mnemonic emblems must be "active" and "striking"—gorgeous or ugly as hell, fantastically garbed or dripping with blood.

No wonder Aristotle warned his readers that memory palaces could leak into the dreams of their creators—adepts of the art were trafficking with the fierce phantasms of the unconscious. Though the classical rhetoricians seem to have deployed these simulacra for purely instrumental purposes, the *ars memoria* eventually took on a more spiritual and occult import. Medieval theologians employed the art to "remember heaven and hell," lodging the Church's innumerable array of vices and virtues within Byzantine psychic architectures, probably not unlike Dante's poetic maps of the afterworld. Though intellectual heavyweights like the Jesuits continued to use the mnemonic art well into the seventeenth century, modern thinkers stopped using such loosely associational networks in order to organize fields of knowledge—part and parcel of their wholesale rejection of the productions of the imagination.

As the historian Dame Frances Yates shows in her classic book *The Art of Memory,* the magical and mystical potentials of these premodern psychic architectures were thoroughly exploited by our old friends the Renaissance Hermeticists. Though magicians had an obvious attraction to creative internal imagery, a more religious reason for their embrace of the art lay in the eleventh treatise of the *Corpus Hermeticum*. In the text, the divine character known as Mind informs Hermes Trismegistus that

you must think of god in this way, as having everything—the cosmos, himself, [the] universe—like thoughts within himself. Thus, unless you make yourself equal to god, you cannot understand god.[169]

For Renaissance intellectuals like Giulio Camillo, Giordano Bruno, and the later Robert Fludd, the implications were clear: The magus must build himself a divine and encyclopedic memory. As the historian Peter French explains, "by inscribing a representation of the universe within his own *mens* [higher mind], man can ascend and unite with God."[170] And what better technology of representation than the art of memory?

After all, your typical aspiring mage was already up to his eyeballs in data. Striving to grok the occult networks that bound together the World Soul, Hermeticists hoarded a stunning amount of information: angelic names, astrological deities, and numerological correspondences; ciphers, signs, and sigils; lists of herbs, metals, and incense. Renaissance tomes like Agrippa's *Three Books of Occult Philosophy* are as packed with charts and lists and instructions as any Macintosh Bible. When it came to spatially organizing this welter of material along the lines of the *ars memoria*, the Renaissance mages turned to the heavens themselves, or more specifically, to the astrological high-rise of Neoplatonic and medieval cosmology. This cosmic map became the macrocosmic "palace" that housed the microcosmic encyclopedia of the world, organized by various hieroglyphic icons that ruled different facets of human knowledge. Though hardly a rigorous taxonomy, this system of symbolic correspondences did possess a certain economy. Regarding such hermetic glyphs, Mark Pesce noted that "You can manipulate a whole bunch of things with one symbol, dragging in a whole idea space with one icon. It's like a nice compression algorithm." As such, the kabbalistic icons utilized by the mages of the *ars memoria* broke down the distinction between literal and figurative. Like the allegedly magical hieroglyphs of the ancient Egyptians, these mnemonic cues both signified and manifested the power they represented; by manipulating sigils and images associated with Venus or Mars, the magus was not just manipulating representations, but trafficking with the forces themselves. Similarly, the icons of hypertext or the World Wide Web simultaneously function as symbols, inscriptions, and operational buttons; they are both a writing and a reality. As Jay David Bolter notes in *Writing Space*, "Electronic writing is more like hieroglyphs than it is like pure alphabetic writing."[171]

This may help explain why the esoteric domains of the World Wide Web are stuffed with sites devoted to Giulio Camillo, whose elaborate wooden memory theaters, encrusted with hermetic images and icons, became the talk of the town in the sixteenth century. But the most sophisticated Renaissance memory hacker was Giordano Bruno, best known for ending his days as Vatican kindling, a "martyr to science" whose heretical advocacy of Copernicanism was actually motivated by his enthusiasm for pagan sun worship. Believing that the astral forces that govern the outer world also operate within, and can be reproduced there to operate "a magico-mechanical memory," Bruno created data-dense memory charts based on a complex Egyptian iconography of star-beings. These fantastic daemons, who should not be confused with Christian demons, were not only "active" and "striking" mnemonic icons, but also living spiritual entities—the intelligent agents of Bruno's universe of knowledge. Bruno also introduced movement into his system through the use of revolving gears of abstract symbols superficially similar to diagrams of symbolic logic. These secret decoder rings derived from the *ars combinatoria* of the thirteenth-century Catalan mystic Ramon Lull, who believed that his logical wheels could automatically demonstrate the divine attributes of God.

It's hardly surprising that Dame Yates, writing in the 1960s, saw a "curiously close" link between Bruno's magico-mechanical memory systems—with their "appalling complexity"—and the "mind machines" discussed in the press, and the German philosopher Werner Künzel eventually translated Lull's art into the computer language COBOL. For Bolter, the connection between the scientist and the Renaissance magus makes sense, for both operators "share the feeling that memory is the key to human knowledge and therefore to human control of the world."[172] Bolter points out that the memory devices of Bruno and others not only reflected the world of sense perceptions but also the "true" metaphysical structure of the cosmos; moreover, the manipulation of this hidden structure would itself open up all the realms of humanly accessible knowledge. So too, Bolter argues, does the computer specialist believe that his computer reflects the true logical structure of the universe, a structure of information that also provides for ultimate control.

So while the technical specs and blueprints of the *ars memoria* dimly anticipate the possible architectures of cyberspace, they even more profoundly reflect the desire we share with the Renaissance Hermeticists: to know the world and its information by capturing it in a virtual representation we can manipulate. The Renaissance might even be defined as a revolution in *point of view*: the discovery of the compass, the invention of perspective drawing, the leap forward in the science of mapmaking, and the mass production of printed images. But these technical developments only indicate a deeper mutation in the human subject: the Renaissance man whose eyes roved far and wide, who explored and mastered what he saw, and whose maps and gadgets helped him dominate the material spaces of the earth. Even if the Internet never achieves any sort of cartographic coherence, it and the myriad offline databases exploiting new visualization tools remain driven by the Hermeticist's desire to master an associational field of icons and data, a mnemonic space where "information is power" and a planet's worth of knowledge is only a click away.

In the Similitude of a Dream

Given all the news feeds, sports stats, and fart jokes available on the Internet, all this talk of wizards and memory palaces may seem a trifle dramatic. But chimeras do inhabit digital space, and to get a good glimpse of them, all you have to do is stroll down to your local software shop. Ignore all the "useful" programs, with their sharp, confident packages and dull, workaday spells of increased intelligence and efficiency. Head for the racks where salivating hellhounds, deep-space cruisers, and legions of marauding orcs hold sway. Head for the computer games.

In many ways, games are to digital technology what porno videos were to the VCR: the "killer app" (or application) that, by stimulating gargantuan desires, creates a mass consumer market for a new media technology. Arcade playstations and Sega/Nintendo/3DO decks suck armies of children into computer codespace for the first time in their lives, providing escapist pleasures and modes of self-definition that comic books and TV shows cannot hope to beat. At the same time, parents fritter away the night running PC games on machines purchased, they would most likely say, for far more sensible purposes. All told, digital games are a billion-dollar industry whose hit products have the capacity to literally addict their users.

Why make some digital games so compulsive? However demanding the strategic challenges of such games are, the pleasures of higher cortical function alone cannot account for their addictive power. In fact, some of the most popular games seem to reach right down to the lizard brain, catalyzing an intense fixation physiologically comparable to a trance state. The Texans behind the phenomenally successful and exuberantly bloody shooting games Doom and Quake were definitely on the right track when they named their company Id—the most primitive character in the Freudian triumvirate of id, ego, and superego. The id is the monstrous unconscious tyke that the good doctor believed our egos must constantly wrestle with in order for civilization to stand. Freud argued that we can never experience the id directly (nor would we want to). But we can track its muddy footprints through slips of the tongue, neurotic compulsions, and dreams, which Freud saw as internal dramas that simultaneously fulfilled and masked the inchoate drives of the unconscious.

The concept of the id has increasingly come under attack, but it continues to inspire the digital entertainment industry. "Psychologists say inside every 18- to 35-year-old male, there lies a potential psychotic killer," states an ad for the Philips games Nihilist and Battle Slayer. "Can he come out to play?" Though computer games are not dreams in any real sense, many a game is both constructed and consumed as what *The Pilgrim's Progress* author John Bunyan might call a "similitude of a dream." Like fantasy literature or visionary art, a good number of games seek to meet the logic of dreams halfway, to attach their surreal images, stark terrors, and otherworldly air of possibility onto compelling narratives or, at the very least, compulsive goals. Sega's 1996 Nights makes a racing game out of the archetypal dream experience of flying, while The Dark Eye exploits the morbid hypnagogic tales of Edgar Allan Poe. The CD-ROM game Myst achieved blockbuster status not because of its somewhat dorky puzzles, but because of its haunting dreamworld imagery of deserted islands, magical books, and baroque machines. It's no wonder that hard-core gamers often report that their screen obsessions seep into REM sleep.

Through networked gameplay, more people are able to share the same simulated dreamscapes at the same time. Multiplayer versions of popular games like Jedi Knight and Ultima Online have colonized the Internet, while companies like Battletech attract kids to theme-park-style centers where teams of players, each encased in individual cockpit pods, attempt to kill each other inside a shared virtual world. The "Freudian" interpretation of computer games as an escape valve for the antisocial id cannot really encompass this suddenly *social* imaginary world (though it certainly helps explain the actions of some of its participants, who can now come one step closer to killing "real" people). Perhaps it's better to take a lesson from the mystics and esoteric psychologists of the ages, for whom the id was not a narcissistic cul-de-sac but a treacherous gateway into the collective planes of the inner worlds. Following the path laid down by earlier Magellans of the mind, Carl Jung described an archetypal world of images and godforms that he believed drew its sap from the most ancient roots of the human mind. Jung named this twilight zone the collective unconscious, though a more evocative and satisfying term was offered up by the Sufi scholar Henry Corbin, who spoke of the *mundus imaginalis,* or imaginal world.

Perhaps what we are building in the name of escapist entertainment are the shared symbols and archetypal landscapes of a tawdry technological *mundus imaginalis.* The evil creatures who must be conquered to advance levels are the faint echoes of the threshold-dwellers and Keepers of the Gates that shamans and Gnostics had to conquer in their mystic peregrinations of the other worlds. Though it's dangerous to add another drop of hype to an industry that rivals Hollywood for commercial crassness and creative sloth, the game designer Brian Moriarty may not have been entirely fatuous when he told a 1996 Computer Game Developers' Conference that "spiritual experiences are, in fact, our business."[173] For all the kick-fighters, F-16s, and football gridirons you find, anyone can see that the digital imaginary is chock-full of images drawn from the depths of myth, cult, and popular religion. This mythopoetic current runs through the Orientalist backdrops of Mortal Kombat, the cartoon animism of kids' software, and the spider demons of Doom. Though most such imagery is juvenile and crude, "mature" works of multimedia also feed on this fantastic stew: Cosmology of Kyoto sets bodhisattvas and folkloric monsters loose inside the cartoon walls of the twelfth-century Japanese capital; Amber explores your past lives; while in Drowned God you uncover the "conspiracy of the ages" by exploring Atlantis, the Bermuda Triangle, and Roswell, New Mexico.

Of all the mythic cosmologies that have been retooled for the purposes of computer play, none can approach the hackneyed majesty of heroic fantasy, the neomedieval genre of strapping swordsmen, bearded wizards, gloating dragons, and D-cup princesses most pungently known as sword and sorcery. Achieving a kind of archetypal quality through the brute repetition of its own clichés alone, the genre has defined the imagery, landscapes, and violent conflicts of countless role-playing adventure games and online MUDs. It also informs the in-jokes, jargon, and even psychology of many computer hackers and hard-core Internet honchos (Katie Hafner and Matthew Lyon's history of the Net is called *Where Wizards Stay Up Late*). It's not too much to say that the phantasms of the Dark Ages form the imaginary bedrock of cyberspace.

As such, sword and sorcery is just one more example of the

neomedieval tapestries that hang in the halls of postmodern civilization. In his essay "Living in the New Middle Ages," Umberto Eco links this curious cultural resonance to a number of shared historical conditions—the rise of cultural tribalism, the insecurities that accompany a collapse of a Great Pax, and the "total lack of distinction between aesthetic objects and mechanical objects."[174] One could also add the increasingly feudal nature of an economy divided between the gated, privately patrolled citadels of the rich and the legions of men and women who strive for corporate peonage or the nomadic pickings of a "freelance" life. Eco also argues that both the medieval era and our own are dominated by the visual communication of images. Elites live in a world of texts and logic, while a less literate mass culture is immersed in a propagandistic sea of images distributed through universal—or "catholic"—communication nets. Eco compares the Gothic cathedral to a comic book in stone, its stained-glass windows to a TV screen flashing Christian advertisements. No doubt Eco would have been amused by a widely distributed 1994 Internet "press release" that announced that Microsoft had acquired the Catholic Church.

Of course, the "Middle Ages" of sword and sorcery has a lot more to do with pulp fiction than with ten centuries of European serfdom lodged between marauding Visigoths and the Black Death. But as Eco points out, the West has been fantasizing about the Middle Ages ever since we thrust ourselves out of its misty womb at the dawn of the Renaissance. In the sixteenth century, Spenser and Cervantes revisited the landscape of chivalry for their own (very different) literary ends; in the midst of the Age of Reason, Walpole's 1764 *Castle of Otranto* sparked the craze for gothic romance, a medievalist genre whose blanched melancholy, brooding spooks, and misty landscapes persist today in horror and science fiction. The Romantics constructed a number of different Middle Ages as bulwarks against the smoke and fury of industrialism, from the leafy odes of Keats and Shelley to the blood-pounding ring cycles of Richard Wagner to the fantasy novels of the socialist reformer William Morris. At the same time, these fictions were also carrying on dialogues with real medieval literature, which was rife with the sorts of miraculous events and magical forces that presumably haunted medieval perception. Despite all their theological product placements, medieval tales often took place in a succulent paganish landscape inherited from Celtic literature, a phantasmagoric realm of spells and sprites and talking trees known at least from Spenser's time as Fairy.

In the twentieth century, the realm of Fairy persists in kids' books, bad movies, and the treacherous Forest of Pulp that makes up the market for contemporary fantasy fiction. And it is in this hackneyed wood that one finds the literary source of digital medievalism: Robert E. Howard, a hard-drinking Texan who spent the 1930s cranking out brutal and necromantic page-turners for pulp magazines like *Weird Tales*. By far his most famous and vivid yarns starred Conan of Cimmeria, a sword-wielding barbarian who lumbered through a cruel landscape of serpent queens and ruined temples. Though a case could be made for Edgar Rice Burroughs, Howard probably earns the credit—or blame— for the creation of sword and sorcery, and his juvenile spirit of bloodthirsty symbolic release lives on in countless computer games today. But Howard's visceral tales probably would have passed from popular memory were it not for the tremendously popular and vastly different work of J. R. R. Tolkien, a mild-mannered Oxford medievalist and staunch Roman Catholic whose *The Lord of the Rings* takes place inside one of the most completely realized worlds in the history of fantastic literature. Tolkien fleshed out his imaginary land of Middle-Earth with its own songs, folklore, and languages; a rigorous social ecology of elves, ents, humans, and hobbits; and an exquisitely crafted topography. Tolkien's work proved the point he himself made in his essay "On Fairy-stories." A great author of fantasy "makes a Secondary World which your mind can enter. Inside it, what he relates is 'true': it accords with the laws of that world. You therefore believe it, while you are, as it were, inside."[175]

Like designers of virtual worlds today, Tolkien knew that successful secondary worlds were not wild flights of fancy, but products of creative method and potent technology—what Tolkien described as an "elvish craft" capable of suspending the disbelief of "both designer and spectator." Tolkien described this art as a kind of magic, but a magic "at the furthest pole from the vulgar devices of the laborious, scientific, magician."[176] Like Jacques Ellul, Tolkien deplored the twentieth century's ugly and vaguely satanic technologies, and his fallen sorcerer Sauron, who forges the rings of power in the volcanic Mount Doom, can be read as a Promethean magus of technique. But though Tolkien had little taste for the modern world, the modern world loved him. *The Lord of the Rings* became a blockbuster hit in the 1960s, spurring a literary (and subliterary) boom in fantasy and science fiction—genres that were gobbled up by, among others, the creative computer geeks growing up in the shadows of the mainframe. Tolkien's imagery also saturated a counterculture that desperately wanted to bring its own magical perceptions to life. Some Berkeley-based science-fiction fans formed the Society for Creative Anachronism to theatrically re-create the Middle Ages, while religious misfits across the land began dabbling with the druid rituals and Celtic mythology that would later sprout into the American Pagan revival. *The Lord of the Rings* didn't just make you want to escape into another world; it made you want to build your own.

Allegorical Machines

Tolkien died in 1973, the same year that two Midwesterners named Gary Gygax and Dave Arneson forged the next link in the chain mail of the technopagan imaginary. Gygax and Arneson were ravenous fans of historically rigorous Avalon Hill strategy games like Gettysburg and Stalingrad, war games played with hexagonal field maps, miniature playing pieces, and byzantine rules meant to simulate the claustrophobic conditions of battle. For a lark, the duo decided to revamp a medieval combat game by introducing fantasy elements that owed as much to Conan the Barbarian as to Frodo the hobbit. The resulting hybrid was the notorious Dungeons & Dragons, better known to its devotees as D&D.

One design feature of D&D would prove particularly important for later computer culture. Rather than control armies from above, participants chose to "play" individual characters created from a menu of races and player classes. You might doff the imaginary cap of a mace-wielding dwarf named Glorp, whose unique characteristics were defined by a statistically determined array of skills, spells, weapons, and traits. Banding together with other role-playing fellows, you and Glorp would explore a neomedieval world filled with underground labyrinths and catacombs. With no ultimate goal in mind, you and your merry crew would scavenge for treasure or magic scrolls, dodge traps, kill enemies, and avoid the death-dealing forces that could ax your character at any moment.

With their invention of the fantasy role-playing game (or RPG), Gygax and Arneson had not simply churned out another world in the Middle-Earth mold. They had built tools for other "subcreators" to use, tools capable of constructing otherworldly realms that transformed players into participants. As a category, the word *fantasy* certainly describes the dark, fairy-tale logic mined by D&D and the lion's share of RPGs that followed in its enormously successful wake. But D&D was also *phantasmic* in its very techniques, for the game "took place" not on a board but in the creative psyches of its players. No longer did combatants loom over strategic maps from the god's-eye view of opposing generals; now they wandered chartless inside a simulated mental world conjured by the godlike game lord and bard known as the Dungeon Master. Acting as oral demiurge, the DM led his players, room by room, through a unique world carved out of his own imagination and D&D's loose rules of composition.

To envision the Dungeon Master's secondary world, D&D players exploited the same powers of creative imagination used and misused by occultists past and present. Indeed, the tips given in the *Advanced Dungeons & Dragons Player's Handbook* sound almost like instructions for a New Age visualization, or a B-movie form of the *ars memoria*:

> As [the Dungeon Master] describes your surroundings, try to picture them mentally. Close your eyes and construct the walls of the maze around yourself. Imagine the hobgoblin as [the DM] describes it whooping and gamboling down the corridor toward you. Now imagine how you would react in that situation and tell [the DM] what you are going to do.[177]

Though most simulation gamers were simply having a blast, many a Pagan was born during those long nights in the den swilling Coca-Cola and eviscerating trolls. Besides the occult arcana that stuff the handbooks of D&D and many RPGs, role-playing games operationally resemble magical rituals, which also take place within a bounded space and time ruled by the imaginative exploration of deeply mythological scenarios. This is not to say that gamers believe in their Secondary Worlds; instead, they *program* them, using an elaborate symbolic machinery in order to solidify and organize the plastic material of the imagination. For most RPGs, this machinery includes thick rulebooks of lore, statistical tables, occasional maps, and a set of weirdly shaped dice that determine the outcome of various contests by forcing the hand of chance.

Tolkien would probably recoil at all this rigmarole, so far from the fairy stories he loved and so reminiscent of the "vulgar devices of the laborious, scientific, magician." But God only knows what the man would have thought of the DEC PDP-10 mainframe computer that would provide the next and arguably strangest operating system for Fairy. In the mid-1970s, a researcher named Don Woods was working at the Stanford Artificial Intelligence Lab—the kind of Californian think tank where the rooms were named after Middle-Earth locales and the printer was outfitted with three elven fonts. Woods came across a primitive text-only adventure game hacked together by Will Crowther, one of the bright guys behind early network computing. Expanding on Crowther's program, Don Woods designed a knockoff of D&D called, variously, ADVENT, Adventure, or Colossal Cave. Unlike D&D combatants, Adventure players went solo into an underworld cartography described by screenfuls of computer text ("YOU ARE IN A MAZE OF TWISTY LITTLE PASSAGES, ALL ALIKE"). Typing simple commands ("GO NORTH," "TAKE WAND," "KILL DRAGON") prompted responses from the impish program ("KILL THE DRAGON WITH WHAT, YOUR BARE HANDS?") and gave you the chance to crack the elaborate puzzles that stood between you and the next treasure chest or underworld chamber. As Steven Levy noted, "Each 'room' of the adventure was like a computer subroutine, presenting a logical problem you'd have to solve."178

Besides laying down the basic framework for hundreds of future adventure games, Adventure showed how successfully a laborious and scientific device like the computer could suspend disbelief and simulate a magical world. The program's well-defined descriptions allowed you to project yourself into the simple prose the way you could dive into a pulpy SF novel, and its logical loops and algorithms brought the "symbolic machinery" of its Secondary World one step closer to natural law. As Julian Dibbell explains, "for anyone in the midst of exploring it, the world of Adventure was as hard-wired as gravity, and almost as convincing."179 By transforming the PDP-10 into both dungeon and dungeon master, Crowther and Woods not only had established a particularly addictive mode of interacting with digital code, but had forged a new kind of imaginal space in the bowels of the computer.

With the blessings of its creators, pirate copies of the program rapidly circulated through various research communities linked through the ARPAnet, the ancestor of today's Internet. According to Dave Lebling, "All work ceased throughout almost the entire country at these research sites. It was almost like an infection."180 Recognizing a potentially lucrative addiction when he saw one, Lebling later took Colossal Cave out of its open network environment and retooled it into Zork, a successful consumer product that helped kick-start the computer game industry.

While the vivid and engrossing graphics of today's games have pushed text-based adventures like Zork to the margins, the digital imagery of sword and sorcery continues to clang away in such popular fantasy computer games as Dragon Warrior, WarCraft II, War Hammer, and the Ultima series.

Because Adventure does not hide its writing space behind graphic images, the game provides a particularly clear framework for grasping the phantasmic logic that shapes digital space. With that in mind, I ask you to dwell for a moment on one of the most archaic and venerable images in the history of computer culture, which also happens to be the first scene that Adventure throws the errant player's way:

YOU ARE STANDING AT THE END OF A ROAD BEFORE A SMALL BRICK BUILDING. AROUND YOU IS A FOREST. A SMALL STREAM FLOWS OUT OF THE BUILDING AND DOWN A GULLY.

At once schematic and concrete, these words conjure up the kind of internal landscape that you want to explore. But if we let the image sound the depths of literary memory, it takes us back to another traveler, stepping off of another road, about to begin another underworld quest:

When I had journeyed half our life's way,
I found myself within a shadowed forest,
for I had lost the path that does not stray.[181]

And so does Dante begin his descent into the colossal caverns of the *Inferno*, the first third of his *Divine Comedy*, the great allegorical poem of the Middle Ages.

Though it's somewhat ridiculous to compare an Olympian work of imaginative poetry with a goofy computer game, the Dantesque link to digital space is compelling. For one thing, both the Inferno and Colossal Cave distinctly resemble the virtual data architectures of the *ars memoria*. As Crowther designed it, Colossal Cave actually fulfilled one of the classic recommendations for the old memory palaces: Internalize the structure of an actual place (in this case, Kentucky's Bedquilt Cave), and then add magical elements and properties. Frances Yates suggests that Dante's *Divine Comedy* may well have been a product of the art of memory, arguing that the poet's intensely visual and nearly tactile journey through the structured layers of the afterworld fulfill the classical rule of "striking images on orders of places."[182]

As Dante strolls through his Neoplatonic Catholic cosmology, his movements tell an archetypal narrative about the virtual soul and its passage from sin to salvation. At the same time, the poem's images pack in a small encyclopedia of data: references to ancient mythology, Thomistic philosophy, autobiography, Italian poetry, the politics of Florence. The *Divine Comedy* is a poetic data space, something that the American poet laureate Robert Pinsky recognized in 1984, when he wrote an Adventure-style text-based computer game loosely modeled on the poem. More recently, the Digital Dante Project at Columbia University has begun "translating" Dante's text into a multimedia Web site that incorporates text, audio, video, and images into a nest of hyperlinks drawn from various commentaries. The Project picked the *Divine Comedy* to prototype their "twenty-first-century illumination" because "Dante the poet understood the power of images, the icons of a culture, and architectural spaces."[183]

As such, Dante was also a master of allegory, that literary and pictorial mode that, at one level, uses concrete images, characters, or landscapes to represent the abstract relationship between ideas, usually of a moral or religious nature. For example, the envious souls who expiate their sins on the second terrace of Mount Purgatory have their eyes sewn shut with wire; this bizarre surface detail corresponds to, and reverses, the moral fault of gazing beyond the self with envy. Allegories are thus a rather paradoxical way of explaining concepts with symbols. As the literary scholar Angus Fletcher points out, allegories often take place in fantastic, almost psychedelic environments—a dreamland, a visionary otherworld, or a futuristic scenario where magic appears as super-science. At the same time, and unlike Dante's poetry, allegories are usually dry and schematic, as they tend to follow the abstract or logical relationships between concepts rather than the unique drives of characters or the turbulent power of raw images. John Bunyan's enormously popular Christian allegory *The Pilgrim's Progress* reads like a connect-the-dots catechism. In fact, some characters in allegorical texts are so programmatic that they were known in the trade as "allegorical machines."

In some ways, Adventure (and the countless adventure games it spawned) sticks the user into a first-person allegory. Like Dante or the knights-errant in *The Faerie Queene,* whose environs Coleridge described as "mental space," you wander through a rigorously structured but dreamlike landscape patched together from phantasms. These images usually possess more than a surface meaning, since they conceal clues and abstract relationships that, if figured out, will send you deeper into gamespace. The characters you run into are also literally "machines"—programmed daemonic agents with whom you must struggle to make your way forward.

Of course, Adventure and its more barbaric descendants are hardly religious or even moral universes, though Lucas Arts's 1996 game After Life did ask players to manage souls in a Dantesque world of hell, purgatory, and heaven. But if the images in these games do not encode virtues and vices, then what do they allegorize? Steven Levy gives us a hint in *Hackers:* "In a sense, Adventure was a metaphor for computer programming itself—the deep recesses you explored in the Adventure world were akin to the basic, most obscure levels of the machine that you'd be traveling in when you hacked in assembly code."[184] Sherry Turkle, a psychologist at MIT, also explained that Adventure fans "found an affinity between the aesthetics of building a large complex program, with its treelike structure, its subprograms and sub-subprograms, and working one's way through a highly structured, constructed world of mazes and magic and secret, hidden rooms."[185] Adventure is not an allegorical machine; it's an allegory *of* the machine.

Angus Fletcher defines allegory as "a fundamental process of encoding our speech," and computers are nothing if not hierarchies of encoded language.[186] At the bottom of this digital dungeon lie the physical circuits whose pulses of energy embody the basic binary code. Because the "machine language" that commands this code is hellish to hack, computer scientists long ago invented control jargons like assembly language and higher-order programming codes such as MS-DOS, UNIX, and C++. These latter tongues come relatively close to natural languages like English; a few well-placed words can command gobs of machine code. At the top level of this stack of lingo lies the sunlit world of the user interface, which in the case of Adventure was just a screen full of text and a simple parser that interpreted the actions that players typed in. The user interface is the level most of us noninitiates manipulate, often without a thought of the hairy briar patch lurking below.

In a sense, all user interfaces can be seen as interactive allegories of the computer. When Apple engineers introduced the Macintosh and its graphic user interface (GUI), they replaced the dry world of command lines and DOS prompts with a world of simple simulacra. The Mac cloaked the computer's workings inside an audiovisual "desktop metaphor" whose folders, trashcans, and icons served as active and intuitive representations of the computer's internal processes. These simulacra proved enormously popular among nontechnical people, and as computers and the Internet continue to saturate the world at large, we can expect user interfaces—including Internet browsers, Web sites, and program control panels—to plunge us ever deeper into such iconic simulations, and to pull us further from the binary codespace where the action "really" lies. Perhaps our tame digital metaphors will one day bloom into allegorical landscapes, and desktops, windows, and browsers will open into three-dimensional worlds animated with daemonic agents and interdimensional portals that conceal an underlying layer of purely logical protocols.

Whether or not we are talking about desktop terminals or software packages or Net browsers, good interfaces mediate the hyperspace of information in ways familiar enough to keep us from getting lost but not so familiar that we remain rooted in the habits associated with other media or with the everyday world. Hypertext visionary Ted Nelson observed:

> Once we leave behind "two-dimensionality" (virtual paper) and even "three-dimensionality" (virtual stacks), we step off the edge into another world, into the representation of the *true structure and interconnectedness of information*. To represent this true structure, we need to indicate multidimensional connection and multiple connections between entities.[187]

The notion that information possesses a "true structure" is a major motif in the metaphysics of information, but here Nelson asks a more basic question: How can one represent such a multidimensional world? Hoping to construct a vast and labyrinthine library of interlinked documents, Nelson pushed the envelope with the rather science-fiction notion of placing "wormholes" between documents, but the name of Nelson's project—Xanadu—and the fact that it remains vaporware after decades of research indicate that such representations are still something of a holy grail. In fact, we still have not gotten much farther than the work of Alan Kay, the Xerox PARC researcher who invented the pull-down

menus, folders, and point-and-click icons that Steve Jobs exploited for
the Mac. In an article on interface design published in 1990, Kay was
already criticizing the overreliance on simple visual metaphors like trashcans. Instead, he argued, magic and theater offered better models for the
construction of robust user interfaces. For an example, Kay analyzed the
now completely "natural" metaphor of the terminal screen as a piece of
paper that we mark on. "Should we transfer the paper metaphor so perfectly that the screen is as hard as paper to erase and change? Clearly
not. If it is to be like magical paper, then it is the *magical* part that is all
important."[188]

Kay's emphasis on magic indicates that the supernatural metaphors
that saturate technoculture may have a more substantive basis than the
fondness that many hackers have for Sandman comic books or D&D.
These metaphors arise and take power because, as William Irwin
Thompson noted in a discussion of computer games, "the conventional
worldview of materialism is not subtle enough to deal with the complexities of a multidimensional universe in which domains interpenetrate
and are enfolded in one another."[189] The science-fiction author Vernor
Vinge came to a similar conclusion in "True Names," a brilliant novella
whose vision of a networked virtual world predates *Neuromancer* by
three years. Unlike the bright neon grid of Gibson's cyberspace, the
Other Plane of Vinge's story is a Tolkienesque world of swamps, castles,
and magic, a half-dreamed environment that is generated partly through
electronic cues that stimulate the "imagination and subconscious" of its
electrode-wearing users. The hacker denizens of the Other Plane band
together as covens of witches and warlocks, and at one point, a few of
them discuss how magical metaphors came to dominate "data space":

> The Limey and Erythrina argued that sprites, reincarnation, spells,
> and castles were the natural tools here, more natural than the atom-
> istic twentieth-century notions of data structures, programs, files, and
> communication protocols. It was, they argued, just more convenient
> for the mind to use the global ideas of magic as the tokens to manip-
> ulate this new environment.[190]

One reason for this convenience is that the allegorical and hieroglyphic
language of magic works well with the fact that the Other Plane exists
simultaneously on at least two levels of reality. Describing a character
approaching the Coven, Vinge writes that while his conscious mind

perceived a narrow row of stones, his "subconscious knew what the stones represented, handling the chaining of routines from one information net to another."[191] The Other Plane thus reverses our normal state of mind. Here it is the *conscious* mind that moves through a world of archetypal imagery, while the subconscious concerns itself with logical information processing.

As Vinge suggested, these technomagical conceits also function as strangely fit metaphors for the workaday world of computer programming itself. In *Turing's Man*, Jay David Bolter quotes computer specialist Frederick Brooks: "The programmer, like the poet, works only slightly removed from pure thought-stuff. He builds his castles in the air, from air, creating by exertion of the imagination. . . . Yet the program construct, unlike the poet's words, is real in the sense that it moves and works, producing visible outputs separate from the construct itself."[192] This is not a very satisfying description of poetry, but it certainly describes the virtual aspirations of the magician. No wonder that ace programmers and UNIX weenies have long been called "wizards," or that the semiautonomous UNIX programs that kick into action on their own accord are known as "demons." Steven Levy's *Hackers* drips with loose references to spellcraft, while *The New Hacker's Dictionary* gives definitions for "deep magic," "heavy wizardry," "incantation," "voodoo programming," and "casting the runes."

Such metaphors infected the computer underground of hackers as well. When young digital pranksters started "breaking into" unauthorized computer systems through network dial-ups, they were in many ways simply playing Adventure online. Naturally, such hackers also took on colorful, sardonic nicknames, many plucked from sword and sorcery. Enterprising young men like Erik Bloodaxe, Black Majik, Kerrang Khan, the Marauder, and Knight Lightning would band together in underground groups like the Legion of Doom, the Knights of Shadow, and the Imperial Warlords. In his book *The Hacker Crackdown*, Bruce Sterling notes that the relatively notorious Atlanta hacker Urvile was also a fanatic Dungeon Master who "barely made the distinction" between fantasy games and cyberspace; the Secret Service agents who seized Urvile's personal notes found role-playing scenarios mixed helter-skelter into hand-scrawled records of his intrusions into actual computer systems.

The plot of "True Names" also concerns a conflict between agents of the state and the Other Plane's freewheeling information brokers, a conflict that Vinge stages in terms of cryptography. Vinge's hackers do not use the U.S. government's encryption schemes, but those that had leaked out of academia "over NSA's petulant objections." Vinge was prophetic: over a decade after his story appeared, the federal government and digital libertarians became embroiled in similar debates over encryption standards, privacy, and online security. For their part, the feds stirred up the usual bogeymen (terrorists, drug dealers, pedophiles) to ensure that the NSA and other state agencies would have backdoor access into any computer system or bit of email that intrigued them. In response, a loose network of online advocates, businesspeople, and scruffy "cypherpunks" raised a mighty stink, while powerful home-brewed encryption software slipped into the Net.

Though magic metaphors and secret codes operate according to very different rules, they are hardly historical strangers. Take the incantations of the *Steganographia,* a trailblazing cryptographic text written by the enigmatic Trithemius of Würzberg. Born in 1462, Trithemius was a prodigious scholar and humanist who took over the monastery of Sponheim at the precocious age of twenty-three. Displaying the infomania of so many Hermeticists, Trithemius transformed the monastery's paltry store of forty-eight books into a library of nearly two thousand volumes. His collection of occult texts alone made it one of the greatest libraries in all of Germany. The man was also heavily into creating secret codes; a copy of his *Polygraphia,* an innovative if primitive book of secret writing, is housed today in the NSA museum near Washington, D.C.

Far more curious is the *Steganographia,* which was apparently revealed to Trithemius in a dream. Though the first two books of this popular and influential work appear to be compendiums of spells, they have long since been recognized as systems for encoding messages; the mysterious name that heads each section simply indicates which decipherment key to employ. In the third book, however, Trithemius unveils what seems to be a complex system of astrological magic, one that exploits the sorts of numerological incantations and esoteric alphabets used by sorcerers and Kabbalists to interface with astral intelligences. Trithemius also describes how images of various cosmic forces can be etched into wax in order to capture and manipulate their powers. Apparently, the abbot's goal was nothing less than long-distance communication through the ether; he claimed his wax images and spells would create an astral network that, with the aid of Saturn's angel Orifiel, would allow the delivery of mental messages within the UPS-worthy window of twenty-four hours. Moreover, Trithemius's code was also a means of acquiring universal knowledge, of knowing "everything that is happening in the world." Though the third book of the *Steganographia* was recently discovered to be nothing more than an elaborate cryptogram, this revelation does not entirely banish the shadows that hover around the abbot's code. For why would Trithemius disguise his cryptography as black magic when black magic could (and did) get him into such serious trouble?

For the adventurous mathematical and occult minds of the Renaissance, astral programming was by no means limited to the archons of the Zodiac. Using an elaborate and highly coded system of theurgic magic, the Elizabethan court astrologer John Dee also sought "the company and information of the Angels of God." As faithful messengers of light mediating God's omniscience, angels were the original intelligent agents—immaterial, rational, stripped of human emotion. Contact with them could open the gates to the invisible cosmos of knowledge, those abstract Neoplatonic spheres that, in Dee's mind, were suggested by mathematics and occult lore alike. Dee made his acquaintance with the angels through a rogue named Edward Kelley, who claimed to see the entities in the surface of a "shew-stone." Dee and Kelley communicated with their daemonic companions through a confusing but linguistically consistent angelic language known as Enochian, but Dee still had no way of knowing whether his online buddies were angels or evil demons in disguise. To pierce this virtual ambiguity, which all of us may come to know far too well, the pious Dee spent much of his online time trying to establish the authentic identity of the angelic bots he encountered.

Scholars of the occult continue to debate the psychological status of Dee's experiences, with a number suggesting that he was simply being conned by Kelley. No matter. From the perspective of the digital dreamtime we now stand on the lip of, Dee's Enochian Calls—like Trithemius's astral encryptions, Vinge's Other Plane, Adventure's digital allegory, and Bruno's mechanical memory—provide a compelling snapshot of the strange interzones that erupt when dreams and phantoms invade information space. Whether we want them there or not, magic metaphors seem to arise almost spontaneously when we attempt to interface with the "mental space" of information and to map its "true" interdimensional structure. But what happens when you also get real people moving around inside such consensual hallucinations? To answer that question, we must return to that marvel of engineering that Will

Crowther worked on when he was not spelunking or hacking Adventure: networked computers.

Dungeons & Digizens

In 1979, the same year that Vinge wrote "True Names," two students at Britain's University of Essex named Roy Trubshaw and Richard Bartle built a network gaming system that allowed different people on different computers to occupy the same database at the same time. They called their text-based world the Multi-User Dungeon, or MUD for short, and it transported players logged into the university network into an Adventure-like gamespace known simply as "the Land." As with Adventure, the computer screen served as an evocative textual window onto a world full of spells, treasures, and neomedieval combat. After reading the description of your immediate surroundings (and any objects you might pick up, buy, or steal), you would type the direction you wanted to go, and the screen text would change, providing you a description of your new location. But you would also encounter some rather spunky dwarves and warriors as well, characters animated by real human beings hunched over keyboards somewhere on the Essex network. When two characters crossed paths, they read each other's descriptions, after which they might strike up a keyboard-clattering chat or start swinging battle-axes over loot. And thus it was that Trubshaw and Bartle brought role-playing games online, giving birth to the cyberspace doppelgänger eventually known as the *avatar*: digital doubles that embody the user's point of view and that also represent him or her to the other denizens of the digital environs.

Despite the lag times and the loss of D&D's oral storytelling, role-playing games and networked computers proved to be a match made in purgatory. Bartle exported MUD code across the world, and over the next few years, other codesmiths hacked together similar programming systems with similar greasy-kid-stuff names like MUCK, MUSH, and MOO. These early MUDs were devoted to variations on the sword-and-sorcery theme. Pouring countless hours into the simple but compelling tasks of avoiding death and delivering it, the bloodthirsty undergraduate geeks that made up the bulk of MUDders would gradually accumulate the wealth and experience points that allowed them to climb up the social hierarchy of the MUD. Near the top rung hovered the coveted status of wizard, at which point the MUD gave players some direct control over the MUD database itself. In some systems, even the "wiz" was trumped by the "gods": demiurgic sysops who wrote and administered the world and could change its basic features and rules at will.

MUDs thus functioned as toy cosmologies, their graded levels of personal power mimicking both the ladders of the corporate world and the hierarchical degrees of Freemasonry, where novices ascended through esoteric grades that granted them increasing spiritual powers. Many MUDs also took place within fictional worlds poached from fantasy and science fiction, material like *Star Trek,* Tolkien, or Anne McCaffrey's *Dragonriders of Pern.* Literalizing the medieval perception that the world is a book, these so-called "theme MUDs" redeployed the characters, social conditions, and geographies of genre fiction into an interactive virtual milieu. As with the cosmologies that once saturated premodern societies from end to end, theme MUDs allowed role players to express their individual creativity within the framework of a shared mythos.

Still, with their compulsive drive toward violence, treasure, and increased power, crude "hack-and-slash" games dominated the world of MUDs until 1989, when a Carnegie-Mellon grad named James Aspnes changed the nature of the game. Aspnes's TinyMUD jettisoned strict ranks, ceased logging experience points and killing off characters, and, most notably, allowed players to participate directly in the ongoing construction of the MUDspace themselves. Though not designed to overthrow role-playing games, TinyMUDs nonetheless began attracting netheads, many of them female, who had little interest in skewering trolls. With an egalitarian do-it-yourself creativity programmed into the environment itself, TinyMUDs went social, players became inhabitants, and close-minded contests of mayhem gave way to the open-ended games of life: camaraderie, sex, gossip, debate, and factional politics, most of which tended to revolve around the rules and regulations of the MUD itself.

Though these new worlds distanced themselves from their hack-and-slash ancestors, the tropes of magic continued to come in handy, simply because they fit the weird rules of social reality that define life in a MUD: shape-shifting, teleporting, telepathic communication at a distance, and especially the power of words to shape the world. On MUDs, language is performative—uploading the message that you are squeezing a chicken is the same thing as squeezing a chicken. More technically savvy MUDders also manipulate the hidden programming language that runs the world, fashioning golemlike bots, or doubles of themselves, or roving independent eyes. As Julian Dibbell noted in a *Village Voice* article about a virtual rape on the MUD LambdaMOO, MUD language invokes the pre-Enlightenment principle of the magic word: "The commands you type into a computer are a kind of speech that doesn't so much communicate as *make things happen,* directly and ineluctably."[193] Or as one Pagan MUDder told the author, "If you regard magic in the literal sense of influencing the universe according to the will of the magician, then simply *being* on the [MUD] is magic."

Nonetheless, "social MUDs" rang the death knell for traditional sword-and-sorcery imagery. In anarchic romper rooms like Lambda-MOO and PostModern Culture MOO, users stitched together their avatars from comic books, fashion magazines, or rock lyrics, while the rooms that people built were collages of media references, Lego sets, and conceptual art. Without any shared purpose or mythos, social MUDs became almost as fragmented, heterodox, and ordinary as life on the street—or at least life in a university dorm. This development was not universally appreciated. For many combat MUDders, removing the possibility that your character could die deflated the driving force of MUD life, replacing it with the idle banter of a parlor game or the chat rooms popular in other regions of the Internet. Their argument goes to the heart of avatar ontology: Do we identify with our online selves because they are as liberated as we want to be, or because they are as constrained as we really are? For old school MUDders, the distinction between being IC (in character) and OOC (out of character) was also vital, if not always crystal clear. But social MUDs in many ways erased or merged these two categories, creating strange new possibilities for online identity and interaction.

As Thanatos fled the scene, Eros moved in to take its place. Many social MUDs became hotbeds of romance, and swordplay was replaced with the gropes and thrusts of netsex, the online world's moist and potent blend of phone sex and raunchy pen-pal letters. Nonetheless, this virtual carnality continued to percolate with the occult energy of the phantasm. After all, the Neoplatonic cosmology of the premodern West in many ways "ran" on Eros, in the broad sense of life force and beauty as well as sexual attraction. Eros provided the magnetic lines of energy that alchemists and hermetic magicians tapped to align themselves with cosmic forces and to cast spells on people. Such enchantments have not quit us, however much we have left the hermetic worldview in the dust. For people in the throes of a crush or a sexual obsession, the Other takes on a daemonic intensity that can drive us from all reason, sending us off on adventures that are more often than not fueled by incessant dreams and figments of desire. Just as the arresting phantasms of pornography have taken the Net by storm, so too has the phenomenon of the lustful crush found itself strangely amplified by the disembodied electro-erotic banter in MUDs and online chat rooms. Deprived of visual cues and immersed in the ambiguities of textual self-description, virtual lovers often find themselves in a seductive Rorschach blot of mutual projection and tantric play.

MUDs also awakened a broader range of imaginal desires by allowing people to construct and experiment with new identities within a genuine social space. As Sherry Turkle put it, "When we step through the screen into virtual communities, we reconstruct our identities on the other side of the looking glass."[194] Gender switching is only the most obvious example of the fluidity of the self in MUDspace, where the relatively fixed identities that structure our everyday lives melt into a fluctuating and protean play of masks, characters, and personae. Many MUDders possess more than one character, or "morph" into different characters during the course of a single session: a werewolf, a paramecium, a Japanese schoolgirl named Keiko. In MUDs, we do not just traffic with phantasms—we become them.

This flurry of self-experimentation is taking place at a time when, for many different reasons, human identity seems up for grabs. The visible bouquet of sexual possibilities and body modifications throws our stable images of flesh and gender into doubt, even as advances in biochemistry, genetics, and psychopharmacology argue that many of the elements of personality that we take for granted are nothing more than symphonies of neurochemicals and hardwired genetic habits. Identity is literally fragmenting; cases of multiple personality disorder have risen exponentially since the early 1980s, along with reported incidents of near-death experiences, spirit encounters, and UFO abductions. At the other end of the cultural spectrum, many influential postmodern theorists vociferously attack the notion of an authentic or essential self, arguing that identity is actually a multiplicity, a variable "social construct" hammered together by a host of changing cultural and historical forces.

For the most part these arguments are rather esoteric, but our excessively mediated technological environment could well be mainlining the postmodern identity crisis to the masses. Turkle cites the psychologist

Kenneth Gergen, who describes the "saturated self" that emerges now that communications technologies allow us to "colonize each other's brains." We begin to feel like routers or switches in vast networks of images, voices, and information, as if the boundaries of the self are dissolving into amorphous systems of data flow. Like the "subject" dissected by postmodern theorists, the online self is constantly under construction.

But as the neomedieval origins of the online avatar suggest, the postmodern virtual self may come with a premodern twist. The "morphs" that people inhabit on MUDs recall not only the digital graphics engines that gave us *Terminator 2*'s melting cop, but the pagan transformations of Ovid's *Metamorphoses*. Many MUDders and other online changelings would chime in with the wizard Tuan Mac Cairill's cheer in the Irish tale *The Voyage of Bran:* "A hawk to-day, a boar yesterday, / Wonderful instability!" This is the song of the shaman, whose archetypal popularity in contemporary spiritual culture cannot be chalked up simply to colonizing New Age romanticism. The shaman changes shape, interbreeds with animals and inhuman cosmic forces, and even scrambles gender roles through cross-dressing and other tricks. Moreover, the shaman leaves his or her body to enter an immense and incorporeal soulspace teeming with images, information, and entities, many of them quite hostile and deceptive. Of course, the shaman also returns from the bowels of the earth with medicine to heal the tribe, whereas we return from a night of MUDding or netlust with aching eyes, sore wrists, and often a vaguely hollow feeling of spent life force.

The psychological, social, and even spiritual fallout from the widespread adoption of avatars remains a complex question. Will these masks be shadow selves, wish-fulfillment figures, energy vampires, or disposable video game tokens? How will we relate to them and with them? What is their ontology? In this regard, the fact that digital doubles are called avatars seems more than happenstance. The Hindu religious term was first used by the Lucasfilm creative designer Chip Morningstar to describe the crude cartoon figures that players used to move around Habitat, an extremely popular multiuser graphical virtual world developed in Japan by Fujitsu. The term's popularity spread after Neil Stephenson used it in his hit science-fiction novel *Snow Crash* to describe the home-brewed digital getups and off-the-shelf costumes that people don in the online virtual world he called the Metaverse, a crowded and cacophonous strip mall vastly more believable than Gibson's cool geometric grids. *Avatar* literally means descent, and in Hindu lore, it denotes the various incarnations a god may take in this world—some Hindus believe that both Rama and Buddha are avatars of the creator god Vishnu. Avatars possess a dual identity. On the one hand, they are separate from the godhead, receiving only a portion of its spirit. On the other hand, avatars are also indivisible from the godhead, because the gods remain in constant communication with everything they touch. While replicating this ambiguous overlap of identity and separation, today's digizens have also turned the scheme on its head: We now *disincarnate* into fleshless "godlike" forms, though it remains to be seen whether this projection can be considered an ascent or a descent, a climb through Purgatorio or a plunge into Inferno. For hard-core Hindu yogis, cyberspace might seem like nothing more than a fresh layer of *maya*, the veil of illusion that cloaks and distorts our perception of reality. In their burning eyes, the pocket universes we're building out of protocols and pixel dust might seem like dreams within a dream, a labyrinth of distracting desires leading ever farther from the Source.

the alien call

The chimeras of online life may be tugging at the souls of cybernauts, but they can't hold a candle to the specters that stalk some folks in the world outside. Even as Western commodity culture strives to unite the hearts and minds of earthlings under a single canopy of satellite signals, T-shirt logos, and movie marquees, more and more Americans seem to be dropping out of consensus reality altogether. Literally millions believe that alien craft cruise the skyways, or that psychic phone networks will do them good, or that, as born-again Christians, they will be beamed up by God in the rapture that precedes the imminent conflagration of the apocalypse. Thousands of otherwise ordinary citizens have reported run-ins with luminescent angels, underground satanic cults, the Blessed Mary, black helicopters, chupacabras, and almond-eyed extraterrestrials armed with anal probes.

Most of us feel comfortable chalking up such close encounters to neu-rochemical imbalances, bad lunch meat, lax education, or the editorial philosophy of the *Weekly World News*. But the closer you look at these phenomena, and at many of the people who are captured by them, the more difficult it becomes to completely separate this loopy world from the straight one. After all, we live in a time of strange weather, of sheep clones, Martian rocks, quantum computers, xenotransplants, magnetic mind machines, planet-smashing asteroids, nanotechnologies, and global electronic brains, while all about us the planet seems to be cracking apart at the seams. Reality, it seems, has been deregulated, and nothing is business as usual anymore—least of all business. The horizon of his-tory bends into an asymptote, and at its warping edges, the more wild-eyed and speculative can't help but glimpse the shadows of some imponderable and ominous X leaning in. As the ancient mapmakers wrote when they sketched the edges of the watery unknown, "Here be dragons."

Of all the dragons slouching along the borders of postmodern con-sciousness, none leaves more enigmatic and goofy tracks than the UFO and its trickster crew. Over the last half century, flying saucers and their daemonic occupants have crash-landed, buzzed cornfields, delivered messages of doom and salvation, sucked bovines dry of blood, conspired with military brass, slipped subliminal messages into B movies, stolen embryos from Bible Belt housewives, seduced Brazilian farmers, and explored the orifices of horror-fiction writers. Though public interest and reported sightings have waxed and waned over the last half century, UFOs and ETs are once again riding high as we crest into the millennium, thanks in no small measure to the kind of media presence that would make most Hollywood actors drool.

As the ultimate superscientific machine, the UFO comes straight from the radiating heart of postwar technoculture, and the lore that has grown up around the alien craft, both within and beyond the culture industry, has blossomed into the most visionary pop mythology that directly engages the question of technology. We should not pass lightly over this word *mythology,* however, as if you could stick UFOs on the same shelf as superheroes or sewer alligators. We need to recall that the first mythologists ran into the cave with their eyes bugging, babbling as they pointed at *that thing out there.* For people who possess crystal-clear memories of clammy-fingered ETs gathering at the foot of their bed, science-fiction tropes are not really an issue. At its phenomenological core, the alien encounter exceeds signs and folklore, and this immediacy recalls the basis of myth making and religion alike. As Carl Jung wrote in his prescient 1959 study *Flying Saucers,* which argued that the UFO was a modern archetype squirted out of the collective unconscious, "in religious experience man comes face to face with a psychically overwhelming Other."[195] The high-tech drama of the UFO stages just such a mystical collision, generating otherworldly fabulations that drip with apocalyptic and deeply gnostic motifs.

With such concerns in mind, the question of whether or not UFOs are "real" is, alternately, too crude and too philosophically taxing to broach. For fifty years now, so-called "nuts-and-bolts" ufologists have been scraping turf, making charts, and tracking the comings and goings of what they believe are perfectly material mechanisms from afar. Desperate to make the UFO a legitimate object of scientific study, these investigators simply mirror the literalism of skeptics, whose bulk-rate sociology and rules of evidence inevitably leave the most interesting and ambiguous questions unasked. Much more compelling are the nimble tactics taken by writers like Jacques Vallee, a computer scientist who has written some of the most rigorous, yet open-minded, books on the subject. For Vallee, the conventional story that UFOs are physical craft piloted by beings from other planets is at best a reflection of our own materialism, at worst a ruse. Instead, Vallee peels back the baroque surface details of UFO lore to trace its deeper epistemological and cultural patterns. Unlike those more naive ufologists who hope that the final piece of the puzzle is just around the corner, Vallee points out that the very nature of the phenomenon—its peculiar combination of scant physical evidence, believable eyewitnesses, recognizable patterns, and patent absurdity—seems almost designed to befuddle. All explanations and interpretations are like signals shot into the heavens: They either fade into the stellar maw or bounce back, echoes of our own descriptions.

For nuanced observers like Vallee, the peculiar behavior of these epistemological loops suggests that deeper forces are at work. Some sense a mischievous, deceptive, and coy intelligence lurking behind the stage of the UFO's theater of the absurd, an intelligence whose "message" seems almost intentionally tangled inside a briar patch of rumor and report, pop archetype and con job, evidence and hoax. It is as if the UFO incarnates the trickster spirit of information itself, constantly flip-flopping signal and noise. In his book *Angels and Aliens*, Keith Thompson argues that ufology thus replicates the binary tension found in literary allegory. As in something like Spenser's *Faerie Queene*, the field's "truths" are split between surreal surface details—what appears to be happening—and a deeper structure of possible explication. Debunkers, conspiracy theorists, and investigators all attempt to untangle these two levels of understanding, to get to the heart of the mystery by separating appearance from reality. This process even has a psychological component, as abductees attempt to dig beneath their superficial "screen memories" to recall their "real" abuse at the hands of extraterrestrial mad scientists.

Shifting this allegorical scramble to the level of myth, Thompson accuses most ufologists (pro and con) of a quest for Apollonian truths when the UFOs themselves follow the tangled path of Hermes. Thompson describes the "hermetic intelligence" that UFOs seem to embody: "inherently ambivalent, leaning to this side and that, [it] operates through analogy, intuition, and association, always seeking the larger pattern in the small isolated event."[196] As we've seen throughout this book, such hermetic intelligence has been dogging technologies all along, and we should hardly be surprised that the supreme technological phantasm of the twentieth century moves like a trickster at the crossroads, and demands a similarly mischievous line of hermeneutic attack. This hermetic twist may even explain the mysterious cattle mutilations that have long been associated with alien flybys; after all, as the *Hymn to Hermes* shows, the god is fond of molesting other people's cows.

Saucers Full of Secrets

In his classic study *Passport to Magonia,* Jacques Vallee traces many motifs of UFO lore to the legends, religious texts, and historical accounts of premodern times. In the ninth century, the Archbishop of Lyons mentions the widespread popular belief in manned floating ships; a twelfth-century Japanese record describes a strange "earthenware vessel" flying around Mount Fukuhara; a medieval Irish account claims that a cloudship got its anchor stuck on a church door. Vallee draws particularly striking connections between alien abductions and the fairy lore compiled in ethnographies like Robert Kirk's seventeenth-century *Secret Commonwealth* and Evans-Wentz's massive *The Fairy Faith in Celtic Countries.* In a more than trivial sense, E.T. is only the latest in a procession of fauns, satyrs, leprechauns, incubi, and other spectral critters who have peered through the windows of the human soul, especially when that soul finds itself in a twilight zone where the borders between phantasm and fact are not so tightly policed.

Whatever Mobius twist of mind and matter explains these otherworldly cameos, some of these entities seem particularly fond of reflecting technological evolution. What appeared to medieval witnesses as cloudships with anchors became dirigibles in late-nineteenth-century America, when newspapers across the country reported numerous sightings of manned cigar-shaped airships, some of which featured mechanical turbines, air brakes, and the sorts of headlamps found on locomotives. By World War II, ghost rockets and jetspeed "foo-fighters" were the most popular anomalous sightings, and as countless commentators have noted, flying saucers hit the scene in the radiating wake of the atomic bomb.

The obvious technosociological conclusion is that flying saucers are manifestations of nuclear anxiety. This thesis gained prominence in the 1950s, popping up in the work of debunkers and B movies like *The Day the Earth Stood Still.* But it also made its way into the messages of the Space Brothers themselves. According to early contactees like George Adamski, whose widely publicized and thoroughly ludicrous encounters with Venusians dripped with religious imagery, the aliens decided to drop by for a chat once they realized that humans were capable of blowing the planet to kingdom come.

Keeping midcentury fears about nuclear apocalypse in mind, the UFO must also be seen as a visionary projectile hurtling from the unconscious depths of the information age. The first anomalous objects to be dubbed "flying saucers" were sighted in 1947, in the year that gave us the CIA, information theory, and the transistor, the nerve cell of the modern computer. Flying saucers then and now show a particular fondness for the electromagnetic ether: buzzing TV stations and power plants, causing electrical disturbances in cars and streetlights, and interrupting radio broadcasts with weird voices and strange bursts of static. Even today's SETI program—mainstream science's stab at searching for extraterrestrial life by aiming massive radio discs at distant stars—is based on the faith that information can be distinguished from noise. The UFO, it seems, is a rumor of God stitched into the fabric of the military-industrial-media complex, a complex whose cybernetic tentacles encircle us still.

As a hallucinatory figure of information, the UFO demonstrates the epistemological role that peripheral data and fringe media sources play in constructing alternative, if not heretical, accounts of reality. To seriously track the UFO, you must explore the margins of media: trashy paperbacks, weird Web sites, photocopied "documents," home films and videos, B movies, buff newsletters, and the occasional TV special on the Fox network. In his best-seller *Communion,* which helped spark the alien abduction craze in the late 1980s, Whitley Strieber described the dislocation induced by such ambiguous information: "I found myself in a minefield. Real documents that seemed to be false. False documents that seemed to be real. A plethora of 'unnamed sources.' And drifting through it all, the thin smoke of an incredible story."[197] Like the cyclone of factoids, photos, lab reports, and testimonies that swirl about the assassination of JFK, the thin smoke of data leaking from the exhaust pipes of the UFO has led many a mind, sturdy and not, into information wormholes from which they will never return.

Ufology's grassy knoll is Roswell, New Mexico. During a rash of flying saucer sightings in the summer of 1947, something strange fell out of the sky onto Mac Brazel's ranch, only a short hop from the Roswell Army Air Field. Summoned to the scene, Major Jesse Marcel allegedly discovered a heap of wreckage that included superstrong balsa-wood-like struts and powerful metals that resembled tinfoil, as well as a material that he later described as a nonflammable "parchment" covered with indecipherable "hieroglyphs." The next day, an information officer at Roswell named Walter Haut issued the statement that "the many rumors regarding the flying disc became a reality yesterday," because Roswell's "intelligence office" had actually recovered one. It was the only official military report to date that confirmed the existence of flying saucers. Newspapers across the globe picked up the report, but it was retracted the following day, when military spin doctors identified the object as nothing more than a crashed weather balloon—a claim that Marcel denied to his death.

Needless to say, the story was not over. For one thing, the afterimages left by the air force's swift retraction gave rise to rather contagious speculations about labyrinthine cover-ups. Over the decades, Roswell lore grew more baroque, and rumors spread that the air force had recovered four alien corpses near the crash site. This claim was "substantiated" in 1984 when a TV producer produced a "top secret" stack of documents, allegedly prepared for President-to-be Eisenhower in 1952, that confirmed the discovery of the bodies. These documents, circulated widely in blurry xeroxed copies throughout the UFO community, described the work of Majestic 12, a hush-hush panel of scientists and military men supposedly organized by President Truman in 1947 to study UFOs. Diehard techgnostic conspiracy theorists should note that this panel included Dr. Vannevar Bush, the cybernetics honcho who invented the first electronic analog computer and wrote a famously visionary essay on the future of computing for the *Atlantic Monthly* in 1945.

Even true-blue UFO investigators now regard the MJ-12 documents as fishwrap, but Roswell lore has grown even more intransigent in the popular mind since the 1980s. Roswell-related rumors have popped up in cable docudramas, furnished material for *The X-Files,* and fed the hype surrounding a "newly discovered" film that allegedly records a military autopsy of an alien corpse in the late 1940s—a document whose oozing detail indicates, at the very least, that some talented media pranksters have a lot of time and money on their hands. In the summer of 1997, two weeks before 50,000 people flocked to Roswell for the fiftieth anniversary of Brazel's find, the air force conspicuously released *Roswell Report: Case Closed,* which disclosed, rather anxiously, that the "weather balloon" was actually a top secret high-altitude surveillance device, while the recovered bodies were actually test dummies chucked out of the sky.

Regardless of the facts, the Roswell incident presents a microcosm of the strange loops that information takes in the vicinity of the UFO: news leaks, cover-ups, infectious rumors, high-tech "hieroglyphs," bizarrely timed official retractions, and a perpetual and markedly cheesy afterlife in the fringes of infotainment. Indeed, throughout its history, the flying saucer has been cloaked with spiderwebs of rumor and deception, ruse and hoax, suspicious fact and even more suspicious synchronicity. As an object of information, the UFO is impossible to extricate from visionary noise, but all this hermetic ambiguity weighs heavily on the minds of most ufologists, who want their answers firm and their causal connections clear. Unfortunately, this drive to get to the bottom of things has led a good many ufologists into the very abyss of reason: conspiracy theory.

Though conspiracy theories have always been with us, in one metaphysical guise or another, their logic seems particularly attractive to people who lose their way along the highways and byways of the information age. Even if one is given to only the mildest of suspicions, the systematic and deeply invasive character of mass media induces myriad doubts about who controls what we see and hear, and what hidden agendas they nurse. Moreover, as the production and distribution of information grows exponentially, traditional hierarchies of knowledge collapse, leaving behind a fragmentary but excessively data-saturated world of ambiguous reports, marginal information, and suggestive correspondences. If you find yourself compelled to somehow knit this chaos together, the feverish mechanics of conspiracy theory work like a charm. Every bit of data becomes a link in an expanding network of connections; if tended with the proper amount of credulity, the network will grow into an explanatory weed so virulent that it may invade the entire landscape of the real.

With their obsessive insistence on a secret hermeneutic code that can tie up the loose ends of history, the more extreme or paranoid conspiracy theorists are not so different from religious fanatics or feverish mystics with a Kabbalistic bent. The paranoid knows that *everything fits together,* but unlike the mystic, this knowledge only confirms him in his separate and anxious selfhood. God is gone: The infinite webwork is ruled no longer by a supreme and integrated intelligence, but by an invisible array of nefarious cabals, hidden machineries, and mysterious agents of deception—occult archons rather than omniscient angels. Even the most secular conspiracy theorist is touched with this esoteric psychology; the archons may be secular (the New World Order, the Trilateral Commission, ZOG), but the basic cosmology remains the same. The visible world is controlled by invisible powers, "the rulers of darkness of this world," as the apostle Paul put it in Ephesians 6:12. But unlike the Christian warrior, who puts on the armor of righteous faith to combat this "wickedness in high places," the gnostic conspiracy theorist girds himself with *knowledge:* the information that he collects, organizes, and disseminates.

Needless to say, social, economic, and institutional power often takes the form of conspiracy, and as the psychopolitics of the postwar world amply demonstrate, these conspiracies can get mighty dark. Millions on the far side of the iron curtain took homeopathic doses of paranoia just to survive in a world defined by bald-faced official lies, secret security forces, and history's most insidious reign of social engineering. But postwar America also hosted an octopus of covert agencies, who honed the tools and tactics of domestic destabilization, data collection, electronic surveillance, disinformation, pharmacological manipulation, dirty tricks, and psychological—even psychic—warfare. This is what you might call America's stealth government, a government that remains partly real and partly imagined, and that gets loads of mileage out of the confusion between the two.

As any *X-Files* fan will tell you, the UFO phenomenon is a distorted reflection of this stealth government, and has been so since the beginning. In the 1950s, in fact, it became a core article of UFO faith that agents of the state were consciously deceiving the public by deliberately introducing disinformation into ufological circles—a conviction that had rather significant psychological and epistemological implications. As the CIA well knows, disinformation is a mighty powerful hex. Even the *suspicion* of disinformation has the power to contaminate and destabilize an entire field of knowledge and perception, legitimate or otherwise. Ufology is the proof. With disinformation in the air, ufologists have an airtight explanation for the persistence of hoaxes as well as the lack of definitive proof; evidence that doesn't corroborate their suspicions or delusions is simply written off as subterfuge. With this slippery logic at work, even the most rational UFO buff can sink into the bogs of paranoia, where standards of proof dissolve, agents wear double faces, and red herrings grow to the size of white whales. It is no wonder that some ufology watchers believe that the whole field was engineered by spooks.

Spectral confirmation of such government hanky-panky are provided by the Men in Black, perhaps the most hilarious figures in ufology's archetypal cast of characters. By the late 1950s, hundreds of UFO buffs, witnesses, and amateur investigators had reported visits from strange, swarthy, and vaguely inhuman gentlemen whose characteristic garb— dark suits and sunglasses—gave them their famous name. In a typical encounter, MIBs would drive up in black Cadillacs whose dashboards gave off a weird, purplish glow. Speaking in mechanical voices, the MIBs would claim they were from the CIA or the air force, and then proceed to lie, steal photos, or strong-arm their hosts into not talking about UFOs with the media or other investigators. Though the MIBs' unkind manner and robotic social skills certainly suggested your typical G-men, more savvy observers like John Keel argued that these ridiculous and uncanny figures issued from that same rip in the space-mind continuum that gave us flying saucers and ETs in the first place. Like the unmarked black helicopters glimpsed by today's right-wing militiamen, or the electromagnetic implants that bedevil so many schizophrenics, these Caddie-cruising daemons of disinformation are visionary symptoms of the covert invisibility of postwar power, that rough magic wielded by the archons of America.

These days, however, the Men in Black are movie stars and Saturday-morning cartoon heroes. In the 1990s, the culture industry became obsessed with conspiracy theories, paranormal phenomena, and alien abductions. Our TVs became stuffed with conspiracy fodder like *The X-Files* and *Dark Skies,* "spooky powers" dramas like *Millennium* and *Sliders, Star Trek* spin-offs, home-video reality shows like *Strange Universe,* and docudramas about angels, Roswell, and alien abductions. Our summers became filled with blockbusters like *Independence Day, Contact, Species,* and *Conspiracy Theory*—all outfitted with varying degrees of paranoia, stupidity, and cosmic promise. Given all this strange fruit, it is hardly surprising that some New Agers and UFO conspiracy freaks believe that unseen forces, terrestrial or not, are consciously manipulating pop culture to prepare the human race for the final galactic revelation. In this unconsciously postmodern notion, the scientific debate over the reality of UFOs is nothing more than a ruse: The invasion has *already happened,* through the media and into our psyches. This media myth finds fit corroboration in the film *Contact,* where a digitally sampled image of President Clinton and real anchors from CNN lend credibility to the fiction with their mediated "authenticity." At the end of the film, Jodie Foster takes a wild psychedelic ride to the alien system, where the extraterrestrials, in order to commune with her without completely blowing her mind, construct a kind of virtual reality landscape based on her own memories. The subliminal message? Our perceptions are manufactured, and the digitally tweaked mediascape itself has become the artificial interface between ourselves and a cosmos that has started to take an interest in our obscure little doings.

Recognizing the pregnant connection between kooky media and even kookier popular beliefs, many rationalists and social critics have attacked the entertainment industry for its self-serving and profit-driven willingness to pander to the superstitions and fringe sciences that fascinate the masses. Some of these skeptics lay the blame for modern irrationalism at the feet of those cultural institutions that increasingly mediate our knowledge and perceptions of reality. Though most working scientists would probably be content simply to improve the public's understanding about the basic procedural differences between science and other forms of human knowledge (including religion and science fiction), others adopt a siege mentality, heaping loads of indignation and scorn on those "irresponsible" writers, publishers, TV producers, and filmmakers who misguide, mislead, and exploit the nation's flocks with their dangerous fabulations.

Unfortunately, the relationship between the mediascape and popular perception is a feedback loop, not a one-way street. The culture industry keeps cranking out cartoons of dark powers and visionary encounters because these images persist in us, portions of the larger and far more perennial force of the creative and collective imagination. In the twentieth century, many of the phantasms that formerly inhabited ancestral lore and folktales slipped on new disguises and colonized the fringes and gutters of media: comic books, pulp fiction, monster movies, rock 'n' roll. By virtue of its very marginality, which is rapidly disappearing now that popular culture is feeding on itself and postmodern professors strive to be hip, junk culture has privileged access to those archetypes, fears, and heretical desires that compose the collective unconscious. As the visionary science-fiction writer Philip K. Dick wrote in his masterpiece *Valis,* "the symbols of the divine show up in our world initially at the trash stratum."[198]

Divine trash may not provide a complete balanced breakfast, but it can certainly fertilize the wayward imaginings of the soul. In Robert Anton Wilson's mischievous counterculture classic *Cosmic Trigger: Final Secret of the Illuminati*, the author describes how the densely networked, LSD-drenched, and satirically paranoid *Illuminatus!* novels that he wrote with Robert Shea started to seep into his "real" life. As Wilson's psychoautobiography so seductively shows, catching the eye of the pyramid cabal has a lot to do with your attention; if you consciously tune in to coincidences, stray conversations, and marginal information sources, deeper patterns inevitably begin to emerge. For Wilson, the challenge is not to seek the objective truth, but to avoid being slurped into what he calls "reality tunnels": black holes of self-reinforcing and totalizing convictions that can capture Republican policy wonks and animal rights activists as surely as they do Roswell fanatics. Faced with today's honeycomb of reality tunnels, Wilson advocates a kind of wry schizophrenia, a yin/yang of skepticism and imagination that maintains the mind always at a crossroads, poised between yes and no.

This excluded middle is where the postmodern Hermes is born: a sacred ironist or a visionary skeptic, dancing between logic and archaic perception, myth and modernity, reason and its own hallucinatory excess. And it is precisely this tension, and not some abdication of critical intelligence, that now leads so many intelligent and curious minds to conspiracies, alternative histories, paranormal phenomena, and pop science fiction. They sense that merely modern skepticism has had its day, that it is precisely our rational detachment and liberal common sense that blinds us to the subliminal workings of things. For our monsters are not just bred by the sleep of reason—they are also spawned by the lies of reason, by the coercive rationality that lurks under cover and under our skin, darkly dreaming of total control. Only by carefully integrating the imaginal pathways of the premodern mind, with its symbolic and visionary modes of processing information, can we come to recognize the divine intercessors and the destructive archons for what they are: liminal figures lurking both inside and out.

Thy Alien, Thy Self

In the 1950s, while nuts-and-bolts ufologists fetishized physical evidence and worried about government cover-ups, another breed of buff tried to decode whatever otherworldly messages the little green heralds left in their uncanny wake. Given the awesome weirdness of the "extraterrestrial hypothesis" (the speculation that UFOs were indeed piloted by aliens from other worlds), it is hardly surprising that the meanings people squeezed from flying saucers were mythic and mystical in nature. While writers like Jung, Vallee, and Thompson have gingerly explored this psychospiritual swamp, most of the UFOs' cosmic decoders rehashed familiar elements of the popular religious imagination, producing apocalyptic fairy tales in the language of pop science and pulp fiction.

Delving into this apocrypha, redolent of the electromagnetic imaginary, one discovers a particularly strong obsession with the *technical* dimensions of communication. In 1954, George Hunt Williamson published *The Saucers Speak,* a slim volume that humbly proclaimed itself "a documentary report of interstellar communication of radiotelegraphy." Williamson claimed that a radio operator named Mr. R. had picked up "wireless transmissions" of Morse code from an intergalactic tribunal of extraterrestrials established on Saturn. Mr. R.'s transmissions—most of which were produced through an allegedly "telepathic" form of automatic writing—provided loads of comical information about alien worlds. More significant, *The Saucers Speak* laid down the millennialist blueprint for the scores of alien communiqués that were to follow. The earth was threatened by dark forces, including nuclear power; a glorious "New Age" was about to dawn; the aliens were here to observe, inform, and aid us in the imminent translation; and physical spaceships were on their way, stellar arks that would carry the chosen ones into the cosmos.

UFO debunkers had a field day with this stuff, arguing persuasively that such potted revelations simply expressed irrational yearnings squelched by the machinery of modern civilization and the dominance of scientific materialism. Desperately seeking scientific legitimacy, most ufologists distanced themselves from people claiming to have chatted with aliens, since close encounters tended to churn up precisely the sort of mythologies these investigators were intent on weeding from their data. The most famous of these early contactees was George Adamski, an associate of Mr. R. and, to judge from his writings, a close student of *The Saucers Speak.* With imagery that distantly echoes the visionary chariot flights that littered the apocalypses of late antiquity, Adamski described joyrides on spacecraft, journeys to the lovely Venusian homeworld, and chats with beautiful long-haired Space Brothers who promised to help save the day.

In the hands of other UFO contactees, such visionary kookery congealed into an explicitly religious ufology. In 1954, after visiting Venus's Temple of Solace and participating in a galactic war against an evil intelligence from Garouche, an Englishman named George King founded the Society of Aetherius, named for his 3,456-year-old Venusian spirit guide. Developing what E. R. Chamberlin called, in his book *Antichrist and the Millennium,* a "genuine ecclesia of the technological dispensation," King held that the earth was a self-aware goddess that was soon to take her redeemed place among the Cosmic Masters. Functioning as the Primary Terrestrial Mental Channel for these Masters, King helped assist the coming apocalyptic transformation by channeling eclectic theosophical teachings from etheric entities with names like Mars Sector Six, Jupiter-92, and Jesus. The Aetherian "scriptures" consist of magnetic tape, recordings which include not only the sermons of whatever cosmic Master hijacked King's vocal cords for the day, but also the technical reports made to that Master by spiritual engineers responsible for keeping the transmission link to King up and running against the forces of darkness. No wonder the central object on the Aetherian altar was a microphone.

Though offshoots of the blond Space Brothers continue to channel utopian messages today, contemporary contactees also tell gruesome tales about impassive, almond-eyed, and vaguely malevolent Grays more interested in human flesh than dialogue. Thousands of otherwise well-enough-adjusted Americans have reported being abducted by these uncanny characters, who often strap their human victims down on operating tables and perform bizarre and painful experiments on their reproductive systems. As with "recovered memories" of incest and satanic abuse, most contemporary abduction experiences are reconstructed with the help of sympathetic therapists using hypnosis and other tricks to pierce thickets of denial and "screen memories" (the psychological equivalent of an air force cover-up). Afterward, self-identified abductees find themselves in a subculture that's far more Twelve Step than *Star Trek*—a tightly knit support network that, by accepting the validity of their experiences, perpetuates their reality as well. Some abductees glimpse their Higher Power in those inky almond eyes, but many buy into the straight-to-video plot offered up by ufologist Budd Hopkins, who argues that the aliens are stealing embryos because they need human genes to graft into their own thinning stock.

Most of us understandably prefer to think of the abduction phenomenon as a symptom of some rather tumultuous sociocultural conditions.

But what conditions exactly? Many commentators invoke the rising awareness of child abuse, as well as the cottage industry of therapists exploring and exploiting the ontological vagaries of memory. But the depths of conviction displayed by many abductees point to the deeper fault lines quaking in the foundation of contemporary identity. Abduction experiences partly speak to the subconscious horror induced by the reduction of human identity to a twisted strip of genetic information that can be spliced and diced like a filmstrip. We sense that the ancient thread of human reproduction, a reproduction of both bodies and beings, is unraveling into a technological network of DNA screenings, MRI scans, in vitro fertilization, hormone pills, and the trade in frozen embryos and elite sperm. Just as scientists reach the point of soberly discussing the possibility of raising transgenic pigs to furnish replacement human hearts, the nightside of the human mind hosts alien miscegenations that recall the myths of the gone world, when the Fey snatched babies, the swan took Leda, and the fallen angels raped the daughters of men.

The crack-up of contemporary identity is not limited to the specters conjured by genetic engineering and interspecies mutation. In his book *Virtual Realism,* the cybertheorist Michael Heim outlines what he calls "Alternate World Syndrome," a condition he links to the "relativity sickness" that besets many users of VR and military simulation machines: a profoundly unsettling and frequently nauseating disjunction between the body's kinesthetic self-awareness and the nervous system's perceptual reorientation toward a concocted otherworld. After returning from hours of VR immersion, Heim writes, "primary reality . . . seems hidden under a thin film of appearance." Heim does not believe this ontological instability is restricted to the data goggles of VR, however, and he speculates that if our culture fails to assimilate new technologies of simulation and telepresence, AWS may reach pathological proportions. For Heim, these pathologies already rear their heads most dramatically in the "peripheral perceptions" of the culture, which include the reality slips and alternative dimensions that saturate popular SF movies and TV shows, as well as alien abductions. In the abduction experience, Heim writes,

> We experience our full technological selves as alien visitors, as threatening beings who are mutants of ourselves and who are immersed and transformed by technology to a higher degree than we think

comfortable and who are about to operate, we sense, on the innards of our present-day selves.[199]

Heim thus interprets the abduction scenario as a resistance to our own imminent evolution. At the same time, this psychic disjunction may also result from the fact that our increasingly smart technologies no longer fit the rather humble frameworks of ordinary human consciousness. In the words of the computer scientist Joseph Weizenbaum, "However much intelligence computers may attain now or in the future, theirs must always be an intelligence alien to genuine human problems and concerns."[200] We now face this incipient alien intelligence everywhere we turn; the fact that we are learning to live with it only suggests that anxious metaphors of mutation will continue to spread through the popular mind.

The science-fiction fringe of the New Age community also believes we are mutating in the face of an invading alien intelligence, except that they look forward to this posthuman metamorphosis with open arms. Like the Extropians, many New Agers are entranced with the transformative and apocalyptic possibilities of information—as technology, as genetic identity, as postmodern *logos*. Indeed, New Age culture derives much of its peculiar weightlessness by identifying the self with information. Spiritual transformation thus becomes reimagined as a literal mutation, a remastering of the genetic code at the hands of disincarnate entities from the Pleiades or through humbler catalysts like brain machines and chakra work. Deliverance is also framed in terms of communications metaphors, as if the transmission and reception of spiritual messages is equivalent to embodying those lessons in everyday life. With their mantra of "you create your own reality," New Agers embrace the notion that the frequencies we tune in to actually *produce* the self and its experience of a specific world. Salvation therefore lies in mastering the remote control of reality, tuning in to positive frequencies and drawing enough fellow minds into the picture to make your world resonate and stick.

The gnostic dimension of such signal fetishism comes to the fore in the material churned out by New Age channelers, especially those who give voice to extraterrestrial teachers. Though skeptics tend to discount all channeled entities as fraudulent, some of these beings are no less psychologically "real" than the myriad of daemons that have possessed the human psyche, in rites both religious and occult, over the millennia. Well before the UFO invaded the drive-in mindscape, the magickal rascal Aleister Crowley telepathically contacted a Sirian named Lam (eerily, Crowley's 1919 sketch of Lam reveals the familiar cranial physiognomy of the Gray: a head shaped like a hairless upside-down pear, with slanted eyes, narrow mouth, and barely any nose). The term "channeling" itself is simply electromagnetic jargon for the old Spiritualist trance, and like the celestial telegraphers of the nineteenth century, New Ager channeling buffs are as thrilled with the medium as they are with the message. The culture critic Andrew Ross points out that New Agers celebrate channeling not just for its wisdom, but for its "ability to resolve the technical problems of communication."[201]

Most channeled ET materials have all the literary or spiritual sustenance of a box of tissue, but as techgnostic allegories of the information age, they can sometimes soar. In Barbara Marciniak's best-selling *Bringers of the Dawn,* the enlightened Pleiadians inform us that the Prime Creator delegated the task of cosmic creation to lower-order creator gods. Originally, these savvy demiurges designed human beings with twelve strands of DNA, chunks of which were contributed by races from around the galaxy. This DNA gave us enough wisdom and spunk to build complex and nifty civilizations of love and light. But around three hundred thousand years ago, some wayward cabal took over this power structure in an act the Pleiadians compare to "corporate raiding on Wall Street." Like the Gnostic archons of Valentinus, these beings were not so much evil as "uninformed." Nonetheless, they redesigned us with double-helix DNA that locks in our propensity to generate psychic frequencies of chaos and confusion, energies that the dark forces literally feed upon. The miracles of ancient religions are actually simulacra, "holographic inserts" generated by these cosmic creeps to manipulate and program our psyches—a function that, Marciniak notes, television and corporate computers now fulfill. Luckily, the "Family of Light" is here to coax us into a new round of mutation, at which time we will rebundle our twelve fibers of DNA, beef up the bandwidth of our psychic frequencies, and become active creators of our reality.

Even more overtly apocalyptic sentiments inform *The Starseed Transmissions,* a channeled text transcribed onto a clunky manual typewriter in the 1970s by a rural New England carpenter named Ken Carey. The entities who write the book through Carey, who seem to be at once extraterrestrials and the angels of Western monotheism, claim that they took over the poor carpenter's brain to alert us to the imminent collapse of history, thought, and matter. As with the Extropian event-horizon of the same name, the coming "singularity" is brought about partly through the technologies and economies of the information age. Restrained from actually intervening in terrestrial affairs by something like *Star Trek*'s Prime Directive, the angels hope to show us how to individually and intuitively achieve "direct contact with the source of all information." Because human languages were "designed to facilitate commerce," they are insufficient for this new Word, which Carey's angels call, in an echo of genetic engineering, "Living Information." This organic alien database not only will provide instructions to us during the hair-raising chaos of the apocalypse, but will also awaken memories of our own stellar origins, buried beneath the "spell of matter" induced when we chose to incarnate as human individuals.

Unlike most channeled texts, *The Starseed Transmissions* is unusually self-conscious about its own status as a media signal. As Carey writes in his introduction, "Regardless of one's opinion on the plausibility of extraterrestrial or angelic communion, it might be pointed out that the simple act of structuring information in this manner opens up communicative possibilities that are virtually non-existent in a conventional mode."[202] Moreover, Carey's aliens are quite frank about their roles as cosmic spin doctors, stealthily spreading their infectious data through terrestrial media webs in order to catalyze change subliminally in human minds. As such, *The Transmissions* read more like a set of trigger signals than a collection of beliefs. Like many human potential self-help books, *The Transmissions* are delivered in a first-person voice ("we") directed toward a second-person reader ("you"), a technique of invasive immediacy that actively seeks both to penetrate and reprogram the reader as she's reading:

> It is critical that you remember your origin and purpose. Your descent into Matter has reached its low point. If all that you identify with is not to be annihilated in entropic collapse, you must begin waking up.[203]

By alternately addressing the "you" that is an ordinary human personality, and the "you" that is awakening to its cosmic destiny, the *Transmissions* attempt literally to *alienate* the reader from conventional reality while providing a mystical focus for this new otherworldly identity. As

Carey's numinous corporate deity explains, "This new information is not additional data that you will act upon. It is, rather, the very reality of your new nature. You are not to act upon my information in the future, you are to be my information yourselves."[204]

Needless to say, the apocalyptic information myths woven by Carey and Marciniak drip with gnostic motifs. After all, the ancient Gnostics also held that our spirits are born in a galaxy far, far away; that the world's pain and suffering are due to dark forces that keep us imprisoned in material delusion; and that an incorporeal blast of cosmic knowledge will alchemically transmute the self into a godlike intelligence. Some Gnostics conceived of the agent of salvation as the incandescent code of the Logos, others as "the Alien man." Mandean compositions typically began by invoking "the great first alien Life from the worlds of light," while one myth described how "Adam felt love for the Alien Man whose speech is alien, estranged from the world."[205]

In his book *The Gnostic Religion,* the existentialist Hans Jonas notes that the gnostic conviction that we are strangers in a strange land creates a cosmological framework for the feelings of homesickness and longing that so many humans experience. Besides giving voice to this primal sense of estrangement, which may very well be programmed into consciousness itself, the gnostic lends this alienation mythic power, transforming the feeling of cosmic remove into "a mark of excellence, a source of power and of a secret life unknown to the environment and in the last resort impregnable to it."[206] Many philosophies and religious traditions, especially the more existentially savvy ones, both acknowledge this offworld impulse and temper it, working the desire for transcendence into a balanced engagement with both the real limits of embodied life and the real possibilities of self-development. But in the chaos of postmodern life, whose accelerated tempo and media storms deplete whatever natural ballast once kept the self intact, this transcendental impulse can easily go awry, shooting off into techno-utopian fantasies or New Age delusions or, in the worst case scenario, into the pit of collective suicide.

Level Above

In the spring of 1997, as Christians celebrated Christ's resurrection and the comet Hale-Bopp blazed across the heavens, thirty-nine monks and nuns of the Heaven's Gate cult dispatched themselves with a deadly mixture of vodka and phenobarbital in the hopes of beaming up to a spacecraft they believed was surfing the dusty spray of the comet. Their science-fiction faith notwithstanding, the cult's most striking conviction was their gnostic denial of the flesh: their buzz-cut couture and quest for asexual androgyny, their belief that their bodies were dispensable "vehicles" or "containers" for their cosmic souls, and their (sometimes literally) self-castrating rejection of physical intimacy. With their rigorous vows of chastity and self-denial, and the sharp metaphysical wedge they drove between mind and body, the Heaven's Gate cult recalled nothing so much as a New Age incarnation of some ancient clutch of crabbed and driven cenobites, yearning for release.

Heaven's Gate began in the early 1970s, when a wave of flying saucer cults zoomed into the frazzled spiritual vacuum that followed the collapse of countercultural utopia. Going under the names Bo and Peep, or simply the Two, Marshall Applewhite and his platonic mate, Bonnie Nettles, attracted a number of followers, some of whom stayed on until the end. Insisting on strict discipline and the rejection of emotions and most desires, the Two encouraged the cult members to cease identifying with their ordinary personality traits, and to shift their attention to "the level above human." Neither these militant wake-up tactics nor the Two's promise of an imminent mothership landing was unique for the times. But in 1997, Applewhite and a core crew of his followers chose to boldly go where no UFO cultists had gone before: through the gates of collective annihilation, and into the deliverance of a wandering star.

Along the way, the cult also hurtled themselves into the heart of the collective pop consciousness that now broadcasts its babble across the globe twenty-four hours a day. Within this new psychic geography of infotainment, nothing is as desirable as a media event: a news spectacle that resonates in the mass mind, that draws attention from all quarters, that dominates all channels with the power of a blockbuster film. The cult's collective suicide was definitely such an event, and it grabbed us because it reflected a kaleidoscopic cluster of the culture's own obsessions and media fixations, circa spring of 1997: UFOs, gender meltdown, Hale-Bopp, computers, the right to suicide, *Star Trek,* the cult of efficiency, affluent digs. Even the fresh black Nikes that appeared so prominently in police videos of the aftermath seemed like one of those product placements that infest Hollywood movies.

The suicides also gave the mass media the chance to hallucinate about the Internet, its brash young rival for the public's attention. Because the cult built Web sites for themselves and for commercial clients, and included some computer professionals in their ranks, they were almost instantaneously branded "an Internet cult"—hardly a just appellation, given that the Internet played no apparent role in their cosmology and that the vast majority of the cultists signed up long before the group turned to the World Wide Web as a source of income and evangelical opportunity. But this didn't stop the talking heads from shoveling up dubious assertions about rampant online cult activity and the ease of "recruitment" on Usenet and IRC. For people already worried or ignorant about cyberspace, the Heaven's Gate coverage transformed the Net into a *spiritual* threat, rather than the simply moral or political one constructed by conservative groups fixated on Web porn and bomb recipes.

Faced with this attack, and recognizing that the open structure of the Net erodes the kind of information control that true cults depend on, many digital activists went on the offensive, arguing that the Net cannot be blamed because the Net is "just a tool." Their instincts were commendable, but this mealy chestnut has got to go. The Net is not a tool; it is, pace McLuhan, an environment, a resonating psychic amplifier that, among other things, erodes the barriers that separate center and margin, news and rumor, opinion and advertisement, truth and delusion. This makes it a great breeding ground for alternative accounts of reality, for subculture, and for those infectious mind viruses some call "memes." Detached from a common vision of public space and shared intellectual culture, online society becomes a hive of interest groups, fandoms, data-junkies, manufactured marketing niches, and virtual communities made up of solitary souls. In the words of Tim Berners-Lee, the creator of the World Wide Web, the Web allows people to "develop a pothole of culture out of which they can't climb."[207] In this sense, the Web incarnates the dark intuition that Henry Adams, looking into a future ruled by the dynamo, articulated almost a century ago: that we do not inhabit a universe after all, but a multiverse.

Multiverses are cool in comic books, but they are also dangerous and difficult places to navigate. As the Net increasingly mediates our perception of the world, as well as our social and economic activity, we may come to learn this dizzying condition firsthand. For even as the Web builds links between different worldviews, and encourages us to channel-surf the tangled noodles of the collective mind, the technology may wind up producing a rent in the fabric of consensus reality as wide as the ozone hole over Antarctica. Already we can see the runs: hoaxes and rumors breed true believers, worldviews become worlds, and bad ideas find like minds. No longer held in check by editors or lawyers or the snail's pace of the mail, anonymous and unsubstantiated claims, both spontaneous and engineered, now run like wildfire through the information environment, forcing institutions to issue official reactions and mainstream journalists to treat the rumors themselves as news. Trading gossip around the well of the global village, we have already amplified whispers about evil computer viruses, CIA-crack connections, TWA jets downed by friendly fire, government conspiracies in Oklahoma, and Lexis-Nexis databases that serve up your social security number and your mother's maiden name. The Web is by nature a kind of conspiracy-machine, a mechanism that encourages an ever-broadening network of speculative leaps, synchronistic links, and curious juxtapositions. A "subcultural search engine" called Disinformation even uses a Yahoo-like system to filter the fringes of the Web for dark plots, kook cosmologies, revisionist histories, and the latest signs and portents.

So it is hardly accidental that at least one member of Heaven's Gate, Yvonne McCurdy-Hill, first climbed aboard the Hale-Bopp express through the portals of her Internet browser. Not that the cult restricted its media evangelism to the online marketplace. Convinced that Luciferic forces were on the rise and the planet was about to be spaded over, the group spent their last few years attempting to squeeze their memes through as many delivery channels as possible. They bought a full-page ad in *USA Today,* dabbled with satellite broadcasts, churned out pamphlets and handbills, distributed videotapes, spammed Usenet, and jazzed up their own data-dense Web page with the latest Java applets. But their savviest stunt was hijacking the mass media from beyond the grave. The still-believing survivor Rio DiAngelo told *Newsweek* that his comrades would be "proud" of all the hoopla their suicide generated: "They really wanted the whole world to know this information but couldn't get it out. No one would listen. I think they would be happy."[208]

The most intense advertisements for the cult's parallel worldview were their final dispatches: the handful of farewell messages videotaped just days before departure. Knowing that these documents would find their way onto television, the cultists faced the cameras and addressed *us,* the media-saturated members of a civilization they had abandoned as a lost cause. As Darwin Lee Johnson explained in one of them:

We know that the spin doctors, the people who make a profession out of debunking everybody, will attack what we're doing. . . . They

will say that we're crazy, that we're mesmerized. . . . We know it isn't
true but how can you know that?

That's the million-dollar question, of course, but compared to the smug
psychobabble about mind control that most of the "cult experts" trun-
dled out on the TV news, the tapes succeeded in destabilizing the usual
routine. They provided a very human, if thoroughly disturbing, picture
of what one former member called "the most extraordinary sociological
experiment you could imagine."

The tapes also suggested what later reporting confirmed: that
Heaven's Gate included some pretty hard-core science-fiction fans, at
least of the variety obsessed with the products of Hollywood's dream
factory. Sitting in assigned seats before their communal 72-inch TV, the
cultists drank up *The X-Files* and the various *Star Trek* shows, and
rounded out their fare with videos like *Cocoon, Close Encounters of the
Third Kind,* and the *Star Wars* trilogy. Alongside their Nike trainers, the
most notable aspect of the group's suicide uniforms was the triangular
shoulder patch emblazoned with the phrase "Away Team"—*Trek* jargon
for the small patrols who beam down planetside. Particularly eerie was
the presence among the dead of Thomas Nichols, the brother of Nichelle
Nichols, who played the communications officer Lt. Uhura on the original *Star Trek* series and who currently hawks a psychic hot line on TV.

Captain Applewhite and Away Team didn't take their genre clichés
quite as literally as many supposed. The group admitted ignorance about
whether or not they would wind up in heaven, in another dimension, or
on the bridge of a starship. One of their online screeds also suggests that
the cult self-consciously employed "the 'Star Trek' vernacular" to communicate their apocalyptic religious convictions to mundane minds
steeped in popular culture. After all, science fiction's allegiance to science
is often pared or overshadowed by the genre's exploration of humanity's
lingering desire for symbol, cosmology, and cognitive breakthrough.
Even middle-of-the-road SF can express mystical, if not gnostic, sentiments at times; in *The Empire Strikes Back,* the wizened Jedi guru Yoda
gurgles to Luke Skywalker, "Luminous beings are we; not this crude
matter." Hearing this line, it's hard not to imagine the acolytes of
Heaven's Gate huddled around their TV set just weeks before their suicide run, silently cheering the old Muppet's confirmation of their most
deeply held beliefs.

A most remarkable use of gnostic SF metaphors occurs in Dennis Johnson's farewell videotape, which was aired on *Nightline* soon after the suicides. In it, the forty-two-year-old ex-rock guitarist claims that "laying down these human bodies that we borrowed for this task" will be just as simple as stepping out of the holodeck on *Star Trek: The Next Generation*—a holographic virtual reality room where the crew while away the hours in fabricated worlds or training exercises. Johnson then goes on:

> We figured it out mathematically . . . we've been training on a holodeck for roughly thirty minutes, and now it's time to stop. The game's over. It's time to put into practice what we've learned. So, we take off the virtual reality helmet, we take off the vehicle that we've used for this task. We set it aside, go back out of the holodeck, to reality, to be with the other members on the craft, in the heavens. Call it another dimension, call it another reality, who knows? We're kept blind ignorant here, which is kind of the state [you would expect] with these vehicles.

Johnson ends this remarkable exhortation by insisting that the group is looking forward to their collective suicide for the simple reason that they do not identify with their bodies. "If you could just see it that way," he implores, "if you could just get into our headspace a little bit, and just see how happy we are, how strong willed we are about doing this, how committed we are." Johnson's slang is interesting here, for while "headspace" is a fine West Coast idiom for another person's point of view, getting into one is also an excellent description of virtual reality, the technology that clearly played a significant role in the cult's gnostic imagination.

What is it about virtual reality that can stoke such imaginings? Technologically, VR can be described as an immersive simulation, a digital construct that users engage, as it were, from the inside out. At the very least, VR exploits and even celebrates the phenomenological fact that we are mind as well as body, and that the twain do not always meet. But VR is not simply a technology; it is a concept that exceeds mere gadgetry and all its inevitable bugs and breakdowns. The concept is absolute simulation: a medium so powerful that it transcends mediation, building worlds that can stand on their own two feet. Though existing VR technologies don't really work this way, the belief that VR constructs a *world,* a simulacrum powerful enough to temporarily overwrite our material one, has been embraced as an article of faith by the technology's fans and detractors alike. VR's utopian proponents ground their idealistic visions of the technology in the immersiveness, playfulness, and immediacy of virtual spaces. On the other side of the fence, neo-Luddites deplore what they see as the ultimate expression of technology's insidious drive to replace the Real, to sever thought from embodiment, and to tear apart whatever gossamer threads still bind us to nature and to our material human communities.

For many, VR has thus come to symbolize the demiurgic powers of the computer itself, with its powerful graphics, immersive spaces, and complex, rule-based models and projections. The universal machine, it seems, is capable of building pocket universes. Already the computer has cranked out myriad simulated worlds for science, industry, and entertainment, while powerful PCs and the gaming industry are democratizing and psychologizing this computational creationism. In his book *Out of Control, Wired* editor Kevin Kelly uses the phrase "God games" to describe digital ant farms like Populus and SimEarth, programs that allow users to "grow" toy worlds by altering, for example, levels of carbon dioxide or the rate of urban development. "I can't imagine anything more addictive than being a god," writes Kelly, giving voice to a widespread if often unconscious cultural hunch that there is something actually *ontological* about computer simulation.[209] That is, by simulating the complexity of reality with greater and greater mathematical finesse, computer worlds are actually becoming more real. The proponents of artificial life, for example, hold that by programming the logic of life into a computer simulation and letting it evolve on its own terms, we will wind up with digital entities that are, for all intents and purposes, *alive.* In the culture at large, the future evolution of computer games and VR gear almost guarantees that the worlds concocted on the far side of the looking-glass screen will begin to possess, at the very least, the seductive sense of reality that we associate with powerful dreams.

From the perspective of the mythological imagination, there is nothing particularly new about this ontological funhouse. Celtic fairy lore bulges with enchanted landscapes, while the protagonists of Hindu yarns often find themselves wandering through infinite nests of Borgesian dream worlds. Most famous perhaps is the Taoist trickster Chuang Tzu, who dreamed he was a butterfly, but wondered upon waking whether he was actually a butterfly dreaming that he was a man. The simulacrum has always been an object of fascination and dread, especially when it becomes a world unto its own. Today the mere existence of computer simulations, and especially VR, gives this powerful mythopoetics a *technological* basis. That is, regardless of how convincing or "realistic" VR technology actually is, the presence of such simulating machines releases the metaphysical ambiguities of the simulacrum into the contemporary world, a world whose materialism, both philosophical and consumerist, makes it ill equipped to handle the archaic and tricky power of the phantasm. Michael Heim's "relativity sickness" may become as common as attention deficit disorder.

In this sense, we might see Applewhite's cult members as dark prophets of a time when the alienation from primary physical reality has reached such an all-time high that the world can be written off as a thirty-minute training program whose usefulness has peaked. Indeed, perhaps the most remarkable and least-noticed aspect of the cult's farewell tapes was their backdrop: a green and succulent garden soaking up the lazy Southern Californian sun, with a chorus of songbirds proclaiming the return of spring. It was as if these men and women were subliminally telling us what the Marcionites proclaimed almost two millennia ago: that even natural paradise is a simulacrum, a trap for the luminous beings we are.

While the conviction that the world is a VR game can certainly be chalked up to fringe psychosis, such mad beliefs can also be interpreted as dreamlike symptoms of a more pervasive cultural pathology. Datagloves and head-mounted video displays are visible symbols for a much more immersive "virtual reality": the ersatz electronic environment of images and data that embower our bodyminds and social spaces. The French philosopher Jean Baudrillard diagnosed this condition as a mass infection by the *hyperreal,* which he defined as a social, political, and perceptual organization based on the dominance of technological simulacra. Like an ontological virus, the hyperreal invades and destroys the older frameworks for understanding the real, replacing it with a new order of reality based on simulation. In his 1983 book *Simulations,* Baudrillard argues that Disneyland is the Mecca of this hyperreal civilization: an environment that is neither authentic nor fake, a copy for which there is no original, and the paragon of social control by "anticipation, simulation, and programming." In Baudrillard's deeply apocalyptic view, the mass media have become a kind of orbiting strand of DNA that "mutates" the real into the hyperreal, eroding any space of authentic resistance and establishing the absolute dominion of the society of the spectacle.

Baudrillard's apocalyptic theories can be read as highbrow science fiction, and in the realm of SF, his basic ideas, to say nothing of Marshall Applewhite's, aren't so novel. The idea that virtual technologies are instruments of social control can be traced to Aldous Huxley's dystopian 1932 novel *Brave New World,* in which "feelies" allow the slave society's drugged and genetically engineered populus to "experience" the sensations of actors projected on a large screen. Perhaps the greatest SF novel of such demiurgic media control is Philip K. Dick's *The Three Stigmata of Palmer Eldritch,* written in 1964. To escape the dismal toil of their lives, the human colonists on Mars while away the hours with Perky Pat Layouts, miniature dollhouses complete with Pat and Walt, svelte figurines resembling those postwar archetypes Barbie and Ken. After gathering together in their hovels, the colonists swallow an illegal drug, Can-D, which "translates" them into Pat and Walt's *Baywatch*-like lives for a painfully brief spell. Some colonists view the virtual trip as escapism; others interpret it as a religious experience in which they lose the flesh and "put on imperishable bodies." A satellite radio station owned by Perky Pat Layouts orbits Mars, emitting a stream of ads for new Perky Pat accessories, while the DJs deal Can-D on the side. Even psychic powers are exploited for commercial gain, as "pre-cogs" working for PPL use their gifts to predict which new accessories will score with the colonists.

As the SF critic Peter Fitting points out, *Three Stigmata* paints a picture of a world where "the liberatory potential of the media and new technologies has been completely debased."[210] This world is not light-years away from us. Already networked computer games, theme park rides, and VR entertainment centers seek not merely to distract or entertain, but to immerse us in new, concocted realities. These virtual technologies are on a collision course with Hollywood's dream factory; in this sense, *Star Trek*'s holodeck can be seen as the entertainment industry's own holy grail. Many Hollywood blockbusters already aspire to become theme parks of a sort, either through roller-coaster-like effects *(Twister)* or by constructing stylish worlds that viewers want to stick around in *(Batman)*. Moreover, we are encouraged to bring chunks of these worlds home with us by buying up licensed icons and relics: dinosaur mugs, Godzilla caps, *Star Trek* uniforms, 007 Visa cards. Most children's programming now fuses merchandise and imaginative experience so thoroughly that kids (and their parents) must purchase action figures, clothes, and slimy substances in order to "play." Even the PPL "pre-cogs" in *The Three Stigmata* reflect the sophisticated demographic techniques that market researchers, trend forecasters, and PR flacks now use to anticipate what images and styles will capture the nomadic flows of consumer desire.

The crew of the *Enterprise* always manage to emerge unscathed from whatever psychological or metaphysical disruptions the holodeck introduces between real and virtual life. But the Trekkers in Heaven's Gate did not make it out of their own pocket universe alive; indeed, their otherworld was so immersive that it did not just reconfigure primary reality according to a religious delusion; it *annihilated* that primary reality. As Baudrillard's own work suggests, the simulacrum has an apocalyptic power. By manufacturing a multiverse of virtual realities, simulation can end the world simply by throwing the stability of all worlds into permanent crisis. As Jay Bolter points out, digital worlds wreak havoc with traditional Western metaphysical assumptions about the nature of creation. "The programmer-god makes the world not once and for all but for many times over again, rearranging its elements to suit each new program of creation. The universe proceeds like a program until it runs down or runs wild, and then the slate is wiped clean, and a new game is begun."[211]

Applewhite and his crew checked out because they felt that Terra's reboot was imminent, or at least that the game was growing dull. The cult's trigger signal was an old prophetic standby: the comet in the sky. But even this ancient cosmic clod was touched with the infectious power of the hyperreal. Mopping up after the suicides, investigators found a downloaded picture of Hale-Bopp still glowing on the cult's computer screens, an image originally constructed with the state-of-the-art perceptual technologies of high-tech satellite astronomy. But the nature of the image had changed as it passed through television, newspapers, magazines, and the World Wide Web. For one thing, Hale-Bopp picked up a shadowy "Companion" as it hurtled through the electronic universe: a blurry doppelgänger described and photographed by inept astronomers, but transformed into a spaceship by the robust imaginations of the UFO fringe. In other words, Hale-Bopp became a simulacrum, a virtual reality, and by the time it arrived on the terminal screens of Rancho Santa Fe, the image had exploded into a blazing sigil of posthuman yearning and millennial angst, emotions that inevitably pick up the alien call. The comet became harbinger again: a logo of the latter days, a great swoosh in the sky, a portent of a culture that can't stop cracking up.

IX

datapocalypse

When asked whether he was an optimist or a pessimist, Marshall McLuhan would invariably respond that he was an apocalypticist. This characteristically snappy comeback not only reminds us of McLuhan's devout Catholicism, but gives a hint as to why the man was so loath to take explicit moral or political stances regarding the electronic society he helped bring to public consciousness. To the consternation of his many critics, McLuhan placed himself in the position of a media seer who divined the technological "signs of the times" at an ironic and fatalistic remove from the secular stage of social action and historical conflict. But McLuhan was not so much a technological determinist as a technological exegete; he read the mediascape through the filters of his own extraordinarily erudite imagination, allowing analogies as much as analysis to lead him forward. This method allowed McLuhan to give intellectual voice to a hunch much deeper than the sociopolitical discourse of what most media theorists can articulate: the hunch that human being and human civilization are undergoing a tumultuous transformation, one so total and irrevocable it can barely be seen.

For the true apocalypticist, the sense that history is about to turn a corner conjures up a psychological stance far more complex than optimism or pessimism, because the apocalyptic turn partly derives its power from the commingling and even confusion of salvation and doom. Even the old school visions of the biblical apocalypticists were deeply polarized, split between rapture and plague, the New Jerusalem and the Antichrist, the coming of the Messiah and the final trip to the pit. McLuhan's schizophrenia on this account could be extreme. On the one hand, he could proclaim, as he did to *Playboy* in 1969, that computer networks hold out the promise of creating

> a technologically engendered state of universal understanding and unity, a state of absorption in the logos that could knit mankind into one family and create a perpetuity of collective harmony and peace.

Invoking Dante's belief that humans will live as broken fragments until we are "unified into an inclusive consciousness," McLuhan brought it all down to brass tacks: "In a Christian sense, this is merely a new interpretation of the mystical body of Christ; and Christ, after all, is the ultimate extension of man."[212] But at nearly the same time, McLuhan was capable of nursing vastly darker views about the new technoculture. In a letter to the Thomist philosopher Jacques Maritain, McLuhan flip-flopped on his *Playboy* vision in about the starkest terms imaginable:

> Electric information environments being utterly ethereal foster the illusion of the world as spiritual substance. It is now a reasonable fac-simile of the mystical body [of Christ], a blatant manifestation of the Anti-Christ. After all, the Prince of this world is a very great electric engineer.[213]

Here McLuhan condemns electronic media, not only for encouraging a denial of the material world (by which he meant the gnostic heresy of docetism), but for producing a demonic simulacrum of the very mystical body he invoked in *Playboy*. In the letter to Maritain, he also hints that certain powers and principalities are actually engineering this satanic state of affairs, suspicions nurtured by McLuhan's dabbling interest in Catholic conspiracy theories about cabals of gnostic Illuminati scheming to manhandle the course of history.

McLuhan was hardly alone in his apocalyptic hunches, then or now. Many today feel a sense of vertigo growing at the heart of things, an almost subliminal rumbling along the fault lines of the real. The fringe-watcher Art Bell, who broadcasts news of the weird on his enormously popular talk radio show, calls it the *quickening*. Bell's term is apt, because the mere acceleration of technological and socio-economic change today is enough to lend a surreal and terrifying edge to the social mutations that mark our everyday lives. New technologies are trans-forming war, commerce, science, reproduction, labor, culture, love, and death at a speed that boggles the best of minds. As global flows of information, products, peoples, and simulacra gush into our immediate lifeworlds, they chip away at our sense of standing on solid ground, of being rooted in a particular time and place. The French philosopher Paul Virilio, a curiously postmodern Catholic, argues that the sheer velocity of information, images, and technological metamorphosis is actually dis-solving our sense of historical time. Though we long ago accustomed ourselves to the manic rhythms of modern life, it sometimes seems as if we have been captured by an even deeper and more violent undertow in the tides of time, a ferocious rip that threatens to pull us out to sea.

Of course, our generation would hardly be the first to feel the rumblings of some tectonic shift in the bedrock of history. In fact, it's tough to find a time during the last couple of millennia when some people somewhere *didn't* think that the last days were upon them. Given the right social or psychological conditions, the right degree of utopian passion or violent upheaval and the intense sense of imminence that characterizes apocalyptic time will emerge. Though countless culminating dates have come and gone with nary a hoofbeat or a trumpet call, eschatological prophets refuse to stop second-guessing the calendar. Toss in a major odometer click like 2000, and mirages of Armageddon and the Golden Age are guaranteed to pop up on the horizon.

Perhaps the West has written itself into a narrative trap and cannot escape its old grandiose fairy tale of fulfillment and annihilation, a story that, like all good stories, both demands and staves off its own end. Though the cosmic sense of an ending can be seen as a peculiar pathology of the historical religions, the eschatological imagination long ago leaked into secular myths of history and scientific progress. As we will see in this chapter, technologies are shot through with myths that frame the story of time, myths of utopia and cataclysm alike. So it should not be surprising that many of the stories circulating about the "information revolution" feed off the patterns of eschatological thought, nor that technological images of salvation and doom keep hitting the screens of the social imagination like movie trailers for the ultimate summer blockbuster. Indeed, you need only scratch the surface of technoculture to discover the infectious intuition that, whether angel or antichrist or AI supermind, something mutant this way comes.

Even the most tough-minded engineers are looking toward the year 2000 with dread these days—and for good reason. Countless computer systems across the globe, especially the "legacy systems" that form the primitive strata of many commercial, banking, and governmental institutions, store the given year as a two-digit numeral, and will therefore misread 2000 as 1900, unleashing unpredictable and potentially catastrophic errors in the process. As of this writing, the Y2K glitch is already fomenting anxious fears and paranoid rumors, stories that remind us how tightly we are lashed to time, or rather to the often arbitrary frameworks we use to categorize and control its always imminent flux. The fact that the West's historical odometer was set by Christian bureaucrats with ten fingers doesn't mean that the clock's not ticking.

Here is my humble prediction: the end times will keep beckoning long past Y2K. We must do better than simply snicker about the irrationality of apocalyptic thought, which is no more sensible and no less interesting or convulsive than gambling or good poetry. The really compelling question is how we grapple with the apocalyptic feelings and figments that already crackle through the world. From where I stand, we should no more ignore these ominous signs and wonders than we should interpret them as literal forebodings of a certain fate. As Japan's Aum Shinrikyo cult proved, apocalyptic intimations can be insanely dangerous, but they can also serve as dreamtexts for the zeitgeist. Even more potent is their ability to shatter the illusory sense that the world today is simply muddling on as it always has. This is not the case. We live on the brink in a time of accelerating noise and fury, of newly minted nightmares and invisible architectures of luminous code that just might help save the day. The sense of an ending ruptures the false complacency of the everyday, and allows us to glimpse our global turbulence, if only for a blink of an eye, under the implacable sign of the absolute.

Eschatechnology

In the twelfth century, Joachim of Fiore returned from a tour of the Holy Lands and decided to don the robes of a Cistercian monk. Joachim soon tired of administrative duties and fled the order, retreating to the mountains to take up a fugitive life as a contemplative. By the end of his life, Joachim's popular and visionary works of biblical exegesis, as well as the occasional blasts of illumination he received from on high, won him the mantle of prophet in his own time. But though some popes praised his writings, and Dante stuck him in Paradise, other theological heavyweights were spooked by the revolutionary import of his work and wrote him off as a raging heretic. As far as Catholics are concerned, the jury is still out.

Joachim's questionable theological taste was his obsession with the Book of Revelation, the big-budget apocalypse that ends the Christian Bible. The scripture itself was written at the end of the first century C.E., when the first generation of Christians eagerly expected the imminent and literal return of their messiah. The young cult was undergoing a wave of Roman persecution, and when the Christian prophet John wound up imprisoned on the isle of Patmos, he felt compelled to pen an apocalypse, a vision of the final days. Along with depicting horrendous waves of plagues, battles, and tribulations, John's text centered on a glorious king who would wrestle the Antichrist, stomp out the beastly empires of the world, and set up shop in a redeemed but earthly kingdom known as the New Jerusalem. Centuries later, when the Christian Bible was finally fixed in canonical stone, the Book of Revelation made it in by the skin of its teeth. Already it was something of a thorn in the side of Rome, which was forced to square the book's embattled vision of a future messianic kingdom with the Church's own existence as an established institutional power in a patently unredeemed world. To solve this discrepancy, Saint Augustine declared that John's apocalypse was a purely symbolic allegory, and that the millennial Kingdom of God was already present on earth in the body of the Church.

As a divinely inspired reader, Joachim was not interested in squeezing such pale allegories from Revelation, but in coaxing the spirit of prophecy from the hard rind of the letter. Mystically musing on the hidden allegorical correspondences between the Old and New Testaments, Joachim finally came up, he believed, with the keys to history. Laying the Christian Trinity along a linear time line, Joachim declared history to be the progressive realization of the Father, the Son, and the Holy Spirit. The earliest age of the Father was characterized by the rule of law and the fear of God, while the second age, kick-started by Jesus and signified by the shift from the Old to New Testaments, was the Age of the Son, a time of faith and filial devotion to the gospel and the Church. But Joachim heard a third era knocking on the door: a new age of the Holy Spirit. With its coming, the edifice of the worldly Church, with its institutional sacraments and scriptural law, would give way to a free eruption of love, joy, and wisdom that would endure until the Last Judgment. Joachim's millennial utopia would see "spiritual knowledge" directly revealed into the hearts of all men, a kind of universally distributed, charismatic gnosis that would fulfill Moses' lament in Numbers 11:29: "Would God that all the Lord's people were prophets, and that the Lord would put his spirit upon them!"

Joachim's prophecies were deeply revolutionary in import. They suggested that the world and the people in it were destined to radically improve; more dangerously, they sparked the desire to *accelerate* the arrival of the third age through social change and individual spiritual growth. With Joachim's third age in mind, the Holy Spirit became the religious poster child for any number of perfectionists, visionaries, cranks, and revolutionary monks, including the Franciscans, the Beghards, the antinomian Free Spirit cult, and later the more anarchist Protestant revolts. But the speculative waves from Joachim's work surged beyond theology. By casting history as a self-transcending process, Joachim prepared the way for thoroughly modern ideas about progress, revolution, and social development. As Norman Cohn writes in his classic book *The Pursuit of the Millennium,* "the long-term, indirect influence of Joachim's speculations can be traced right down to the present day, and most clearly in certain 'philosophies of history' of which the Church emphatically disapproves."[214] Joachim helped foster the evolutionary notions of history honed by Hegel and the positivist Auguste Comte, who saw history as an ascent from the theological to the metaphysical to the scientific. Even Marx and Engels, atheists and historical materialists who snippily referred to presocialist utopias as "duodecimo editions of the New Jerusalem," could not escape the millennialist shadow of Joachim's three ages. They believed human social history began with agrarian or primitive communism, passed through the heinous machineries of capitalism, and finally came to rest in a triumphant communism, a classless heaven on earth in which the state withers away, alienation is banished, and the proletariat is free. By the time that the Russian and Chinese revolutions came around, Marxism had bloomed into a thoroughly messianic movement—even if ideologically it remained utterly hostile to the transcendent aspirations of religion.

Communism was not the twentieth century's only encounter with Joachim's "pattern of threes." After Hitler's insanely millennialist Third Reich, Joachim's age of the Spirit pops up in the heart of postwar visions of the information age. In his best-selling and influential book *The Third Wave,* Alvin Toffler proclaimed that we were on the edge of an imminent and astounding phase-shift toward a postagrarian, postindustrial society based on freedom, individualism, decentralization, and mutant machines. Toffler's prophecies were grounded and perceptive enough to be reckoned with, but their speculative breadth was also intoxicating enough to lend an expectant and even prophetic tone to the growing rhetoric of the "information revolution." Prominent surfers on the third wave later included *Wired* magazine, the short-lived Republican Revolution sparked by Newt Gingrich, and the high-octane business books and seminars of George Gilder, Tom Peters, and any number of technocapitalist gurus and visionaries. Gilder, for one, waxes quite mystical at times. Besides praising the literally divine ingenuity of technowiz start-ups, Gilder even implies that the rapid shrinking of the microchip is leading our civilization to the brink of some magnificent incorporeal transformation.

Though the revolutionary rhetoric of digital technocapitalism has been attacked for its hubris, myopia, and blind insensitivity to the corporeal problems of the world, it also signifies a truth with considerable consequences: the scientific and technological development that has characterized Western culture for centuries is infused with millennialist fervor. As the historian David Noble shows in his revelatory book *The Religion of Technology,* Joachim's drive to perfect history fed directly into the medieval world's changing notions of technology, as monasteries began incorporating the once lowly "mechanical arts" into their otherworldly labor. Besides embodying man's God-given rational superiority to the rest of nature, technology enabled him to dominate and transform the fallen world. Following the Renaissance, the West committed itself to what Michael Grosso calls "the slow apocalypse of progress," as science and technology took on the task of regenerating the earth and revealing its secrets. In Noble's words, technology became eschatology, with the result that the technomania of our contemporary world "remains suffused with religious belief."

Consciously or not, much of this exuberance is linked to the final reel of the Book of Revelation, when, after a series of baroque calamities, the New Jerusalem finally descends from heaven. Alongside Plato's philosophical Republic, the New Jerusalem is the theological prototype of utopia: an adamantine urban jewel of spiritual design and revolutionary moral import. Though the river of life percolates along its golden streets, and fruit trees bloom with genetically engineered reliability, the Heavenly City's layout and materials are anything but natural. Radiant and transparent, the burg has no need of sun or moon because "the glory of God is its light." Moreover, its touchdown is accompanied by a total cosmic transformation, the emergence of "a new heaven and a new earth."

Despite twentieth-century thrill rides like Hiroshima, Chernobyl, and Bhopal, the most evangelical proponents of science and technocapitalist progress continue to spout perfectionist promises about the new earth that lies just around the corner. Nanotechnology proselytizers declare that molecular machines will soon give us unimaginable creative power over material reality, while some DNA researchers suggest that the decoding of the human genome will allow us to perfect the species, if not conquer death itself. A few visionary scientists and mathematicians even talk about the coming Singularity, a point on the near horizon when the rapid developments in artificial intelligence, robotics, microchip power, and biotechnologies will converge, producing an unimaginable change of state that will erase the logic of human history and render all prognostications mute.

Though reproductive technologies and genetic engineering may well end up influencing the shape of the future far more intensely than computers, the machineries of information and communication continue to carry many of today's headiest eschatechnological fantasies. As we saw in chapter II, communications technology has carried a millennialist charge since media started tapping into electricity, the symbolic material of enlightenment both sacred and profane. We already heard the American congressman F. O. J. Smith's claim that, by "annihilating space," the telegraph would cause "a revolution unsurpassed in moral grandeur by any discovery that has been made in the arts and sciences."[215] The evangelist and technological prophet Alonzo Jackman was similarly enthused when he proclaimed in 1846 that the electrical telegraph would allow "all the inhabitants of the earth [to] be brought into one intellectual neighborhood and be at the same time perfectly freed from those contaminations which might under other circumstances be received."[216]

These speculations introduce a number of startlingly familiar motifs into the technoutopian rhetoric of new communications technologies: moral revolution, the global village, the apocalyptic collapse of time and space, even the hygiene of purely virtual contact. Bell's telephone brought a more democratic factor into the equation; in 1880, the august *Scientific American* anticipated "nothing less than a new organization of society—a state of things in which every individual, however secluded, will have at call every other individual in the community."[217] When the French Bishop of Aix consecrated an electrical plant to God's work, the writing was on the wall: Electricity not only signified the sublime and spectacular, but would do the work of building a millennial kingdom of light. These electrical dreams leaked into the electromagnetic spectrum as well; Tesla wrote that the wireless would be "very efficient in enlightening the masses, particularly in still uncivilized countries and less accessible regions, and that it [would] add materially to general safety, comfort and convenience, and maintenance of peaceful relations."[218]

It does not take a Joachim to see where all this is heading. Today, we are saturated with the rhetoric of "mythinformation," which the social critic Langdon Winner defines as "the almost religious conviction" that a widespread adoption of computers, communications networks, and electronic databases will automatically produce a better world for humanity. With the growth and interbreeding of the Internet, wireless satellite networks, global media, and the myriad worlds of the computer, the communications utopia arises yet again. With astounding predictability, we tell ourselves (and are told) that the digital age is an evolutionary leap forward for humanity, one that will help empower the individual, restore community, aid the infirm, overcome prejudice, turbocharge democracy, make us smarter and richer, and maybe even spark world peace. "Something is happening," promises an IBM TV spot, as a montage of the world's myriad peoples zeroes in on a wise old African man. "Just plug in, and the world is yours." In an MTV-flavored television advertisement for the MCI Network, which informs us that the information superhighway is open to all colors and ages, we see the word "utopia?" typed out on a terminal screen; "No, the Internet," a voice-over tells us.

In his cornerstone essay for the influential collection *Cyberspace: First Steps,* the architecture professor Michael Benedikt points out that the cultural myth of cyberspace owes much of its resonance to the image of the Heavenly City. Like the New Jerusalem, cyberspace promises weightlessness, radiance, palaces within palaces, the transcendence of nature, and the pleroma of all cultured things. Benedikt goes so far as to offer an informational vision of fleshless redemption, suggesting that the "realm of pure information" may

> decontaminat[e] the natural and urban landscapes, redeeming them, saving them . . . from all the inefficiencies, pollutions (chemical and informational), and corruptions attendant to the process of moving information attached to things—from paper to brains—across, over, and under the vast and bumpy surface of the earth.[219]

Benedikt acknowledges that his visions of cyberspace remain pipe dreams. On the other hand, he makes the equally valid point that the power and persistence of such ancient "mental geographies" and salvational myths ensure that, for all the silicon snake oil and corrosive applications that accompany digital communications, cyberspace will continue to retain a degree of "mytho-logic."

In the next section, we will look more closely at the religious and apocalyptic myths that inform our fascination with communication and its technologies. But it's crucial to note that the euphoria of the information age also emerges from the sense of rupture that powerful new media introduce into society. As I have suggested throughout this book, different forms of communication—oracular performance, writing, print, television, email—shape social and individual consciousness along specific lines, creating unique networks of perceptions, experiences, and interpersonal possibilities that help shape the social construction of reality. From this it follows that when a culture's technical structure of communication mutates quickly and significantly, both social and individual "reality" are in for a bit of a ride. To borrow an image from the Kabbalah, powerful new media "break the vessels," opening up novel and unmapped regions of the real. The social imagination leaps into the breach, unleashing a torrent of speculation, at once cultural, metaphysical, technical, and financial. These speculations inevitably take on a utopian and feverish edge. As David Porush writes, "As technology manipulates and alters human nature, and human nature adapts itself to the new technosphere, new versions of utopia arise, which in turn promote new technologies, which in turn change the context for defining human nature, and so on."[220] However much we aspire to embody the rationalism of our machines, we cannot escape this feedback loop between techne and dream.

Amplifying these feedback loops with abandon, the Internet has certainly broken the vessels. Once beefed up with the World Wide Web, the Net became the most enchanting medium of our times, and now seems destined to give Gutenberg's printing press a run for the money as a major technocultural mutagen. Those fortunate enough to get online can, as at no other time in history, resonate with like minds across the planet, mine rich veins of unexpected information and images, and respond to the frazzled chaos of life with constructive communication and a plethora of points of view. As the EFF's Mike Godwin puts it, the Internet "is the first medium that combines all the powers to reach a large audience that you see in broadcasting and newspapers with all the intimacy and multi-directional flow of information that you see in telephone calls. It is both intimate and powerful."[221]

This conjunction of power and intimacy explains much of the utopian enthusiasm that first greeted the medium in the early to mid-1990s. Without sacrificing the intimate scale we cherish as individuals, the Net allowed us to reconnect with a much larger world, to occupy, at least potentially, a place of noncoercive communicative power. Both the popularity of the personal home page and the rhetoric of virtual community expressed the desire to overcome the alienation of modern life by plugging some portion of the self into a network technology. Symbolically if not actually, the Net thus provided a fragmented and malleable halfway home for the postmodern self to get back on its feet. Millions were also attracted to the Net's literally free exchange of ideas, expertise, and creative labor. Even if users were forced to sift through piles of chaff, this gift economy existed outside the market. The virtual trade in knowledge, skills, and experience not only added novelty and happenstance to online life; it also engendered a kind of public space that blocked, for a time, the mighty waves of commodification and marketing that have soaked nearly every pocket of contemporary life with the trace of lucre. Even the first Internet entrepreneurs—ISPs, hardware manufacturers, publishers, consultants—made their money around or beneath the Net, not on it.

The Dutch media activist Geert Lovink calls the initial years of the Net's mass popularity Dream Time: "a short period of collective dreaming, passionate debates, gatherings, and quick money to be made." Unfortunately, such periods do not last long before they succumb to the tug of more prosaic historical forces, and especially to the powerful undertow of money and power. In different ways, this has been the sad story of communication utopias from the telegraph to radio to television. Creative possibilities and novel social forms are winnowed and routinized; technologies are packaged for consumers rather than hacked; commercial interests and the state alike colonize the new communications space as a "natural" extension of their domains.

Whether or not the Internet will simply replicate this admittedly simplistic scheme remains to be seen. Since the printed book, few technologies have come along that have had a better potential for engendering a genuinely creative and democratic environment of debate, knowledge amplification, alternative visions, new mediations of community, and novel comminglings with the world offline. I fear that if the Internet becomes dominated by the microbeasts of twenty-first-century power, then the efforts of global citizens to create a viable and humane techno-logical culture, and to maintain our pinkies on the guidance system of spaceship earth, will be severely impaired. Many argue that we must now integrate the Net as efficiently as possible into the global economy, to make it as safe for credit card addiction as we can, to pave the way for mega-TV, and to privatize both the network and our online transac-tions and identities. Perhaps these developments are inevitable, and even necessary, but it seems to me that we must continue to dream as well, and to do so in as public a manner as possible. We cannot pretend to resuscitate Lovink's Dream Time, a period of naive and newborn utopian glee that is already gone. But perhaps we can tool cyberspace into some urban remix of the aboriginal Dreamtime: a virtual ecology of mind, an electronic agora, a collective metamap that supplements rather than replaces the real.

The Net, after all, is still under construction, and therein lies its strength. Rather than frustrating utopian possibilities, the Internet's per-petual imperfections, its leaky pipes and exposed wires, may serve to keep the medium's wilder, more alchemical, and more socially innovative possibilities alive. The gaps and ruptures that the technology's endless mutations create hopefully will help frustrate consumer culture's pre-dictable imperative to transform cyberspace into a mall. The endless pro-cession of bugs, viruses, and incompatible protocols may also keep the lines noisy enough to prevent us from being mesmerized by whatever ersatz wonderlands appear, and to remind us that utopia does not lie beyond the magic mirror, but in the virtual images we carry inside our potential, and increasingly collective, selves.

. . . And Knowledge Shall Be Increased

Angels are everywhere these days. All across America, ordinary people are reporting lifesaving heavenly interventions and profound inward encounters with mysterious beings of light. A veritable angel industry has emerged, with seraphim pins, self-help manuals, lavishly illustrated Pre-Raphaelite daybooks, cards and calendars, and the hit CBS series *Touched by an Angel*. Though the angel remains a powerful and uncanny figure, many of our contemporary examples are little more than chubby tykes and anorexic New Age sylphs. One looks in vain for the blazing hulks of Blake, the sublime intelligences of Pseudo-Dionysus, or the dazzling forms of the Shi'ite Sufis. Though mystics and ceremonial mages describe the encounter with one's Holy Guardian Angel as a seriously spine-chilling experience, the sorts of intercessors we hear about on *Oprah* or the *Weekly World News* too often seem content to make sure the airbags work.

Still, it would be a failure of the imagination to chalk up the return of Thrones and Dominions to the economic tightening of the Bible Belt or to Christian envy at all the press that ETs garner. Something else is afoot. *Angelos* means messenger in Greek, and angels have traditionally been considered luminescent agents of the logos, figures of order, communication, and knowledge. Manifesting the helpful side of Hermes, angels mediate between an inaccessible but omniscient godhead and the earthly spheres where humans lumber along in the dark. It's for this reason that so many magicians and Kabbalists have burned the midnight oil attempting to contact these incandescent bureaucrats; like John Dee, they sought "the company and information of the Angels of God." So perhaps it is no accident that these mediators have come again in our datapocalyptic days, for they form blazing icons of the only faith that many people now hold: that information and communication will somehow save us.

Indeed, Langdon Winner was more correct than he knew when he described the "almost religious conviction" society now has in the efficacy and goodness of information machines. At root, the popular and even utopian hopes invested in information technology, and especially in the Internet, derive from a profound faith in the power and value of human communication, its ability to reach across borders, touch minds, inspire intelligence, and both expand and strengthen the boundaries of self and community. Communication is an enormously complex and tangled affair, of course, full of tricks and noise, and our contemporary ideology of efficient and productive information exchange often ignores this rich and troubling ambiguity. But even if communication has become a rather one-dimensional fetish, our passion for it runs deep.

The American pragmatist John Dewey gave voice to this passion when he wrote that "of all affairs communication is the most wonderful. That the fruit of communication should be participation, sharing, is a wonder by the side of which transubstantiation pales."[222] On the surface, Dewey's is an eminently secular American sentiment, at one with libraries, town halls, and freedom of the press, all of which help construct the democratic ideal of a public space of voices that enables communities to cohere and individuals to represent themselves. But while this conception of communication remains a secular ideology, part and parcel of our pluralistic world of clamorous democracy and hypermedia, its wondrous ability to bring minds into mutual connection invests it with a spiritual power. Communication continues to attract us partly because it carries within it the seeds of communion: of overcoming loneliness and alienation, and of drawing us together into collective bodies based on compassion, intelligence, and mutual respect. Symbolically speaking, this promise of communication draws much of its energy from the very religious tradition that free-speech advocates and other communication liberals now so often confront across the picket lines: Christianity.

Dewey's contrast between communication and the miracle of transubstantiation conceals this deeper sympathy. Transubstantiation is the Catholic doctrine which holds that by participating in the Eucharist, the ritual consumption of wine and bread that forms the interactive heart of the Mass, we experience holy communion with the body of Christ. Protestants rejected this mystical belief in literal communion, arguing that the Eucharist is a symbolic act. But all Christians resonate with the narrative root of the ritual: the last supper, when Jesus broke bread and shared a cup of wine with his friends and disciples the night before he died. Despite the agony and betrayal implied in the scene (or perhaps because of it), Jesus' odd invitation to share in his body and blood remains a powerful symbol of the communion of beings. When the early Christians instituted the Eucharist, the holy meal was more than a mystical invocation or a simple memorial act; it was also a potluck feast, a deeply human celebration of community identity, and thus the very image of the participation and sharing that Dewey identifies as the fruit of communication.

In sharp contrast to the liberal and secular aims of pluralism, however, Christians have been so convinced of the value of their particular feast that they have regularly insisted that every human being must dig in or be damned. Indeed, despite the rift between the Eastern and the Roman church, and the nearly infinite splinterings of Protestantism, Christianity remains, along with Islam, the religion with the most global and totalizing aspirations. More Christians now walk the earth than followers of any other religious faith, and the religion continues to expand, especially in areas outside the Near Eastern and European climes that nursed it. Historically speaking, Christianity owes much of this global reach to violence: its savage intolerance of pagans, Jews, and infidels within the borders of Christendom, and its collusion with colonial power beyond those borders, where the conquest of other cultures generally meant their forced conversion as well. But any reckoning of the religion's phenomenal success must also take Christianity's intense communicative power into account. Ever since the first evangelists wandered about the Roman Empire announcing the *kerygma,* the "good news" of God's redemptive activity through Christ, priests and missionaries have devoted themselves to proselytizing and preaching the gospel, in all its multifaceted forms, with a fervor unmatched in the history of religion. Though all but the most isolated humans have probably gotten the message by now, evangelism remains a powerful religious calling for many Christians, especially Protestants. Evangelical activity has taken many contradictory forms throughout the complex history of Christianity, but it also must be seen as part of a corporate communications project: the global broadcast of the gospel.

And this broadcast began with a bang. Before the resurrected Christ took to the skies, he told his disciples that the Holy Ghost would soon arrive and baptize them, giving them the power to preach the gospel "unto the uttermost part of the earth." Ten days after Christ's ascension, the disciples gathered for the harvest feast of Pentecost:

> And when the day of Pentecost was fully come, they were all with one accord in one place. And suddenly there came a sound from heaven as of a rushing mighty wind, and it filled all the house where they were sitting. And there appeared unto them cloven tongues like as of fire, and it sat upon each of them. And they were all filled with the Holy Ghost, and began to speak with other tongues, as the Spirit gave them utterance. And there were dwelling at Jerusalem Jews, devout men, out of every nation under heaven. Now when this was noised abroad, the multitude came together, and were confounded, because that every man heard them speak in his own language. (Acts 2:1–6)

There are around 120 disciples at this point, all feasting together "with one accord." But when the Holy Spirit arrives, it shatters this merely human harmony with a ferocious noise, the sound of a turbulent storm. The disciples are touched with supernatural tongues, tongues that are both visual (like fire) and verbal. The Spirit seizes their vocal cords and begins spontaneously channeling information about the works of

God to a multinational audience. More magically still, these listeners hear the Spirit speak *in their own language,* as if the ancient curse of Babel has temporarily been lifted, or at least something like *Star Trek's* universal translator has kicked in. Pentecost is a communications mystery: A chaos of noise comes bearing the ecstatic tongues of the Spirit, which transmit the Word to a global public in all frequencies of human speech.

Such immediate intensity cannot be sustained indefinitely, of course, and so the Holy Ghost, or rather the men behind it, soon took up the writing machine to amplify the gospel's broadcast power. Despite the romantic picture of early Christianity as an unmediated culture of oral spontaneity, Christians were concerned with reading, writing, and citing texts from the beginning. For one thing, the earliest Christians were believing Jews, and they wanted to write themselves into the Jewish messianic tradition by demonstrating on a line-by-line basis how Christ fulfilled scriptural prophecies of a coming king; evidence suggests that some Christians compiled relevant samples of Hebrew texts into handy notebooks for use during preaching and debate. Later, the Gospels would employ a variety of literary devices to structure and stage the conversion of their readers. From the moment that Saint Paul began cranking out epistles to the far-flung congregations of the first century, letters that would be declaimed before the community and that would eventually be committed to the bound book, Christians exploited the technology of the Word as a vehicle for the living Logos.

By the Middle Ages, the Catholic Church had ensconced the Bible inside an immense exegetical and liturgical apparatus, restricting its access to priests, monks, and scholars schooled in Latin. But when the Protestant reformers of the sixteenth century took on the medieval Church, they attempted to recover the spirit of early Christianity by radically reimagining the role of scripture. To restore a more direct connection between the Word and the souls of ordinary men and women, they translated the Bible into vernacular languages. The sacredness of Latin was overturned; unlike the scriptures of Jews and Muslims, whose holy tongues remain in essence untranslatable, the Protestant word was so intensely immediate it could transcend the distortion and error introduced by translation—a perfect expression of the globalizing myth of Pentecost. Over the centuries, many Protestants also came to emphasize the value of internalizing scripture, of developing a personal relationship to the text.

As every student of the writing machine knows, the Protestants probably could not have pulled off their Reformation without the newfangled
printing press, which Luther himself called "God's highest act of grace."
The printing press blasted the Word in all directions at once, forever
fracturing the unity of Christendom while also allowing sects to regulate
the internal lives of believers through standardized materials like the
Book of Common Prayer. Even in 1455, Johannes Gutenberg already
recognized the evangelical power of his invention:

> Let us break the seal which seals up the holy things and give wings to
> Truth in order that she may win every soul that comes into the world
> by her word, no longer written at great expense by hands easily
> palsied, but multiplied like the wind by an untiring machine.[223]

Whether or not Gutenberg was thinking of the mighty wind of Pentecost
here, he clearly wants to imply that the supernatural hand of the Holy
Spirit guided his machine. After all, by transcending the imperfect labor
of human scribes, the printing press cheaply and tirelessly multiplied the
Word, and thereby accelerated and intensified the process of evangeliz-
ing the planet.

The fact that this little technocultural prayer appears at the Web site
for Logos Research Systems, a Christian infotech firm that produces
data-packed biblical CD-ROMs, only proves that new technologies of
the Word continue to hold a powerful spiritual allure for many Christians. Indeed, one suspects that Pentecost's primal scene of ecstatic
communication continues to subliminally spur the utopian enthusiasm
and universal rhetoric of the information age. It certainly influenced
McLuhan's *Playboy* vision, which held that computer networks would
allow us to bypass language in favor of "a technologically engendered
state of universal understanding and unity, a state of absorption in the
logos that could knit mankind into one family."[224] In a crude sense,
the binary code is the closest we've yet come to something like a universal tongue.

In any case, the Pentecostal fire most certainly inspired modern Pentecostalism, perhaps the fastest-growing and most media-savvy Christian
religious movement of the twentieth century. Like the disciples at their
harvest feast, Pentecostals combine an evangelical urge to convert everybody in sight with an ecstatic embrace of the more mystical gifts of the
spirit: healing, prophesying, and especially "speaking in tongues," the

spontaneous eruption of that incomprehensible otherworldly lingo known as glossolalia. In many ways, Pentecostals are the epitome of Harold Bloom's gnostic "American Religion": They embrace the sanctified self within, the self that walks with Jesus and knows the Spirit in all its transhistorical immediacy.

The spark of modern Pentecostalism first touched down in Topeka, Kansas, in 1901, but its most sustained outbreak took place in Los Angeles a few years later, when a black Holiness preacher named William Seymour began a revival so intense that its participants believed that apostolic times had come again, and that history had dissolved into biblical spirit. From there Pentecostalism spread rapidly across the globe, even though the movement was roundly criticized by more staid and mainline believers. Today Pentecostals and other charismatic Christians form a significant proportion of the Christian evangelical community, and the worldwide numbers of Pentecostals alone is nearing the two hundred million mark. Pensacola, Florida, recently hosted the longest-running Pentecostal revival since Seymour's day, and the enthusiastic movement is spreading like wildfire across Asia, Africa, and especially Latin America, where it has already transformed the religious landscape.

Along with fundamentalists like Jerry Falwell, with whom they are too often identified, Pentecostals are resolutely antimodernist. In contrast to liberal Christians and critical scholars, they completely reject the idea that the Bible is a human and historical document; instead, they attempt to read it as an error-free manual of literal truth. But like the Ayatollah Khomeini, whose rise to power was facilitated by the clandestine cassette-tape distribution of the exiled cleric's fiery speeches, Pentecostal evangelists have also shown that antimodern messages and modern media can be a match made in heaven. Indeed, both Pentecostals and fundamentalists have embraced electronic media with an unparalleled intensity and panache. The mediagenic Pentecostal flapper Aimee Semple McPherson took to the L.A. airwaves in the 1920s, drowning out other stations' frequencies and telling concerned FCC regulators that "you cannot expect the Almighty to abide by your wavelength nonsense." Though loads of sober and mainstream Christian programs appeared on radio and television over the ensuing decades, Pentecostals and fundamentalists dominated the broadcast spectrum by the 1970s, when televangelists took the idiot box by storm.

Though televangelists benefited from the deregulation of the airwaves, their media success had deeper roots. Evangelicals understood the spectacular and infectious language of TV, and they exploited its immediacy and gaudy sensationalism with a primitivist professionalism. Focusing on the intense emotions, healing powers, and biblical word-jazz of the preacher, as well as showing the spirit working through the live audience, these "electronic churches" staged media events that transformed home viewers from spectators into participants. With their calls for immediate conversion, not to mention their pledge drives and twenty-four-hour prayer hot lines, televangelists turned the television into an "interactive" medium, and they garnered millions of check-writing viewers as a result. The Texas preacher Robert Tilton even claimed he could cure his viewers' ills by placing his healing hand on the live television camera and passing spiritual forces directly to the surface of the home TV screen. And though the scandals surrounding Jimmy Swaggert and Jim and Tammy Faye Bakker brought the house of cards crashing down in the late 1980s, slicker outfits like Pat Robertson's Christian Broadcasting Network, which owns cable's Family channel and broadcasts its *700 Club* newsmagazine across the globe, are still going strong. Christian evangelists have diversified their media as well, moving into cartoons, comic books, videotape distribution networks, shortwave and AM radio talk shows, rap music, fax circles, email prayer networks, and the Internet.

Whether motivated by religious conviction, right-wing politics, or greed, evangelical Christians pounce on new communications technologies for the same reason that advertisers and advocacy groups do: These technologies are a great way of spreading memes. Now a rather trendy concept in cybercircles, the meme can be defined as the mental equivalent of a gene: an idea or learned behavior that seeks to propagate itself in the competitive environment of culture. In his book *The Selfish Gene,* the evolutionary biologist and notorious atheist Richard Dawkins quotes N. K. Humphrey, the creator of the concept:

> . . . memes should be regarded as living structures, not just metaphorically but technically. When you plant a fertile meme in my mind you literally parasitize my brain, turning it into a vehicle for the meme's propagation in just the way that a virus may parasitize the genetic mechanism of a host cell . . . the meme for, say, "belief in life after death" is actually realized physically, millions of times over, as a structure in the nervous systems of individual men the world over.[225]

Hard-core materialist philosophy like this often becomes rather ham-fisted when it comes to the life of the mind, and the reductionist concept of the meme is no exception. Though useful for tracking the infectious quality of ad slogans and sitcom haircuts, the meme stumbles when it attempts to explain complex cultural artifacts and traditions, to say nothing of the often highly intrapersonal reasons that men and women come to lead religious lives. The fact that some materialists attempt to write off subjectivity itself as nothing more than a "meme complex" is probably the best demonstration of the concept's fundamental weakness.

Nonetheless, the meme does give us a handy tool for understanding two related dimensions of evangelical communication: the almost technical desire to spread the Word, and the organic, infectious, and sometimes ecstatic power the Word has on many individuals. Evangelical language is itself thoroughly saturated with biblical code, and some preachers transform particular units of scripture into conversion slogans that can be propagated on tracts, in person, or on TV. The placards for John 3:16 that once invaded mass sporting events are only one example of this viral, almost Madison Avenue–worthy logic, a logic that scripture itself sometimes seems to support. Consider Isaiah 55:10–11, where the Lord proclaims:

> For as the rain and the snow come down from heaven, and return not thither but water the earth, making it bring forth and sprout . . . so shall my word be that goes forth from my mouth; it shall not return to me empty, but it shall accomplish that which I purpose, and prosper in the thing for which I sent it.

With such infectious notions in mind, it hardly seems accidental that the idea that Humphrey chose as an example of a meme is the basic religious belief in life after death. As a materialist, Humphrey no doubt picked the example to take a potshot at believers, but I suspect that, for good or ill, his own memes may prove to be dodo birds compared to many of humanity's most basic religious convictions. After all, these notions, and the experiences they help engender, have been coevolving with human beings for millennia, and in the end, it is they who may come the closest to achieving eternal life.

If nothing else, the power of the evangelical meme, and its successful interbreeding with electronic media, reminds us that communication always has an ecstatic, nonrational dimension. Pentecostals spread glossolalia as well as doctrine, and speaking in tongues can be considered communication so otherworldly that it transcends semantics entirely. In this sense, advanced telecommunication networks may only amplify the raptures and fears that ride the carrier wave of our more reasonable communication codes. This also happens to be one of the main themes of Neil Stephenson's 1992 *Snow Crash,* perhaps the most vibrant bit of cyberpunk mythology written since Gibson's *Neuromancer* trilogy, and one that uncorks the notion of Pentecostal memes with a devilish wit.

Set in a dystopian near-future of franchise governments, suburban enclaves, and a strip mall cyberspace known as the Metaverse, the novel revolves around a conspiracy set in motion by the powerful and wealthy evangelist L. Bob Rife, who represents postmodern mind control at its worst. Besides his Scientological name and his global media empire, which includes the fiber-optic networks that support the Metaverse, Rife controls a number of his followers through radio antennas implanted directly into their cortexes. (Stephenson was prophetic: Some members of Japan's apocalyptic Aum Shinrikyo cult wore Perfect Salvation Initiation headgear in order to electronically synchronize their brain waves with those of their guru, Shoko Asahara.) But Rife's main technology of mind control is Snow Crash, a "metavirus" that breaks down the distinction between computer and biological code. On the street, Snow Crash takes the form of a drug; in the virtual reality of the Metaverse, it exists as a computer virus that online avatars pick up visually, at which point the virus crashes the system and infects the user's brain. Once infected, people go blank, lose their defenses against suggestion, and begin speaking in tongues, which the novel claims is the irrational language that lurks in the deep structure of the human brain.

According to the memetic mythology that Stephenson unfolds during the course of his book, all humans once spoke this primal Adamic tongue, which enabled our brains to be easily controlled by the biomental viruses propagated by ancient Sumerian priests. To become self-conscious, innovative, and ultimately rational beings, we had to repress this universal tongue. "Babel-Infocalypse," the moment when human speech became mixed up and multiple, was thus a liberating event, because it delivered us from the old viral trance and forced us to consciously learn skills, to think, and to stand on our own two feet. The religions of the Book also kept this trance at bay through hygienic codes of behavior and the "benign virus" of the Torah, whose integrity was maintained through strict rules concerning its replication. Nonetheless, the old metavirus continues to lurk in the margins of human culture, where it rears up in phenomena like Pentecostal glossolalia and, one might add, the nostalgic dreams of universal and perfect communication that drive Western mystics and techno-utopian globalists alike. But Stephenson warns that we can only recover this Adamic state of collective mind at the price of our rational self-consciousness—a telling lesson in an era of worldwide communication nets and powerful media memes.

Stephenson uses the term *Infocalypse* to suggest the tendency of languages and information systems to diverge, to explode into mutually incomprehensible complexity. But for some technosavvy evangelicals, his term would take on a far different meaning. In Matthew 24:14, Jesus promises that "this gospel of the kingdom shall be preached in all the world for a witness unto all nations; and then shall the end come." Many premilliennialist evangelicals interpret this to mean that Christ will not hit the return button until every person living on Earth has been exposed to the Word—a situation that media-equipped Christians are hoping to bring about as fast as possible. Globally minded ministers like Pat Robertson, who adopted Matthew 24:14 as the corporate motto of CBN, have thus reimagined the technology of communication itself as a kind of apocalyptic trigger. In his McLuhanesque book *The Electric Church,* Ben Armstrong, the former head of the televangelist consortium known as the National Religious Broadcasters, cites Revelation 14:6:

> And I saw another angel fly in the midst of heaven, having the ever-lasting gospel to preach unto them that dwell on the earth, and to every nation, and kindred, and tongue, and people.

With the almost cartoon literalism common to many evangelicals, Armstrong suggests that this angel symbolizes the satellites that now broadcast the gospel to a sinful planet.

Curiously enough, John of Patmos, the visionary author of Revelation who concocted this image of the geosynchronous angel in the first place, is himself notably self-conscious about the mechanics of information propagation. His apocalypse is laced with images of literary materials. A seven-eyed lamb cracks open the seven seals of a divine book, unleashing the four horsemen of the Apocalypse, while later the heavens roll up like a scroll. John also frames his drama with language that focuses somewhat obsessively on the process of reading and writing. In the vision that opens the text, Jesus Christ announces himself as the Alpha and Omega (the first and last letters of the Greek alphabet), and then orders John to "Write what you see in a book, and send it to the seven churches" (Rev. 1:11). As Harry Gamble argues in his history of early Christian writings, "[John's] prophecy is not a visual apprehension or an oral message subsequently preserved in writing: the text is what was originally intended."[226] That is, John's book is not a recollected reflection, but the site of divine revelation itself.

Given that his revelation foretold the imminent end of the world, John was understandably compelled to get the word out as fast as possible. The time was at hand, and Christ had enjoined him to "not seal up the words of the prophecy of this book." John thus explicitly framed his text as a letter, and he blessed "he who reads aloud the words of the prophecy, and . . . those who hear, and who keep what is written therein" (Rev. 1:3). The historian W. M. Ramsay argues that John chose the particular seven churches he did because each was located at a natural center of communication and was thus ideally located for circulating copies of Revelation throughout the Christian community. Given the fact that copying introduces noise and distortion, John sought to control the replication of his text by warning the potential reader or scribe not to alter any of his words, because otherwise "God will add to him the plagues described in this book." The success of John's memetic endeavor can be measured by the simple fact that Revelation made it into the final cut of the Bible, over and against any number of more manageable contenders.

Needless to say, the first generations of Christians did not live to see the Second Coming. But though the orthodox Church tried to clamp down on millennialist fever, John's almost hallucinogenic guidebook continued to feed the fires of apocalyptic expectation throughout the course of Christian history. John's cast of characters were particularly intriguing: Exactly who were the great whore of Babylon, the false prophet, the two witnesses, and the seven-headed beast? Though many Christians interpreted Revelation as allegory or impenetrable mystery, it was tough for some to suppress the hunch that John's text, along with the apocalyptic prophecies of Ezekiel and Daniel, encoded specific information about actual events on the historical horizon. Given that John's elaborate symbolic language forms a kind of literary Rorschach blot, countless self-appointed prophets through the ages have been able to find apocalyptic significance in current events, from the crowning of the Holy Emperor Frederick II to the Gulf War. The Book of Revelation itself can thus become a kind of metavirus. By drawing readers into the apocalyptic time of the text, it encourages them to uncover the true meaning of John's eschatological drama by matching it to living history. In other words, Revelation reveals itself as a code to be cracked.

Though many Bible-crackers stick to the narrative imagery of biblical prophecy, others have treated the text of scripture itself as a literal cipher. As we saw in chapter 1, Jewish Kabbalists squeezed additional meanings out of the Torah with techniques such as Temurah, the transposition of letters, or Gematria, which uses the numbers associated with each Hebrew letter to suggest esoteric correspondences between words (for example, the Hebrew words for serpent and messiah both equal 358). Much of this code-breaking has been directed toward mystical ends, but countless exegetes have deciphered literal historical predictions as well, and continue to do so today. In Michael Drosnin's best-selling 1997 book *The Bible Code,* for example, the author claims that by rearranging the Torah into a kind of crossword puzzle, all sorts of curious words and correspondences pop out: Kennedy is near Dallas, Newton intersects gravity, and Hitler looms only twenty rows away from Nazi. Though Drosnin doesn't do anything as audacious as date the Eschaton, he does claim that the Torah is "an interactive database" that predicts the future. His metaphor is not altogether out of place; the impressive if ultimately empty synchronicities he discovered are based on statistical analyses performed by Israeli scientists using massive number-crunching computers. It seems that the vision of computer-aided Kabbalah that Umberto Eco spun in *Foucault's Pendulum* has become a reality; in fact, Hebrew hermeneuts can download Gematria software from the Internet.

As Edward Rothstein pointed out in the *New York Times,* the phenomenal worldwide success of Drosnin's book comes at a time when society has become utterly enthralled by the idea of the code. "The scientific and the speculative, the devotional and the kooky: everywhere in our religious beliefs and cultural enterprises, we are preoccupied with discerning codes."[227] Rothstein suggests that, in part, we have latched onto the code because we no longer believe that human nature and society are quite as malleable as we once had hoped. Genetic engineers are mapping the human genome, and every week brings a new announcement linking some physiological malady or psychological quirk to DNA, which from the beginning of its public career was fetishized as the "code of creation." Cognitive scientists and artificial intelligence wizards claim to be cracking the assembly language of thought; at the same time, we hand more and more of our decisions over to coded systems of cybernetic control, information processing, and statistical analysis. Though moderns have long trumpeted the ambiguity and contingency of the world, nowadays it sometimes seems that everything has already been written, or at least programmed in advance.

The pop fascination with *The Bible Code* also conceals the old dream of the universal book: the Torah that creates the world, the book of Nature that mirrors the logos of God, or the great tome that Dante glimpsed in the empyrean of Paradise: "I saw buried in the depths, bound with love in one volume, that which is scattered through the universe."[228] Attempting to make this dream a reality, the scholar theologians of the Middle Ages produced great *summae,* theological texts that attempted to demonstrate the fundamental unity of all things by philosophically organizing them according to the great chain of being. By the time of the Enlightenment, when scientists had taken over the labor of decoding the world, the summa had mutated into the secular encyclopedia, which organized human knowledge according to rational categories, alphabetical listings, and indexes. In the age of the Internet, when information moves too fast for the codex and even the *Encyclopaedia Britannica* has gone online, Dante's universal book has returned in the fantasized and idealized image of the universal hypertext: an infinite network that links documents, images, and fragments of knowledge and news into a constantly mutating multidimensional library that divinely ingathers the evolving cosmos. The Internet has become infected with this dream, which in theological terms seeks to mirror the mind of God. As Paul Virilio told the online journal CTHEORY, "The research on cyberspace is a quest for God . . . and deals with the idea of a God who is, sees, and hears everything."[229]

Perhaps the manic enthusiasm for information, for producing, packaging, transmitting, and consuming scattered fragments of a coded world, is partly motivated by an unconscious desire for a totalizing revelation, an incandescent apocalypse of knowledge. After all, the word *apocalypse* simply means an uncovering or revealing. As a literary genre, the apocalypse presents itself as a kind of visionary freedom of information act, with God granting the sect a glimpse of his multimedia, literally all-time book of the world. All apocalyptic writings are shot through with the desire for the transparency and fullness of knowledge, a yearning for that time when all will be revealed, when a truer Torah will emerge, when light will come to the hidden things in the dark. In Matthew 10:26, Jesus even sounds like a pundit for the open surveillance society, promising that, in the last days, "there is nothing covered up that will not be uncovered, nothing hidden that will not be made known." But of all prophetic intimations of the information age, the most suggestive remains Daniel 12:4, at least in its squirrelly and much-loved King James translation. After proclaiming the future resurrection of the dead, when the "wise shall shine as the brightness of the firmament," the messiah tells the exiled prophet to seal up his book until the time of the end, when "many shall run to and fro, and knowledge shall be increased."

Now there's a vision that most of us can get behind. Today we are drowning in an information glut, and the faster we move about, in meatspace or cyberspace, the more ferocious the flows become. In this sense, our high-speed information overload is itself generating an ersatz apocalyptic buzz, though not quite the way that Daniel envisioned. As we wire ourselves into the buzzing networks of information exchange, we give ourselves over to the time-splicing, space-shrinking, psychic intensification of the whole giddy and heedless rush of Progress, its hidden eschatological urges laid bare at the very moment they become the most profane. We can no longer even keep time with the modern sense of history, because its feisty rhythms were still very much a product of books and material memory, both of which are now evaporating into the sound-bite, quick-cut, self-referential "now" of the ever-forgetting electronic universe.

In one of his apocalyptic theoretical tracts, Jean Baudrillard called this mediated rapture "the ecstasy of communication." He argues that the "harsh and inexorable light of information and communication" has now mastered all spheres of existence, producing an omnipresent system of media flows that has colonized the interior of the self. Passion, intimacy, and psychological depth evaporate, and we wind up "only a pure screen, a switching center of all the networks of influence." No longer subjects of our own experience, we abandon ourselves to a cold and schizophrenic fascination with an infoglut he likens to a "microscopic pornography of the universe." Though one suspects that Monsieur Baudrillard might do well to cancel his premium cable service, his dour prophecy certainly resonates. Many of us have indeed enclosed our nervous systems within a vibrating artificial matrix of cell phones, pagers, voice mail systems, networked laptops, and ever-present terminal screens, which monitor us as much as we monitor them. As we attempt to micromanage this onslaught of sound bites, emails, temporal disjunctions, and data dumps, we lose the slower rhythms and gnawing silences of the inner world. We lose the capacity to speak and act from within, and communication is reduced to a reactive, almost technical operation. And so we drown, believing that to drown is to surf.

The problem with the totalizing pessimism of Baudrillard and other technological doomsters is that humans remain protean beings, blessed with enormous elasticity and a profound potential for creative adaptation. Indeed, I suspect we will hack this phase-shift in our own tangled way, and that part of this adaptation may actually involve moving the ecstasy of communication to a higher ground, where we might grab the visionary bull by the horns. Along the multiplying planes of information and communication, we may learn to move like nomads, becoming errant seers despite ourselves, just to grapple with it all. And in the periphery of perception, where all the networks intersect, we may glimpse the outlines of some nameless Matrix emerging, some new structure of being and knowing that undergirds the merely material real, a vast webwork of collective intelligence within which we are at once on our own and one with the immense ecology of a conscious cosmos.

Needless to say, the ecstasy of communication still leaves one dazed and confused when the morning comes. That is our human lot, after all, to fall to earth. But to see just *how* dazed and confused a close encounter with the information eschaton can be, we need to turn to one of the most sublime and crackpot tales in the annals of techgnosis: the strange and visionary case of Philip K. Dick, who wrestled with the information angel and woke up battered and bruised, wondering if it was all just a dream. Or a trick.

Divine Interference

On February 2, 1974, Philip K. Dick was in pain. That particular day he did not care that his darkly comic tales of androids, weird drugs, and false realities were already recognized as some of the most visionary that science fiction had yet produced. He had just had an impacted wisdom tooth removed, and the sodium pentothol was wearing off. A delivery woman arrived with a package of Darvon, and when Dick opened the door, he was struck by the woman's beauty and the attractive golden necklace she wore. Asking her about the curious shape of the pendant, Dick was told it was a sign used by the early Christians. Then the woman departed.

All Americans who drive cars know this fish well, as its Christian and Darwinian mutations wage a war of competing faiths from the rear ends of Volvos and Hondas across the land. As a Christian logo, the fish predates the cross, and its Piscean connotations of baptism and magical bounty (the miracle of loaves and fishes) reach back to the time when the persecuted cult secretly gathered in Alexandrine catacombs. *Ichthus,* the Greek word for fish that's often inscribed within the symbol, is itself a kind of code, a Greek acrostic of the phrase "Jesus Christ, Son of God, Savior." One apocryphal story claims that Christians would clandestinely test the allegiance of new acquaintances by casually drawing one curve of the ichthus in the dirt. If the stranger was in the know, he or she would complete the image.

For Dick, the ichthus was a secret sign of an altogether different order. Like the winged letter that appears in the Gnostic "Hymn of the Pearl," the delivery woman's necklace served as a trigger for mystical memory. As Dick wrote later in a personal journal:

> The (golden) fish sign causes you to remember. Remember what? . . . Your celestial origins; this has to do with the DNA because the memory is located in the DNA. . . . You remember your real nature. . . . The Gnostic Gnosis: You are here in this world in a thrown condition, but are not *of* this world.[230]

Once Dick's brain was zapped by the fish sign, it went on to host a remarkable series of revelations, hallucinations, and vatic dreams that lasted off and on for years. In particular, Dick's vision put him in direct contact with a force he described as a "vast active living intelligence system"—VALIS for short. In his 1980 quasi-autobiographical novel of the same name, Dick defined VALIS as a "spontaneous self-monitoring negentropic vortex . . . tending progressively to subsume and incorporate its environment into arrangements of information." Sounding rather like a mystic's take on the Internet, VALIS is in some ways the ultimate techgnostic vision: an apocalyptic matrix of living information that overcomes entropy and redeems the fallen world. In essence, Dick's mystic glimpse differs little from *The Starseed Transmissions* that Ken Carey channeled only a few years after Dick's VALIS experiences. But unlike Carey, who was content to simply transmit his cosmic information, Dick wove his visions into the tangled, complex, and far more human struggles of his narratives: strange, powerful, and deeply ironic fables concerning the psychic turmoil and hilarious double binds that ordinary humans find themselves in as they struggle for love and justice in a world ruled by the absurd simulacra and alienating tyrannies of post-industrial life.

Besides working elements of the events he came to call "2-3-74" into a number of his later novels, Dick also cranked out the "Exegesis," a couple million mostly handwritten words that restlessly elaborate, analyze, and pull the rug out from under his own weird experiences. To judge from those portions that have seen the light of day, the Exegesis is an alternately powerful, boring, and disturbing document. Sparkling metaphysical jewels and inspiring chunks of garage philosophy swim in a turbid and depressing sea of speculative indulgence and self-obsession hermeneutics in amphetamine overdrive. In his "Tractates Cryptica Scriptura," which are excerpts from the Exegesis appended to *Valis,* Dick crystallized the paranoid and redemptive themes of info-gnosis. Like Ed Fredkin's computational physics, the "Tractates" hold the view that the universe is composed of information. The world we experience is a hologram, "a hypostasis of information" that we, as nodes in the true Mind, process. "We hypostasize information into objects. Rearrangement of objects is change in the content of information. This is the language we have lost the ability to read."[231]

As we saw earlier, the notion of a lost Adamic language is an old one in Western esoteric lore. For Dick, the scrambling of the Adamic code meant that both ourselves and the world as we know it are "occluded," cut off from the brimming matrix of cosmic data. Instead, we are trapped in the Black Iron Prison, Dick's image for the satanic mills of illusion, political tyranny, and oppressive social control that keep our minds in manacles. More than a merely paranoid motif, Dick's Black Iron Prison can be seen as a mythic expression of the "disciplinary apparatus" of power analyzed by historian Michel Foucault, who showed that prisons, mental institutions, schools, and military establishments all organized space and time along similar lines of rational control. Foucault argued that this "technology of power" was distributed throughout social space, enmeshing human subjects at every turn, and that liberal social reforms are only cosmetic touch-ups of an underlying mechanism of control. Though Foucault saw this as an eminently modern architecture, Dick's religious imagination rocketed him back to the ancient world. Rome became the paragon of this Empire, and as Dick put it, "The Empire never ended." The feverish Dick even recognized its archetypal lineaments in the Nixon administration.

In one of Dick's myriad metaphysical scenarios, VALIS surreptitiously invades this spurious world of control to liberate us. Like the letter in "The Hymn of the Pearl" that lay on the side of the road, Dick's God "presumes to be trash discarded, debris no longer noticed," so that "lurking, the true God literally ambushes reality and us as well."[232] Birth from the spirit occurs when this metaphysical "plasmate" replicates in human brains, creating hybrids Dick called "homoplasmates." In *Valis,* Dick claims that the last homoplasmates were killed off when the Romans destroyed the Second Temple in 70 C.E., at which point, "real time ceased." The gnostic plasmate did not reenter human history until the watershed year of 1945, when the codices of Nag Hammadi were uncovered. Dick's plasmate mythology thus injects the postwar world with the apocalyptic expectations of late antiquity, while spiritualizing the notion of an information virus. Though antagonistic atheists like Richard Dawkins use the materialistic idea of the meme in order to attack religion, Dick's plasmate redeems the world through the very materiality of its infectious code.

However intriguing his visions, Dick obviously logged a lot of hours on the far side of kooky. Sometimes VALIS struck him as a pink beam of esoteric data, or spoke to him with a compassionate "AI voice" from outer space. Other times, Dick felt that he was in telepathic communication with a first-century Christian named Thomas, and at one point, the surrounding landscape of early-seventies California "ebbed out" while the landscape of first-century Rome "ebbed in." Dick also picked up strange signals from electronic devices, messages of salvation and threat trickling out of the old electromagnetic imaginary. Once, when listening to the Beatles' "Strawberry Fields Forever," the strawberry-pink light informed him that his son Christopher was about to die. Rushing the kid to a physician, Dick discovered that the child had a potentially fatal inguinal hernia, and the boy was soon operated on.

Clearly the bizarre events of 2-3-74 avail themselves equally to the languages of religious experience and psychological pathology, although they seem too fractured for the one, and too rich and even visionary for the other. Dick himself recognized this ambiguity, and until his untimely death in 1982, he never stopped mulling over his VALIS experience, not only because he could never make up his mind, but because he recognized even in his looniness that metaphysical certainty is a dire trap. Unlike the whole disturbing march of mystagogues and prophets through the ages, Dick remained ambivalent about his creative cosmologies, and in this ambivalence he speaks volumes about the nature of religious experience in the age of neurotransmitters and microwave satellites. Dick distrusted reification of any sort (his novels constantly wage war against the process that turns people and ideas into things), and he accordingly refused to solidify his tentative notions into a rigid belief system. Even in his private journals, he constantly liquefied his own revelations, writing with a skeptic's restless awareness of the indeterminacy of speculative thought. In the end, though, 2-3-74 recalls nothing so much as the ontological paradoxes of a Philip K. Dick novel, where the spurious realities that often surround his characters can collapse like cardboard, and metaphysical break-ins are generally indistinguishable from psychological breakdowns. Even if Dick suffered something like temporal lobe epilepsy (which his biographer Lawrence Sutin argues is the most likely somatic explanation), his earlier books prove that 2-3-74 erupted from his own creative daemon.

In 1970's *A Maze of Death*, for example, a character's quest for self-knowledge stages a techgnostic metafable that mixes "The Hymn of the Pearl" with Pirandello's *Six Characters in Search of an Author*. The 1970 novel opens with a group of colonists congregating on a lush, leafy planet named Delmak-O. As soon as they arrive, the taped instructions that the colonists were promised when they embarked for the planet are found mysteriously erased. Much of the remaining plot resembles Agatha Christie's *And Then There Were None*, as one by one the colonists are murdered or mysteriously die. For the reader, it is impossible to tell what is "really" happening, since each colonist also sinks deeper and deeper into his or her own subjective worldview, losing the ability to communicate with one another and to maintain a consensus about the reality of Delmak-O.

One cognitive map that is shared by all the colonists is the theology of A. J. Specktowsky's *How I Rose from the Dead in My Spare Time and So Can You*. Specktowsky's book describes a universe ruled by four deities: the Mentufacturer (the creative demiurge), the Form-Destroyer (death, entropy), the Walker-on-Earth (an Elijah-like prophet), and the Intercessor (the Christ figure or Redeemer). As Dick writes in a note that precedes the narrative, this theology resulted from his own attempt to "develop an abstract, logical system of religious thought, based on the arbitrary postulate that God exists." The cybernetic underpinnings of this faith are symbolized by the transmitter and the relay network that the colonists initially use to send their prayers to the god-worlds.

Of course, this system almost immediately breaks down. The colonists then discover that only some aspects of their supposedly natural environment are organic, while others, particularly the insects, are technological. There are camera-bees, flies with speakers and musical tapes, and fleas that endlessly reprint books. Examining a miniature building under a microscope, Seth Morley discovers amidst its circuitry the phrase "Made at Terra 35082R." Soon afterward, Morley's growing doubts about the reality of Delmak-O produce a paranoid breakthrough:

> [It is] as if, he thought, those hills in the background, and that great plateau to the right, are a painted backdrop. As if all this, and ourselves, and the settlement—all are contained in a geodesic dome. And . . . research men, like entirely deformed scientists of pulp fiction, are peering down on us. . . .[233]

The remaining colonists soon come to believe that they are being used as lab rats in some debased social scientific experiment, and that the malfunction of their initial instruction tapes was deliberate. They conclude that they are actually on Earth, inmates of an insane asylum who have had their memories erased by the military. These suspicions are confirmed when they spot uniformed guards and flying helicopters moving through the landscape of Delmak-O.

At this point, the colonists enter a full-fledged paranoid scenario, which includes many elements common both to pulp fiction and to actual conspiracy theories (Men in Black, blocked memories, "bugs" and other hidden surveillance devices). But Dick is not satisfied with this answer to the riddle of Delmak-O, and neither are the colonists, who still can't explain why each of them is tattooed with the phrase "Persus 9." Banding together, they approach the tench, an uncanny local creature who, earlier in the narrative, offered oracular *I Ching*–like answers to their questions. But when the colonists ask the tench what Persus 9 means, the thing explodes in a mass of gelatin and computer circuitry, initiating a chain reaction that results in the apocalyptic destruction of the planet.

In the following chapter, we discover that Persus 9 is the name of a disabled spaceship, hopelessly circling a dead star. To maintain sanity as they drift to their certain doom, the crew had programmed their T.E.N.C.H. 889B computer to generate virtual worlds that the men and women would then enter through "polyencephalic fusion." Delmak-O was based on a few basic parameters initially established by the group—including the same postulate that the author Dick claims he used to create the theology of Specktowsky's book: that God exists.

As postmodern allegories go, *A Maze of Death* cuts to the bone. Incapable of altering the destructive course of our dysfunctional technological society, we resort to what media critic Neil Postman called "amusing ourselves to death." Like the Perky Pat Layouts in *The Three Stigmata of Palmer Eldritch*, the T.E.N.C.H. symbolizes a culture based on "mentufactured," or imagineered, distractions. In his later essay "How to Build a Universe That Doesn't Fall Apart Two Days Later," Dick explicitly applies the false worlds of his fiction to contemporary American life:

> Today we live in a society in which spurious realities are manufactured by the media, by governments, by big corporations, by religious groups, political groups . . . unceasingly we are bombarded with pseudo-realities manufactured by very sophisticated people using very sophisticated electronic mechanisms. I do not distrust their motives; I distrust their power.[234]

As I have suggested throughout this book, the gnostic mythology of the archons is in some ways an appropriate image of power in an age of electronic specters and high-tech propaganda, an environment of simulation whose slipperiness can twist even the most noble of motives. For those so inclined, the mythology of the archons instills a hermeneutics of suspicion, one that questions the hidden agendas that lurk beneath the mediascape even as it runs the risk of lapsing into paranoia. And indeed, in both his fictions and his life, Dick could become quite paranoid about the invisible wardens of this Black Iron Prison. But like the Gnostics of old, Dick also flip-flopped in his vision of the archons. Sometimes he saw them as evil, other times as aberrant and selfish products of their own ignorance and power. The difference is crucial: The Manichean notion that good and evil are absolute contraries sucks the self into a harsh and paranoid dualism, while the other, more "Augustinian" mode of gnosis opens the self into the continual labor of awakening that holds out the possibility of enlightening even the archons, who in the end are no other than ourselves. This is the story of Delmak-O, a simulation orchestrated not by a conspiracy of evil military scientists, but by people's alienated desires and their unwillingness to confront death.

Though Morley's gnostic quest for true identity succeeds in rending illusions, it appears to offer no ascent, only a frank awareness of the slow drift toward oblivion. But *A Maze of Death* is a Philip K. Dick story, which means that the story is never really over. Once Morley awakens on the spaceship, he feels depressed to the point of suicide. As the rest of the crew prepare to enter another simulation, he wanders into a corridor where he encounters a strange figure that calls himself the Intercessor. Morley doesn't buy it. "But we invented you! We and T.E.N.C.H. 889B." The Intercessor does not explain himself as he leads Morley "into the stars," while the rest of the crew find themselves once again stuck on Delmak-O.

As a literal deus ex machina, Dick's preprogrammed savior does make for a rather dissatisfying conclusion to the narrative. On the other hand, the Intercessor does create a numinous gap in Dick's otherwise bleak scenario, an ontological rupture that allows the phantasm, the simulacrum, to reveal its uncanny and potentially redemptive power. In a sense, Morley enters a different order of the virtual, one that exists above the technologies of simulation. This is the virtual that has always been with us, that needs no gadgets to intercede in our lives, that arises from the "arbitrary postulates" of our cultural software even as it transcends them. As the British SF author Ian Watson notes, "One rule of Dick's false realities is the paradox that once in, there's no way out, yet for this very reason transcendence of a sort can be achieved."[235]

Sensing the potential metaphysical and political fallout of a society whose perceptions were increasingly engineered, Dick used his pulp fables to redeploy the old gnostic struggle for authenticity and freedom within the hard-sell universe of technological simulacra. Despite the transcendental temperament of his later days, Dick did not follow other technodualists in condemning the flesh or the material world. Instead, the demiurgic traps in his novels are human constructions, figments we build out of media technologies, commodity hallucinations, emotional lies, and our desire to lose ourselves in a good tale. The life of authenticity begins when these illusions collapse. "I will reveal a secret to you," Dick writes in the essay cited above. "I like to build universes that *do* fall apart. I like to see them come unglued, and I like to see how the characters in the novels cope with this problem."[236]

By cracking apart his own fictional worlds, Dick left us fractured fables about the hilarious, bleak, and occasionally liberating interpenetration of VR and real life. His characters are us, constantly tripping over ourselves as we slip back and forth, with or without technologies, between the virtual world of spirit and that material world where all things die. Though Dick heard VALIS's negentropic call of information redemption, he also recognized that entropy is what kills our illusions, and that such dark and ironic liberations may become even more important in a hyperreal world that disguises the devastating consequences of its technologies with the bright and shiny packaging of techno-utopia. Of course, we cannot know whether the information web destined to gird the earth will be an electronic asylum or a holistic society of mind, a "vast active living intelligence system" or an infinite nest of Perky Pat Layouts. But even if we find ourselves absorbed into some bountiful network of collective intelligence, then you can guarantee that the network will inevitably go on the fritz.

Faced with the failure of all totalizing and redemptive schemes, Dick came down to nothing more than the drive to remain human in an often inhuman world. In contrast to the exhausted skepticism of the postmoderns or the juvenile glee of the posthumans, Dick never abandoned his commitment to the "authentic human," which he tentatively described as the viable and elastic being that can "bounce back, absorb, and deal with the new." Perhaps the greatest strength of Dick's wildly inventive, choppy, and humorously bleak narratives lies in his intimately rendered portrait of human beings, and especially of the jury-built and fiercely creative measures that we hack together when metaphysical and technological solutions to our psychological and social ills collapse at our feet. Though Dick's fiction shares some gnostic SF notions with L. Ron Hubbard's writings, Dick's characters are the absolute opposite of the superheroes of Scientology; they are bumbling Joes and Janes, struggling with moral ambiguity, poverty, drugs, invasive institutions, credit agency robots, and shattered headspaces. They live in worlds where commodities have supplanted community, where androids dream, and where God lurks in a spray can. The most divine communications in such a world aren't carried in a pink blast of otherworldly gnosis, but in that most telepathic of human emotions: empathy.

third mind from the sun

When the Jesuit paleontologist Pierre Teilhard de Chardin shuffled off this mortal coil in New York City on Easter Sunday, 1955, few people noticed. Though the priest was known as a scientist of sorts, the writings that would bring him posthumous fame—incandescent and poetic speculations about cosmic history and the future of humanity—remained largely unpublished. The reason was simple: The essays of his that *had* seen the light of day were so weird that certain Catholic bureaucrats had begun to murmur about excommunication. Rather than take this drastic step, Teilhard's superiors simply prohibited him from publishing.

They also effectively banished him to China for many years, where he dated fossils, sifted through Gobi Desert dust, and helped dig up the Peking man. Teilhard was living in the East when his spiritual meditations on the history of Earth led him to write *The Phenomenon of Man*, a masterwork of mystical science whose giddily optimistic view of humanity's role in the evolution of cosmic consciousness has come to inform one of the most important questions that now tugs on hearts and minds around the planet: What is the nature of the new global space we now find ourselves within? Attempting to come to grips with the more cosmic and incorporeal dimensions of our networked world, a variety of techno-utopians, New Agers, and cybertheorists have crafted different visions of Gaian minds and global brains. But they all owe a debt to Teilhard, whose sweeping vision of planetary consciousness can still leave one wondering if he did not indeed possess a prophetic eye.

Critics of Christianity often accuse the religion of institutionalizing a dangerous rupture between humanity and nature. But Teilhard argued the opposite: Humanity, including its art, gadgets, and religions, was part and parcel of the planet's evolutionary game plan. Though maintaining a measure of dualism between mind and body, Teilhard rejected the bitterness of Manichean myth and proclaimed "the spiritual value of matter." He saw evolution as the progressive unfolding of biochemical complexity, a process that, in turn, generated ever-greater organizations of consciousness. As evolution creaked forward from rocks to plants to the beasts of land and sea, consciousness simultaneously grew into ever more novel and complex architectures of mind, architectures that he believed were intrinsic and internal to material forms. Eventually, this twofold process resulted in the subjective dimension of the human brain that allows you to understand these words. Thus for Teilhard, the emergence of the human psyche and its collective networks of culture and civilization were more than serendipitous froth on the surface of Darwin's random soup. These structures of consciousness constituted the leading edge of the evolutionary wave of Earth itself, a planet that Teilhard saw, in a prescient intuition of James Lovelock's Gaia hypothesis, as a "super-organism."

Teilhard was not the most rigorous of scientists, however, and he lost major points with his embarrassing and rather murky involvement with the Piltdown man—the purported "missing link" discovered in an English gravel pit that turned out to be a human skull cap mischievously arranged with the jaw of an orangutan. On the other hand, Teilhard's evolutionary speculations were more than just the foamings of a preternaturally enthusiastic spirit, and other scientists of the early twentieth century anticipated some of his views. The brilliant Russian mineralogist Vladimir Vernadsky also regarded the Earth as a total living system, and held that planetary evolution was passing from a stage determined by biological laws to one molded by conscious human activity. The eminent biologist Sir Julian Huxley, son of the great Darwinian cheerleader Sir Thomas Huxley and brother to the novelist and philosopher Aldous, held a similar position. Huxley argued that "It is only through social evolution that the world-stuff can now realize radically new possibilities. . . . For good or evil, the mechanism of evolution has in the main been transferred onto the social and conscious level. . . . The slow methods of variation and heredity are outstripped by the speedier processes of acquiring and transmitting experience."[237]

Teilhard had no doubts that this transfer was all for the best, because in the long run, human activity was going to awaken the physical planet itself. From its very beginnings, the Jesuit believed, the human mind wove itself into a collective matrix of culture and communication, an etheric web of consciousness that not only linked individual humans but was destined to cloak the entire biosphere like an onion skin. Teilhard called this cerebral crown of creation the "noosphere," a collective psychic entity that emerged from the same organic and symbiotic drive toward unity and complexity that initially led freelance chemical elements to band together as molecules and cells. In the noosphere, however, the binding units are not chemicals but human minds, the accumulated accretions of imagination, language, and thought. The noosphere itself evolves, and as it continues "adding its internal fibers and tightening its network," it will rope human individuals into increasingly collective forms of consciousness. Sounding a note that McLuhan would later trumpet, Teilhard argued that the noosphere's thick tangle of economic, social, and information networks would submerge us into "an enforced resonance" with all the thoughts, wills, and passions of our fellow creatures.

Hold on to your hats, though, for this evolutionary process will not quit until matter achieves the ultimate state of superorganization and complexity. At that point, Terra herself achieves consciousness, and collective humanity will kick up its heels for the final number in the Time and Space Review. With matter and mind narrowing to a single point of what technology gurus still call "convergence," we will find ourselves sliding down a cosmic wormhole that Teilhard dubbed the "Omega point." At that node of ultimate synthesis, the internal spark of consciousness that evolution has slowly banked into a roaring fire will finally consume the universe itself. Christ will "blaze out like a flash of lightning," and our ancient itch to flee this woeful orb will finally be satisfied as the immense expanse of cosmic matter collapses like some mathematician's hypercube into absolute spirit.

At this point in his conceptual journey, Teilhard had clearly drifted far from the Galápagos Islands. The Jesuit offered empirical evidence for the rise of biochemical complexity throughout planetary history (an argument that nouveau Darwinians like Stephen Jay Gould resoundingly reject), but Teilhard's evolutionary road show boils down to a deeply Christian mysticism that is apocalyptic at its core. Though he tap-danced on the thin ice of heresy, Teilhard was thinking as a Catholic when he came up with the notion of the noosphere. "Catholic" literally means "deriving from the whole," and Teilhard's holistic vision of planetary consciousness derives from the orthodox image of the institutional Church as a universal spiritual body that seeks to absorb every unique human individual into its millennial flesh, topped with the head of Christ. Fans of Western philosophy will also recognize the dim shadows of Hegel's idealism in Teilhard's thought, with its similar hunger for absolute synthesis and its conviction in the ultimate absorption of matter into spirit.

Though it would be wrong to accuse Teilhard of practicing science, the man was certainly enthusiastic about synthesizing spirit with the technoscientific project of the modern world. In a revealing passage in *The Future of Man,* Teilhard argued that the mystical experiences undergone by the yogis of the East were actually emanations from the Omega point, but that the sages misinterpreted the message when they rejected the material possibilities of the world in order to cultivate transcendent reality. In contrast, Teilhard was a global perfectionist who believed that the divine progressively realized itself through the lumbering machinery of history, technological as well as natural. Teilhard's mysticism thus fused two contradictory vectors of the Western spirit: the world-denying ascent toward transcendence and the headlong plunge toward the total domination of matter. "God awaits us when the evolutionary process is complete: to rise above the World, therefore, does not mean to despise or reject it, but to pass through it and sublime it."[238] Proclaiming that we move "upward by way of forward," Teilhard honed a kind of theological Extropianism. In this sense, Teilhard's work must be seen as a visionary response to one of the most pressing existential needs in twentieth-century thought: to find in the sloppy mechanics of evolution a positive basis for human life, some cosmic pattern or pulse that might enable us to see ourselves, our minds and cultures, as more than blind flukes doomed to bow down before the entropic second law.

With a winning combination of optimism, scientific enthusiasm, and mystical authority, Teilhard molded together Darwin and the divine. This synthesis of science and spirit, heretical to many on both sides of the divide, attracted legions of postwar readers, including Mario Cuomo and the New Age policy wonk Al Gore. In *Earth in the Balance,* Gore's attempt to create a Green philosophy that won't clog the pipes of the new world order, the vice president hopes that Teilhard's "faith in the future" will inspire humanity to resanctify Gaia while taking technological responsibility for it. In his book *The Phenomenon of Science,* whose title consciously twists Teilhard's famous work, the Russian cyberneticist Dr. Valentin Turchin attempts to describe the laws that drive the emergence of new phases of evolution, or what he calls a "meta systems transition." Though eschewing Teilhard's mysticism for the language of equations, Turchin still concludes that technology is launching us into a new phase of cultural evolution, one which will lead to the creation of a cybernetic superhuman organism, possibly through the mediation of the Internet. Traces of Teilhard even appear in the work of physicist Frank Tipler, who claimed in *The Physics of Immortality* that the anti-entropic forces of the universe are driving all things toward the ultimate improbability: an "Omega Point" supermind that will banish the forces of heat death and place the cosmos under the control of consciousness.

You don't have to go as far out as Tipler to hear echoes of Teilhard in contemporary science. Like many thinkers attempting to construct an integral philosophy of mind and nature, Teilhard would have felt right at home with systems theory, that interdisciplinary tradition that has already reared a few of its hydra heads in this book. As we discussed earlier, systems theorists de-emphasize the usual reductionist tack of dividing the fluctuating webwork of reality into isolated chunks of stuff. Instead, they look at the world as a nest of holistic and interdependent processes, a cosmos characterized by pattern and flow rather than form and matter. Systems theory began in the early part of the century with the biologist Ludwig von Bertalanffy and the engineers behind cybernetics, and today finds one of its fullest expressions in the complexity theory that tantalizes scientists and researchers at places like New Mexico's Santa Fe Institute. Generally speaking, complexity theorists study systems, like the weather or the economy, that are neither excessively ordered nor wildly stochastic, but dynamically arise in the liminal zone that fluctuates between these two relatively simple conditions. Between the yin and yang of randomness and determinism, something like the Tao of becoming emerges: the propensity of certain systems to "self-organize," to spontaneously generate novel patterns of behavior at precisely the moment they appear to be slipping into chaos. Whirlpools emerge in turbulent rivers, chemical regularities pop up in soups of random particles, bees swarm, and ants create cities. The Santa Fe heavyweight Stuart Kauffman calls these kind of emergent properties "order for free," and however rigorously they are charted and described, they seem to manifest the creative mind of nature herself, a mind we may also meet when immersed in artistic labor or the sensual poetry of perception.

Aiming for a language of pattern and process universal enough to be able to explain everything from L.A. traffic patterns to the distribution of galaxies, complexity theorists deal with terms and definitions that are necessarily slippery. In fact, one of the Santa Fe Institute's grails is a rigorous definition of what exactly makes a system *complex* in the first place. As scientists wander through a tangled forest of fuzzy guesses and abstract terminology, it remains unclear whether "complexity" is completely quantifiable or appears partly in the eye of the beholder. According to the physicist and Santa Fe Institute associate Dr. Dan Stein, "Complexity is still almost a theological concept."[239] One suspects that this tricky, metaphysical air derives partly from the subtle cracks that complexity theory introduces into the mechanistic and reductive view of the universe that has dominated the Western world-picture for centuries. What Gregory Bateson called "the pattern that connects" invariably draws the human mind into the web. And indeed, some complexity theorists consider consciousness itself to be the ultimate emergent property, the ultimate face of complexity—and Teilhard would surely have agreed.

As we noted earlier, one of the great conceptual leaps made by cybernetics was to characterize both living creatures and artificial gadgets as systems of information flow. Today this breakdown between the made and the born is cascading into a paradigm shift. Once life and mind are described as properties of complex systems, then complex systems, whether biological, ecological, or technological, begin to take on qualities of life and mind. We find ourselves faced with the image of the "organic information machine," an image realized in the science of artificial life. By using powerful computers to simulate evolutionary processes, especially replication, mutation, and selection, Santa Fe researchers like Chris Langton are attempting to breed novel and unpredictable digital critters inside the superfast Darwinian boxing ring of their computers. With his Tierra program, the biologist Thomas Ray has created digital microworlds capable of evolving an impressive array of creatures and parasites that compete for the "energy" of CPU time. As you might expect, organic metaphors abound in the A-Life community, and scientists like Ray and Langton consider their progeny to be, in principle at least, living beings. When Ray booted up his program for the first time, he said that "the life force took over," making him the creator, or at least the midwife, to an altogether new order of life.[240] Like the Kabbalists whose knowledge of the hidden Torah enabled them to create the mythical golem, the great android of Western esoteric lore, the wizards of artificial life use the spells of digital code to breed apparently autonomous beings on the other side of the looking glass. As the A-Life researcher Daniel Hillis proclaimed, "We can play God."[241]

Once again, we find a form of animism arising through the mediation of our most artificial and abstract of machines, a scientific animism bound up with the computer's ability to act as a replicating demiurge. For though A-Life hackers may play God, the computer does the lion's share of the work. Indeed, like chaos theory and most complexity research, A-Life could not exist without digital computation. With their number-crunching prowess and their ability to conjure up graphic simulations that model millions of parallel elements, computers can reveal patterns and properties impossible to notice in earlier times, when a line of inquiry might result in nothing more than a spew of apparently random numbers or the outlines of impossible equations. In a review of James Gleick's popular best-seller *Chaos,* the mathematician John Franks compared the computer to the microscope, arguing that digital computation allowed access to heretofore invisible dimensions of natural and mathematical phenomena. In this sense, chaos, which is really a name for the order lurking in the apparently random, is the child of the computer. But artificial gods like Langton and Ray aren't just looking at the world through digital glasses—they are engineering the world they see, channeling the life force into the virtual worlds of computer code.

Given the pivotal role that computers play in our understanding of chaos, complexity, and artificial life, it is hardly surprising that these sometimes rather speculative sciences have also turned around and started to influence how people think about the social, cultural, and economic dimension of computers. In *Out of Control,* the flagship volume of this technological post-Darwinism, *Wired* editor Kevin Kelly argues that we are heading into a neobiological civilization defined by organic technologies, machinelike biologies, and the prevalence of networks and hive minds. In this Teilhardian world, evolution and engineering become two sides of the same out-of-control force of adaptive learning and holistic feedback loops. Amassing loads of research, Kelly attempts to convince the reader that the spontaneous, symbiotic, and self-organizing capacities of complex systems amount to nothing less than an "invisible hand" of evolution—one that he thinks should be allowed to run riot. Instead of musty old governments, outmoded humanist philosophies, and moribund social institutions, the creative novelty of the universe itself should guide technological development, economic networks, and human culture. Kelly would bridle at the label of metaphysician, but he closes his book with some neo-biological rules of thumb, bumper-sticker slogans like "seek persistent disequilibrium" and "honor your errors" that he calls the "Nine Laws of God." Though Kelly himself is a born-again Christian, his God is in many ways the polar opposite of the top-down lawgiver of traditional biblical faith. Instead, his Nine Laws recall the process theology that has quietly built up steam in some twentieth-century religious circles, a theology that supplants the transcendent one-shot Platonic Creator with a more Taoist and Heraclitan sense of creative evolution and constant becoming.

Like Kelly, Teilhard extended his evolutionary optimism to encompass the pell-mell march of twentieth-century technology. The Jesuit praised all those possessed by the "demon (or angel) of Research" because they recognized that the world is a "machine for progress—or rather, an organism that is progressing." Anticipating the conceptual fusion (and confusion) of the made and the born that characterizes so many cyborganic thinkers today, Teilhard argued that technologies are now directly participating in their own evolution. Machines will continue to beget machines with the persistence of biblical patriarchs, and their interlinking progeny will eventually intertwine into "a single, vast, organized mechanism." But unlike the materialist techno-Darwinians, Teilhard believed that the outward complexification of material form is always accompanied by the internal growth of consciousness. For Teilhard, then, technologies are not simply human tools, but vessels of the expanding noosphere, the body and nervous system of a world consciousness striving to be.

As we saw earlier, electric infotech has been considered a kind of "nervous system" since the days of the telegraph, and, not surprisingly, Teilhard emphasized the role that electronic media played in the development of his technological "brain of brains." Writing in the early 1950s, he underscored the global reach of radio, cinema, and television, while also drawing attention to "the insidious growth of those astounding electronic computers." In a sense, Teilhard recognized the emergent outlines of a worldwide electronic and computational brain at a time when few engineers were even thinking about the possibilities of networked computers. Or as Jennifer Cobb Kreisberg bluntly declared in *Wired,* "Teilhard saw the Net coming more than half a century before it arrived."[242]

Cobb later expanded her theological ideas about the sacred pulse of technological development in her book *Cybergrace,* but it is no accident that her thoughts first appeared in *Wired.* From its first issue, the magazine's infectious and often absurdly gung ho enthusiasm for both the Internet and the global technoeconomy has been informed with a kind of secularized Teilhardian fervor. Along with Kevin Kelly's paeans to the coming neo-biological civilization, *Wired* regular John Perry Barlow is also a hard-core Teilhard fan, who announces in the magazine's pages that "the point of all evolution up to this stage is the creation of a collective organization of Mind."[243] And in an online interview, the magazine's cofounder Louis Rossetto tipped his hat to Teilhard and the Jesuit's influence on Internet culture. "What seems to be evolving is a global consciousness formed out of the discussions and negotiations and feelings being shared by individuals connected to networks through brain appliances like computers. The more minds that connect, the more powerful this consciousness will be. For me, this is the real digital revolution—not computers, not networks, but brains connecting to brains."[244]

Even trippier scenarios emerge from the brain of Mark Pesce, the VRML wizard we met in chapter VII. For Pesce, the astounding growth of the Net over the last decade can mean only one thing: Teilhard's noosphere is striving to know itself. In the capstone address before a VRML World Movers conference, Pesce explained that the noosphere, having saturated the electrical communication technologies of the pre-digital age, has begun to turn inward, ingesting "all human knowledge and all human experience." Using complexity-theory lingo, Pesce explained that, sometime in the early 1990s, the networked noosphere began an irreversible process of self-organization. "The first of its emergent properties was the World Wide Web, for it first needed to make itself comprehensible—that is, indexible—to itself." For proof of this rather mystical concrescence, Pesce pointed to the astronomical growth rate of the Web: "How else to explain a process that magically began everywhere, all at once, across the length and breadth of the Internet?" He called this phenomenon "the Web that ate the Net," and predicted that a similar transformation lies in the near future, when the Web will unfold into a three-dimensional cyberspace, courtesy of VRML or some other 3D Net protocol. "VRML is the porthole cut into the noosphere, the mirror which lets the seer see our self."[245]

Clearly, the notion that computer networks are booting up the mind of the planet is not a technoscientific scenario at all, however much the language of complex systems or artificial intelligence may help us get a handle on the Internet's explosive, out-of-control growth or its possible mindlike properties. The leap from the global brain to the Gaian mind remains an essentially metaphysical move—which doesn't mean that the leap isn't worth hazarding. For whether or not we take Pesce literally, his vision of the online noosphere gives voice to a growing if inchoate intuition that computer networks and virtual technologies have opened up what amounts to a new category of knowing and being, a unique and unparalleled global space of intelligence, experience, terror, and communion. On the other hand, even if we accept the outlandish supposition that Gaia is indeed waking up and rubbing her satellite eyes, we cannot assume that this electronic consciousness will be unified to itself, let alone achieve a state of mystical perfection. This is the lesson of Gibson's *Neuromancer* myth: The cyberspace AI that achieves technological godhead at the end of his first novel cannot maintain its omniscient infinity, and it fragments into the crafty polytheistic subroutines of Haitian Vodou. Or as Louis Rossetto put it, the emergence of a *single* global mind is no more likely than the discovery that a single human mind lurks within our own skulls: "We actually have a bunch of different 'minds,' which negotiate with each other."[246]

Rossetto's quip reminds us that the Gaian mind is really a story about our minds. In particular, it is about what is happening to those minds as we intertwine them through computer networks and global media flows, through beepers, faxes, satellites, and cell phones, through emerging electric structures of work, education, and play. And from this perspective—a neuron's eye view of the global brain, so to speak—the noosphere does not begin with a state of mystical absorption, but with an identity crisis. Nowadays, it no longer seems as if we own our own minds. From cognitive science to postmodern psychology, it seems that the self has lost its bearings; the subject deconstructs itself and the society of mind devolves into a rabble.

Technology plays a privileged role in this identity meltdown, as the massive influx of media and information overwhelms the containers of consciousness, particularly, it seems, on the Internet. As the MIT sociologist Sherry Turkle argues in *Life on the Screen*, a savvy ethnography of online society—the virtual self is fragmented, fluid, and always under construction. Many computer users play with the malleable qualities of online identity: inhabiting different characters, histories, and genders; multiplying the self into a host of handles and log-ons; engineering autonomous digital doppelgängers. Turkle suggests that the multiplicity of online identity may actually enhance our ability to creatively explore and develop our personalities and relationships at a time of profound social dislocation; less generous observers might characterize the Internet as one cause of that dislocation, a false and fractured infinity that encourages people to avoid or postpone the ethical decisions, internal reflections, and acceptance of limitations that frame a life and give it shape and depth.

At the same time, the very multiplicity and fluidity of online identity opens up the possibility of new forms of human communion. On listservs, MUDs, and bulletin boards, our thoughts and personalities are woven into communities of virtual intelligence, where we are defined as much by the links and networks we bring with us as by the peculiar discursive fingerprints we leave on information space. Online, we colonize each other's brains, or at least the texts and images that flow through and shape those brains, and this mutual infestation breeds what Howard Rheingold calls "grass-roots group minds": new computer-mediated modes of collaboration, education, art, and decision making that may amplify and synthesize individual intelligence and creativity. In this sense, the Gaian mind is simply a mythic metaphor for a process that has begun much closer to home: the construction of networked environments and virtual spaces that knit our minds into transpersonal spaces of knowledge and experience potentially greater than the sum of their parts.

The cyberphilosopher Pierre Lévy calls this process the emergence of "collective intelligence." In an optimistic and incisive book of the same name, Lévy argues that computer networks, virtual environments, and multimedia tools will not simply amplify our individual cognitive powers, but will give rise "to a qualitatively different form of intelligence, which is added to personal intelligences, forming a kind of collective brain, or hypercortex."[247] This hypercortex is not just a new machinery of thought, but an *environment,* "an invisible space of understanding, knowledge, and intellectual power, within which new qualities of being and new ways of fashioning a society will flourish and mutate."[248] This "knowledge space" signifies nothing less than a new chapter of the human story, following on the heels of a number of anthropological spaces that humans have explored over the millennia: the nomadic earth of hunter-gatherers, the bounded territorial spaces of agricultural societies and the state, and the "deterritorialized" spaces of commodity flows introduced by capitalism. Lévy does not believe the knowledge space will erase these earlier environs, but he does hope that the digital terra incognita will allow us to overcome their limitations. Virtual interfaces and other forms of visualization will transform the collective networks of information into a navigable and nomadic "cosmopedia," a constantly unfolding space that will enable us to rise above the worlds of consumerism, political parochialism, and the mass media, and to develop the kind of radically democratic and transpersonal smarts we will need to confront the enormous difficulties that lie just around the bend.

Lévy is a philosopher, and he does not invoke the sorts of mystical forces that animate the thought of Teilhard de Chardin and other Gaian mind visionaries. On the other hand, he recognizes that the peculiar qualities of information space and virtual reality resurrect metaphysical concerns and the spiritual imagination alike. In his chapter "Choreography of Angelic Bodies," Lévy resuscitates medieval Islamic theology in order to apply Neoplatonic conceptions of the angel to the development of collective intelligence. As we saw in earlier chapters, Neoplatonist philosophers and mystics imagined the cosmos as a multistoried highrise. The closer a level stands to the transcendent godhead, the more perfection and unity it has. As you might expect, our world is in the basement, a ball of multiplicity and confusion where the transcendental call of the divine intellect must battle the chaos of fragmentation, ignorance, and wayward human passions. As Lévy explains, angels act as mediators and transformers within this hierarchy of spiritual reality; they collect the divine sparks of the level below them, including our world, and they fuse and direct these sparks toward the more synthetic planes of divine intelligence.

For Lévy, the Angel that medieval thinkers glimpsed hovering above our world returns today as the archetypal image of the collective intelligence that technologies are now creating. Theology becomes technology, once again. But in a crucial theoretical move, Lévy turns the metaphysical architecture of the Neoplatonic cosmos on its head, transforming transcendence into immanence and redirecting divine intelligence back toward the embodied human world we actually inhabit. Once the Angel is recognized as virtual rather than divine, it no longer lures us onto the Platonic space shuttle of world-loathing transcendence, but instead reflects our own active and angelic intelligence back onto the earth. "The angels of the living unite to perpetually form and re-form the Angel of the collective, the moving and radiant body of human knowledge. The

Angel does not speak. It is itself the aggregate voice or choral chant that rises from an acting and thinking humanity."[249] The Angel is not a tyrannical hive-mind. Our own angelic natures, our own active powers of intelligence, are amplified but not swallowed up by the "inverse cathedral" of the digital knowledge space.

Lévy suffers from a typically Gallic love of abstraction, and the more you try to imagine how Lévy's luminous vision of collective intelligence might actually unfold within the clamorous conditions of our workaday lives and technologies, the more difficult it is to hold on to. Contemplating such utopian and metaphysical possibilities in the light of today's information politics is like listening to the "Sanctus" of Bach's B-minor Mass on a cheap home stereo system: You feel swallowed up within a shimmering mathematical cathedral of the collective human voice, only to hear the glorious chorus fade into speaker buzz and the noise of car alarms outside. But Lévy's attempt to imagine the new space of information through the Angel of the collective remains highly compelling. Lévy acknowledges that spiritual and transpersonal possibilities continue to beckon the human mind, and that these possibilities have been triggered anew by our technologies—or rather, by what our technologies are doing to our minds. At the same time, Lévy resists the temptations of transcendence, of the fallacy that technology or metaphysical truths will deliver us to the level above human. If a postmodern World Soul is indeed emerging from the electronic hypercortex of information networks, then we must make sure that soul keeps its feet on the ground.

In this sense, it's important to see the myth of the Gaian mind, not in the virtual light of collective intelligence, but in the shadows of a more urgent and pressing condition: globalization. The telecommunication and computer networks that envelop the earth are only the most hardwired expression of what amounts, in the end, to a single planetary system blanketing Terra's multiple cultures and nations. Capitalism and communications have been shrinking the world for centuries, of course, but this new global space intertwines us as never before with its increasingly dynamic flows of capital, goods, immigrants, pollution, software, refugees, pop culture, viruses, weapons, ideas, and drugs. It is a world where warming trends spurred by industrial nations swallow islands in Polynesia, where governments pay more attention to CNN than to ambassadors, where a single bank clerk in Singapore can bring down a financial institution on the other side of the planet.

For Teilhard, Pesce, and other Gaian minders, the fact that the world is now wired into a collective web of interconnections suggests that evolutionary or even mystical forces are leading us into something like a global village. But as any anthropologist would tell you, villages can be pretty back-biting, oppressive, and paranoid places. Even Marshall McLuhan recognized the frightening claustrophobia of the global village he first described. As early as 1962, McLuhan argued that as the modern individual slips into the intensely participatory echo chamber of global electronic culture, we risk an eruption of violence, mental breakdowns, and societywide pathologies. "As our senses have gone outside us, Big Brother goes inside," he claimed, warning that unless we remain aware of this dynamic,

> we shall at once move into a phase of panic terrors, exactly befitting a small world of tribal drums, total interdependence, and superimposed coexistence. . . . Terror is the normal state of any oral society, for in it everything affects everything all the time.[250]

Mystical reports to the contrary, it seems that the realization that "everything affects everything all the time" is not always such a great release. For many global citizens anyway, the perception of total interdependence brings with it a dark and paralyzing fear, at the root of which lies the awareness that there is *no escape*. That's why so many of our panic terrors today cluster around the threat of contagion: Ebola plagues, AIDS, computer viruses, soul-rotting media memes, deadly *E. coli* outbreaks, even the infectious financial downturns of 1997's "Asian flu."

Most ominous of all is the possibility that total interdependence will mean new forms of totalitarian control. Though thinkers like Teilhard and Lévy go out of their way to avoid the suggestion that the global mind would transform the world into a high-tech anthill, such implications are unavoidable. The book jacket of Kevin Kelly's *Out of Control*, which is meant to reassure us that networking is definitely the way to go, pictures a swarm of half-virtual bees flitting about a honeycomb of MultiHyve computer monitors. Even the angels that Lévy hopes will help save us from this fate have something of the Stasi to them. In Islamic lore, for example, the winged guardians operate as holy spy-cams, invisible witnesses that hover about us during our daily trials, recording all our actions in a file to be sealed unto Judgment Day. Now we have digitized these recording angels, who are now fit to track, reconstruct, and issue judgment on our identities and actions as we move through an infosphere of databases, electronic transactions, demographic tracking software, and surveillance cameras.

Given the collapse of most overtly totalitarian regimes on the planet, fears of the dawning surveillance society might be seen as nothing more than phantasms that stand at the gates of a new mode of collective interdependence, paranoid projections our anxious egos cast as they shuffle, willingly or not, into the global village. But these ominous specters also signify very real possibilities—and actualities. Every phase of human development has its dark side, but the midnight face of technological globalization is as black as pitch. Given the amount of globalist cheerleading we hear from politicians, marketeers, and the media, there is a pressing need for critical, skeptical, and suspicious voices in the global debate, though such voices must transcend the easy pessimism of many neo-Luddites, with their Rousseauist fatalism and fear of change. Indeed, the social critics of the twenty-first century might even renew their own messianic and prophetic pact with the angels, recalling that, like Jacob, we are called to wrestle with these agents of the possible, not to emulate them.

Whether or not we feel that globalization is a "natural" phase of human evolution, the phenomenon is real, and we will need more than a hermeneutics of suspicion to nurture the productive and humane opportunities of these turbulent times. In a speech made at Harvard in 1995, Václav Havel described his quest for a deeper dimension of global political engagement. Acknowledging the emergence of a single planetary civilization, Havel pointed out that this civilization still amounts to a thin technological epidermis stretching over an immense variety of cultures, peoples, religious perspectives, and traditions, all rooted in very different historical experiences and geographic climes. Based on his own globe-trotting experiences, Havel argued that this diverse and often hidden human "underside" of the global village is now gaining a second wind, especially as the promises of secular modernity collapse. Even as the strip malls of global civilization spread, "Ancient traditions are reviving, different religions and cultures are awakening to new ways of being, seeking new room to exist, and struggling with growing fervor to realize what is unique to them and what makes them different from others." For perfectly understandable reasons, quite a number of these countries and cultures are rejecting many of the Euro-American political and social values that, to varying degrees, accompany globalization. Some of the fiercest opponents of McWorld resort to violent struggle, often deploying technologies—radar, computers, lasers, nerve gas—that owe their existence to the very civilization whose paradigm lies in their crosshairs.

Given all the tensions pulling beneath Gaia's new fiber-optic skin, Havel argues that we need to adopt a basic code of ethics and mutual coexistence, a strongly pluralistic perspective that will allow a genuinely open and multicultural society to flourish. But if we think that this code lies in commodity culture or market discipline or Western legal concepts, Havel warns, then we might as well pack it in. An ethics capable of reorienting the world within its new global framework cannot be another "universal idea" churned out by the rationalist West; nor can it be programmed through social engineering; nor can it be crafted and disseminated like Coca-Cola ads or condoms. Speaking with a candor, humility, and personal authority altogether foreign to today's politicians, Havel called on humans to plunge much deeper into the spiritual dimension that undergirds all of our diverse cultural histories:

> We must come to understand the deep mutual connection or kinship between the various forms of our spirituality. We must recollect our original spiritual and moral substance, which grew out of the same essential experience of humanity. I believe that this is the only way to achieve a genuine renewal of our sense of responsibility for ourselves and for the world. And at the same time, it is the only way to achieve a deeper understanding among cultures that will enable them to work together in a truly ecumenical way to create a new order for the world.[251]

Havel is not asking anyone to abandon the noble features of the modern mindframe and return to tribal idols, absolute truths, or the consoling fairy tales we once told ourselves to keep the cold and dark at bay. Instead, Havel is gesturing toward a "post-religious" spirituality, one that can thrive in a pluralistic third millennium alongside science and technology and all that pesky capital. Wisely, he does not tell us anything about where this spirituality would come from or what it would look like. Instead, he simply asks a question:

Don't we find somewhere in the foundations of most religions and cultures, though they may take a thousand and one distinct forms, common elements such as respect for what transcends us, whether we mean the mystery of Being, or a moral order that stands above us; certain imperatives that come to us from heaven, or from nature, or from our own hearts; a belief that our deeds will live after us; respect for our neighbors, for our families, for certain natural authorities; respect for human dignity and for nature; a sense of solidarity and benevolence towards guests who come with good intentions?[252]

This is not exactly the kind of stuff you expect from a man like Havel— a chain-smoking politician, an avant-garde humanist, and a hard-core Frank Zappa fan. But as with countless people across the world, Havel's gut tells him that we are at a crossroads, and that we will need the full range of human capacities to confront the catastrophes looming just around the bend.

Meet the Beast

In the mid-1990s, an amazing technological artifact started making the rounds of the electronic art shows and media exhibitions that now pop up from Helsinki to Buenos Aires. Created by the Berlin design group Art+Com, T_Vision brought the idea of a "virtual world" onto a new level of graphic realization. Here's the setup: you stand before a large screen on which hovers a fat, photo-realistic image of planet earth—an image seamlessly woven together from a twenty-gigabyte database of aerial shots, topographical information, and high-resolution satellite images. With a large plastic "earthtracker," you can rotate this virtual Terra like a basketball, in any direction you choose. Or you can use the "space mouse" to plunge toward a specific landmass, zooming continuously down into a shifting patchwork of increasingly localized high-resolution images. Spinning the earth, you feel like a god; plunging toward its surface, like a falling angel.

T_Vision provides a visceral experience of what Fredric Jameson would identify as the postmodern version of the technological sublime. As we saw in earlier chapters, we got our first big rush of the technological sublime in the late nineteenth and early twentieth centuries, when grand canals, electrical grids, continental railroads, and the great bridges and dams could trigger an almost terrifying sense of grandeur and awe.

But these monuments of industrial prowess no longer move us much; China's massive Three Gorges Dam now strikes us as an ecological disaster, a devastating act of nationalistic hubris. We are no longer enchanted by production, but by the *re*production of images and information. Our icon is not the dam, but the terminal screen, behind which lies an immense global matrix of databases, images, real-time information feeds, and communication networks—a matrix that is, quite literally, impossible to represent.

Because human brains cannot satisfactorily compass this hyperspace of collective information, it takes on the uncanny aura of the sublime, an aura that, in turn, enchants the screens and gadgets with which we attempt to interface with the new information environment. As Jameson writes, "The technology of contemporary society is therefore mesmerizing and fascinating not so much in its own right but because it seems to offer some privileged representational shorthand for grasping a network of power and control even more difficult for our minds and imaginations to grasp: the whole new decentered global network of . . . capital itself."[253] William Gibson's image of cyberspace dazzled so many because it suggested that individual "minds and imaginations" could navigate a virtual representation of these decentered networks and flows. The exalted grandeur of Gibson's image disguise its dark ironies, though one of *Neuromancer*'s Rastafarian characters sums them up in a word: "Babylon." Like Jameson, Gibson suggests that we may be approaching the apogee of technological alienation, a point that is sublime only because it is terrifying.

Though T_Vision does not explicitly represent the global networks of capital and communication, it does give us a hint of how the Gaian mind might start to interface with our minds. As some cyberthinkers argue, we will only begin to master the overwhelming confusion of networked information environments when we learn to build virtual architectures that can map the myriad data flows that currently define information space. With T_Vision partly in mind, Mark Pesce argues that the handiest and most appropriate memory palace we might employ for this purpose is, of course, the globe itself. Given the amount of real-time data and satellite imagery already available on the Internet, it's not too tough to imagine a day when something like a real-time T_Vision will be accessible online; the resulting interactive global information system would be similar to the earth database that pops up in Neil Stephenson's *Snow Crash*.

With Teilhardian optimism, Pesce argues that by transforming the planet into the ultimate virtual database, we will bolster our awareness of the interdependent bonds that define the global community. Such an image would help us, for example, to "see" the environmental devastation that currently threatens to knock the biosphere out of whack, and to lobby global agencies and track the perpetrators with a newfound sense of urgency and commitment. On a more ethical, if not mystical, level, such an image might also hardwire the realization that the world and the people in it are cut of one cloth, and that all of us must learn to get along within the finite framework of spaceship earth. Al Gore must have been nursing a similar hunch when he pushed for Earth-Span, a satellite system that would continuously beam high-resolution photos of the turning earth to Web sites and cable stations around the world. In this triumphant symbolic paradox, the abstract grid of media space, which is perhaps the most artificial and disembodied of human artifacts, would thus allow Gaia to reassert herself as the ultimate field and limit of the real.

The photographs of the planet that graced the early covers of *The Whole Earth Catalog* remind us that this utopian hope is not altogether new. Captured by NASA astronauts, images of the "big blue marble" floating against the inky abyss of space became ubiquitous pop icons in the late 1960s and early 1970s, and were embraced by many environmentalists and peaceniks as salvational images of ecological unity and human community. But as the deep ecologist and critic Michael Zimmerman writes, "The technical accomplishments required to build the spacecraft from which to take those photos . . . were made possible by the same objectifying attitude that discloses Earth as a stockpile of raw materials for enhancing human power."[254] When Martin Heidegger saw NASA's first images of Earth on television in 1966, he proclaimed that "the uprooting of man has already taken place. . . . This is no longer the earth on which man lives."[255] In other words, we cannot hope to discover a deeper sense of being and connection through a technological system that engages the earth as an object to be dominated and used, whether as a mass media image, a mine of materials, or a visual database. For many, T_Vision conjures up a Heideggerian wave of ontological nausea; the godlike blast of power and omniscience one tastes with the act of spinning a real-time image of the earth seems about as Faustian as multimedia gets these days.

Even more disturbing is the degree to which T_Vision draws its visual power from an essentially military model of surveillance, an abstract system of power, vision, and information control that Michel Foucault would have traced back to Jeremy Bentham's panopticon. As Foucault described it, the panopticon, a prison building whose peculiar architecture allowed guards to constantly observe prisoners in their cells, created an abstract space of surveillance that enabled authorities to control people, not through physical force, but by constantly reminding them that they were under observation—a fact that the prisoners themselves would then psychologically internalize. T_Vision globalizes this Black Iron Prison, or, more accurately, it presents a crude video game reflection of the planetary panopticon that already exists. With the spread of the Global Positioning System, the launch of commercial spy satellites like EarthWatch, and our heedless devotion to information retrieval by any means necessary, it is clear that the eye in the sky will only sharpen its focus as we spin into the twenty-first century. We indeed may bring light to the hidden things of darkness, but that only begs the question of who holds the light.

One defense of T_Vision and its inevitable descendants is simply that, given the reality of spy satellites and the privatization of military surveillance, we might as well make the world's flows of information as open and democratic as possible. As one component of the politics of the "open society," this vision holds that social activists, environmentalists, and ordinary people will be empowered by, in essence, *spying back*. Perhaps this is the most realistic conclusion, but it remains a deeply disturbing one, because it acknowledges the extent to which privacy is becoming a thing of the past as we pass into a world of vast interlinked databases, James Bond spycraft, ubiquitous news cameras, and tracking devices for felons and children. Already the rituals of popular television reflect this profound mutation in social space, as the private tragedies and tribulations of ordinary people are laid bare for all to see in the voyeuristic video-cam spectacles of *Cops* and *Real TV* or the talk-show tribunals led by Maury Povich and Montel Williams. We may yet find ourselves wired into a Borg-like collective beehive of information and image, an essentially totalitarian apparatus of perpetual surveillance without, as yet, a totalitarian command center.

Teilhard de Chardin also believed that human history was marching toward a vast collective society, one in which individuals would begin to resonate and fuse with the lives, emotions, and desires of their fellows.

He even came to the rather disturbing conclusion that the various total-itarian regimes that slouched their way across the battlefields of the twentieth century were actually "in line with the essential 'trend' of cos-mic evolution." In fact, Teilhard held that our only real hope lay in the absolute triumph of holistic collectivization. "If we are to avoid total anarchy . . . we can do no other than plunge resolutely forward, even though something in us perish, into the melting-pot of socialization."[256] Assuring his readers that they will learn to love this rather creepy state of affairs, Teilhard proclaimed that true union actually differentiates us and that our plunge toward planetary convergence "must have the effect of increasing the variety of choice and the wealth of spontaneity."[257]

Though such promises strangely resemble the corporate hype that now sugar-coats the rapacious growth of transnational capitalism, Teil-hard is really speaking as a hard-core mystical Catholic, with a profound faith in the collective body of awakened souls and the essentially open and evolutionary character of the universe. But the Christian imagina-tion is a coat of many colors, and some of its patches take on far darker and more violent hues. Some Christians, especially those with a brute Protestant conviction in the rock-solid inerrancy of the biblical word, would concur with Teilhard that our headlong flight toward planetiza-tion is part of a master plan. But they would strongly disagree about the major actors involved. Knowing that you can't tell the players without a scorecard, they would reach for John of Patmos's Book of Revelation:

> I stood upon the sand of the sea, and saw a beast rise up out of the sea, having seven heads and ten horns, and upon his horns ten crowns, and upon his heads the name of blasphemy. (Rev. 13:1)

Meet Mr. Antichrist, the vassal of the dragonlord Satan. Though John's description resembles some Industrial Light & Magic monster movie morph, most fundamentalist prophecy buffs believe that this beast is actually a man, a supernaturally gifted orator who blasphemes the Lord, restores a number of ancient empires through political unification, and establishes power "over all kindreds, and tongues, and nations." The Antichrist is not alone, however, and soon after the beast comes up from his dip, John sees another creature sprouting out of the earth, a monster who wears the horns of a lamb and speaks like a dragon. This is the false prophet who will seduce "all that dwell upon the earth" into worshiping the Antichrist, apparently by dazzling us with "great wonders" that include fire that falls from heaven and various other sham show-biz miracles. But then things get *really* weird:

> And he causeth all, both small and great, rich and poor, free and bond, to receive a mark on their right hand, or in their foreheads: And that no man might buy or sell, save that he had the mark, or the name of the beast, or the number of his name. (Rev. 15–17)

As anybody with a decent collection of heavy metal CDs can tell you, the number of the beast is 666.

Levelheaded scholars would remind us that all this daemonic imagery poured out of John's skull at the end of the first century, when the addle-brained Roman emperor Domitian started hounding Christians again after decades of relative conviviality. The above passages almost certainly reflect the Christian horror of institutionalized Caesar worship, and their antiglobalist sentiments probably stem from the young cult's almost anarchistic rejection of Rome's arrogantly universal state. Using the number-crunching techniques favored by esoteric biblical exegetes, most scholars conclude that the beast himself was probably Nero.

But as we saw in the last chapter, the allegorical outlines of John's apocalyptic spectacle are so large and vibrant that they can fit almost any era—most certainly including the information age. The evangelical community first started getting worked up about computers in the early 1970s, when the striped, computer-friendly bar codes of the now ubiquitous UPC (Universal Product Code) symbols started popping up on salable goods. These weird sigils were interpreted by many as forerunners of the mark of the beast, and some Christians feared that we would soon be forced to have them etched into our flesh. Later scares along similar lines include reports that a Belgian computer called The Beast was being programmed with the name of every living earthling; that Procter & Gamble's man-in-the-moon logo proved that the corporation was in cahoots with the Church of Satan; that Saturday morning kid shows were witchcraft propaganda; and that the numerological value of "computer" is 666.

Such a paranoid style of reading the commodity symbolism and technological systems of contemporary society certainly qualifies as unintended eschatological camp, but these visionary suspicions nonetheless pack a certain imaginative punch. Paranoid prophecy can generate vibrant examples of what William Irwin Thompson calls epistemological-cal cartoons—superficially garish myths that allegorize more subtle and significant realities. For with their apocalyptic imaginations, Christian prophecy buffs draw attention to many of the technological transformations of society that the rest of us generally ignore, accept, or embrace without a second thought. In their exposé *The Mark of the Beast: Your Money, Computers, and the End of the World,* the evangelical brother team Peter and Paul Lalonde argue that a variety of cutting-edge technologies—debit cards, smart cards, smart roads, biometrics, databanks, microchip tracking implants—suggest a definite programmatic shift toward the world order of the Antichrist, a world order in which all movement, buying, and selling will be tracked and controlled. Unlike more hysterical purveyors of what they call "mark-of-the-beast malarkey," the authors, who also host the cable show *This Week In Bible Prophecy,* stick to solid information sources like *Card Technology Today.* More important, they place their factoids within a sociopolitical context not so far removed from the analyses promulgated by pessimistic social critics. Peter and Paul call it the "last days system"—a world in which cash disappears, information technology foments invisible and diabolical concentrations of power and wealth, and the vagaries of digital identity allow and justify invasive forms of electronic social control and the insidious spread of surveillance devices.

By using the apocalyptic imagination to interrogate the infrastructure of the information age, the Lalondes and their ilk do more than give voice to the powerlessness, anxiety, and fear that many postmodern citizens feel. Their prophetic paranoia also punctures the blasé belief that the current technological metamorphosis of everyday social reality is simply business as usual. Through their wild eyes, we glimpse how readily we have handed over little freedoms in the name of safety, efficiency, and convenience—and how little choice in the matter we actually have. With every electronic transaction, we are projecting our identities into a virtual labyrinth of interlinked databases stuffed with financial, medical, legal, and travel information. From debit card swipes to identity authentication to electronic ticketing to automatic toll roads, we now leave bread crumbs of bits along every trail we take.

Even if the Lalondes' image of a bat-winged Big Brother seems ridiculously over the top, their concerns about our beastly virtual economy are not. With the collapse of the Soviet empire and the dismantling of the old totalitarian states, the capitalist world of global trade, consumer

media, and international finance is indeed poised to dominate "all kindreds, and tongues, and nations." The idea that smart cards are a tool
of the Antichrist, or that European Union bureaucrats are restoring
imperial Rome, is simply a popular allegory of this capitalist imperium.
Clearly, conspiracy theories that claim to describe some secret, invisible,
and deeply unwholesome cabal lurking behind the rhetoric of the New
World Order are basically delusions. But they are often oracular delusions, dream communiqués from the historical subconscious. The
"occult" qualities of the current shift in global power have little to do
with the Illuminati, the Trilateral Commission, or the secret rites performed in the Bohemian Grove. With the meltdown of the nation-state
and the virtualization of the economy, power now transcends the visible
space of representative democracy. It disappears in broad daylight, a
vanishing that is aided by the bewitchments of a media industry dominated by fewer and fewer major corporations, and which devotes much
of its time, consciously or not, to what Noam Chomsky calls "the manufacturing of consent."

The dark vision of the last days system puts a markedly different
mythic spin on globalization than the Gaian mind does, and its lineaments are worth keeping in mind as the machineries of capitalism extend
their extracting claws into every fold and crevice of the planet: the deep
sea floor, the Communist fortress of China, the genes of rain forest
plants and peoples. For now, it is clear that profit, and not cosmic evolution, is the driving spirit of planetization—its major metaphor, its
omnipotent and universal truth. As the techno-logic of the market
increasingly infects all spheres of human existence, from politics to education to the family, it achieves an unparalleled domination. Boundaries
of time and space that once kept the demands of the market at bay are
dissolving into an enveloping sea of silicon, as information technology
extends the competitive empire of work into the nooks and crannies of
our personal lives. The message of those arcadian TV spots showing
folks hanging out on tropical beaches with their laptops and cell phones
is simple and tyrannical: We are only free and fulfilled when we remain
on the grid, on schedule, on call. According to the philosopher Gilles
Deleuze, Foucault's disciplinary panopticon has already been superseded
by a more invasive and perpetually morphing mode of coercion. "The
operation of markets is now the instrument of social control and forms
the impudent breed of our masters. Control is short-term and of rapid

rates of turnover, but also continuous and without limit. . . . Man is no longer man enclosed, but man in debt."[258]

While making millions richer, the worldwide economic polarization that electronic capital has helped produce may prove calamitous for humanity as a whole, especially for that half of the population who has never even picked up a phone. In societies across the globe, the widening gap between rich and poor has taken on an intensity so neofeudal in flavor that a few gloomy prophets have dubbed our future the New Dark Ages. Social critics direct our attention to the darkening landscape of inner-city decay, social breakdown, and the gangster of capitalism in Russia and other Eastern European countries. In developed nations, hard-won labor conditions and social safety nets are being undermined in the name of efficiency and profit, while developing countries are witnessing the explosion of industrial shantytowns so foul they make the grinding poverty of village life almost seem like Club Med. For all the hearty entrepreneurs who can bootstrap themselves and "surf the chaos," the hard-core beneficiaries of globalization remain the electronic elect that Arthur Kroker calls the "virtual class": an oligarchic transnational elite with so little connection to local cultures, real workers, or immediate ecosystems that they might as well live in orbit—or at least a gated, privately patrolled, and totally wired citadel. You don't need to be a science-fiction writer or a futurist in a bad mood to picture how chilling this volatile, undemocratic, and profoundly unbalanced condition might become.

Of course, it's easy to get bent out of shape by the ominous image of the New World Order, of brain lords and cyborg drones, not to mention the already clichéd bogeyman of the global multinational corporation. Many pragmatists claim that global trade agreements like GATT, NAFTA, and the Maastricht Treaty promise nothing more harrowing than the McWorld described by social theorist Benjamin R. Barber: a plastic purgatory of global chain stores, fast food, cable TV, CDs, freeways, fax machines, billboards, blue jeans, cell phones, and computer monitors. Given the genocidal horrors that have marked the twentieth century, one suspects there are worse planetary fates than finding ourselves inside a global mall of rootless cosmopolitans more keyed on consumption than conflict. Over a century ago, when industrial capitalism waxed triumphant and Western gunboats kept the restless natives in check, a contributor to *Cosmopolitan* magazine wrote that:

[T]oday the inhabitants of this planet are rapidly approximating to the state of a homogenous people, all of whose social, political and commercial interests are identical. Owing to the unlimited facilities of intercommunication, they are almost as closely united as the members of a family; and you might travel round the globe, and find little in the life, manners and even personal appearance of the inhabitants to remind you that you were remote from your own birthplace.[259]

Needless to say, this family of commerce is white, urban, and Western under the skin, its global sway dependent on the extraordinary violence and racism of colonialism. But the key McWord here is "homogenous," a term verily prophetic of the flattening effect that today's global shopping center introduces into the myriad lifeworlds of humankind. What thrilled the *Cosmo* writer, the possibility of traveling everywhere without ever leaving home, rightly strikes many of us with horror, because that everywhere increasingly feels like nowhere, an immense labyrinth of chain stores, strip malls, and major airport lobbies.

Whether or not the planet itself can handle globalization is another question. Any serious observer must find herself questioning the sustainability of our extractive, industrial, and agricultural practices, our levels of consumption, and our myopic insults to the biosphere. All the cool commodities in the world cannot compensate for a future that promises a massive extinction of plants and creatures, the devastating loss of topsoil and rain forest, a cornucopia of pesticide-laden monocrops and lab-engineered Frankenfoods, and the climatic instabilities of global warming. And while globalization may thrust some social groups and regions into relative affluence, such prosperity could prove to be an ecological time bomb if the exuberant consumption patterns of the West are simply replicated on a global scale. Of course, globalization has also been accompanied by a growing awareness of the bio-physical limits that hamstring spaceship earth. People across the world are opening their eyes to the larger circle of life that humans can neither escape nor afford to ignore. Unfortunately, international eco-conferences seem so far incapable of mustering the will for substantive stewardship, even as global regulatory agencies like the WTO ditch the progressive environmental standards of many Western countries in the name of "restraint of trade." The global economy has also created an even more propitious climate for rapacious multinationals and corrupt local officials to accelerate their plunder, precisely because they operate on an international scale that's nearly impossible to regulate or police. While some believe that breakthrough technologies will swoop in like Superman to save the day, many of the "soft path" technological solutions to ecological problems that already exist remain unexploited because of corporate resistance and political inertia.

One irony in the rise of ecological thought is that its organic models and holistic metaphors are also used to justify the unfettered excesses of the global market and its technological engines. Many technolibertarians and proponents of the "new economy" espouse a kind of "market animism" that takes shape along neo-Darwinian lines. Exploiting the language of systems theory and emergent properties discussed earlier, these enthusiasts envision a self-organizing and infinitely expanding economy built on feedback loops, symbiotic technologies, decentralized control, organic information flows, and, of course, the absence of "artificial" intervention by states and regulatory mechanisms. As John Perry Barlow forcefully put it in a post to the nettime listserv:

> Nature is itself a free market system. A rain forest is an unplanned economy, as is a coral reef. The difference between an economy that sorts the information and energy in photons and one that sorts the information and energy in dollars is a slight one in my mind. Economy *is* ecology.

The British critic Richard Barbrook calls this kind of rhetoric "mystical positivism," because its appeal to cosmic forces is couched in scientific terms. Barbrook points out that hymns to the coral reef economy not only obfuscate the manipulative power of financial elites, but ignore the immensely productive role that states, regulatory agencies, and other rationalized public institutions can and do play in the information economy. Nor can nature be blamed for the rapid and decisive spread of neoliberal market economies through the post–cold war world, as if global capital was a jungle finally reclaiming the archaic, bloody temples of the nation-state. Many countries whose economies are now splayed before the hungry eyes of global investors got that way through the perfectly artificial politics of debt; once in thrall to international agencies like the World Bank and the IMF, the governments of many developing countries have been basically forced to accept neoliberal market policies that, in many cases, line the pockets of the international banking community rather than address the immediate social, political, and ecological needs of the country in question.

But perhaps the market animists are right. Perhaps the global economy is in some sense alive, and the undeniable creativity, resiliency, and profit-making power of the market are evidence of the emergent properties of neo-biological evolution. After all, interest has always been a kind of artificial life; even Thomas Aquinas, who lived at a time when usury was considered a sin, recognized that "a kind of birth takes place when money grows from [other] money." Of course, Aquinas did not embrace the dynamic disequilibrium of modernity's socioeconomic transformations, which would have struck him as perverse. He believed that the self-multiplying power of money "is especially contrary to Nature, because it is in accordance with Nature that money should increase from natural goods and not from money itself."[260]

Obviously we cannot and should not return to the static cosmology of the Middle Ages, but we still might ask ourselves what sort of monsters are breeding in our midst. Take, for example, the volatile and increasingly virtual global financial markets, whose jangling nervous system consists of metastasizing information networks whose combined traffic probably dwarfs the bitstreams of the Internet. Over a trillion dollars circulate through foreign exchange markets every diurnal spin, and less than 5 percent of this frantic activity represents actual cash transactions; the rest of it zips through an abstract digital hyperspace of volatile feedback loops whose instability and interdependence make them both profitable and potentially catastrophic. Money has gone gnostic, detaching itself from the fleshy vehicle of material goods and production to become a metaphysical chaos of pure information. This is great news if you can run with the bulls, but when the economies of entire nations can be deconstructed in a matter of days, it is increasingly unclear what all this activity has to do with building a better world. As the old animists of the bush would remind us, the fact that the environment is alive doesn't mean that it's always got our best interests at heart.

Or as Gilles Deleuze put it in the early 1990s: "We are [now] taught that corporations have a soul, which is the most terrifying news in the world."[261] One particularly scary sidebar to this news report is the post-modern return of social Darwinism, the noxious nineteenth-century philosophy that used the idea of the "survival of the fittest" to justify the robber barons and appalling working conditions of the industrial revolution. Nowadays, "selfish genes" and the amoral search for "fitness" are invoked to justify the social policies (or lack thereof) of technocapitalist evolution. Some libertarians and market animists believe that, once freed from progressive pieties and the illusions of social engineering, the market itself will act as an enormous selection mechanism, naturally sifting innovative humans from the unambitious ones, the superbrights from the slothful, the transhuman from the luckless and all-too-human.

That such a sad doctrine could return to the margins of the wired world only indicates how desperately we need to revivify the social imagination, a revival that may very well demand a rekindling of some basic "religious" convictions about the purpose of life and the value of individual souls. When Julian Huxley argued over half a century ago that the mechanism of evolution had passed into human society, he did so not because he thought we should start emulating the slow and sloppy excess of natural selection, with its drunken symbiosis and wayward violence. Instead, we could and should attempt to *redeem* that process:

> As far as the mechanism of evolution ceases to be blind and automatic and becomes conscious . . . it becomes possible to introduce faith, courage, love of truth, goodness—in a word moral purpose—into evolution. It becomes possible, but the possibility has been and is often unrealized.[262]

Teilhard de Chardin also saw man's awakening to the reality of evolutionary processes as the opportunity for a profound social transformation. Though committed to a deterministic vision of natural evolution so expansive it included the second coming of Jesus Christ as well as multicellular organisms and TV sets, Teilhard never abandoned the ethical foundations without which mysticism so easily coagulates into cosmic cant. As Teilhard proclaimed toward the close of *The Phenomenon of Man,* "The outcome of the world, the gates of the future, the entry into the super-human—these are not thrown open to a few of the privileged nor to one chosen people to the exclusion of all others. They will open only to an advance of *all together,* in a direction in which *all together* can join and find completion in a spiritual regeneration of the earth."[263]

For the mystical paleontologist, the merciless Darwinian picture of evolution as a selfish, purposeless, and amoral process could never tell the whole story, precisely because it left out the inner spirit of humans and things, the breath and breadth of mind and soul that fills, and fulfills, creation.

the path is a network

Mahayana legend has it that after Shakyamuni Buddha achieved his insight into the nature of things, he whipped off a phone book–sized scripture known as the *Flower Garland Sutra*. Easily the most cosmic and psychedelic of the writings attributed to Buddha, the *Flower Garland Sutra* features droves of enlightened beings, with sci-fi names like Matrix of Radiance and Space Eye, endlessly expounding the dharma in myriad buddhaworlds festooned with garlands of gems and flowers as numberless as the pores on an infinite Buddha's skin. The sutra also unfolds perhaps the greatest vision of the network found in any religious text. According to the Hua-yen philosophers who obsessed over the sutra in seventh- and eighth-century China, the text's immense cosmological vision is contained in the image of the Net of Indra. Here is Francis Cook's description:

> Far away in the heavenly abode of the great god Indra, there is a wonderful net which has been hung by some cunning artificer in such a manner that it stretches out infinitely in all directions. In accordance with the extravagant tastes of deities, the artificer has hung a single glittering jewel in each "eye" of the net, and since the net itself is infinite in dimension, the jewels are infinite in number. There hang the jewels, glittering like stars of the first magnitude, a wonderful sight to behold. If we now arbitrarily select one of these jewels for inspection and look closely at it, we will discover that in its polished surface there are reflected all the other jewels in the net, infinite in number. Not only that, but each of the jewels reflected in this one jewel is also reflecting all the other jewels, so that there is an infinite reflecting process occurring.[264]

For the Hua-yen philosophers, Indra's holographic net symbolized the mutual identity and mutually interpenetrating nature of all phenomena. That is, in its static aspect, everything in the universe ultimately boils down to everything else; but in its dynamic aspect, the universe is an interdependent network of insubstantial agents that are constantly affecting and being affected by other agents. "Thus each individual is at once the cause for the whole and is caused by the whole, and what is called existence is a vast body made up of an infinity of individuals all sustaining each other and defining each other."[265] The net of Indra preserves the fluctuating multiplicity of reality while acknowledging its ultimately nondual nature, always beyond and in between subject and object, self and other.

All this is a bit dizzying, but the contemporary Vietnamese monk and peace activist Thich Nhat Hanh brings Indra's net down to earth, or rather, down to a simple piece of paper. If you look at the paper with the eyes of a poet, Hanh says, you will realize that it contains within it all the elements that the paper itself depends upon; on its milky surface you will see clouds, forests, sunshine, loggers. "And if you look more deeply, with the eyes of a bodhisattva, with the eyes of those who are awake, you see not only the cloud and the sunshine in it, but that everything is here: the wheat that became the bread for the logger to eat, the logger's father—everything is in this sheet of paper."[266] The universe is a self-organizing network of infinite relationship, a symphony of interdependent becoming—and all of it can be accessed through the polished jewel-screen of a single awakened mind.

As we suggested in an earlier chapter, there is more than a little cybernetics implied in the Buddhist view of mutual interdependence. As Joanna Macy argues, both cybernetic systems theory and Buddhist philosophy can be said to characterize the world as a nonlinear dance of mutually modulating feedback loops. This "chaosmos" does not proceed from a first cause or the divine word of a creator, but endlessly combines and recombines forms and forces into a perpetual collage of creation and decay. Indra's net is an image of totality, but unlike Teilhard's vision of the Omega point, this holism does not depend upon some apocalyptic moment of future synthesis. In the Hua-yen view, reality is *already* a totally interdependent matrix, and this unity does not and cannot cancel out difference, the blooming multiplicities that compose each individual event.

As both the Asian scholar Edward Conze and the Zen master Robert Aitkin have pointed out, Buddhism's quest for awakening, for realizing Indra's net, can be seen as a path of *gnosis,* of the saving knowledge of the self. But because this self is not separate from the totality of the real, it can be saved only by being seen through, like a jewel polished until it becomes translucent, or a pair of sunglasses, or a mind that breaks through the desiccated concepts that always seek to order and stratify the chaosmos. In this sense, the practice of meditation, which is of course a whole garden shed of practices that various Asian contemplative traditions honed with an unparalleled sophistication, is the ultimate gnostic technology. Often caricatured as narcissistic navel gazing or ascetic withdrawal, the meditation path that leads to Indra's net actually winds up affirming the immanent networks of material, social, and mental forces that constantly breed our interdependent world. Once the Buddha opened his deep-space dharma eye, he did not climb mountaintops to gaze longingly into the heavens; he touched the earth in the shadow of a tree. The drama of phenomenal existence, with its quasars, frogs, and fiber-optic cables, is impossible to separate from transcendent reality.

One does not need to head East to catch wind of this visionary rumor. In *The Gospel of Thomas,* discovered in Nag Hammadi's cache of gnostic memes, Jesus' followers ask him when the messianic kingdom will come. "It will not come by watching for it," Jesus says. "It will not be said, 'Look, here it is,' or 'Look, there it is.' Rather, the father's kingdom is spread out upon the earth, and people do not see it."[267] How does one see this kingdom, at once otherworldly and immanent? Beats me, but many Buddhists say that you can do worse than to practice mindfulness, a term which encompasses a variety of techniques for cultivating attention. Mindfulness is a *techne,* neither a philosophy nor a passive trance but an active practice of probing and witnessing experience. The practice begins when we sharpen our awareness of the moment-to-moment flux of thought and sensation as it weaves itself through the warp and woof of body and mind. Slowly, we may begin to see how much of our reality can be traced to delusional projections, cultural programming, or the repetition of mechanical habits of categorization, emotional fixation, and greed. We begin, ever so slightly, to decondition ourselves, and another world begins to emerge, a world that is nonetheless basic and familiar: a world always on the fly, a self-organizing network of flows and events drawn through the shuttle of the passing present. By helping us become intimate with this endless brocade, mindfulness cultivates a kind of mobile center that can pliably and creatively interact with the morphing demands of a perpetually decentered world.

Whether or not such gnostic technology can pilot one to the nondual shores of the Buddhaverse, mindfulness practice does have some pretty nifty side effects along the way. As many have pointed out, the currency of the Net is attention, an insight that holds true as well for the expanding empire of signs, data, and virtualities of which the Net is both part and paragon. Mindfulness cultivates and sharpens attention, clarifying the often largely automatic process wherein we "choose" to notice, to react, to link, to pass on by. The more intelligent and crisp attention becomes, the less susceptible one grows to mechanical habits and programmed phantasms, not to mention the dangerous attractors that lurk, as they always have, in virtual space, waiting to draw our bodyminds into downward spirals. The contemporary rise of attention deficit disorder, a condition seemingly linked to the ubiquity of media nets, only underscores how much we need to treat attention as a craft, at once a skill to be learned and a vessel in flight. But the name of this chronic syndrome also contains a clue. For it is precisely *disorder* that we need to learn to pay attention to, because in that turbulence lies our own future manifold. The mind is an instrument, and we practice scales so that we may begin to improvise with spontaneous grace.

As you might expect, Western Buddhists nursing the digital dharma can hardly avoid making the punning leap between Indra's net and the Internet, another cunning artifice whose dynamic mesh of mind and photons takes the form of a nonlinear, hyperlinked, many-to-many matrix. For some, the formal resemblance between the Hua-yen vision and our planetary trellis of fiber-optic cables, modems, microwaves, screens, and servers suggests that, in a symbolic sense at least, we may now be hardwiring a network of connections that reflects the nondual interdependence of all reality. At the same time, of course, the digital Overmind also reflects the anger, delusion, and greed that Buddhists claim drive the miseries of human existence. An immense digital gizmo populated by human minds cannot magically cause those minds to transcend their shuttered worldviews, to lighten their compulsions or assuage their fear and loathing. Without turning to face our own terminal screens, without sharpening critical wisdom and cultivating compassion, the Internet may only become a new brand of bondage.

The net of Indra works its real magic by dissolving our habitual tendencies to divide the world into separate and autonomous zones: inside and out, self and other, online and off-, machines and nature. So the next time you peer into the open window of a Web browser, you might ask yourself: Where does "the network" end? Does it cease with the virtual words, images, and minds of cyberspace, or with the silicon-electronic matrix of computing devices, or with the electrical grid that powers the show with energies extracted from waterflow and toxic atom? Perhaps the network extends further—to the Jacquard looms and American war machines that loosed the historical dynamic that eventually plopped a PC with a netlink on your desk, to the billionfold packet-switching meshwork of human neurons that shape and submit to information space, to the capital flows that animate the quick hands of young Filipinas who wire up semiconductors for dollars a day. As you contemplate these widening networks, they may alter the granularity and elasticity of the self that senses them, as well as changing the resilience and tenderness of the threads binding that self to the mutant edge of matter and history. I suspect there is no end to such links, and that this immanent infinity, with its impossible ethical call, makes up the real worldwide web.

Tough-minded readers may find this interdependent vision of mystic materialism a bit of a stretch, but it's important to note that something quite like the net of Indra also pops up in the metaphysics of Leibniz, one of the supreme philosophers of Enlightenment rationalism. Leibniz's researches into symbolic logic, calculating machines, and binary numbers (whose invention he credited to the Chinese sages behind the *I Ching*) helped lay the groundwork for today's digital computers. Leibniz also dreamed of arithmetizing the totality of human thought, a dream touched with more than a little techno-utopianism. By inventing a set of common symbols that could represent the workings of the mind, he thought he could, in principle, calculate the solution to all the problems that beset the fractious Europe of his day—moral, political, and metaphysical.

Leibniz insisted on the intimate relationship between human minds and logical machines, and he followed Descartes in holding that the activity of animal and human bodies was basically no different from the tickings of a clocklike automaton. But Leibniz was not a pure mechanist; not unlike the Hua-yen philosophers, he believed that the cosmos boiled down to the relationships that form between different nodes of perception—i.e., souls. In his *Monadology*, Leibniz described the universe as a vast matrix of these individual perceptual units, which he called "monads." Unlike the jewels in the net of Indra, monads are ultimately solitary and permanent entities—as souls, they have "no windows." But the monads do carry within themselves representations of the entire universe, representations that are mediated and coordinated by the big monad known as God. For Leibniz, God ensures that communication and truth are possible because he maintains what amounts to an immense logical apparatus of perception.

Leibniz's pious rationalism was destined to be skewered on the twin post-Enlightenment prongs of skepticism and positivism, but according to the cyberspace philosopher Michael Heim, the monadology nonetheless foreshadows the incorporeal matrix of the Internet, just as Leibniz's research into symbolic logic and binary notation anticipates digital microprocessors. Certainly online surfers can relate with the stance of the monad: though plugged into a "universal" network of servers, we stare into our terminal screens as solitary individuals, hoping that the logic of the network will ensure that our perceptions accord and our messages make it through. But the monadology also reminds us that, while the Internet may be described as a totalizing logical machine that amplifies the organic computers in our skulls, our *phenomenological* experience of both these calculating devices can never be entirely reduced to mechanist explanations. In his *Monadology,* Leibniz makes this point with a thought experiment: "Supposing that there were a machine whose structure produced thought, sensation, and perception, we could conceive of it as increased in size with the same proportions until one was able to enter into its interior, as he would into a mill. Now, on going into it he would find only pieces working upon one another, but never would he find anything to explain Perception."[268] For Leibniz, even if the mind machine is treated as a virtual machine that we can hack to bits, we will still not uncover the gear of our own awareness. We may construct testable explanations for consciousness, but we will never reduce the sprightly play of the mind in the world—a play that both Leibniz and the Hua-yen philosophers would argue unfolds as a collective network of perception.

As the archetype of the network comes to infiltrate contemporary conceptions of brains, ecology, and technology, monads and jewel nets arise in the realm of virtual possibility. Of course there are problems with such monumental metaphysical systems. Indra's net, for example, is a firmly holistic vision, and there are always holes in holism. Ecologists and network architects would be the first to point out that, while everything is ultimately connected to everything else, some things are definitely more connected than others. The Hua-yen vision is essentially static as well; although it allows for the dynamic interplay of individual agents, it does not make much room for the dynamic and developmental contradictions that characterize much of history, natural and human alike. As an image, the net is a webwork wafting in space rather than an arrow of turbulent time, a closed hologram rather than an irreversible and open chain of mutation. An infinite lattice of interdependence does not express the complex surprises that our expanding cosmos so generously spits out—a failing that should particularly concern human beings, who balance some of the most complex and surprising objects in the universe atop their towering spines.

Are such evolutionary surprises evidence of cosmic progress, or are they simply wayward mutations? Today it is mighty hard to swallow grand tales of teleology and universal goals; with postmodernists to the left of us and hard-core Darwinians to the right, the evolutionary perfectionism of a Teilhard de Chardin goes down like tepid science fiction. Nonetheless, our global civilization continues to bank on the revolutionary promise of progressive technological change, a quintessentially modern perspective that may nonetheless draw from deeper springs. In essence, the notion of historical evolution is a quest narrative. Before Joachim of Fiore loosed the myth of progress into the bloodstream of the Christian West, men told tales of a hero, with a thousand and one faces, restlessly seeking a redemptive goal: the golden fleece, the elixir of immortality, the holy grail. Whether taking form as Gilgamesh, a Round Table knight, or Ulysses, the man of many devices, the hero plunges ever forward, riding his vector of yearning, though his linear track often leads him into the traps and cul-de-sacs of an ensnaring nature he must constantly resist. Salvation is not within but ahead: a finger of land on the distant edge of the sea, an unearthly silver light piercing the mulchy forest gloom.

I suspect that one of the reasons that the story of technological progress continues to hold such power is that it literalizes a quest myth we can no longer take seriously in ourselves. Machines articulate and define themselves against the messiness of organic nature, a world whose laws and limits they both exploit and conquer through control, manipulation, and speed. As David Noble has shown, the Western image of technological progress draws from profoundly Christian notions of dominion and millennialist perfectionism. The errant knight of medieval lore has morphed into a machine-man, his grail now the Singularity that visionary engineers claim lies just over the horizon, a blazing point of technological convergence that will finally master the rules of the known.

If the relentless vector of technological development embodies a heroic narrative of power, mastery, and self-definition, what does it mean that this ultimately phallic quest now finds itself in a chaotic postmodern techno-jungle characterized by the massive and impossibly tangled intersection of networks? The networks that have come to dominate so many technological, scientific, and cultural discourses and practices—communication webs, cognitive neural nets, interlinked computers, parallel processors, complex institutional frameworks, transnational circuits of production and trade—are not linear vectors or stable expressions of control. They are complex weavings, crisscrossed webworks, complex fabrics of unpredictable and semiautonomous threads. The network is a *matrix,* a womb, the mother-matter that spawns us all, and the matrix was always wired. Despite its biological roots, the word itself now denotes a host of technological tools and practices: a metal mold or die; a binding substance, like cement in concrete, or the principal metal in an alloy; a plate used for casting typefaces; a rectangular grid of mathematical quantities treated as a single algebraic entity; and, of course, the dense pattern of connections that link up computer systems. The matrix forms the context for emergence; it is the medium, the motherboard, through which events, objects, and new linkages are grown.

Obviously, today's technological matrices cannot simply be characterized as "feminine" spaces or the rebirth of Dame Nature's modus operandi. Such systems are perfectly capable of sustaining linear goals of individual aggrandizement, hierarchical control, and patriarchal power plays—not to mention war. Nonetheless, if we allow ourselves a sip or two of zeitgeist liqueur, it seems hardly coincidental that the network becomes a dominant technological archetype at the same time that society hosts the rise of environmental activism, deep ecology, Gaia hypotheses, and goddess religion, to say nothing of the extraordinary success of modern feminism, which has unleashed women in the workplace and generated a sustained critique of the oppressive social arrangements that for so long sustained the West's pretensions of enlightened progress.

In her book *Zeros + Ones,* Sadie Plant unlocks the secret history of women and machines, brilliantly rewriting the history of digital technology as a cyberfeminist yarn: "neither metaphorical nor literal, but quite simply material, a gathering of threads which twist and turn through the history of computing, technology, the sciences and arts."[269] Taking inspiration from the ancient female labor of the loom, Plant's book is a crazy quilt of history and postmodern futurism that shuttles between witches and telephone operators, textile production and online sexuality. She gives particular pride of place to Ada Lovelace, the razor-sharp daughter of the poet Lord Byron. In the mid-1800s, Lovelace became the world's first computer programmer when she analyzed and described the computational possibilities of Charles Babbage's never-completed Analytical Engine, a gadget which Lovelace claimed "weaves algebraic patterns just as the Jacquard loom weaves flowers and leaves."[270] The history of technologies, it seems, spills us onto an unexpected shore: not the world of Odysseus and his many devices, but of Penelope at her loom, biding her time, weaving and unweaving an endless cloth to undermine the stratagems of men.

Though technology and engineering have historically been considered masculine provinces, Plant argues that digital networks, and the imbrication of those networks with culture, economy, and DNA, are undermining a patriarchal agenda she identifies with control, identity, and individual agency. Network technologies and computational devices breed multiplicities, not stable identities, although established structures of power constantly try to constrain and exploit this turbulence. All along, working women have been forced to engage the nitty gritty labor of the network: telephone switches, typewriter keys, microprocessor assembly, the proto-algorithms of the loom, even the multitasking of domestic labor. Decades before men invented electronic brains, women who performed calculations for a living were known as "computers." Nowadays, when the complexity of technologies designed to increase human control instead breeds an unpredictable chaos, digital women may find themselves strangely fit for the new environment.

Plant's exuberant vision can be seen as a futuristic retort to eco-feminists, who often embrace nonhierarchical systems thinking in the name of Romantic images of women, nature, and the Goddess. Plant too is a kind of pagan, but a technological pagan who recognizes that we cannot know what alliances the earth's chthonic energies and alien intelligences may have already made with machines. Alchemy begins as a metallurgic art, after all, its later dreams of mystic redemption and trans-Uranium elements forming atop an archaic engagement with animist matter. We still divide ancient times into ages of copper, bronze, and iron, as if human history itself was a froth given off by the intelligent evolution of metals, a process that today transcends metallic elements, as we pass into an age defined by silicon, bio-chips, crystalline lattices, and the bizarre substances leaking out of materials science. Teilhard may have been right to see technologies as part and parcel of Terran evolution, an artificial life striving toward complexity and even mind. But he may have grossly overestimated humanity's role in the plan. Perhaps we are nothing more than meat-brained midwives, "sex organs," as McLuhan said, "of the machine world."

As below, so above: our cultural and psychic lives increasingly reflect the patterns and temporal signatures of this machine world and its expanding networks. Though Brian Eno was right to complain that computers still do not have enough Africa in them, the contraptions are definitely learning to pound out polyrhythms. Mainframes are mutating into networked workstations; robots learn to probe the world through decentralized neural nets; communication fragments into packet-switched data transfers; the centralized Von Neumann architecture of early computing begins to give way to massively parallel structures that distribute control and multiply connections. Our bodyminds are struggling to adapt to these new multiplicities. Just listen to the dance music that samplers and digital microprocessors churn out today: Electronic beats once characterized by their precise "mechanical" monotony have flowered into the chaotic, rhythmic swarms of drum 'n' bass or experimental techno, while garage producers and DJs cut and splice sonic Frankensteins out of myriad strands of musical and aural code. This is the metal machine music for a liquid silicon world, whose inhabitants are learning to follow the beats of many different drummers *at once*.

Multiplicity also rules the Internet, with its growing variety of media types, its lack of a controlling center, and the horizontal links it establishes between various networks, autonomous programs, and genres of expression. Though the narrow social makeup of Net users worldwide dampens the technology's wildest potential, the Internet nonetheless sets the cultural and psychic stage for a multitasking maelstrom of voices and machines, a meshwork of interchanges that undermines, to widely varying degrees, stable notions of knowledge, authority, and cultural production. Source code and shareware spread like dandelion tufts; facts and opinions float free of academia or the fourth estate; exploding populations of mathematical creatures compete and replicate; Hot Wheels fanzines and remote-control gardens lie a keystroke away from genealogical databases or the latest shots of stellar nebulae. On the surface, at least, it looks a lot like chaos.

Or maybe it looks like the nihilistic free fall known as the postmodern condition. After all, postmodernists tell us that the "master narratives" that once organized the story of modern civilization into stable categories of knowledge and identity have now spent their force without achieving their goals. Language is no longer a field for truth and expression but a labyrinthine network of referential ambiguities and structural codes that can never be resolved or mastered. As such, the West's canons of cultural authority and its "logocentric" discourses of truth and knowledge are little more than strategies of power, provisional and problematic, if not actually tyrannical. In their place, postmodernists offer up a decentered world of endless fragmentation, a field where human identity becomes a moving target and history dissolves into a pandemoniac play of signs and simulacra.

In the 1980s, writers and artists influenced by poststructuralist philosophy started wrestling with electronic text, computer networks, and digital culture, and many found that these "discursive objects" absorbed the new monster slang like a sponge. Obsessed with technologies of power and violently allergic to humanism, poststructuralists felt at home amid symbionts and abstract machines; deconstruction in particular seemed like a virus specifically designed to infect the Borgesian library of hypertext. A subgenre of cybertheory arose, with Donna Haraway finishing off an enormously influential manifesto proclaiming she'd rather be a cyborg than a goddess. But one of the most compelling poststructuralist images to wend its way into digital culture was sampled from the old book of nature. In contrast to the tree, whose rooted and vertical unity has long made it a favorite map for the hierarchical organization of knowledge and patriarchal authority, cyberculture embraced the rhizome. As Sadie Plant explains, "Grasses, orchids, lilies, and bamboos have no roots, but rhizomes, creeping underground stems which spread sideways on dispersed, horizontal networks of swollen or slender filaments and produce aerial shoots along their length and surface as distribution of plants. They defy categorization as individuated entities."[271] And so do the myriad networks that make up the Internet, that wild digital weed whose very name underscores the interruptions and interbreeding that give postmodernists such interminable delight.

In the long run, I suspect that some of the most valuable and productive aspects of postmodern thought may lie in its confrontation with digital technology, whose alien cunning it helped to articulate and whose posthuman possibilities it helped to unfold. The symbiotic relationship between French-fried discourse and the new machines cuts both ways, of course: cyberculture also embodies the channel-surfing decadence, depthless fragmentation, and smug obsession with self-referential codes and jargon that characterize postmodern culture at its worst. But post-modernism is a phase to pass through, culturally and intellectually, not to reject in the name of corroded certainties or feeble moral plaints. Already the infectious memes of postmodern thought are losing their vir-ulence, as the cultural bloodstream begins to absorb and adapt to their biting half-truths, becoming cannier and more robust in the process. The fact that Parisian intellectuals and the new machines were unknowingly moving in tandem is itself evidence of the larger choreographies of his-tory that such theorists deny.

Peering into the haze ahead, the postmodern interpretation of the Internet as a transgendered interzone of cyborgs and ruptures seems no more definitive than the middle-of-the-road vision embodied by ESPN SportsZone, Expedia, and the boring search categories of Yahoo. We have only begun to explore the creative forms of knowledge and experi-ence that cross-pollinated virtual multimedia data-structures like the Internet will birth. These omnivorous systems can render almost any conceivable object into a shared language of bits: images, text, voice, architecture, real-time data feeds, video, animation, sound, VR, artificial life, interactive maps, autonomous algorithms and codes. As more and more dimensions of the real are translated into the Boolean Esperanto of binary code, we open up the possibility for utterly unexpected modes of synthesis to arise, patterns of connection and integration that for now seem barely conceivable. But how could we know them in advance? If they come, they will emerge from a vibrating matrix of information, image, and mathematical mutation whose processing powers and uni-versal scale have simply never existed before. Of course they will arise as an imagination. Of course they will take the form of *surprise.*

Pierre Lévy calls one possible representational matrix the "cosmope-dia": a dynamic and kaleidoscopic space of knowledge that provides new ways of understanding the world and of being in the world. In this cosmic and cinematic encyclopedia, the collective knowledge of the thinking community, a category which must include machines as well, becomes materialized "in an immense multidimensional electronic image, perpetually metamorphosing, bustling with the rhythm of quasi-animate inventions and discoveries."[272] In contrast to the fragmented hypertext that defines what Lévy calls "commodity space," the cosmo-pedia will provide "a new kind of simplicity," a simplicity that arises from the principles of organization native to knowledge space: the fold, the pattern, the resonating crystal. The chaos may unfold a cosmos after all.

Herman Hesse provided a literary and mystic glimpse of Lévy's cosmopedia in *The Glass Bead Game,* whose publication in 1943 helped win Hesse a Nobel Prize. Set in a distant future devoid of the usual science-fiction trappings, Hesse's novel presents itself as a biography of Joseph Knecht, a master of the Glass Bead Game and a leader of Castalia, a utopian community of scholar-monks and contemplative aesthetes. But perhaps the most interesting "character" in the book is the eponymous Game itself, whose spiritual roots, we are told, can be traced back to ancient China, the Hellenistic Gnostics, and the golden age of Islamic-Moorish culture. First appearing as an abacus-like rack of glass beads used by students of music to represent and recombine various themes and contrapuntal structures, the Game eventually developed into an interdisciplinary device whose hieroglyphic language of "symbols and formula" enabled aficionados to play with elements drawn from the entire range of thought and expression.

> All the insights, noble thoughts, and works of art that the human race has produced in its creative eras, all that subsequent periods of scholarly study have reduced to concepts and converted into intellectual property—on all this immense body of intellectual values the Glass Bead Game player plays like an organist on an organ. And this organ has attained an almost unimaginable perfection; its manuals and pedals range over the entire intellectual cosmos; its stops are almost beyond number. Theoretically this instrument is capable of reproducing in the Game the entire intellectual content of the universe.[273]

We are told that an individual game might begin with an astronomical configuration, or the theme of a Bach fugue, or a sentence out of Leibniz or the Upanishads. Players would then use allusions, intuitive leaps, and formal correspondences in order to develop their chosen theme through kindred concepts, while also juxtaposing themes with contrary images or equations in order to weave a kind of cognitive counterpoint. One could imagine playing links between Indra's net and the monadology, for example, and then introducing the Borg as an ironic twist.

Allowing the Game's own magic of intuitive leaps to infect our minds, it is not so hard to see why Hesse's fabulous instrument has inspired a number of computer visionaries and network minds. Today we are faced with the enormous challenge of how to sort, index, search, link, and navigate through multidimensional fields of data that crisscross a variety of different formal genres: text, sound, image, algorithm. Indeed, the creative design of interactive hypermedia databases has become one of the key arts of the age. This emerging craft is more than a matter of library science; it is a work redolent of profound psychological, cultural, and even philosophical implications. Charles Cameron, one of a host of game designers currently constructing playable versions of the Glass Bead Game, argues that Hesse's "virtual music of ideas" adds a distinctly aesthetic dimension to this task, suggesting an open-ended and fluid structure for associative thought and learning. Pattern recognition has always drawn some of its power from the imagination and its dreamlike interface to art and archetype. Though reasoning by analogy has been a major bugaboo of upright minds since Western science began, it makes sense for hunter-gatherers attempting to survive the postmodern forest of symbols and data. We must learn to think like DJs, sampling beats and voices from a vast cornucopia of records while staying true to the organic demands of the dance.

For Hesse, this dance was ultimately cosmic, Shiva's jig of perpetual creation and destruction. In his novel, the residents of Castalia treat the contemplation of individual bead games as a meditative practice, one that ultimately leads "to the interior of the cosmic mystery, where in the alternation between inhaling and exhaling, between heaven and earth, between Yin and Yang, holiness is forever being created."[274] In this sense, the Glass Bead Game can be seen as a musical counterpoint to the hermetic dreams that have popped up throughout this book: the cosmic memory palace, the noosphere, the apocalyptic tome. The fact that the Game so strongly anticipates the World Wide Web only shows how much these transcendent (and psychedelic) aspirations continue to magnetize cyberspace. Blending together mind and techne, image and code, the Internet arises as the Great Work of engineering, a computational matrix that forms the tentative framework for a new phase of cultural evolution, an alchemical beaker within which we toss anything and everything that can be reduced to binary code. Because it is composed of concept and imagination as much as logic machines and electromagnetic pulses, cyberspace sidesteps Einsteinean space-time, giving birth to a kind of digital metaphysics—or, perhaps more properly, "netaphysics."

Those drawn to the uncharted waters of netaphysics should proceed as wary experimentalists, playful and ironic rather than apocalyptic, and ever mindful of the dark dragons of technopolitics that lurk below the waves they surf. No one can claim to speak in the name of cosmic evolution or the Gaian mind; we can only draw new networks and judge the results by criteria both aesthetic and pragmatic, criteria that will themselves inevitably mutate. Information is more like a jungle than an infinite library, and we cultivate as we navigate, forever divorced from a god's-eye view. We are back to pacts, and lore, and guiding intuitions. A kind of madness lurks this way as well, an excess of meaning that can send thought hurtling into a black hole. Networks are systems of organization, after all, and when they start feeding off the deep and amorphous forces of the human psyche, paranoia and paralysis await. Even Hesse saw the dark side of his infinite game, and in the end Joseph Knecht quits Castalia's contemplative utopia, abandoning its rarefied and disembodied pursuit of Mind for an offline life in the gritty world outside.

Netaphysicians cannot expect anything like salvation or final knowledge from their encyclopedic Overmind, because to do so is to make the same visionary error we have been tracking throughout this book: mistaking technological possibilities for social or spiritual ones. Nonetheless, for all its bankrupt absurdities, technomysticism arises because humans remain, in some mercurial sense, spiritual beings, and this curious twist of human nature will express itself wherever it can. The self has always been something of an engineering project, after all, a virtual reality molded by the myriad conditions that compose its becoming. Some of these conditions are hardwired genetic instructions; others are echoes of past decisions and experience; still others take the form of vast social and cultural systems that cultivate, map, and discipline the bodymind. But the self is also a spark crackling with being, with intuition and dream, and with the activity of perception which Leibniz could nowhere find as he wandered through the reductive mill of a thinking machine. The self is the alchemical vessel, and it is shaped by the practices our bodyminds engage in: art, diet, sex, dance, learning, sport, contemplation, friendship, ethics. Such technologies of the self are often largely automatic, but when the practices themselves begin to awaken and integrate, they become spiritual, in the broadest sense of the term. The postmodern avatars of fragmented identity ultimately lose the thread: the self has many avenues and powers, but this multiplicity is raw material that allows creative modes of integration to emerge. Not mutation, but trans-mutation.

As the high-tech juggernaut careens into the third millennium, I sus-pect we may need to open to such possible transmutations: to fire up the alembics of the imagination, to tune in to the pagan pulse of planetary life, to wire up the diamond matrix within. For many earthlings, there is simply not much choice in the matter: A turning is in the air. Slowly, ten-tatively, a "network path" arises from the midst of yearning and confu-sion, a multifaceted but integral mode of spirit that might humanely and sensibly navigate the technological house of mirrors without losing the resonance of ancient ways or the ability to slice through the greed, hate, and delusion that human life courts. Against the specter of new and renewed fundamentalism, people both inside and outside the world's religious traditions are trying to cut and paste a flood of teachings, tech-niques, images, and rites into a path grounded enough to walk upon. Who knows what virtualities will arise along the way? This path is a matrix of paths, with no map provided at the onset, and no obvious goal beyond the open engagement with whatever arises. "A path is always between two points," Deleuze and Guattari write, "but the in-between . . . enjoys both an autonomy and direction of its own."[275]

The network path does not swerve from psychology, from natural and human history, from cognitive science, anthropology, or nanotech-nology. Science and engineering are not enemies—how could they be? The disenchanted investigation of empirical and psychological phenom-ena, the canny co-creation of an evolving world, the death of (our con-ceptions about) God—all of these are stations, or rather nodes, of the path. The network path only blossoms when we accept that we will not transcend the sometimes agonizing disjunctions between our various structures of belief and practice. We will not simply sew up the conflicts between faith and skepticism, the stones and the stories, the incandes-cence of the absolute and the mundane absurdity of an everyday life growing more bizarre and frightful by the minute. Instead, these tensions and conflicts become dynamic and creative forces, calling us to face oth-ers with an openness that does not seek to control or assimilate them to whatever point of view we happen to hold. By replacing the need for a common ground with an acceptance and even celebration of our com-mon groundlessness, the network path might creatively integrate these gaps and lacunae without always trying to fill them in. You can no more banish the noise on this network than you can banish the void from a cup—nor would you want to. You just attend to the chaos that comes until something unexpected blooms: a dilation in the mind, a dawning in the heart, and a shared breathing with beings so deep it reaches down to sinew.

How can I speak of such things in this cynical day and age, when economy is god and the enormity of the world's ills seems matched only by our incapacity to deal with them? Unmoored from folkways, grasping after figments, addicted to the novelty and compulsions of a hyperactive society, we drift in overdrive through the mounting wreckage. Amidst all the distracting noise and fury, the hoary old questions of the human condition—*Who am I? Why am I here? How do I face others? How do I face the grave?*—sound distant and muffled, like fuzzy conundrums we have learned to set aside for more pragmatic and profitable queries. Waking up is hard to do when we rush about like sleepwalkers on speed. I suspect that unless we find clearings within our little corners of space-time, such questions will never arise in all their implacable awe. Media machines will no more deliver these pregnant voids than the purchase of a sports utility vehicle will unfurl one of those open roads they show on the idiot box. Such clearings lie off-road, off the grid, offline. They are beyond instrumentality. They are the holes in the net.

On the other hand, the fact that technology has already catalyzed so much soul-searching suggests how mischievous and sprightly a role it plays in the mutual unfolding of ourselves and the world. As I announced at the outset, technology is a trickster. We blame technologies for things that arise from our social structures and skewed priorities; we expect magic satisfactions from machines that they simply cannot provide; and we remain consistently hoodwinked by their unintended consequences. Technologies have their own increasingly alien agenda, and human concerns will survive and prosper only when we learn to treat them, not as slaves or simple extensions of ourselves, but as unknown constructs with whom we make creative alliances and wary pacts. This is particularly the case with information machines. Whatever social, ecological, or spiritual renewal we might hope for in the new century, it will blossom in the context of communicating technologies that already gird the earth with intelligence and virtual light. Prometheus is hell-bent in the cockpit, but Hermes has snuck into Mission Control, and the matrix is ablaze with entangling tongues.

ENDNOTES

1. Bruno Latour, *We Have Never Been Modern,* trans. Catherine Porter (Cambridge, Mass.: Harvard University Press, 1993), 7.

2. Ibid., 75.

3. Samuel C. Florman, *The Existential Pleasures of Engineering* (New York: St. Martin's Press, 1976), 109.

4. Edith Hamilton, *Mythology* (New York: Mentor, 1969), 69.

5. Charles Boer, trans., *The Homeric Hymns* (Woodstock, Conn.: Spring Publications, 1970), 36.

6. Karl Kerényi, *Hermes: Guide of Souls,* trans. Murray Stein (Dallas: Spring Publications, 1976), 84.

7. Norman O. Brown, *Hermes the Thief* (Great Barrington, Mass.: Lindisfarne, 1990), 39, 61.

8. L. Sprague de Camp, *The Ancient Engineers* (New York: Ballantine, 1974), 258.

9. Robert S. Brumbaugh, *Ancient Greek Gadgets and Machines* (New York: Thomas Y. Crowell, 1966), 94.

10. E. R. Dodds, *Pagan & Christian in an Age of Anxiety* (New York: W. W. Norton, 1970), 133.

11. Antoine Faivre, *The Eternal Hermes,* trans. Joscelyn Godwin (Grand Rapids, Mich.: Phanes Press, 1995), 88.

12. David Abram, *The Spell of the Sensuous* (New York: Pantheon, 1996), 131.

13. Walter J. Ong, *Orality and Literacy* (New York: Methuen, 1982), 78.

14. Abram, *The Spell of the Sensuous,* 112.

15. "Interview with Marshall McLuhan," *Playboy,* March 1969, 59.

16. David Porush, "Hacking the Brainstem," in *Virtual Realities and Their Discontents,* ed. Robert Markley (Baltimore: Johns Hopkins University Press, 1996), 124.

17. B. T. Sotah, 20a.

18. Cited in Gershom Scholem, *Major Trends in Jewish Mysticism* (New York: Schocken Books, 1946), 76.

19. Harry Y. Gamble, *Books and Readers in the Early Church: A History of Early Christian Texts* (New Haven, Conn.: Yale University Press, 1995), 141.

20. Cited in Antoine Faivre, *Access to Western Esotericism* (Albany, N.Y.: SUNY Press, 1994), 41.

21. Garth Fowden, *The Egyptian Hermes* (Princeton, N.J.: Princeton University Press, 1986), 81.

22. Giovanni Pico della Mirandola, *Oration on the Dignity of Man,* trans. A. Robert Caponigri (Chicago: Gateway Editions, 1956), 7.

23. Frances A. Yates, *The Art of Memory* (Chicago: University of Chicago Press, 1966), 224.

24. Frances A. Yates, *Giordano Bruno and the Hermetic Tradition* (Chicago: University of Chicago Press, 1964), 156.

25. Ioan Couliano, *Eros and Magic in the Renaissance,* trans. Margaret Cook (Chicago: University of Chicago Press, 1987), 104.

26. Lama Anagarika Govinda, *The Way of the White Clouds* (Boston: Shambhala, 1970), 107.

27. Ibid.

28. Cited in Latour, *We Have Never Been Modern,* 93.

29. Dennis Stillings, introduction, Ernst Benz: *The Theology of Electricity,* trans. Wolfgang Taraba (Allison Park, Penn.: Pickwick Publications, 1989), xii.

30. Ernst Benz, *The Theology of Electricity,* trans. Wolfgang Taraba (Allison Park, Penn.: Pickwick Publications, 1989), 18.

31. Christopher Smart, "Jubilate Agno," in *The Norton Anthology of Poetry,* 3rd edition (New York: W. W. Norton, 1983), 471.

32. Benz, *The Theology of Electricity,* 57.

33. Cited in Jonathan Cott, *Stockhausen* (New York: Simon & Schuster, 1973), 15.

34. James Wyckoff, *Franz Anton Mesmer: Between God and Devil* (Englewood Cliffs, N.J.: Prentice-Hall, 1975), 37.

35. Robert Fuller, *Mesmerism and the American Cure of Souls* (Philadelphia: University of Pennsylvania Press, 1982), 11.

36. Ibid., 60.

37. Cited in Arthur Zajonc, *Catching the Light* (New York: Bantam, 1993), 145.

38. http://hoohana.aloha.net/~htoday/June95txt.html

39. William Irwin Thompson, *Passages About Earth: An Explanation of the New Planetary Culture* (New York: Harper & Row, 1973), 51.

40. William Irwin Thompson, *Coming into Being* (New York: St. Martin's Press, 1996), 223–24.

41. Steven Lubar, *Infoculture* (Boston: Houghton Mifflin, 1993), 76.

42. Ibid., 81.

43. Ibid., 86.

44. Marshall McLuhan, *Understanding Media* (reprint, Cambridge, Mass.: MIT, 1994), 247.

45. Ibid., 252.

46. Ruth Brandon, *The Spiritualists* (New York: Knopf, 1983), 13.

47. Joscelyn Godwin, *The Theosophical Enlightenment* (Albany, N.Y.: SUNY, 1994), 188.

48. Emma Hardinge, *Modern American Spiritualism* (1869; reprint, Hyde Park, N.Y.: University Books, 1970), 29.

49. R. Laurence Moore, *In Search of White Crows* (New York: Oxford University Press, 1977), 100.

50. Brandon, *The Spiritualists,* 43.

51. Roy Stemman, *Spirits and Spirit Worlds* (Garden City, N.Y.: Doubleday, 1976), 40.

52. Carolyn Marvin, *When Old Technologies Were New* (New York: Oxford University Press, 1988), 57.

53. Avital Ronell, *The Telephone Book* (Lincoln: University of Nebraska Press, 1989), 367.

54. Ibid., 240.

55. Ibid., 250.

56. Ibid., 245.

57. Sadie Plant, *Zeros + Ones* (New York: Doubleday, 1997), 114.

58. Margaret Cheney, *Nikola Tesla: Man Out of Time* (New York: Dell, 1981), 22.

59. Marvin, *When Old Technologies Were New,* 100.

60. Ibid., 137.

61. F. David Peat, *In Search of Nikola Tesla* (Bath, Great Britain: Ashgrove, 1983), 43.

62. http://www.neuronet.pitt.edu/~bogdan/tesla

63. Ronell, *The Telephone Book,* 259.

64. Peat, *In Search of Nikola Tesla,* 83.

65. Cited in "Electroacoustic Music in the 21st Century," http://www.zynet.co.uk/steel wolf/ezine005/articles/electro.html

66. June Singer, "The Evolution of the Soul," in *The Allure of Gnosticism,* ed. Robert Segal (Chicago: Open Court, 1995), 55.

67. "Gospel of the Egyptians," James M. Robinson, *The Nag Hammadi Library,* trans. Members of the Coptic Gnostic Library Project of the Institute for Antiquity and Christianity (New York: Harper & Row, 1978), 205.

68. Albert Speer, *Inside the Third Reich,* trans. Richard and Clara Winston (New York: Avon, 1974), 653.

69. Theodore Roszak, *The Cult of Information* (New York: Pantheon, 1986), 14.

70. Norbert Wiener, *The Human Use of Human Beings* (New York: Doubleday Anchor Books, 1954), 17.

71. Dorothy Nelkin and M. Susan Lindee, *The DNA Mystique: The Gene as Cultural Icon* (New York: W. H. Freeman, 1995), 53.

72. Plotinus, *The Enneads,* trans. Stephen MacKenna (New York: Larson Publications, Burdett, 1992), 313–14 [IV.3.17].

73. Wiener, *Human Use of Human Beings,* 101–102.

74. Ibid., 36.

75. Ibid., 34.

76. Ibid., 36.

77. Hans Jonas, *The Gnostic Religion* (Boston: Beacon, 1963), 45.

78. *Hermetica,* trans. Brian P. Copenhaver (Cambridge: Cambridge University Press, 1992), 41.

79. Harold Bloom, *The American Religion* (New York: Simon & Schuster, 1992), 30.

80. "The Hymn of the Pearl," in Willis Barnstone, ed., *The Other Bible* (New York: Harper & Row, 1984), 311–12.

81. Jonas, *Gnostic Religion,* 77.

82. Ibid., 195.

83. Ioan Couliano, *The Tree of Gnosis* (New York: HarperCollins, 1992), 125.

84. Bloom, *The American Religion,* 31.

85. Stephan Hoeller, *Freedom: Alchemy for a Voluntary Society* (Wheaton, Ill.: Quest, 1992), xv.

86. Ibid., 173.

87. David Noble, *The Religion of Technology* (New York: Knopf, 1997), 82.

88. Catherine Albanese, *Nature Religion in America* (Chicago: University of Chicago Press, 1990), 65.

89. Ibid., 8.

90. http://www.eff.org/~barlow/library.html

91. Ibid.

92. Hoeller, *Freedom,* 13.

93. Ibid., 226.

94. Ibid., 140.

95. *Encyclopaedia Britannica,* 15th ed., s.v. "Anarchism," vol. 1, p. 812.

96. Hoeller, *Freedom,* 230.

97. Cited in Benjamin Woolley, *Virtual Worlds* (London: Penguin, 1992), 212.

98. Hakim Bey, "The Information War," in *Mediamatic* 8, no. 4 (1996): 61.

99. Ibid., 59.

100. Mark Dery, *Escape Velocity* (New York: Grove Press, 1996), 248.

101. http://www.extropy.com/~exi

102. Ibid.

103. Ed Regis, *Great Mambo Chicken and the Transhuman Condition* (Reading, Mass.: Addison-Wesley, 1990), 150.

104. Ibid., 176.

105. "Synopsis of the Entire System According to Augustine," in Willis Barnstone, ed., *The Other Bible* (New York: Harper & Row, 1984), 41.

106. William Irwin Thompson, *The American Replacement of Nature* (New York: Doubleday, 1991), 123.

107. Roszak, *The Cult of Information,* 113.

108. Jay Bolter, *Turing's Man* (Chapel Hill: University of North Carolina Press, 1984), 74.

109. Regis, *Great Mambo Chicken,* 153.

110. Hoeller, *Freedom,* 165.

111. *Time,* Special Issue, 148, no. 14 (Fall 1996): 29.

112. Marshall McLuhan and Quentin Fiore, *War and Peace in the Global Village* (New York: Bantam, 1968), 18.

113. P. D. Ouspensky, *In Search of the Miraculous* (New York: Harcourt, Brace & World, 1949), 47.

114. Ibid., 59.

115. Stewart Lamont, *Religion Inc.: The Church of Scientology* (London: Harrap, 1986), 28.

116. Ibid., 28.

117. Jon Atack, *A Piece of Blue Sky* (New York: Lyle Stuart, 1990), 157.

118. http://www.demon.co.uk/castle/xenu/xenu.html

119. Lowell D. Streiker, *Mind-Bending* (New York: Doubleday, 1984), 80.

120. The Lama Foundation, "Cookbook for a Sacred Life," in *Be Here Now* (San Cristobal, N.M.: Lama Foundation, Year of the Earth Monkey), 1.

121. Cited in Douglas Rushkoff, *Cyberia* (San Francisco: HarperSan Francisco, 1994), 67.

122. "What Does Being a Buddhist Mean to You?" *Tricycle* 6, no. 1 (Fall 1996): 41.

123. Timothy Leary, Ralph Metzner, and Richard Alpert, *The Psychedelic Experience* (reprint, New York: Citadel Underground, 1995), 61.

124. Jay Stevens, *Storming Heaven* (New York: Harper & Row, 1987), 248–49.

125. Dery, *Escape Velocity*, 29.

126. Tony Schwartz, *What Really Matters* (New York: Bantam, 1996), 150.

127. Ibid., 154–55.

128. Fuller, *Mesmerism and the American Cure of Souls*, 87.

129. Charles T. Tart, *Waking Up* (Boston: Shambhala, 1987), 23.

130. John C. Lilly, *The Center of the Cyclone* (New York: Bantam, 1972), xv.

131. Ibid., 9.

132. Timothy Leary, *Exo-Psychology* (Los Angeles: Starseed/Peace Press, 1977), 104.

133. Ibid., 114.

134. http://www.factory.org/nettime/archive/1140.html

135. Dery, *Escape Velocity*, 22.

136. Robert Pirsig, *Zen and the Art of Motorcycle Maintenance* (New York: Bantam, 1974), 16.

137. Cited in Roszak, *The Cult of Information*, 148.

138. Dery, *Escape Velocity*, 33.

139. Kevin Kelly, *Out of Control* (Reading, Mass.: Addison-Wesley, 1994), 127.

140. McLuhan and Fiore, *War and Peace*, 83.

141. Jacques Ellul, *The Technological Society* (New York: Knopf, 1964), 423.

142. Cited in Florman, *The Existential Pleasures of Engineering*, 54.

143. McLuhan and Fiore, *War and Peace*, 25.

144. Ibid., 72.

145. Cited in William A. Covino, *Magic, Rhetoric, and Literacy* (Albany, N.Y.: SUNY Press, 1994), 23.

146. William A. Covino, *Magic, Rhetoric, and Literacy* (Albany, N.Y.: SUNY Press, 1994), 8.

147. Michel de Certeau, *The Practice of Everyday Life*, trans. Steven Rendall (Berkeley: University of California Press, 1984), xxiv.

148. T. M. Luhrmann, *Persuasions of the Witch's Craft* (Cambridge, Mass.: Harvard University Press, 1989), 106.

149. Margot Adler, *Drawing Down the Moon* (Boston: Beacon, 1986), 397.

150. Cited in Robert Anton Wilson, *Cosmic Trigger* (Phoenix: Falcon Press, 1977), 18.

151. Ronald Grimes, *Beginnings in Ritual Studies* (Washington, DC: University Press of America, 1982), 54.

152. Interview with author, September 1996.

153. Interview with author, October 1994.

154. Philip K. Dick, *The Shifting Realities of Philip K. Dick*, ed. Lawrence Sutin (New York: Pantheon, 1995), 183.

155. William Gibson, *Neuromancer* (New York: Ace Books, 1984), 51.

156. Margaret Wertheim, "The Medieval Return of Cyberspace," in *The Virtual Dimension,* ed. John Beckmann (New York: Princeton Architectural Press, forthcoming).

157. William Gibson, *Mona Lisa Overdrive* (New York: Bantam, 1988), 13.

158. James Burke and Robert Ornstein, *The Axemaker's Gift* (New York: Grosset/Putnam, 1995), 281.

159. Ibid., 308.

160. Cited in Dery, *Escape Velocity,* 55.

161. Wertheim, "The Medieval Return of Cyberspace."

162. William Gibson, *Count Zero* (New York: Ace, 1986), 119.

163. Interview with author, May 1989.

164. Ed Morales, "Circle of Fire," *Village Voice,* March 19, 1996, 37.

165. Yates, *The Art of Memory,* 47.

166. http://www.pathfinder.com/ time/magazine/1997/dom/ 970519/tech.the_man_who-i. html

167. Yates, *The Art of Memory,* 17.

168. Ibid., 2.

169. *Hermetica,* 41.

170. Peter J. French, *John Dee* (London: Routledge & Kegan Paul, 1972), 71.

171. Jay David Bolter, *Writing Space* (Hillsdale, N.J.: Erlbaum, 1991), 60.

172. Bolter, *Turing's Man,* 164.

173. http://marlowe.wimsey.com/ ~rshand/streams/gnosis/ cyber.html

174. Umberto Eco, *Travels in Hyperreality,* trans. William Weaver (New York: Harcourt Brace Jovanovich, 1986), 82.

175. J. R. R. Tolkien, "On Fairy-stories," in *The Tolkien Reader* (New York: Ballantine, 1966), 37.

176. Ibid., 10.

177. Gary Gygax et al., *Advanced Dungeons & Dragons Player's Handbook,* 2nd ed. (Lake Geneva, Wis.: TSR, 1995), 10.

178. Steven Levy, *Hackers* (New York: Dell, 1984), 141.

179. Julian Dibbell, *My Tiny Life* (New York: Owl Books, forthcoming).

180. http://www.csd.uwo.ca/
~pete/Infocom/Articles/
lebling.html

181. Dante, *Inferno*, trans. Allen
Mandelbaum (New York:
Quality Paperbook Book Club,
1980), canto 1, line 1.

182. Yates, *The Art of Memory*,
95.

183. http://www.ilt.columbia.edu/
projects/dante/

184. Levy, *Hackers*, 141.

185. Sherry Turkle, *The Second Self*
(New York: Simon & Schuster,
1984), 80.

186. Angus Fletcher, *Allegory*
(Ithaca, N.Y.: Cornell
University Press, 1964), 3.

187. Theodor Holm Nelson, "The
Right Way to Think About
Software Design," in *The Art
of Human-Computer
Interface*, ed. Brenda Laurel
(Reading, Mass.: Addison-
Wesley, 1990), 241.

188. Alan Kay, "User Interface: A
Personal View," in *The Art of
Human-Computer Interface
Design*, ed. Brenda Laurel
(Reading, Mass.: Addison-
Wesley, 1990), 199.

189. Thompson, *The American
Replacement of Nature*, 41.

190. Vernor Vinge, *True Names . . .
and Other Dangers* (New
York: Baen Books, 1987), 81.

191. Ibid., 60.

192. Bolter, *Turing's Man*, 168.

193. Julian Dibbell, "A Rape in
Cyberspace," *Village Voice*,
December 12, 1993, 42.

194. Sherry Turkle, *Life on the
Screen* (New York: Simon &
Schuster, 1995), 177.

195. Carl Jung, *Flying Saucers*,
trans. R.F.C. Hull (New York:
Signet, 1969), 50.

196. Keith Thompson, *Angels and
Aliens* (Reading, Mass:
Addison-Wesley, 1991), 93.

197. Whitley Strieber, *Communion*
(New York: Avon, 1987),
229.

198. Philip K. Dick, *Valis* (New
York: Bantam, 1981), 212.

199. Michael Heim, *Virtual Realism*
(New York: Oxford University
Press, 1997), 144.

200. Joseph Weizenbaum,
*Computer Power and Human
Reason* (San Francisco: W. H.
Freeman, 1976), 213.

201. Andrew Ross, *Strange Weather*
(New York: Verso, 1991), 37.

202. Ken Carey, *The Starseed
Transmissions* (New York:
HarperCollins, 1982), 1.

203. Ibid., 35.

204. Ibid., 75.

205. Jonas, *The Gnostic Religion*,
76.

206. Ibid., 50.

207. http://www.pathfinder.com/
time/magazine/1997/dom/
970519/tech.the_man_who-i.
html

208. "Secrets of the Cult,"
Newsweek, April 14, 1997,
30.

209. Kelly, *Out of Control*, 233.

210. Peter Fitting, "Reality as
Ideological Construct," in
R. D. Mullen et al., eds., *On
Philip K. Dick* (Terre Haute,
Ind.: SF-TH Inc., 1992), 101.

211. Bolter, *Turing's Man*, 187–88.

212. "Interview with Marshall
McLuhan," 72.

213. Matie Molinaro, Corinne McLuhan, and William Toye, eds., *Letters of Marshall McLuhan* (New York: Oxford University Press, 1987), 370.

214. Norman Cohn, *The Pursuit of the Millennium* (New York: Oxford University Press, 1961), 109.

215. Lubar, *Infoculture,* 81.

216. Marvin, *When Old Technologies Were New,* 201.

217. Ibid., 65.

218. Ibid., 192.

219. Michael Benedikt, "Introduction," *Cyberspace: First Steps* (Cambridge, Mass.: MIT, 1992), 3.

220. Porush, "Hacking the Brainstem," 122.

221. http://www.hotwired.com/ wired/3.08/departments/cyber. rights.html

222. John Dewey, *Experience and Nature,* 2nd ed. (LaSalle, Ill.: Open Court, 1929), 138.

223. http://www.logos.com

224. "Interview with Marshall McLuhan," 72.

225. Richard Dawkins, *The Selfish Gene* (New York: Oxford University Press, 1976), 192.

226. Gamble, *Books and Readers in the Early Church,* 104.

227. Edward Rothstein, "Is Destiny Just a Divine Word Game?" *New York Times,* August 12, 1997, C1.

228. Cited in Bolter, *Writing Space,* 104.

229. http://www.ctheory.com/ a-cyberwar_god.html

230. Lawrence Sutin, *Divine Invasions: A Life of Philip K. Dick* (New York: Harmony Books, 1989), 210.

231. Dick, *Valis,* 219.

232. Ibid., 63.

233. Philip K. Dick, *A Maze of Death* (New York: Daw, 1970), 101.

234. Philip K. Dick, "How to Build a Universe That Doesn't Fall Apart Two Days Later," in *I Hope I Shall Arrive Soon,* ed. Mark Hurst and Paul Williams (New York: St. Martin's Press, 1985), 4.

235. Ian Watson, "The False Reality as Mediator," in *On Philip K. Dick: 40 Articles from Science-Fiction Studies* (Greencastle, Ind.: SF-TH Inc., 1992), 67.

236. Dick, "How to Build a Universe That Doesn't Fall Apart Two Days Later," 5.

237. *Encyclopaedia Britannica,* 12th ed., s.v. "nature, philosophy of," 873.

238. Pierre Teilhard de Chardin, *The Future of Man,* trans. Norman Denny (New York: Harper Torchbooks, 1964), 82.

239. "Researchers on Complexity Ponder What It's All About," *New York Times,* May 6, 1997, B9.

240. Turkle, *Life on the Screen,* 150.

241. Ibid., 160.

242. Jennifer Cobb Kreisberg, "A Globe, Clothing Itself with a Brain," *Wired,* June 1995, 108.

243. Ibid.

244. http://www.netizen.com/ cgi-bin/interact/view_stitch? msg.25901

245. http://www.hyperreal.com/
~mpesce

246. http://www.netizen.com/
cgi-bin/interact/view_stitch?
msg.25901

247. Pierre Lévy, *Collective
Intelligence,* trans. Robert
Bononno (New York: Plenum,
1997), 105.

248. Ibid., xxv.

249. Ibid., 104.

250. Marshall McLuhan, *The
Gutenberg Galaxy* (Toronto:
University of Toronto Press,
1962), 32.

251. http://www.czech.cz/infosrc/
hrad/havel/speeches/eng/95/
0806ang.htm

252. Ibid.

253. Fredric Jameson,
*Postmodernism: The Cultural
Logic of Late Capitalism*
(Durham, N.C.: Duke
University Press, 1991),
37–38.

254. Michael Zimmerman,
Contesting Earth's Future
(Berkeley: University of
California Press, 1994),
75.

255. Ibid., 76.

256. Teilhard de Chardin, *The
Future of Man,* 54.

257. Ibid., 56.

258. ftp://etext.archive.umich.edu/
pub/Politics/Spunk/anarchy
_texts/misc/Spunk962.txt

259. Marvin, *When Old
Technologies Were New,* 202.

260. Cited in Dante, *The Divine
Comedy,* trans. and ed. Charles
Singleton (Princeton: Princeton
University Press, 1970), pt. 2,
182.

261. ftp://etext.archive.umich.edu/
pub/Politics/Spunk/anarchy
_texts/misc/Spunk962.txt

262. *Encyclopaedia Britannica,*
12th ed., s.v. "nature,
philosophy of," 873.

263. Pierre Teilhard de Chardin,
The Phenomenon of Man,
trans. Bernard Wall (New
York: Harper, 1959), 244.

264. Francis Cook, *Hua-yen
Buddhism* (University Park,
Penn.: Pennsylvania State
University Press, 1977), 2.

265. Ibid., 3.

266. Thich Nhat Hanh, "Engaged
Buddhism," in *Entering the
Stream,* ed. Samuel Bercholz
and Sherab Chödzin Kohn
(Boston: Shambhala, 1993),
248.

267. *The Gospel of Thomas,* trans.
and ed. Marvin Meyer (San
Francisco: HarperSanFrancisco,
1992), 65.

268. Cited in George Dyson,
Darwin Among the Machines
(Reading, Mass.: Addison-
Wesley, 1997), 51.

269. Sadie Plant, *Zeros + Ones* (New
York: Doubleday, 1997), 12.

270. Raymond Kurzweil, *The Age
of Intelligent Machines*
(Cambridge, Mass.: MIT Press,
1990), 165.

271. Plant, *Zeros + Ones,* 124.

272. Pierre Lévy, *Collective
Intelligence,* 217.

273. Herman Hesse, *Magister Ludi,*
trans. Richard and Clara
Winston (New York: Bantam,
1969), 6–7.

274. Ibid., 105.

275. Cited in Plant, *Zeros + Ones,*
123.

INDEX

About the Author

Erik Davis is a fifth-generation Californian who currently resides in San Francisco. His work has appeared in *Wired, The Village Voice, Gnosis,* and other publications, and he has lectured internationally on techno-culture and the fringes of religion. He can be contacted at his Web site: http://www.levity.com/techgnosis/